Growing Smarter

DATE DUE

MAR 28 2010	
JAN 3 2011	
MAR 01 2011	

BRODART, CO. Cat. No. 23-221-003

Urban and Industrial Environments

Series editor: Robert Gottlieb, Henry R. Luce Professor of Urban and Environmental Policy, Occidental College

Sustainable Metropolitan Communities books

Robert D. Bullard, ed., *Growing Smarter: Achieving Livable Communities, Environmental Justice, and Regional Equity*

Related Urban and Industrial Environments series books

Keith Pezzoli, *Human Settlements and Planning for Ecological Sustainability: The Case of Mexico City*

William A. Shutkin, *The Land That Could Be: Environmentalism and Democracy in the Twenty-First Century*

Robert Gottlieb, *Environmentalism Unbound: Exploring New Pathways for Change*

Matthew Gandy, *Concrete and Clay: Reworking Nature in New York City*

David Naguib Pellow, *Garbage Wars: The Struggle for Environmental Justice in Chicago*

Julian Agyeman, Robert D. Bullard, and Bob Evans, eds., *Just Sustainabilities: Development in an Unequal World*

Jason Corburn, *Street Science: Community Knowledge and Environmental Health Justice*

Barbara L. Allen, *Uneasy Alchemy: Citizens and Experts in Louisiana's Chemical Corridor Disputes*

Steve Lerner, *Diamond: A Struggle for Environmental Justice in Louisiana's Chemical Corridor*

Peggy F. Barlett, ed., *Urban Place: Reconnecting with the Natural World*

Eran Ben-Joseph, *The Code of the City: Standards and the Hidden Language of Place Making*

Julie Sze, *Noxious New York: The Racial Politics of Urban Health and Environmental Justice*

Growing Smarter

Achieving Livable Communities, Environmental Justice, and Regional Equity

Edited by
Robert D. Bullard

The MIT Press
Cambridge, Massachusetts
London, England

MIT Press books may be purchased at special quantity discounts for business or sales promotional use. For information, please e-mail ⟨special_sales@mitpress .mit.edu⟩ or write to Special Sales Department, The MIT Press, 55 Hayward Street, Cambridge, MA 02142.

This book was set in Sabon on 3B2 by Asco Typesetters, Hong Kong.
Printed on recycled paper and bound in the United States of America.

Library of Congress Cataloging-in-Publication Data

Growing smarter : achieving livable communities, environmental justice, and regional equity / edited by Robert D. Bullard.
    p.   cm. — (Urban and industrial environments)
Includes bibliographical references and index.
ISBN 978-0-262-02610-9 (alk. paper)—ISBN 978-0-262-52470-4 (pbk. : alk. paper)
1. Cities and towns—United States—Growth. 2. Sustainable development—United States. 3. Environmental justice—United States. 4. Social justice—United States. 5. Regional disparities—United States. 6. Minorities—Civil rights—United States. I. Bullard, Robert D. (Robert Doyle), 1946–

HT384.U5G76   2007
307.76—dc22   2006046670

10 9 8 7 6 5 4 3 2 1

Contents

Foreword   vii
Carl Anthony

Acknowledgments   xiii

List of Abbreviations   xv

Introduction   1

I   Race, Smart Growth, and Regional Equity

1   Smart Growth Meets Environmental Justice   23
Robert D. Bullard

2   Race, Poverty, and Urban Sprawl: Access to Opportunities through
Regional Strategies   51
john a. powell

3   ¿Quién es Más Urbanista? Latinos and Smart Growth   73
Manuel Pastor, Jr.

4   Sprawl and Civil Rights: A Mayor's Reflections   103
William A. Johnson, Jr.

II   Land Use and the Built Environment

5   Nashville: An Experiment in Metropolitan Governance   127
David A. Padgett

6   Smart Growth and the Legacy of Segregation in Richland County,
South Carolina   149
Maya Wiley

7   Food Justice and Health in Communities of Color   171
Kimberly Morland and Steve Wing

8   Washed Away by Hurricane Katrina: Rebuilding a "New" New
Orleans   189
Beverly Wright and Robert D. Bullard

III Transportation Equity

9   Confronting Transportation Sprawl in Metro Atlanta   215
Robert D. Bullard, Glenn S. Johnson, and Angel O. Torres

10 Environmental Justice and Transportation Equity: A Review of
MPOs   249
Thomas W. Sanchez and James F. Wolf

11 Beyond Dirty Diesels: Clean and Just Transportation in Northern
Manhattan   273
Swati R. Prakash

12 Linking Transportation Equity and Environmental Justice with
Smart Growth   299
Don Chen

IV Growing Smarter for Livable Communities

13 Building Regional Coalitions between Cities and Suburbs   323
Myron Orfield

14 Smart Growth Tools for Revitalizing Environmentally Challenged
Urban Communities   345
Daniel J. Hutch

Afterword: Growing Smarter and Fairer   371
Robert D. Bullard

Contributors   379

Index   381

Foreword

Carl Anthony

This remarkable book, *Growing Smarter: Achieving Livable Communities, Environmental Justice, and Regional Equity*, edited by Robert D. Bullard, is the first in a series of Sustainable Metropolitan Communities books to be published by The MIT Press, as an imprint within the Urban and Industrial Environments series, edited by Robert Gottlieb. Professor Bullard, an environmental sociologist, is the author of numerous books on environmental justice, transportation, race, planning, and urban development. In this collection, he brings together important new essays that place struggles for racial justice and livable communities for poor and marginalized populations in the context of an exciting new discourse concerning metropolitan regional equity.

The public discourse about metropolitan development is changing. Advocates of social, racial, and environmental justice must seek to understand the new meanings embodied in this changing rhetoric. New language reflects new political alignments. The term *smart growth* is a response to the growing awareness of the significance of planning for natural disasters such as hurricanes and earthquakes, public opposition to sprawl development on the metropolitan fringe, and resistance to infill projects that do not represent the needs of the communities where they are located. Contrary to much discussion of the so-called free market, the forms, patterns, and potential benefits or burdens of a particular development are shaped as much by public policy as they are by the private sector.

Concepts like *sustainable development* and smart growth are important because they are beginning to provide a political foundation for a new generation of public policy. The generally recognized definition of sustainable development is development that meets present needs without compromising the potential of future generations to meet their needs. This definition often sidesteps the question of whose present needs, and which future generations are to benefit from any proposed development. For many environmental groups and private developers, these terms mean a blending of environmental and private real estate goals; they do not, however, include social justice or racial equity. Advocates of sustainable development often agree that cities and suburbs should evolve in ways that enhance everybody's quality of life. But people of color are not usually in the room when these agreements take place.

Thus, smart growth can mean gentrification, the displacement of low- and moderate-income families in existing older neighborhoods, or public subsidies for transportation investments that further isolate low-income populations from regional opportunity. On the other hand, advocates for regional equity and environmental justice insist that smart growth must include racial justice and the full participation of communities of color in decisions that affect their quality of life. As the concepts of smart growth and sustainable development evolve, they may represent either a threat to the well-being of poor people or important opportunities for previously marginalized communities to have a say in shaping patterns of development throughout the metropolitan region.

A key concept of smart growth is the idea of promoting livable communities. Such communities are based on pedestrian scale, a diversity of populations, mixed incomes, and mixed uses. Although the quest for livable communities is often associated with the new urbanism movement of architects, planners, and developers that emerged in the 1990s, it also has deep, if forgotten, roots in the 1960s. The civil rights insurgency inspired innovations in the fields of architecture, landscape architecture, and urban planning. Designers, as members of professions whose role it was to give material form to the longings and desires of communities, were offered opportunities because of the civil rights movement to open community spaces for new forms of social life with the goal of developing more livable communities for poor and marginalized populations. Community design centers sprouted across the country. The concept of advocacy planning—meaning the provision of architectural and planning services for vulnerable groups resisting destructive schemes by planning authorities, government agencies, or similar bodies—was developed. Citizen participation in urban design decision making, now standard practice by groups like the Urban Land Institute, emerged as a new tool within the field. Architects began to pay more attention to individual user needs in contrast to an earlier focus on monumental designs. Community development corporations were formed as innovative institutions to address the needs of marginalized urban and rural neighborhoods.

Livable communities are the opposite of the dominant paradigm of today's metropolitan development based on sprawl. Sprawl is frequently defined as poorly planned, land-consumptive development at the edges of cities, surrounding suburbs, or in rural fringes within commuting distance of metropolitan centers. Opponents of sprawl, most often affluent suburban residents or environmental groups, are aware that sprawl is growing much faster than the population. For example, between 1960 and 1990 the amount of developed land in U.S. metropolitan areas more than doubled, while the population grew by less than half. Opponents of sprawl know well that it creates automobile dependence and longer driving distances. They are also aware of the negative impact of sprawl on natural resources.

Opponents, however, are not often aware of its shadow side: the abandonment of inner-city neighborhoods, older suburbs, and rural areas. Thousands of vacant properties in cities like Philadelphia, Baltimore, and Detroit as well as in rural areas around the country are caused by overinvestment in poorly planned suburbs. And let us not forget the destruction of New Orleans and the contamination of 80 percent of its neighborhoods in the aftermath of Hurricane Katrina. The way New Orleans and communities along the Gulf Coast region get rebuilt has implications for other U.S. cities and metropolitan regions.

These investments impose heavy costs on local governments and the residents left behind. Vacant buildings are sites for illegal drug activity, theft, violence, and arson. The demolition of vacant buildings and cleaning of vacant lots require public expenditures by jurisdictions strapped for cash. Homes in abandoned neighborhoods lose their property values. Thus, a basis exists for a coalition between opponents of sprawl and opponents of urban and rural abandonment—the quest for regional equity.

The movement for environmental justice exploded on the scene during the 1980s, as communities of color all across the United States fought to protect themselves against the unequal distribution of environmental hazards undermining the health of people forced to live in neighborhoods with locally unwanted land uses. This movement quickly expanded to confront a wide variety of hazards: pesticides, air pollution, lead poisoning, toxic waste production and disposal, garbage dumps, and occupational hazards.

The pursuit of metropolitan regional and neighborhood equity is, in many ways, an extension of the movement for environmental justice. It is a mobilization led by social justice advocates, civil rights organizations, and labor unions concerned with issues of fairness in the way metropolitan regions grow. It seeks to address not only what communities are against but also what they are for: healthy neighborhoods with convenient access to good schools, affordable housing, parks, and grocery stores; equitable public investments; and access to opportunity. This movement responds to two challenges that poor and marginalized communities and neighborhoods face as they seek to improve their quality of life. The first is that the larger patterns of metropolitan development have undermined past neighborhood-based efforts to remedy concentrated urban poverty, socioeconomic issues, and racial isolation. The second challenge is to find systemic ways to link poverty alleviation to the larger, society-wide patterns of social, economic, and environmental development.

The advocates of regional and neighborhood equity perhaps are the fastest-growing part of the smart growth movement. But they have been critical of both environmental groups and the conventional development industry for their lack of attention and responsiveness to issues of race, class, and poverty. They recognize, though, that public debate about smart growth and the new metropolitan agenda provides a political context to build new allies in the effort to address the unmet needs of poor people, working people, and people of color in ways that improve the quality of life for everyone.

The way we build and live in cities has a profound impact on society's use and misuse of natural resources. It also profoundly affects social, economic, and racial justice outcomes. It is important to realize that in a globalizing world, the real city is the whole metropolitan region, made up of many jurisdictions, including the central city, its suburbs, and the rural and wilderness areas under its influence. Private developers focus on the shape of individual projects within a particular jurisdiction. But the public sector must fairly represent the interests of populations both positively and negatively impacted by a given development. This is an especially critical responsibility when public subsidies are involved. Decisions made by one jurisdiction have spillover effects on neighborhoods and ecosystems throughout a region. Public actions that define land use must incorporate civic engagement for all affected residents, including communities of color throughout a whole region, in ways that shape the behavior of private market forces to achieve fair outcomes for all.

The books in the Sustainable Metropolitan Communities series are crafted at the intersection of engagement with these issues of the environment, metropolitan development, and race. The series and *Growing Smarter* are especially timely given the rebuilding and redevelopment of New Orleans and the Gulf Coast region after Hurricane Katrina. Despite the obvious fact that these issues are connected in everyday life, and that policymakers and practitioners advocating for one or more of these concerns often find themselves in deep conflict over their outcomes, publications most frequently treat such issues in silos. *Growing Smarter* breaks down the silos in this extraordinary initial contribution to the Sustainable Metropolitan Communities book series. The authors inspire a new generation of academics, policymakers, and coalitions in their efforts to improve the quality of life for all of our communities

Acknowledgments

I would like to thank a number of individuals and organizations whose hard work and dedication made this book possible. In particular, I want to thank the contributors, who not only wrote chapters but also endured constant nagging about deadlines. A special nod goes out to Carl Anthony and Michelle DePass of the Ford Foundation for support of this book project as part of the workplan of the African American Forum on Race and Regionalism (AAFRR), of which I serve as cochair. I also want to thank Deeohn Ferris, who facilitated the work of the AAFRR, and the other two AAFRR cochairs, Angela Glover Blackwell of PolicyLink, Inc., and john a. powell of the Kirwan Institute for the Study of Race and Poverty at Ohio State University, who provided guidance in this undertaking.

Finally, I owe special gratitude to my colleagues Glenn S. Johnson and Angel O. Torres at the Environmental Justice Resource Center, who were able to juggle their regular work schedules, supervise two major book projects—including this one—and follow up with the contributors and keep us on track. Lastly, I want to thank two other center staff, Lisa Sutton and Michelle Dawkins, who also assisted with tracking the mountains of paperwork associated with an edited volume.

List of Abbreviations

AASHTO	American Association of State Highway and Transportation Officials
ACIR	Advisory Commission on Intergovernmental Relations
ADA	Americans with Disabilities Act
AQMD	Air Quality Management District
ARB	Air Resources Board
ARC	Atlanta Regional Commission
ATL	Hartsfield-Jackson Atlanta International Airport
bhp	Brake-Horsepower
CAA	Clean Air Act
CBD	Central Business District
CBO	Community-Based Organization
CDC	Centers for Disease Control and Prevention
CLRP	Constrained Long-Range Plan
CMAQ	Congestion Mitigation and Air Quality
CNG	Compressed Natural Gas
COG	Council of Governments
CT	Census Tract
CWSRF	Clean Water State Revolving Fund
DEP	Diesel Exhaust Particles
DFW	Dallas–Fort Worth International Airport
DNL	Day-Night Average Sound Level
DOT	Department of Transportation

EGR	Exhaust Gas Recirculation
EPA	Environmental Protection Agency
EPD	Environmental Protection Division
FEMA	Federal Emergency Management Agency
FHA	Federal Housing Administration
FHWA	Federal Highway Administration
GIS	Geographic Information System
GISL	Geographic Information Sciences Laboratory
GPS	Global Positioning System
HAPs	Hazardous Air Pollutants
HBCUs	Historically Black Colleges and Universities
HOLC	Home Owner Loan Corporation
HUD	Housing and Urban Development
IOM	Institute of Medicine
ISTEA	Intermodal Surface Transportation Efficiency Act
LDEQ	Louisiana Department of Environmental Quality
LULUs	Locally Unwanted Land Uses
MALDEF	Mexican American Legal Defense and Education Fund
MARTA	Metropolitan Atlanta Rapid Transit Authority
MBTA	Massachusetts Bay Transit Authority
MPO	Metropolitan Planning Organization
MSA	Metropolitan Statistical Area
MTA	Metropolitan Transit Authority
NALEO	National Association of Latino Elected and Appointed Officials
NAACP	National Association for the Advancement of Colored People
NATA	National Air Toxics Assessment
NEPA	National Environmental Policy Act
NFHA	National Fair Housing Alliance
NIMBY	Not in My Backyard
NOx	Nitrous Oxide

NRDC	Natural Resources Defense Council
PAHs	Polycyclic Aromatic Hydrocarbons
PM	Particulate Matter
RTA	Rapid Transit Authority
SAFETEA-LU	The Safe, Accountable, Flexible and Efficient Transportation Equity Act—A Legacy for Users
SBA	Small Business Administration
SD	Superdistrict
SEMCOG	Southeast Michigan Council of Governments
TAC	Toxic Air Contaminant
TDOT	Tennessee Department of Transportation
TEA-21	Transportation Efficiency Act for the Twenty-First Century
TIF	Tax Incremental Financing
TIP	Transportation Improvement Program
TRI	Toxic Release Inventory
TSU	Tennessee State University
TVA	Tennessee Valley Authority
ULI	Urban Land Institute
USCCR	United States Commission on Civil Rights
USDOT	United States Department of Transportation
UZO	Urban Zoning Overlay
VA	Veterans Administration
VMT	Vehicle Miles Traveled
VOC	Volatile Organic Compounds
WE ACT	West Harlem Environmental Action, Inc.
ZEV	Zero-Emission Vehicles

Growing Smarter

Introduction

A growing antisprawl movement has emerged over the past decade under the broad umbrella of smart growth. Suburban sprawl is fueled by the "iron triangle" of finance, land use planning, and transportation service delivery. Sprawl and smart growth mean different things to different people. In *The Limitless City*, Oliver Gillham (2002, 8) defined sprawl as "a form of urbanization distinguished by leapfrog patterns of development, commercial strips, low density, separated land uses, automobile dominance, and a minimum of public open space."

Sprawl is growth characterized by inadequate accessibility to essential land uses such as housing, jobs, and public services that include schools, parks, green space, and public transportation. Suburban sprawl is not new. It is an extension of long-established patterns of suburbanization, decentralization, and low-density development (Bullard, Johnson, and Torres 2000). Sprawl has even been defined as a fundamental civil rights issue (Johnson 2002). Sprawl-driven development has "literally sucked population, jobs, investment capital, and tax base from the urban core" (Anthony 1998).

It is clear that in order to access many of these new suburban developments, one must have access to an automobile, since public transit is usually inadequate or nonexistent. Sprawl creates a car-dependent citizenry. Urban sprawl is consuming land faster than the population is growing in many cities across the country. Communities from coast to coast are engaged in heated debates about whether this type of growth is good or bad.

Growth and sprawl are not synonymous. Nevertheless, suburban sprawl has been the dominant growth pattern for nearly all of the metropolitan regions in the United States for the past five decades (Orfield 1997). Urban land area nearly quadrupled, from 18.6 million to 74 million acres in the contiguous United States, between 1954 and 1997 (U.S. Department of Agriculture 1997). Historically, the decentralization of employment centers has had a major role in shaping metropolitan growth patterns as well as the location of people, housing, and jobs.

Government policies buttressed and tax dollars subsidized suburban sprawl through new roads and highways at the expense of public transit (Bullard and Johnson 1997; Conservation Law Foundation 1998). Local governments also influenced private investment decisions through roads, sewers, parks, and schools. Tax subsidies made it possible for new suburban employment centers to become dominant outside of cities, and to pull middle-income workers and homeowners from the urban core (Schmidt 1998). Federal housing and highway policies helped subsidize a sizable share of the middle-class move to suburbia, while at the same time promoting policies that concentrated pubic housing and poor people in the crumbling urban core.

The infrastructure in most U.S. cities is crumbling. The physical infrastructure includes such things as roads and bridges, housing stock, schools, public buildings, parks and recreational facilities, public transit, water supply, wastewater treatment, and waste disposal systems. Billions of public dollars spent on infrastructure bias private real estate markets in favor of exurban development (Richards 2001). Taken as a whole, infrastructure decline has a negative impact on people's well-being and the quality of life for everyone—not just individuals who live in central cities. Poor infrastructure conditions in urban areas are a result of a host of factors including the distribution of wealth, uneven development, racial and economic discrimination, redlining, housing and real estate practices, the location decisions of industry, differential enforcement of land use regulations, and unrestrained suburban growth.

The smart growth movement is in part a response to suburban sprawl along with the kaleidoscope of urban problems related to housing markets, business location, migration, land use, transportation, pollution, conservation, and environmental protection (Wolch, Pastor, and Dreier 2004). The movement also seeks to manage growth while creating healthy, livable, and sustainable communities (Bollier 1998). Many localities are limiting subsidies that fuel dispersed development, and channeling these resources into growth management plans and regulations that encourage a balance of housing, transportation, commercial, and community choices. The overall goal is to shape where and how growth occurs (Richards 2001).

Generally, smart growth tools and methods concentrate largely on the physical environment and land use politics (Wolch, Pastor, and Dreier 2004, 281). Smart growth is "development that serves the economy, the community, and the environment" (U.S. Environmental Protection Agency 2001, 1). Smart growth attempts to achieve economic development and jobs, strong neighborhoods, transportation choices, and healthy communities. Generally, smart growth strategies include "mixed land use, decreased automobile dependence balanced by transportation alternatives (walking, bicycling, and transit), and increased density balanced by preservation of green spaces" (Frumkin, Frank, and Jackson 2004, 207).

Growing Smarter

Smart growth has failed to adequately address social equity, especially the plight of poor people and people of color (Wolch, Pastor, and Dreier 2004, 281). The movement has only scratched the surface of the artificial barriers (that is, housing, employment, education, transportation, land use and zoning, health and safety, public investments, and so on) that limit the social and economic mobility of racial and ethnic groups. Historically, people of color have had fewer housing and residential choices than whites. Their communities have been redlined, abandoned, and targeted for locally unwanted land uses or LULUs. Smart growth initiatives have turned the spotlight back on many urban core neighborhoods, accelerating gentrification and the displacement of incumbent residents. Many of the "rediscovered" and "revitalized" neighborhoods are priced well beyond the economic reach of longtime residents.

Smart growth advocates are gradually moving their plans into action. Unfortunately, many marginalized groups are left out altogether. Smart growth does not necessarily translate into fair or equitable growth. Equity issues have received little attention in the smart growth dialogue.

Like its mainstream environmental movement counterpart, much of the smart growth conversations, meetings, and action agendas have only marginally involved people of color, the working class, and low-income persons. In short, the emerging smart growth movement has bypassed the rich ethnic and economic diversity that characterizes many central cities, metropolitan regions, and the nation.

Addressing Race and Regional Equity

Race and place in urban America are deeply connected (Frazier, Margai, and Tettey-Fio 2003). Race continues to polarize and spatially divide cities, suburbs, and exurbs (Farley, Danziger, and Holzer 2002). Place affects access to jobs, education, public services, culture, shopping, level of personal security, and medical services (Dreier, Mollenkoph, and Swanstrom 2001). For example, African American homeowners pay an 18 percent "segregation tax" for living in segregated neighborhoods (Rusk 2001). Race maps closely to economic geography. Racialized space creates perpetual demarcations (powell 2000). The redlining practices used by insurance companies, banks, and mortgage companies are built largely around racialized zip codes (Bullard, Johnson, and Torres 2000).

People of color comprise a majority of the population in nearly half of the nation's one hundred largest cities. The Census Bureau predicts that people of color will make up over half of the U.S. population by 2050. Some employers use space as a "signal" associated with perceptions about race, class, worker skills, and attitudes (Tilly et al. 2003, 306). Using these signals, many employers often recruit white suburban workers, while avoiding central city black workers. In metropolitan Atlanta, for example, space "inside" and "outside" of I-285 (a perimeter highway that encircles the city) has become racialized. Businesses and employers are keenly aware of and contribute to racialized space (Tilly et al. 2003, 313). A business location advertised as "inner-city and inside the perimeter" is code for black, while a location defined as "outside the perimeter" connotes suburban and whites.

Many urban problems do not stop at the city limits; some require regional solutions. Before Hurricane Katrina emptied New Orleans of its more than four hundred thousand inhabitants in August 2005, it was the largest city in the United States without a meaningful master plan. Economist David Rusk (2005b) described the pre-Katrina New Orleans area problem as follows:

Oil and chemical firms and land developers are so influential that local "plans" have been slavish reflections of whatever business wanted to do. The Regional Planning Commission (RPC) is the New Orleans region's MPO. Its membership covers only five of the nine parishes of the New Orleans region. Its board has five members from each jurisdiction (the mayor/parish council president, two council-members, and two citizen members); thus, Plaquemines Parish (27,332) has the same voting representation as New Orleans (473,681). Like most MPOs, RPC is weak and, though my report on the New Orleans region recommended major reforms to strengthen RPC, to my knowledge, none were implemented.

These problems are not unique to New Orleans. The question is how will the nation forge equitable and inclusive solutions to address disparities in transportation, housing, economic opportunity, land use, infrastructure, education, environmental justice, and health. As a start, the Ford Foundation began investing in regional equity demonstrations in five cities: Camden, New Jersey; Detroit, Michigan; Baltimore, Maryland; Richmond, California; and Atlanta, Georgia. University of New Hampshire professor Cynthia M. Duncan (2004), the former director of the Ford Foundation's Community and Resource Development unit, described the role of regional equity in addressing long-standing racial disparities:

Many of the problems in distressed, racially segregated inner-city neighborhoods in the United States, and increasingly in older, inner-ring suburbs, are rooted in seemingly benign—but effectively racist—housing, school and transportation policies that emerged after World War II. These policies subsidized suburbanization and resulted in severe inequities in access to good schools, decent housing and transportation to good jobs.

Today there are opportunities for reinvestment and potential new allies to call for it. Many middle-class suburbanites are worried about congestion and sprawl and the effects that a culture built on the automobile is having on the environment. Business leaders are worried about workers being able to afford housing reasonably near their work. Public and private leaders are calling for a smarter approach to growth. Inner-city groups are organizing to promote healthy communities and environmental justice. The regional equity approach to development combines community efforts to build strong institutions and better infrastructure with regional policies to foster equitable public and private investment. The aim is achieving lasting community change that is racially and economically just and environmentally sustainable.

Regional equity is built around three basic premises. First, regional health depends on the health of all sectors of the region. Second, central cities and declining suburbs cannot confront the problems of racialized concentrated poverty independently—that is, without a regional focus. Third, a regional approach to equity issues must support rather than undermine the political power, social cohesion, and sense of place of all residents of the region, but particularly those who have long been denied an effective voice as a result of regional forces (powell 2000; PolicyLink, Inc. 2002).

Rusk sees "measuring regional equity" as an important step in delineating the problem and formulating solutions. He focuses mainly on socioeconomic, educational, and fiscal outcomes (for jurisdictions). For Rusk, regional equity outcomes can be measured on three different levels: individual, group, and jurisdictional outcomes. His regional equity measures do not deal with disparities in physical environmental conditions (for instance, air and water pollution, toxic waste, and so forth) and health disparities—issues central to the environmental justice movement (Rusk 2005a).

One regional equity goal is to reduce residential segregation by race. Racial segregation in housing, as well as schools and jobs, is fundamental to the geography of the modern U.S. city. Spatial and social mobility are interrelated. Sociologists Douglas Massey and Nancy Denton (1993) contend that segregation constitutes a powerful impediment to black socioeconomic progress. Residential integration is more of a dream than a reality. Generally, whites live in neighborhoods where there are few people of color. People of color live in more integrated neighborhoods than whites:

The typical white lives in a neighborhood that is 80.2% white, 6.7% black, 7.9% Hispanic, and 3.9% Asian. The typical black lives in a neighborhood that is 51.4% black, 33.0% white, 11.4% Hispanic, and 3.3% Asian. The typical Hispanic lives in a neighborhood that is 45.5% Hispanic, 36.5% white, 10.8% black, and 5.9% Asian. The typical Asian lives in a neighborhood that is 17.9% Asian, 54.0% white, 9.2% black, and 17.4% Hispanic. (Logan 2001, 3)

Race matters in cities, suburbs, and rural areas. The color line is no imaginary one in the United States. This country has never been color blind (Brown et al. 2003). Middle-income homeowners in black neighborhoods have fewer services, retail stores, banks, good schools, and other residential amenities than are commonly found in most middle-class neighborhoods—amenities that white homeowners take for granted (Cashin 2004). Discrimination in real estate and mortgage markets as well as educational environments robs current and future generations of African Americans of important wealth-creating opportunities. Racial and economic segregation exacerbate inner-city poverty (Jargowsky 1997).

Most growth in metropolitan regions is occurring outside of central cities—away from where people of color are concentrated. Over 80 percent of the country's future growth (if current trends hold) is expected to occur in "edge cities" and other suburbs (Diamond and Noonan 1996). Nationally, 32 percent of Americans live in central urban areas, 32 percent live in urban fringe areas, 25 percent live in rural areas, 6 percent live in small towns, and 5 percent live in midsize towns.

Cities only seem to get attention after conditions reach some crisis state, or when human frustration spills over into major uprisings or race riots. Americans who have the economic means continue to leave our central cities. Higher-income households are leading this flight. Although affluent households (that is, persons making $60,000 and over) make up only 24 percent of households in the nation's larger cities, they account for over 40 percent of the 1.2 million net out-migrants.

Every decade or so Americans rediscover the city and close-in neighborhoods. They soon find that living in the city has many advantages. Over the past five decades, government-subsidized initiatives have cleared "blighted" neighborhoods and slums under various urban renewal programs. Successive waves of urban revitalization programs all resulted in the "urban removal" of large numbers of renters, poor people, and black residents, followed by gentrification. Gentrification refers to the tearing down of housing and buildings that accommodate the poor, usually blacks, and the construction of new, upscale housing and other amenities in their place that cater to a new group of usually white, middle-class residents. It is the back-to-the-city movement of capital (Smith 1996). Gentrification fuels a "growth machine" that defines place as a commodity (Logan and Molotch 1988).

Jurisdictions often compete in a "race to the bottom" by reducing taxes, lowering wage standards, and easing environmental regulations in order to lure new investments (Pastor et al. 2000, 155). Angela Blackwell and her colleagues at PolicyLink, Inc. (2002, 7), a think tank based in Oakland, California, see "community based regionalism" as an important strategy for promoting equitable development and sustainable solutions to regional disparities and injustice. Similarly, john a. powell in *Racism and Metropolitan Dynamics* (2002, 232–36) calls for a racially just "federated regionalism." As powell (2002, 5) writes:

Racially just "federated regionalism" is a model in which a regional authority controls access to the opportunities that have regional dimensions, but local authorities control other matters. This way identity, governmental responsiveness, and community are preserved. Regionalism—specifically a racially just form of regionalism that not only facilitates access to fundamental life opportunities but protects against harm and nourishes political power and community strength—is simply a tool to gain greater traction and results on existing efforts.

The absence of a national urban policy has left hundreds of financially strapped cities and their aging first-ring suburbs increasingly resource poor, while developing and sprawling suburbs grow richer. The socio-spatial layout and negative relations between cities, older suburbs, and newer suburbs resulted from decades of policies and practices to isolate poor people of color (Jargowsky 1997, 193). Over the years, central cities and suburbs have become more alike. Many of the social ills such as poverty, unemployment, infrastructure decline, environmental degradation, crime, and drugs once associated with big cities now are commonplace in many older suburbs.

Reducing inequities within regions makes economic, social, environmental, and health sense since the future of cities and suburbs are inextricably interdependent. The United States needs it cities. The fate of business is linked with the workforce, and the middle class with that of the poor (Pastor et al. 2000, 157). Central city poverty and inequality (education, income, employment, housing, environment, land use, transportation, taxes, and so on) across a region can stifle a whole region's development. Problem-ridden cities and declining suburbs are two sides of the same coin. They are interconnected across the metropolitan landscape because of region-level economic restructuring.

Organization of This Book

Growing Smarter brings together in one volume several themes addressed in a series of books that I have written, edited, or coedited over the past two decades. In *Invisible Houston* (Bullard 1987), *Houston: Growth and Decline in a Sunbelt Boomtown* (Shelton et al. 1989), and *In Search of the New South* (Bullard 1989), the central theme revolved around urban growth, migration, and inequitable access to opportunities in the South and Sun Belt. Housing segregation, redlining, urban disinvestments, and neighborhood revitalization strategies formed the core issues in *Residential Apartheid* (Bullard, Grigsby, and Lee 1994).

The link between race, environmental protection, civil rights, and sustainable development was sharpened with the publication of *Dumping in Dixie* (Bullard 2000), *Confronting Environmental Racism* (Bullard 1993), *Unequal Protection* (Bullard 1994), *Just Sustainabilities* (Agyeman, Bullard, and Evans 2003), and *The Quest for Environmental Justice* (Bullard 2005). Finally, transportation equity, sprawl, and smart growth were addressed in *Just Transportation* (Bullard and Johnson 1997), *Sprawl City* (Bullard, Johnson, and Torres 2000), and *Highway Robbery* (Bullard, Johnson, and Torres 2004).

All of my books examine the continued significance of race and class factors in shaping the lives and livelihoods of low-income, working-class, and people of color communities. Times have changed, but the issues remain the same in the early years of the twenty-first century. In some instances, urban ills have worsened and expanded beyond the central city into the suburbs. Crime, drugs, concentrated poverty, unemployment and idleness, poor-quality schools, inadequate housing, abandoned buildings, and declining infrastructure are no longer considered inner-city problems. Smart growth, environmental justice, and regional equity frameworks all recognize the connection between development and the quality of life.

The contributors to this volume include urban planners, sociologists, economists, educators, lawyers, health professionals, and environmentalists. All of the authors place equity at the center of their analysis of environmental justice, livable communities, smart growth, and regionalism. The contributors adopt an environmental justice framework that defines the environment as "where we live, work, play, go to school, and worship as well as the physical and natural world."

Our core analysis examines the impact of the built environment on access to economic opportunity and quality of life. We also explore the costs and consequences of uneven urban and regional growth patterns, suburban sprawl and public health, transportation investments and economic development, and enduring inequalities of place, space, and race. For this volume, a conscious effort was made to assemble a multidisciplinary team of scholars who would blend their work into a coherent and readable book. The authors also agreed not to dance around the fact that all communities are not created equal. Inequality is real.

The volume sets out to answer specific questions: Are metropolitan regions working optimally for *anyone*? What changes and new paradigms can be offered that will improve the quality of life, and create healthy and livable metropolitan regions for *everyone*? How does the built environment impact health? How do current trends in racial and income segregation in metropolitan areas affect the process of urban redevelopment? How do government policies (that is, housing, education, finance, land use planning, and transportation policies) aid, and in many cases subsidize, separate and unequal economic development and segregated neighborhoods? How can regional transportation investments and decision making be used to promote opportunity? What lessons can be applied from the environmental justice movement to other movements (regional equity, smart growth, and so on) to address racism and injustice against other people of color, the poor, and other disenfranchised groups?

In fourteen chapters and an afterword, the authors cover a wide range of topics, and describe factors that continue to shape the quality of life in our nation's cities, suburbs, and metropolitan regions. The authors examine the role government plays in fostering equal opportunity and civil rights laws without regard to race, color, or national origin. They also look at regional strategies used to address concentrated poverty, segregation, and social isolation (tax credits, developer incentives, urban growth boundaries, revenue sharing, city-county consolidation, and fair share housing law) along with their advantages and weaknesses.

Chapter 1 explores the notion that all communities are *not* created equal. I contend that sprawl-fueled growth is widening the gap between the haves and have-nots, and builds a case for linking the principles of smart growth with environmental justice. Also, I show that suburban sprawl has clear social and environmental effects. The social effects of suburban sprawl include the concentration of urban-core poverty, closed opportunity, limited mobility, economic disinvestment, social isolation, and urban/suburban disparities that closely mirror racial inequities. The environmental effects of suburban sprawl include urban infrastructure decline, increased energy consumption, automobile dependency, threats to public health and the environment—including air pollution, flooding, and climate change—and threats to farmland and wildlife habitat.

Chapter 2, by john a. powell, demonstrates the need for social justice and urban civil rights advocates to focus on sprawl as well as concentrated poverty. Powell provides strong evidence that racialized, concentrated poverty is both a cause and a product of sprawl, and that due to this interrelationship, concentrated poverty cannot be addressed without addressing sprawl. To examine this relationship, the author explores how the phenomena of gentrification and the revitalization strategy of infill operate differently in rich, middle-class, and poor cities. Finally, powell argues that concentrated poverty and sprawl are regional issues that can only be addressed on a regional level, and that it is a mistake for social justice and urban civil rights advocates to leave the regional discussion only to environmentalists and land use planners.

In chapter 3, Manuel Pastor, Jr., analyzes the factors that make regions prosper. He maintains that with the changing demographics and "new faces" of the suburbs, regions must provide and preserve opportunity for all citizens and communities. His analysis also offers a new vision of community-based regionalism that links cities and suburbs with an emphasis on equity, arguing that metropolitan areas must reduce poverty in order to grow, and that low-income individuals and people of color must make regional connections in order to escape poverty. Finally, Pastor calls for new policies and politics to address social, economic, and racial/ethnic disparities in our nation's multiethnic and multicultural metropolitan regions.

In chapter 4, William A. Johnson, Jr., argues that sprawl is fundamentally a civil rights issue and that the emerging smart growth movement can be harnessed to advance equal opportunity. He offers a unique view on urban growth issues—as seen through the personal perspective of an African American mayor with a strong civil rights background. Johnson contends that the burdens of sprawling metropolitan growth fall disproportionately on people of color living in cities. He draws directly from his personal experiences in dealing with the effects of sprawl as the mayor of Rochester, New York.

Johnson describes the city government of Rochester as a model of workplace diversity. Superbly qualified persons of color are generously represented at all levels of the organization. Nevertheless, after saying good-bye to each other at a city hall exit, white employees head for the buses that lead to the predominantly white east-side neighborhoods or the suburbs. African American employees wait for the buses that will carry them in a different direction. Rarely do blacks and whites share the same bus or bus stop, let alone the same neighborhood. For eight hours a day—at work or in school—many Americans experience racial and ethnic diversity. For the balance of the day—at home—most Americans lead extremely segregated lives.

In chapter 5, David A. Padgett focuses on applications of geographically and spatially based methods in assessing the impact of suburban sprawl on Nashville's African American population. In June 1962, Tennessee voters in Nashville and Davidson County approved the creation of a metropolitan government. Although other cities had partially consolidated already, Nashville was the first U.S. city to achieve true consolidation. Today, there are some seventeen consolidated governments in the United States out of over three thousand county units. Most of these metropolitan governments use a variation of the 1962 Nashville plan. Between 1980 and 2000, the Nashville Metropolitan Statistical Area (MSA) surpassed the Memphis MSA as the most populous in Tennessee.

In 2004, *Black Enterprise* magazine named Nashville the fourth-best city for African Americans in its "Top Ten" ranking. In a real sense, Nashville is a tale of two black communities: one having moved to outlying areas and the suburbs, and enjoying the fruits of a booming economy as well as explosive growth and opportunities; and the other experiencing a questionable future as it struggles to get the attention of those leaving it behind.

Chapter 6, by Maya Wiley, examines the dynamics of sprawl and the policy responses to it in Richland County, South Carolina. Wiley's analysis helps sharpen the focus of race and sprawl in a rural-urban context. Richland County is growing fast in terms of population, and even faster in relation to residential and retail strip mall construction. But it is a county with a significant rural character. Like much of the South, its metropolitan area has an urban core, Columbia, and rural areas. The southeastern end of the county, Lower Richland, which represents a large portion of the county's landmass, is rural and predominantly black. Former plantation lands are now small parcels owned by the descendants of slaves, many of them low income with no other assets, and where communities lack many basic services and have received few county infrastructure investments or the opportunities that come with them, in stark contrast to traditionally white parts of Richland County.

The Richland County Council's smart growth plan seeks to restrict rural development, thereby angering black landowners, who see the restrictions as ending any hope of appreciation of their one real asset and threatening their tradition of subdividing property for the benefit of their children. The county's land use vision permits sprawl to continue where it is occurring, while restricting development in poor African American communities, where development and access to opportunities within the metropolitan region are sorely needed. The anger and distrust engendered by land use planning in Richland County may not be unique in the southern black belt. Where low-income people of color own land and homes in rural areas, attempts to control sprawl by limiting growth and development may produce destructive results in already-impoverished communities.

In chapter 7, Kimberly Morland and Steve Wing examine the location of supermarkets, restaurants, and other food sellers in 216 neighborhoods in Maryland, Minnesota, Mississippi, and North Carolina. The retail sector has been affected by economic policies that support corporate retail chains, public- and private-sector loan policies that favor homeownership for white Americans, and land use policies that facilitate the development of predominantly wealthy and white suburban neighborhoods.

The authors show that wealthier neighborhoods have more than three times as many supermarkets as poor ones, limiting access for many people to the basic elements of a healthy diet. When broken down by race, not just wealth, there are four times as many supermarkets in mainly white neighborhoods as in black neighborhoods. Black households are less likely to have a car or truck available. The lack of private transportation and supermarkets in low-wealth and predominantly black neighborhoods suggests that residents of these neighborhoods may be at a disadvantage when attempting to achieve a healthy diet.

Chapter 8, which I coauthored with Beverly Wright, looks at the smart growth and environmental justice debate after Hurricane Katrina destroyed New Orleans and ravaged the Louisiana, Mississippi, and Alabama Gulf Coast on August 29, 2005. We examine the rebuilding of New Orleans and the Gulf Coast region against a range of indicators, including housing, economic development, insurance settlements, loans, environmental cleanup, transportation, access to jobs, and health. Some smart growth principles are making their way into the rebuilding of New Orleans and the hurricane-ravaged Gulf Coast region. On the other hand, developers and government officials make their deals while environmental justice principles appear to be buried with the millions of tons of hurricane debris.

In chapter 9, coauthors Glenn S. Johnson, Angel O. Torres, and I examine the major factors that contributed to Atlanta being dubbed the sprawl "poster child." Traffic gridlock and polluted air help make Atlanta one of the "most sprawl-threatened" large cities in the United States. The boundaries of the Atlanta metropolitan region doubled in the 1990s. The region measured 65 miles from north to south in 1990. The ten-county metropolitan region had a population of over of 3.7 million people as of April 1, 2003.

Today, Atlanta's economic dominance reaches well beyond 110 miles from north to south. As we illustrate, much of Atlanta's sprawl development was fueled by the iron triangle of finance, land use planning, and transportation service delivery. Finally, as Hartsfield-Jackson Airport became the busiest in the world and a major economic powerhouse in the Atlanta region, "runway sprawl" displaced, destabilized, and destroyed the airport's primarily African American neighborhoods.

In chapter 10, Thomas W. Sanchez and James F. Wolf discuss the extent to which large MPOs incorporate environmental justice concerns into their planning processes. They look at three dimensions: (1) efforts targeted at assessing the fairness of planning outcomes and the promotion of social equity, (2) public participation in MPO processes, and (3) analysis of the extent to which MPO boards underrepresent social, economic, and ethnic/racial groups. The authors rely on existing research for background on MPO structures and responsibilities, and then present the results of a survey to examine the types of equity planning conducted by MPOs, the forms of public participation efforts, and the representation of voting board members.

Chapter 11, by Swati Prakash, focuses on the health impacts of transportation-related pollution, and analyzes how people of color, the poor, children, and the elderly are disproportionately exposed to and affected by toxic diesel fumes (primarily from on-road sources) in urban areas—with an emphasis on northern Manhattan. It also examines the federal regulations related to reducing exposure to diesel exhaust, assesses the available and emerging clean fuel alternatives and technologies for reducing diesel emissions, and makes recommendations for improvements in policy. Finally, Prakash reviews the major challenges and opportunities to systematically clean up or replace diesel fuel in our nation's fleets of trucks and buses, and proposes organizing and coalitional strategies to effectively advance this at the local, state, regional, and national level.

In chapter 12, Don Chen explores smart growth as one component of a livable communities framework. For generations, coming to the United States has meant that no matter what your social standing, religion, race, ethnicity, language, or political beliefs, you could gain access to the good life if you worked hard and played by the rules. Today, equal access to opportunities and fair play are still cherished values. But all too often, discriminatory barriers have kept the American dream out of peoples' reach—especially for low-income people—preventing them from gaining access to a good education, quality health care, affordable housing, a clean environment, and decent jobs.

Chapter 13, by Myron Orfield, examines the core reasons for building coalitions to address regional problems created or exacerbated by suburban sprawl. The author details a comprehensive regional agenda for addressing the growing social and racial separation and the wasteful sprawling development that limits opportunity for the poor (particularly for people of color) and threatens the environment. He offers solutions for land use planning from a regional perspective, greater fiscal equity among local governments (with an emphasis on reinvestment in the central cities and older suburbs), and improved governance at the regional level that will help facilitate the development of policies to benefit all types of metropolitan communities. Orfield argues that coalition-building efforts that stress the links between core cities and suburbs can bring about reforms to increase equity for an entire region.

In chapter 14, Daniel J. Hutch covers the relationship of smart growth and land use issues to disadvantaged communities (low-income ones as well as communities of color), and highlights the tools and opportunities to better achieve more equitable and sustainable outcomes in land use investment decisions. The author contends that there is still a large disconnect between regional land use decisions, including smart growth policies, and the interests of economically disadvantaged communities. The challenge for urban advocates is to rebalance growth to benefit older inner-ring communities while appealing to broader concerns, including environmental, social, fiscal, and equity issues. Providing alternative choices to existing low-density development in outlying or fringe areas would not only better protect green space and the quality of our environment (land, air, and water) but would also benefit the region as a whole.

In the afterword, I draw on the chapters in this volume to provide a summary, synthesis, and policy options. I argue that the smart growth and environmental justice movements should join forces to become a potent force in shaping needed change in our central cities and suburbs. Such an alliance would also move metropolitan regions a long way toward breaking down the mistrust, stereotypes, myths, and a litany of other artificial social and economic barriers that divide us as a nation.

References

Agyeman, J., R. D. Bullard, and B. Evans. 2003. *Just Sustainabilities: Development in an Unequal World.* Cambridge, MA: MIT Press.

Anthony, C. 1998. Suburbs Are Making Us Sick: Health Implications of Suburban Sprawl and Inner City Abandonment on Communities of Color. In *Environmental Justice Health Research Needs.* Atlanta: Environmental Justice Resource Center.

Bollier, D. 1998. *How Smart Growth Can Stop Sprawl: A Briefing Guide for Funders.* Washington, DC: Essential Books.

Brown, M. K., M. Carnoy, E. Currie, T. Duster, D. B. Oppenheimer, M. M. Schultz, and D. Wellman. 2003. *Whitewashing Racism: The Myth of a Color-Blind Society.* Berkeley: University of California Press.

Bullard, R. D. 1987. *Invisible Houston: The Black Experience in Boom and Bust.* College Station: Texas A&M University Press.

Bullard, R. D., Ed. 1989. *In Search of the New South: The Black Urban Experience in the 1970s and 1980s.* Tuscaloosa: University of Alabama Press.

Bullard, R. D., Ed. 1993. *Confronting Environmental Racism: Voices from the Grassroots.* Boston: South End Press.

Bullard, R. D., Ed. 1994. *Unequal Protection: Environmental Justice and Communities of Color.* San Francisco: Sierra Club Books.

Bullard, R. D. 2000. *Dumping in Dixie: Race, Class, and Environmental Quality.* 3rd ed. Boulder, CO: Westview Press.

Bullard, R. D. 2005. *The Quest for Environmental Justice: Human Rights and the Politics of Pollution.* San Francisco: Sierra Club Books.

Bullard, R. D., J. E. Grigsby III, and C. Lee, eds. 1994. *Residential Apartheid: The American Legacy.* Los Angeles: UCLA Center for African American Studies.

Bullard, R. D., and G. S. Johnson, eds. 1997. *Just Transportation: Dismantling Race and Class Barriers to Mobility.* Gabriola Island, BC: New Society Publishers.

Bullard, R. D., G. S. Johnson, and A. O. Torres, eds. 2000. *Sprawl City: Race, Politics, and Planning in Atlanta.* Washington, DC: Island Press.

Bullard, R. D., G. S. Johnson, and A. O. Torres, eds. 2004. *Highway Robbery: Transportation Racism and New Routes to Equity.* Boston: South End Press.

Cashin, S. 2004. *The Failures of Integration: How Race and Class are Undermining the American Dream.* New York: Public Affairs.

Conservation Law Foundation. 1998. *City Routes, City Rights: Building Livable Neighborhoods and Environmental Justice by Fixing Transportation.* Boston: Conservation Law Foundation.

Diamond, H. L., and P. F. Noonan. 1996. *Land Use in America.* Washington, DC: Island Press.

Dreier, P., J. Mollenkoph, and T. Swanstrom. 2001. *Place Matters: Metropolitics for the Twenty-First Century*. Lawrence: University Press of Kansas.

Duncan, C. M. 2004. Green Growth: Environmentalism and Economic Development Can Make a Powerful Partnership. *Ford Foundation Report* (Fall). Available at ⟨http://www.fordfound.org/publications/ff_report/view_ff_report _detail.cfm?report_index=535&print_version=1⟩.

Farley, R., S. Danziger, and H. J. Holzer. 2002. *Detroit Divided*. New York: Russell Sage Foundation.

Frazier, J. W., F. M. Margai, and E. Tettey-Fio. 2003. *Race and Place*. Boulder, CO: Westview Press.

Frumkin, H., L. Frank, and R. Jackson. 2004. *Urban Sprawl and Public Health: Designing, Planning, and Building for Healthy Communities*. Washington, DC: Island Press.

Gillham, O. 2002. *The Limitless City: A Primer on the Urban Sprawl Debate*. Washington, DC: Island Press.

Jargowsky, P. 1997. *Poverty and Place: Ghettos, Barrios, and the American City*. New York: Russell Sage Foundation.

Johnson, W. A., Jr. 2002. Sprawl as a Civil Rights Issue: A Mayor's Reflection. Paper presented at the George Washington University Center on Sustainable Growth, Washington, DC.

Logan, J. 2001. *Ethnic Diversity Grows, Neighborhood Integration Lags Behind*. Albany, NY: Lewis Mumford Center, University of Albany.

Logan, J. R., and H. L. Molotch. 1988. *Urban Fortunes: The Political Economy of Place*. Berkeley: University of California Press.

Massey, D. S., and N. A. Denton, eds. 1993. *American Apartheid and the Making of the Underclass*. Cambridge, MA: Harvard University Press.

Orfield, M. 1997. *Metropolitics: A Regional Agenda for Community and Stability*. Washington, DC: Brookings Institution Press.

Pastor, M., Jr., P. Dreier, J. E. Grigsby, and M. Lopez-Garza. 2000. *Regions That Work: How Cities and Suburbs Can Grow Together*. Minneapolis: University of Minnesota Press.

PolicyLink, Inc. 2002. *Promoting Regional Equity: A Framing Paper*. Miami, FL: Funder's Network for Smart Growth.

powell, j. a. 2000. The Racial Justice and Regional Equity Project. Available at ⟨http://www1.umn.edu/irp/rjrewhatis.html⟩.

powell, j. a. 2002. *Racism and Metropolitan Dynamics: The Civil Rights Challenge of the 21st Century*. Minneapolis: Institute on Race and Poverty, University of Minnesota.

Richards, L. 2001. Alternatives to Subsidizing Edge Development: Strategies for Preserving Rural Landscape. *Terrain.org: A Journal of the Built and Natural Environment* 10 (Fall/Winter).

Rusk, D. 2001. *The Segregation Tax: The Cost of Racial Segregation on Black Homeowners.* Washington, DC: Brookings Institution Center on Urban and Metropolitan Policy.

Rusk, D. 2005a. Measuring Regional Equity. Working paper, May 27.

Rusk, D. 2005b. Measuring Regional Equity in the New Orleans Area: An Unsentimental Assessment. Working paper, September 15.

Schmidt, C. W. 1998. The Specter of Sprawl. *Environmental Health Perspective* 106 (June): 274.

Shelton, B. A., J. E. Feagin, R. D. Bullard, N. Rodriguez, and R. Thomas. 1989. *Houston: Growth and Decline in a Sunbelt Boomtown.* Philadelphia: Temple University Press.

Smith, N. 1996. *The New Frontier: Gentrification and the Revanchist City.* New York: Routledge.

Tilly, C., P. Moss, J. Kirschenman, and I. Kennelly. 2003. Space as a Signal: How Employers Perceive Neighborhoods in Four Metropolitan Labor Markets. In *Urban Inequality: Evidence from Four Cities,* ed. A. O'Connor, C. Tilly, and L. D. Bobo. New York: Russell Sage Foundation.

U.S. Department of Agriculture. 1997. Major Land Use Changes in the Contiguous 48 States. In *Agricultural Resources and Environmental Indicators (AREI) Updates, No. 3.* Washington, DC: USDA, Economic Research Service, Natural Resources and Environmental Division.

U.S. Environmental Protection Agency. 2001. About Smart Growth. Available at ⟨http://www.epa.gov/smartgrowth/about_sg.htm#what_is_sg⟩.

Wolch, J., M. Pastor Jr., and P. Dreier. 2004. *Up against Sprawl: Public Policy and the Making of Southern California.* Minneapolis: University of Minnesota Press.

I

Race, Smart Growth, and Regional Equity

1

Smart Growth Meets Environmental Justice

Robert D. Bullard

Suburban sprawl impacts the daily lives of everyone—including poor people and people of color. Sprawl has social and economic consequences. It is linked to poverty and inequality, and heightens the separation between income classes (Jargowsky 2002). Sprawl development exacerbates school crowding, heightens the disparities between urban and suburban schools, accelerates urban infrastructure decline, concentrates poverty, creates a spatial mismatch between urban workers and suburban job centers, intensifies racial disparities, and negatively impacts public health.

This chapter explores the underlying themes that the smart growth and environmental justice movements have in common. It also examines barriers that keep these diverse movements apart. Can the nation's metropolitan areas, many of which are polarized by race, class, and politics, provide opportunities and quality environments for all of their residents—whether they live in the rural fringe, suburbs, or central cities? This question rests at the heart of the regional equity debate.

Bridging the Gap

Why should environmental justice advocates care about suburban sprawl, smart growth, or regional equity? The smart growth movement is beginning to influence what happens in communities all across the United States. Many core smart growth principles focus on protecting the environment, using resources wisely, facilitating cooperation between cities and suburbs, and investing in and rebuilding our inner-city older suburbs. Numerous studies show that smart growth development can minimize air and water pollution, encourage brownfields cleanup and re-use, preserve open space and farmland, increase transportation choices that alleviate traffic congestion and enhance transportation efficiency, and save tax dollars (Gibson and Taft 2001).

Smart growth and environmental justice have many compatible goals. Both movements are built around a set of principles that recognize the interconnection between humans and the environment. Both movements also recognize that where we live impacts the quality of our lives and our life opportunities. And the framers of both movements also encourage community and stakeholder collaborations in planning and decision making. Smart growth and environmental justice are *not* antigrowth, antidevelopment, and antisuburbs. Both movements offer opportunities for building coalitions and alliances to break down artificial barriers in housing, employment, education, transportation, land use and zoning, health and safety, and urban investment (Bullard, Johnson, and Torres 1999).

Breaking out of the "race" trap is easier said than done. Today, as was true a decade ago, the smart growth movement is largely a white one, while the environmental justice movement in made up of a majority of people of color. The leadership of both movements generally reflects the constituency base. Even though whites and people of color may have common interests when it comes to urban growth issues, they seldom have opportunities in common meetings to make these converging interests known. We are not only residentially segregated but also highly segregated organizationally as a nation. More often than not, highly charged urban growth and development issues get reduced to race and class interests (Bullard, Johnson, and Torres 2000).

An increasing number of suburbanites are opting to live in central city neighborhoods, placing tremendous pressures on the environment where people of color, poor people, and working-class people live, work, play, and attend school. One need not have an advanced degree in urban and regional planning to understand that some Americans live in good neigh-borhoods and communities that provide them with all sorts of advan-tages and amenities, while others live in not-so-good neighborhoods and communities that impose an array of disadvantages, burdens, and costs on them (Dreier, Mollenkoph, and Swanstrom 2001, 56). Living on the "wrong side of the tracks" can be hazardous to one's health, well-being, and life changes.

It is no accident that people of color and poor people inhabit some of the most environmentally degraded and economically segregated communities in the country. Smart growth policies offer opportunities to address a range of problems, including environmentally degraded land, polluted air, traffic congestion, loss of green space, concentrated poverty, urban disinvestments, housing abandonment, bank and insurance redlining, and growing social and economic polarization (Bullard, Johnson, and Torres 2000; Orfield 2003).

Borrowing heavily from the civil rights movement, environmental justice activists in the late 1980s and early 1990s challenged mainstream environmentalists to rid their movement of institutionalized racism, elitism, sexism, and paternalism. They sent letters to the "Big Ten" environmental groups, and pressed their position at local gatherings as well as national and international meetings, to demand that these mostly white groups, which purported to represent everybody, diversify their staff, boards, and agendas (Bullard 1996). To date, no organized letter-writing campaign has been directed at the mainstream smart growth groups.

Environmental Justice Principles
The environmental justice movement was founded on the principle of "people speaking for themselves" (Alston 1990). Although it is usually unwritten, that slogan literally translates into "people of color and poor people speaking for themselves" since too often middle-class white environmentalists, planners, political and business elites, government officials, and industry representatives sat at decision-making tables and made policy *for* people of color and the poor, not with them. Two decades of struggle have taught us that if poor people and people of color are not at the table when plans are developed or decisions are made, their interests may not be well served. Of course, getting a seat at the table is not sufficient. The voices of marginalized groups must be heard and respected, and their vision must be acted on before real change takes hold.

The environmental justice framework incorporates other social movements and principles (for example, the precautionary principle) that seek to prevent and eliminate harmful practices in land use, industrial planning, health care, waste disposal, and sanitation services (Bullard 1993). In 1994, recognizing that the environmental protection apparatus was broken in many low-income and people of color communities across the country, and after much prodding from environmental justice leaders, the U.S. Environmental Protection Agency (EPA) acknowledged its mandate to protect all Americans.

The dominant environmental protection paradigm institutionalizes unequal enforcement, trades human health for profit, places the burden of proof on the victims and not the polluting industry, legitimates human exposure to harmful chemicals, pesticides, and hazardous substances, promotes risky technologies, exploits the vulnerability of economically and politically disenfranchised communities, subsidizes ecological destruction, creates an industry around risk assessment and risk management, delays cleanup actions, and fails to develop pollution prevention as the overarching and prevailing strategy (Bullard 2000).

The question of environmental justice is not anchored in a debate about whether or not decision makers should tinker with risk assessment and risk management. The framework rests on developing tools and strategies to eliminate unfair, unjust, and inequitable conditions and decisions (Bullard 1996). It also attempts to uncover the assumptions that may contribute to and produce differential exposure and unequal protection, and thus bring to the surface the ethical and political questions of who gets what, when, why, and how much.

The U.S. EPA (1998, 1) defines environmental justice as the

fair treatment and meaningful involvement of all people regardless of race, color, national origin, or income with respect to the development, implementation, and enforcement of environmental laws, regulations and policies. Fair treatment means that no group of people, including racial, ethnic, or socioeconomic groups should bear a disproportionate share of the negative environmental consequences resulting from industrial, municipal, and commercial operations or the execution of federal, state, local, and tribal programs and policies.

In response to growing public concern and mounting scientific evidence, President Bill Clinton on February 11, 1994 (the second day of the national health symposium) issued Executive Order 12898, "Federal Actions to Address Environmental Justice in Minority Populations and Low-Income Populations." This order attempts to address environmental injustice within existing federal laws and regulations. It reinforces the Civil Rights Act of 1964, Title VI, which prohibits discriminatory practices in programs receiving federal funds. The order also focuses the spotlight back on the National Environmental Policy Act (NEPA), a twenty-five-year-old law that sets policy goals for the protection, maintenance, and enhancement of the environment. NEPA's goal is to ensure for all Americans a safe, healthful, productive, and aesthetically as well as culturally pleasing environment. NEPA requires federal agencies to prepare a detailed statement on the environmental effects of proposed federal actions that significantly impact the quality of human health (Council on Environmental Quality 1997).

The executive order also calls for improved methodologies for assessing and mitigating environmental impacts, the health effect from multiple and cumulative exposure, the collection of data on low-income and minority populations who may be exposed to substantial environmental risks and the impacts on consumption patterns of populations who principally rely on fish and wildlife for subsistence. It also encourages participation of the impacted populations in the various phases of assessing impacts—including scoping, data gathering, alternatives, analysis, mitigation, and monitoring.

Documenting Disparities

Numerous studies document that people of color have borne greater health and environmental risks than society at large, independent of income and class status (Institute of Medicine 1999). They also face elevated health risks from workplace hazards, municipal landfills, incinerators, abandoned toxic waste dumps, and polluting industries (Bullard 2000; Commission for Racial Justice 1987; Goldman and Fitton 1994). Many of the nation's environmental policies distribute costs in a regressive pattern while providing disproportionate benefits to individuals who fall at the upper end of the education and income scale.

From New York to Los Angeles, grassroots community resistance has emerged in response to the practices, policies, and conditions that residents have judged to be unjust, unfair, and illegal. Some of these conditions include: the unequal enforcement of environmental, civil rights, and public health laws; the differential exposure of some populations to harmful chemicals, pesticides, and other toxins in the home, school, neighborhood, and workplace; faulty assumptions in calculating, assessing, and managing risks; discriminatory zoning and land use practices; and exclusionary practices that limit some individuals and groups from participation in decision making (Cole and Foster 2001; Agyeman, Bullard, and Evans 2003).

A 1992 *National Law Journal* study uncovered glaring inequities in the way the federal EPA enforces its laws (Lavelle and Coyle 1992). The study found a racial divide in the way the U.S. government cleans up toxic waste sites and punishes polluters. White communities get faster action, better results, and stiffer penalties for polluters than communities of color do. This unequal protection occurred whether the community was wealthy or poor. The *National Law Journal* study also reinforced what many grassroots activists have known for decades—all communities are not treated the same (Lavelle and Coyle 1992). Communities that are located on the wrong side of the tracks are at greater risk from exposure to lead, pesticides (in the home and workplace), air pollution, toxic releases, water pollution, solid and hazardous waste, raw sewage, and pollution from industries (Goldman and Fitton 1994).

The National Academy's Institute of Medicine (IOM) also discovered environmental and health disparities across various ethnic groups. The IOM (1999) scientists confirmed that people of color and low-income communities are (1) exposed to higher levels of pollution than the rest of the nation, and (2) experience certain diseases in greater number than the more affluent, white communities. The study concluded that government, public health officials, and the medical and scientific communities need to place a higher value on the problems and concerns of environmental justice communities.

The U.S. Commission on Civil Rights (USCCR) held hearings on environmental justice where experts presented evidence of environmental inequities in communities of color, including disproportionate incidences of environmentally related disease, lead paint in homes, hazardous waste sites, toxic playgrounds, and schools located near Superfund sites and facilities that release toxic chemicals. In its report *Not in My Backyard*, the USCCR (2003, 27) concluded that "minority and low-income communities are most often exposed to multiple pollutants and from multiple sources.... There is no presumption of adverse health risk from multiple exposures, and no policy on cumulative risk assessment that considers the roles of social, economic, and behavioral factors when assessing risk."

It is ironic that environmental justice at the EPA was initiated under the George H. W. Bush administration. Environmental justice, however, has faltered and all but become invisible at the EPA under the George W. Bush administration. The title of an EPA Office of Inspector General report, *EPA Needs to Consistently Implement the Intent of the Executive Order on Environmental Justice*, sums up the treatment of environmental justice under George W. Bush. After a decade, the EPA (2004, 1) "has not developed a clear vision or a comprehensive strategic plan, and has not established values, goals, expectations, and performance measurements" for integrating environmental justice into its day-to-day operations.

A U.S. General Accountability Office (2005) report, *Environmental Justice: EPA Should Devote More Attention to Environmental Justice When Developing Clean Air Rules*, also criticized the EPA for its handling of environmental justice issues when drafting clean air rules. And in July 2005, the EPA was met with a firestorm of public resistance when it proposed eliminating race and income from its Environmental Justice Strategic Plan. The proposal was described as "a giant step backward" and "a road map for other federal agencies to do nothing" (Bullard 2005a, 1). One must ask, What would the government response be if the victims of environmental injustice were disproportionately white and affluent?

In December 2005, the Associated Press released results from its study *More Blacks Live with Pollution*, which showed that African Americans are 79 percent more likely than whites to live in neighborhoods where industrial pollution is suspected of posing the greatest health danger (Pace 2005). Using the EPA's own data and government scientists, the study revealed that in nineteen states, blacks were more than twice as likely as whites to live in neighborhoods where air pollution seems to pose the greatest health danger.

The Associated Press analyzed the health risk posed by industrial air pollution using toxic chemical air releases reported by factories to calculate a health risk score for each square kilometer of the United States. The scores can be used to compare risks from long-term exposure to factory pollution from one area to another. The scores are based on the amount of toxic pollution released by each factory, the path the pollution takes as it spreads through the air, the level of danger to humans posed by each different chemical released, and the number of males and females of different ages who live in the exposure paths (Pace 2005).

Land Use Zoning

Zoning has shaped much of the urban built environment. It is probably the most widely applied mechanism to regulate urban land use in the United States. Zoning laws broadly define land for residential, commercial, or industrial uses, and may impose narrower land use restrictions—for example, the minimum and maximum lot size, the number of dwellings per acre, and the square feet and height of buildings (Haar and Kayden 1999).

Zoning laws and regulations influence land use and in turn have important environmental justice implications. Local land use and zoning policies are the "root enabling cause of disproportionate burdens and environmental injustice" in the United States (Maantay 2002). A National Academy of Public Administration (2003, 50) report, *Addressing Community Concerns: How Environmental Justice Relates to Land Use Planning and Zoning*, found that most planning and zoning board members are men; more than nine out of ten members are white; most members are forty years old or over; and boards contain mostly professionals and few, if any, nonprofessional or community representatives.

Exclusionary zoning (and rezoning) has been a subtle form of using government authority and power to foster and perpetuate discriminatory practices—including environmental planning. Exclusionary zoning has been used to zone against something rather than for something. On the other hand, "expulsive" zoning has pushed out residential uses and allowed "dirty" industries to invade communities (Rabin 1999, 106–8). Largely the poor, people of color, and renters inhabit the most vulnerable communities. Zoning laws are often legal weapons "deployed in the cause of racism" by allowing certain "undesirables" (immigrants, people of color, and poor people) and operations (polluting industry) to be excluded from areas (Rabin 1999, 25).

With or without zoning, deed restrictions, or other devices, various groups are unequally able to protect their environmental interests. More often than not, people of color and low-income communities get short-changed in the neighborhood protection game (Pastor, Sadd, and Hipp 2001; Faber and Krieg 2001). Zoning ordinances, deed restrictions, and other land use mechanisms have been widely used as a not in my backyard (NIMBY) tool, operating through exclusionary practices. Nevertheless, zoning has been ineffective in protecting some communities and populations from environmental threats from unregulated and unplanned sprawl-driven growth.

No amount of zoning has insulated the most vulnerable communities from the negative impacts of sprawl, whose costs and consequences fall disproportionately on individuals and communities at the lower end of the economic spectrum. Moreover, government regulations have not provided equal protection to all communities mainly because the current environmental protection apparatus manages, regulates, and distributes risks (Bullard 1996, 2000; Agyeman, Bullard, and Evans 2003). Because low-income, working-class, and people of color families are disproportionately and adversely affected by the environmental problems resulting from sprawl, it is not difficult to define sprawl as an environmental justice problem, and smart growth and regional equity as the solution.

One of the foremost obstacles affecting the revitalization of many urban communities is environmental degradation. As older industries have closed permanently, or left the central city to relocate to more "suitable" areas, they have left behind sites that are frequently contaminated by years of pollution. Decades of "look-the-other-way" industrial policies have subsidized threats to human health and the natural environment.

The urban landscape is dotted with brownfield sites (Bullard 2000). Brownfields are abandoned or underutilized industrial or commercial facilities where redevelopment is complicated by real or perceived environmental contamination. The U.S. General Accounting Office (1995) estimates that there are between 130,000 and 450,000 brownfield sites across the United States, and that they will cost $650 billion to clean up. Others have estimated that there are currently 500,000 or more brownfield sites, and that they will cost approximately $600 billion to clean up (Twombly 1997).

A large share of the brownfield sites are located in underserved inner-city communities heavily populated with either African Americans or Hispanics. A study by the *Dallas Morning News* (2000) and the University of Texas–Dallas found that some 870,000 of the 1.9 million (46 percent) housing units for the poor—mostly for minorities—sit within about a mile of factories that reported toxic emissions to the EPA. Many of the abandoned sites and brownfields are located in areas that have received empowerment and/or enterprise zone status. Residents in these communities, more often than not, are unemployed or under-employed, live below the poverty level, live in substandard housing, receive public assistance, and lack a high school education.

No Safe School Zone

All school environments are not created equal. Students of color comprise a majority of the students enrolled in fifteen of the sixteen Sierra Club (1998) "most sprawled-threatened" large cities. These cities include Atlanta (93.2 percent), Saint Louis (81.6 percent), Washington, DC (95.5 percent), Cincinnati (74.3 percent), Kansas City (83.1 percent), Denver (78 percent), Seattle (60 percent), Minneapolis (67.9 percent), Saint Paul (64.7 percent), Fort Lauderdale (58.8 percent), Chicago (90.4 percent), Detroit (96.3 percent), Baltimore (89.2 percent), Cleveland (80.7 percent), Tampa (48.2 percent), and Dallas (92.2 percent). The minority enrollment ranges from a low of 48.2 percent in Tampa-Hillsborough schools to 95.5 percent in Washington, DC, schools (U.S. Department of Education 2004).

In 1999–2000 more than six hundred thousand students in Massachusetts, New York, New Jersey, Michigan, and California were attending nearly twelve hundred public schools located within a half mile of federal Superfund or state-identified contaminated sites (Child Proofing Our Communities Campaign 2001). No state except California has a law requiring school officials to investigate potentially contaminated property, and no federal or state agency keeps records of public or private schools that operate on or near toxic waste or industrial sites (Lazaroff 2000).

Schools play a major role in where families with children decide to settle. The drift toward racially segmented metropolitan areas is most pronounced in public education. Author Myron Orfield (1997, 3) contends that "schools are the first victims and the most powerful perpetrator of metropolitan polarization." A 2002 Harvard Civil Rights Project study, *Race in American Public Schools: Rapidly Resegregating School Districts*, reports that the nation's school districts are becoming more diverse and more segregated (Frankenberg and Lee 2002).

Race played a big part in white middle-class flight from cities and urban school districts. In 2000, over 70 percent of black students attended schools where students of color were in the majority; 40 percent of black students attended schools that were 90 to 100 percent black; and over 80 percent of white students attended schools where more than 80 percent of the students were white (Orfield 2003). Black-white school segregation is most pronounced in districts with either no desegregation or where the courts rejected a city-suburban desegregation.

Latino student segregation has been steadily rising since the 1960s. Today, Latino students are the most segregated ethnic minority in the country. The Latino share of the nation's students almost tripled since 1968. Black student enrollment increased by 30 percent and white student enrollment decreased by 17 percent over the same period. Over 37 percent of Latino students attend schools where 90 to 100 percent of the pupils are students of color. The average Latino student is enrolled in a school that is less than 30 percent white.

Huge economic disparities exist between affluent suburban schools and their poor inner-city counterparts. These disparities are buttressed by the archaic school property tax financing method (U.S. Department of Education 2004). Our current taxing system encourages speculation, creates artificial land scarcity, rewards infrastructure abandonment, fosters scattered development, and promotes urban sprawl (Kunstler 1996, 27). Sprawl development has now forced many suburban school districts to come face-to-face with overcrowding and inadequate infrastructure problems—problems long associated with cities.

Transportation Sprawl

U.S. transportation policies, at least in the figurative sense, still relegate African Americans to the back of the bus. For more than a century, African Americans and other people of color have struggled to end transportation discrimination on buses, trains, and highways (Bullard and Johnson 1997). This form of racial apartheid, which clearly violates constitutionally guaranteed civil rights, was codified in 1896 by *Plessy v. Ferguson*, a U.S. Supreme Court decision that upheld Louisiana's segregated "white" and "colored" seating on railroad cars, ushering in the infamous doctrine of "separate but equal." *Plessy* not only codified apartheid for transportation facilities but also served as the legal basis for racial segregation in education until it was overturned in 1954 by *Brown v. Board of Education of Topeka*, another U.S. Supreme Court decision.

The modern civil rights movement has its roots in transportation. In 1953, nearly half a century after *Plessy v. Ferguson*, African Americans in Baton Rouge, Louisiana, staged the nation's first successful bus boycott. Two years later, on December 1, 1955, Rosa Parks refused to give up her seat at the front of a Montgomery city bus to a white man. In so doing, Parks ignited the modern civil rights movement. By the early 1960s, young "Freedom Riders" risked death by riding Greyhound buses into the Deep South as a way to fight transportation apartheid and segregation in interstate travel. Writing in the foreword to *Highway Robbery: Transportation Racism and New Routes to Equity*, Congressperson John Lewis (2004) summed up the challenge that lies ahead, "Our struggle is not over. The physical signs are gone, but the legacy of 'Jim Crow' transportation is still with us" (viii).

Lest anyone dismiss transportation as a tangential issue, consider that Americans spend more on transportation than any other household expense except housing—indeed, more than they do on food, education, and health care (Bullard 2005b). On average, Americans spend nineteen cents out of every dollar earned on transportation expenses. Transportation costs ranged from 17.1 percent in the Northeast to 20.8 percent in the South—where 54 percent of African Americans now reside. The nation's poorest families spend more than 40 percent of their take-home pay on transportation. Households that earned less than $20,000 saw their transportation expenses increase by 36.5 percent between 1992 and 2000. On the other hand, households with incomes of $70,000 and above only spent 16.7 percent more on transportation in 2000 than they did in 1992 (Sanchez, Stolz, and Ma 2004).

The private automobile is still the most dominant travel mode of every segment of the U.S. population. Private automobiles provide enormous employment access advantages to their owners. Nationally, only 7 percent of white households do not own a car, compared with 13 percent of Asian American households, 17 percent of Latino households, and 24 percent of African American households (Pucher and Renne 2003). The lack of car ownership and inadequate public transit service in many central cities and metropolitan regions exacerbate social, economic, and racial isolation, especially for low-income African Americans who already have limited transportation options.

Follow the Dollars

Follow the transportation dollars, and one can tell who is important and who is not. Congress passed the Intermodal Surface Transportation Efficiency Act (ISTEA) in 1991 to improve public transportation necessary "to achieve national goals for improved air quality, energy conservation, international competitiveness, and mobility for elderly persons, persons with disabilities, and economically disadvantaged persons in urban and rural areas of the country." In 1998, Congress reauthorized the transportation act under the Transportation Equity Act for the Twenty-First Century (TEA-21). From 1998 to 2003, TEA-21 spending amounted to $217 billion, the "largest public works bill enacted in the nation's history" (Gardner 1998, 1099–101).

TEA-21 expired in September 2003, and Congress then passed six temporary extensions. The latest extension carried spending through the end of May 2005 with the Federal Highway Administration (FHWA) getting $24.5 billion and transit $5.2 billion. TEA-21 created thousands of job opportunities. The U.S. Department of Transportation (USDOT) estimates that every $1 billion invested in public transportation infrastructure supports approximately 47,500 jobs.

Most of the transportation funds are distributed through state DOTs and local MPOs for each city. Generally, MPOs are not known for their diversity. The "one area, one vote" structure significantly underrepresents the racial minorities and urban areas of large MPOs, and overrepresents white constituents. Local bodies (and officials) are not representative due to persisting racism as well as the social and institutional barriers encountered by racial minorities (Sanchez, Stolz, and Ma 2004).

The current federal funding scheme is biased against metropolitan areas. The federal government allocated the bulk of transportation dollars directly to state DOTs. Many of these state road-building fiefdoms are no friend to urban transit. Nationally, 80 percent of all surface transportation funds are earmarked for highways and 20 percent are earmarked for public transportation. States generally spend less than 20 percent of their federal transportation funding on transit (Sanchez, Stolz, and Ma 2004). Although local governments within metropolitan areas own and maintain the vast majority of the transportation infrastructure, they receive only about 10 percent of every dollar they generate (Ashe 2003). Only about 6 percent of all federal highway dollars are suballocated directly to the metropolitan regions (Puentes and Bailey 2003).

A third of the $133 billion available to highway spending in 2001 came from federal and state gas taxes (Puentes and Prince 2003). Thirty states restrict the use of the gasoline tax revenue to funding highway programs only, thereby limiting these states' ability to finance and invest in mass transit options as well as air quality improvements in their cities and suburbs. Many of the states that restrict the use of the gas tax are also home to majority black cities, as in Alabama (Birmingham, 75.5 percent), Arkansas (Pine Bluff, 65.9 percent), Georgia (Atlanta, 61.4 percent; Savannah, 57.1 percent; and Macon, 62.5 percent), Indiana (Gary, 84 percent), Mississippi (Jackson, 70.6 percent; Greenville, 69.6 percent; and Meridian, 54.4 percent), Missouri (Saint Louis, 51.2 percent), Ohio (Cleveland, 51 percent), and Tennessee (Memphis, 61.4 percent). There is little doubt that such cities are getting shortchanged when transportation spending is tilted toward rural and far-flung suburban road pavement (Hill et al. 2003).

The nation's skewed gas tax distribution system creates "donor regions." Rural Harrison County in Ohio, with a population of a mere fifteen thousand people, receives the same level of funding from the county share as Cuyahoga County (Cleveland), which has 1.4 million urban residents (Hill et al. 2003). According to the *Atlanta Journal-Constitution*, Georgia's "funding formula steers cash to rural highways at the expense of gridlocked Atlanta motorists." From July 1999 through September 2003, Georgia spent $620 for every resident in the thirteen-county Atlanta region—a region with the state's worst congestion and the dirtiest air. In contrast, Georgia spent $1,000 per resident in the rest of the state (Stanford 2003). During the late 1990s, only about 17 percent of the gas tax revenues were returned to the thirteen Atlanta metropolitan counties—a region that generates 40 percent of the state's collection.

This problem is not unique to metropolitan Atlanta. Commuters in 176 metropolitan areas paid $20 billion more in federal gas taxes than they received in federal highway trust fund monies for both transit and highways from 1998 through 2003 (Environmental Working Group 2004). Taxpayers in fifty-four metropolitan areas lost an estimated $100 million during that same six-year period. The top gas tax losers were Los Angeles, Dallas–Forth Worth, Phoenix, Atlanta, Detroit, and New Orleans. New Orleans, with an astounding 27.9 percent poverty rate, received only fifty-three cents on each dollar paid.

Dismantling Transportation Apartheid
All across the nation, community groups are challenging local, metropolitan, state, and federal transportation agencies to strengthen intermodal options that sustain communities. These groups are also demanding that urban planners and policymakers think beyond cars and roads, and make transportation a *bridge* and not a *barrier* to opportunity. Too often public transit in many U.S. cities is stigmatized as "poor people" transportation or "transportation for losers" (Bullard, Johnson, and Torres 2004, 179).

Nationally, just 5 percent of all Americans use public transit to get to work (U.S. Bureau of the Census 2000). Most transit systems have tended to take their low-income and people of color "captive riders" for granted, and have concentrated their fare and service policies on attracting middle-class and "discretionary riders" out of their cars. Urban transit is especially important to African Americans because over 88 percent live in metropolitan areas and over 53 percent live inside central cities.

African Americans are almost six times as likely as whites to use transit to get around. In urban areas, African Americans and Latinos comprise over 54 percent of transit users (62 percent of bus riders, 35 percent of subway riders, and 29 percent of commuter rail riders). Nearly 60 percent of transit riders are served by the ten largest urban transit systems and the remaining 40 percent by the other five thousand transit systems (Sanchez, Stolz, and Ma 2004).

In December 2005, the nation celebrated the fiftieth anniversary of the Montgomery bus boycott. Rosa Parks, however, would have a difficult time sitting at the front or the back of a Montgomery bus today, since the city dismantled its public bus system in 1997—a transit agency that served mostly blacks and poor people (Stolz 2000). The cuts in the Montgomery bus system were made at the same time that federal tax dollars boosted the construction of the region's extensive suburban highways.

In January 2000, a study determined that the Demand and Response Transit (DART) system was not serving the citizens of Montgomery in an effective and efficient manner. On February 2, 2000, the Montgomery City Council voted to establish, on a trial basis, three new fixed routes to begin on March 6, 2000. The trial run of the fixed route service proved to be more effective and efficient in serving the transportation needs of the citizens of Montgomery. The new fixed route system was such a success that the City of Montgomery approved six additional fixed routes. The Montgomery Area Transit System is still today owned by the City of Montgomery and operated by First Transit Group Incorporated through contract (Montgomery Area Transit System 2006).

From New York to California, African Americans and other people of color are demanding an end to transportation policies that aid and abet the flight of people, jobs, and investments to the suburban fringe. In 1994, the Labor/Community Strategy Center and Bus Riders Union, along with the Korean Immigrant Workers Advocates and Southern Christian Leadership Conference, represented by the NAACP Legal Defense and Educational Fund, brought suit against the Los Angeles Metropolitan Transit Authority (MTA), charging it with violating Title VI of the 1964 Civil Rights Act. The coalition won a historic out-of-court settlement against the MTA in 1996 (Bullard, Johnson, and Torres 2004).

Even though the Bus Riders Union has won repeatedly in court, as recently as January 2004, it have had to wage an uphill battle to get the MTA to comply with the ten-year federal consent decree (Streeter 2004).

Community groups all across the country are fighting to end the kind of transit racism that killed seventeen-year-old Cynthia Wiggins of Buffalo, New York (Collison 1996). Wiggins, an African American, was crushed by a dump truck while crossing a seven-lane highway, because Buffalo's Number Six bus, an inner-city bus used mostly by African Americans, was not allowed to stop at the suburban Walden Galleria Mall. The bus stopped about three hundred yards away from the mall. Cynthia, not able to find a job in Buffalo, had secured work at a fast-food restaurant in the suburban mall.

The Wiggins family and other members of the African American community charged the Walden Galleria Mall with using the highway as a racial barrier to exclude some city residents (Chen 1999). The high-profile trial began on November 8, 1999. The lawsuit was settled ten days later when the mall owners, Pyramid Companies of Syracuse, agreed to pay $2 million of the $2.55 million settlement, over time, to Wiggins's four-year-old son. The Niagara Frontier Transportation Authority agreed to pay $300,000, and the driver of the truck agreed to pay $250,000.

Job Flight and Spatial Mismatch

In 2000, no other group in the United States was more physically isolated from jobs than African Americans (Raphael and Stoll 2000). University of California at Los Angeles scholar Michael Stoll's research reveals that more than 50 percent of blacks would have to relocate to achieve an even distribution of blacks relative to jobs. The comparable figures for whites are 20 to 24 percentage points lower.

In 2004, *Black Enterprise* magazine ranked Atlanta, Georgia, the number one city for African Americans, driven primarily by entrepreneurial opportunities, earnings potential, and cultural activities (Padgett and Brown 2004). Yet the majority of entry-level jobs in metro Atlanta are not within a quarter mile of public transportation. Households in the Atlanta region pay an extra $300 per month for the lack of transportation choices. This translates to $3,600 per year that households could be using for other expenses (Center for Neighborhood Technology 2004). This is not a small point since African Americans in metropolitan Atlanta earned only $703 per $1,000 earned by whites in 2000.

Suburbs are increasing their share of office space, while central cities see their share declining (Lang 2000). A 2000 Brookings Institution study, *Office Sprawl: The Evolving Geography of Business*, reported the suburban share of the metropolitan office space at 69.5 percent in Detroit, 65.8 percent in Atlanta, 57.7 percent in Washington, DC, 57.4 percent in Miami, and 55.2 percent in Philadelphia (Lang 2000, 5). Getting to many suburban job centers without a car is next to impossible.

It is no accident that Detroit leads in suburban office sprawl. Detroit is one of the most racially segregated big cities in the United States (Logan 2003). It is also called the "Motor City," and is the only major metropolitan area without a regional transit system. Heaster Wheeler (2004), executive director of the Detroit NAACP, the largest branch in the country, summed up the plight of his Motor City neighbors:

One out of three Detroit households don't own cars and they rely very heavily on public transportation. Unfortunately, our current transportation system does not take you anywhere. You cannot get to the airport, you cannot get to the mega-malls on the outskirts of the region (such as Twelve Oaks, Great Lakes Crossing, and Somerset), and they are located in areas that currently enjoy significant job growth. Detroiters pay disproportionate taxes to support transportation but get very little in return to support their transit needs. Over 50 percent of the new jobs that have come to our region in the last twenty-five years are located in areas not served by transit systems. The challenges of concentrated poverty are made worse by this lack of transportation and the benefits are extended to the communities that enjoy concentrated wealth.

Because of auto insurance redlining, the cost of owning and insuring an automobile for the working poor and working class is cost prohibitive. Many times, the cost for insurance is more than the average automobile payment, thus exacerbating the need for transit that will take you somewhere. You can literally be a convicted drunk driver living in the suburbs and pay less for auto insurance than a perfect driver living in the city. If state government mandates auto insurance coverage they should mandate rate fairness. Auto insurance premiums should be based on individual driving records and not zip codes, and not creditworthiness. Regional transportation systems fuel revitalization and attract economic activity and prosperity. For urban centers, we either constantly work to attract prosperity or we simply learn to manage more poverty.

Clearly, transportation is an essential ingredient in moving low-income families from poverty and dependency to self-sufficiency. Transportation investments, enhancements, and financial resources, if used properly, can bring new life and much-needed revitalization to urban areas, and can aid in lifting families out of poverty. Race and class dynamics operate to isolate millions of African Americans in central cities and away from expanding suburban job centers.

Transportation dollars have fueled suburban highway construction and job sprawl. Transportation investments are key ingredients in building economically viable and sustainable communities. State DOTs, MPOs, and transit providers have a major responsibility to ensure that their programs, policies, and practices do not discriminate against or adversely and disproportionately impact people of color and the poor.

The Right to Clean Air

Urban air quality is of major concern to people of color since they are disproportionately concentrated in the nation's nonattainment areas. Air pollution is not randomly distributed. National Argonne Laboratory researchers report that 57 percent of whites, 65 percent of African Americans, and 80 percent of Hispanics live in 437 counties with substandard air quality (Wernett and Nieves 1992). Sprawl-driven road programs add to this air pollution quagmire. Ground-level ozone is the primary ingredient of smog. Children are at special risk from the ozone (Pribitkin 1994).

Transportation sources nationally account for 80 percent of carbon monoxide (CO), 45 percent of nitrous oxide (NOx), 36 percent of hydrocarbons (HC), 32 percent of carbon dioxide (CO_2), 19 percent of particulate matter (PM), and 5 percent of sulfur dioxide (SO_2) emissions (White et al. 1994). Motor vehicles emit one-third of the nation's CO_2, one-quarter of all chlorofluorocarbons (CFC), 40 percent of NOx, and most of the CO (Kay 1997). A five-mile commute in a car annually releases 110 pounds of CO pollution into the air. The same commute on a train releases only one-half ounces of the same pollution per passenger.

Air pollution from vehicle emissions causes significant amounts of illness, hospitalization, and premature death. Although it is difficult to put a single price tag on this cost, estimates range from $10 billion to $200 billion a year (Bollier 1998). Air pollution exacerbates asthma and other respiratory illnesses. Inner-city children have the highest rates for asthma prevalence, hospitalization, and mortality (Centers for Disease Control and Prevention 1995).

Asthma, not gunshot wounds or drive-by shootings, is the number one reason for childhood emergency room visits in most major cities in the country. For millions, asthma is not only about health and the environment but also about civil and human rights. The hospitalization rate for African Americans is three to four times the rate for whites. In 2003, the Centers for Disease Control and Prevention (CDC 2004) reported that African Americans had an asthma death rate 200 percent higher than whites. Asthma is the most common chronic disease of childhood and the fourth-leading cause of disability among children less than eighteen years old in the United States (Centers for Disease Control and Prevention 1995). As of 1998, African Americans were almost three times more likely than whites to die from asthma (Centers for Disease Control and Prevention 2000).

A 2002 study in *Lancet* reported a strong causal link between ozone and asthma (McConnell et al. 2002, 386–91). Ground-level ozone may exacerbate health problems such as asthma, nasal congestions, throat irritation, respiratory tract inflammation, reduced resistance to infection, changes in cell function, loss of lung elasticity, chest pains, lung scarring, formation of lesions within the lungs, and premature aging of lung tissues (U.S. EPA 1996; Ozkaynk et al. 1995).

Air pollution claims seventy thousand lives a year, nearly twice the number killed in traffic accidents. Vehicular traffic along freeways and major thoroughfares produce harmful noise and pollution. Students attending schools closer to major thoroughfares have higher incidences of respiratory distress (van Vliet et al. 1997). Emissions from "dirty" diesel vehicles also pose health threats to nearby residents, including premature mortality, aggravation of existing asthma, acute respiratory symptoms, chronic bronchitis, and decreased lung function. Long-term exposure to high levels of diesel exhausts increase the risk of developing lung cancer (U.S. EPA 2002; Health Effects Institute 1995).

Diesel PM alone contributes to 125,000 cancers in the United States (State and Territorial Air Pollution Program Administrators 2000).

Adults and children living, working, or attending school within three hundred meters of major roadways are significantly more likely to get asthma, other respiratory illnesses, or leukemia, and may have a higher incidence of cardiovascular disease. Children are at special risk from the ground-level ozone—the main ingredient of smog (Pribitkin 1994). One of every four U.S. child lives in an area that regularly exceed the EPA's (2000) ozone standards.

In New York City, six out of eight of the MTA's diesel bus depots are located in northern Manhattan, a low-income community of color, while citywide twelve of twenty depots are in communities of color. In addition, five of the depots in northern Manhattan are in residential communities, within two hundred feet of people's homes. Diesel bus fumes from two thousand buses housed in the area inflict life-threatening pollution on West Harlem residents. In 1998, West Harlem Environmental Action, Inc. (WE ACT), a local environmental justice organization, won a campaign to get one bus depot converted to natural gas.

Are Smart Growth and Environmental Justice Compatible?

Clearly, the smart growth and environmental justice movements have a lot in common. The environment includes "where we live, work, play, go to school, as well as the physical and natural world" (Bullard et al. 2000). Both movements have set out the clear goals of addressing urban quality of life issues, including the protection of the environment, using resources wisely, cooperation between cities and suburbs, brownfields cleanup and reuse, open space and farmland preservation, transportation choices that alleviate traffic congestion and enhance transportation efficiency, affordable housing, expanded employment opportunities, and investing in and rebuilding communities.

Both movements allow for community collaborations in planning and decision making, and provide opportunities for building coalitions and alliances among diverse stakeholders. The mostly white smart growth movement and the mainstream environmental movement have a long way to go before they overcome their middle-class suburban bias. Yet both movements have made modest progress in building social equity principles into their agenda. They have done even less in bringing to the surface the deeply ingrained racial and class barriers in the United States that polarize urban and suburban residents. The environmental justice movement has provided the leadership in redefining environmentalism to include social equity and racial justice.

Persistent residential segregation has made it difficult for blacks and Hispanics to move to better-quality neighborhoods. Separate neighborhoods translate to unequal neighborhoods even for the most successful black and Hispanic households (Logan 2002). Getting a seat at the smart growth table has been problematic for many low-income and people of color urban residents.

While some individuals have taken an "integrationist" approach, others have opted to build smart growth and equitable development components into their environmental justice organization framework in their fight to secure safe and sanitary housing and toxic-free neighborhoods. A growing network of groups have pushed for tougher enforcement of clean air regulations, and campaigned to get dirty diesel buses and bus depots from being dumped in their neighborhoods. Still others have focused their energies on transportation-oriented development, linking public transit systems with jobs and economic activity centers, as well as representation on boards and commissions, in order to get their fair share of public infrastructure investments and to ensure that workers get paid a livable wage so that they can also have options—including homeownership and a car. Both smart growth and environmental justice advocates should commit to working on joint projects while including stakeholders from both movements.

References

Agyeman, J., R. D. Bullard, and B. Evans. 2003. *Just Sustainabilities: Development in an Unequal World*. Cambridge, MA: MIT Press.

Alston, D. 1990. *We Speak for Ourselves: Social Justice, Race, and the Environment*. Washington, DC: Panos Institute.

Ashe, V. H. 2003. Testimony to the U.S. House of Representatives Transportation and Infrastructure Committee. May 7. See ⟨http://www.house.gov/transportetion/highway/05-07-03/ashe.html⟩.

Bollier, D. 1998. *How Smart Growth Can Stop Sprawl: A Briefing Guide for Funders*. Washington, DC: Essential Books.

Bullard, R. D. 1993. Race and Environmental Justice in the United States. *Yale Journal of International Law* 18 (Winter): 319–335.

Bullard, R. D. 1996. *Unequal Protection: Environmental Justice and Communities of Color*. San Francisco: Sierra Club Books.

Bullard, R. D. 2000. *Dumping in Dixie: Race, Class, and Environmental Quality*. 3rd ed. Boulder, CO: Westview Press.

Bullard, R. D. 2005a. EPA's Draft Environmental Justice Strategic Plan—A Giant Step Backward. July 15. Available at ⟨http://www.ejrc.cau.edu/BullardDraftEJStrat.html⟩.

Bullard, R. D. 2005b. Transportation Policies Leave Blacks on the Side of the Road. *Crisis* 112, no. 1 (January–February): 21–22, 24.

Bullard, R. D., and G. S. Johnson, eds. 1997. *Just Transportation: Dismantling Race and Class Barriers to Mobility*. Gabriola Island, BC: New Society Publishers.

Bullard, R. D., G. S. Johnson, and A. O. Torres, eds. 1999. Atlanta: Megasprawl. *Forum: Applied Research and Public Policy* 14, no. 3:17–23.

Bullard, R. D., G. S. Johnson, and A. O. Torres, eds. 2000. *Sprawl City: Race, Politics, and Planning in Atlanta*. Washington, DC: Island Press.

Bullard, R. D., G. S. Johnson, and A. O. Torres, eds. 2004. *Highway Robbery: Transportation Racism and New Routes to Equity*. Cambridge, MA: South End Press.

Center for Neighborhood Technology. 2004. *Making the Case for Mixed-Income and Mixed-Use Communities*. June 1. Atlanta, GA: Atlanta Neighborhood Development Partnership Inc.

Centers for Disease Control and Prevention. 1995. Asthma: United States, 1982–1992. *Morbidity and Mortality Weekly Report* 43:952–955.

Centers for Disease Control and Prevention. 2000. *Death Rates from 72 Selected Causes by Year, Age Groups, Race, and Sex: United States, 1979–98*. Hyattsville, MD: National Center for Health Statistics.

Centers for Disease Control and Prevention. 2004. Asthma Prevalence, Health Care Use, and Mortality, 2000–2001. Available at ⟨http://www.cdc.gov/nchs/products/pubs/pubd/hestats/asthma/asthma.htm⟩ (accessed September 19).

Chen, D. W. 1999. Suit Accusing Shopping Mall of Racism over Bus Policy Settled. *New York Times*, November 18, B11.

Child Proofing Our Communities Campaign. 2001. *Poisoned Schools: Invisible Threats, Visible Actions*. Falls Church, VA: Center for Health, Environment, and Justice.

Cole, L., and S. R. Foster. 2001. *From the Ground Up: Environmental Racism and the Rise of the Environmental Justice Movement*. New York: New York University Press.

Collison, K. 1996. Mall Bus Policy Called Anti-City; Death Raises Bias Question. *Buffalo News*, January 28, 1A.

Commission for Racial Justice. 1987. *Toxic Wastes and Race in the United States*. New York: United Church of Christ.

Council on Environmental Quality. 1997. *Environmental Justice: Guidance under the National Environmental Policy Act*. Washington, DC: Council on Environmental Quality.

Dallas Morning News. 2000. Study: Public Housing Is Too Often Located near Toxic Sites. October 3. Available at ⟨http://www.cnn.com/2000/NATURE/10/03/toxicneighbors.ap/⟩.

Dreier, P., J. Mollenkoph, and T. Swanstrom. 2001. *Place Matters: Metropolitics for the Twenty-First Century*. Lawrence: University Press of Kansas.

Environmental Working Group. 2004. Metropolitan Areas Get Short End of Federal Gas Tax Funds. Available at ⟨http://www.ewg.org/reports/gastaxlosers/analysis.php⟩.

Faber, D. R., and E. J. Krieg. 2001. *Unequal Exposure to Ecological Hazards: Environmental Justice in the Commonwealth of Massachusetts*. Boston: Northeastern University.

Frankenberg, E., and C. Lee. 2002. *Race in American Public Schools: Rapidly Resegregating School Districts*. Cambridge, MA: Harvard Civil Rights Project.

Gardner, D. C. 1998. Transportation Reauthorization: A Summary of the Transportation Equity Act (TEA-21) for the Twenty-First Century. *Urban Law Journal* 30:1097, 1099–1101.

Gibson, T., and G. A. Taft. 2001. Making the Brownfields-Transportation Link: Smart Growth Options for States and Metropolitan Areas. *ECOStates: Quarterly Journal of the Environmental Council of the States* (Spring). See ⟨http://www.epa.gov/opei/ecoso/0611.htm⟩.

Goldman, B., and L. J. Fitton. 1994. *Toxic Wastes and Race Revisited*. Washington, DC: Center for Policy Alternatives, NAACP, United Church of Christ.

Haar, C. M., and J. S. Kayden, eds. 1999. *Zoning and the American Dream: Promises Still to Keep*. Chicago: American Planning Association.

Health Effects Institute. 1995. *Diesel Exhaust: A Critical Analysis of Emissions, Exposure, and Health Effects*. Cambridge, MA: Health Effects Institute.

Hill, E. W., B. Geyer, K. O'Brien, C. Robey, J. Brennan, and R. Puentes. 2003. *Slanted Pavement: How Ohio's Highway Spending Shortchanges Cities and Suburbs*. Washington, DC: Brookings Institution.

Institute of Medicine. 1999. *Toward Environmental Justice: Research, Education, and Health Policy Needs*. Washington, DC: National Academy Press.

Jargowsky, P. A. 2002. Sprawl, Concentration of Poverty, and Urban Inequality. *Urban Sprawl: Causes, Consequences, and Policy Responses*, ed. G. D. Squires, 39–71. Washington, DC: Urban Institute Press.

Kay, J. H. 1997. *Asphalt Nation: How the Automobile Took over America and How We Can Take It Back.* New York: Crown Publishers, Inc.

Kunstler, J. H. 1996. *Home from Nowhere: Remaking Our Everyday World for the Twenty-First Century.* New York: Simon and Schuster.

Lang, R. E. 2000. *Office Sprawl: The Evolving Geography of Business.* Washington, DC: Brookings Institution.

Lavelle, M., and M. Coyle. 1992. Unequal Protection. *National Law Journal*, September 21, 1–2.

Lazaroff, C. 2000. Pesticide Exposure Threatens Children at School. *Environmental News Service*, January 5.

Lewis, J. L. 2004. Foreword. *Highway Robbery: Transportation Racism and New Routes to Equity*, by R. D. Bullard, G. S. Johnson, and A. O. Torres. Boston: South End Press.

Logan, J. R. 2002. *Separate and Unequal: The Neighborhood Gap for Blacks and Hispanics in Metropolitan America.* Albany, NY: Lewis Mumford Center for Comparative Urban and Regional Research, University of Albany.

Logan, J. R. 2003. *Ethnic Diversity Grows, Neighborhood Integration Lags Behind.* Albany, NY: Lewis Mumford Center for Comparative Urban and Regional Research, University of Albany.

Maantay, J. 2002. Zoning, Law, Health, and Environmental Justice: What's the Connection? *Journal of Law, Medicine and Ethics* 30, no. 4 (Winter): 572.

McConnell, R., K. Berhane, F. Gilliland, S. J. London, T. Islam, W. J. Gauderman, E. Avol, H. G. Margolis, and J. M. Peters. 2002. In Exercising Children Exposed to Ozone: A Cohort Study. *Lancet*, 359, 386–391.

Montgomery Area Transit System. 2006. "History." Available at ⟨http://www.montgomerytransit.com/History/history.html⟩ (accessed on May 19, 2006).

National Academy of Public Administration. 2003. *Addressing Community Concerns: How Environmental Justice Relates to Land Use Planning and Zoning.* Washington, DC: NAPA.

Orfield, G., and S. E. Eaton. 2003. Back to Segregation. *Nation*, March 3. See ⟨http://www.thenation.com/doc/2003030/orfield⟩.

Orfield, M. 1997. *Metropolitics: A Regional Agenda for Community and Stability.* Washington, DC: Brookings Institution Press.

Ozkaynk, H., J. D. Spengler, M. O'Neil, J. Xue, H. Zhou, K. Gilbert, and S. Ramstrom. 1995. Ambient Ozone Exposure and Emergency Hospital Admissions and Emergency Room Visits for Respiratory Problems in Thirteen U.S. Cities. In *Breathless: Air Pollution and Hospital Admissions/Emergency Room Visits in 13 Cities.* Washington, DC: American Lung Association.

Pace, D. 2005. AP: More Blacks Live with Pollution. *ABC News*, December 13. Available at ⟨http://abcnews.go.com/Health/wireStory?id=1403682&CMP=OTC-RSSFeeds0312⟩.

Padgett, D., and C. M. Brown. 2004. Top Cities for African Americans. *Black Enterprise* 34, no. 12:78–103.

Pastor, M., Jr., J. Sadd, and J. Hipp. 2001. Which Came First: Toxic Facilities, Minority Move-Ins, and Environmental Justice. *Journal of Urban Affairs* 23, no. 1:3.

Pribitkin, A. E. 1994. The Need for Revision of Ozone Standards: Why Has the EPA Failed to Respond? *Temple Environmental Law and Technology Journal* 13:104.

Pucher, J., and J. L. Renne. 2003. Socioeconomics of Urban Travel: Evidence from the 2001 NHTS. *Transportation Quarterly* 57 (Summer): 49–77.

Puentes, R., and L. Bailey. 2003. *Improving Metropolitan Decision Making in Transportation: Greater Funding and Devolution for Greater Accountability.* Washington, DC: Brookings Institution.

Puentes, R., and R. Prince. 2003. *Fueling Transportation Finance: A Primer on the Gas Tax.* Washington, DC: Brookings Institution.

Rabin, Y. 1999. Expulsive Zoning: The Inequitable Legacy of Euclid. In *Zoning and the American Dream: Promises Still to Keep*, ed. C. M. Haar and J. S. Kayden. Chicago: American Planning Association.

Raphael, S., and M. A. Stoll. 2000. *Modest Progress: The Narrowing Spatial Mismatch between Blacks and Jobs in the 1990s.* Washington, DC: Brookings Institution.

Sanchez, T. A., R. Stolz, and J. Ma. 2004. *Moving to Equity: Addressing Inequitable Effect of Transportation Policies on Minorities.* Cambridge: Harvard Civil Rights Project.

Sierra Club. 1998. *The Dark Side of the American Dream: The Cost and Consequences of Suburban Sprawl.* College Park, MD: Sierra Club.

Stanford, D. 2003. Metro Roads Shortchanged: Funding Formula Steers Cash to Rural Highways at the Expense of Gridlocked Atlanta Motorists. *Atlanta Journal-Constitution*, September 28, p. A1.

State and Territorial Air Pollution Program Administrators and the Association of Local Air Pollution Control Officials. 2000. Cancer Risk from Diesel Particulate: National and Metropolitan Area Estimates for the United States.

Streeter, K. 2004. For the MTA, the Bucks Start Here. *Los Angeles Times*, January 13.

Stolz, R. 2000. Race, Poverty, and Transportation. *Poverty and Race* (March–April). See ⟨http://www.prrac.org/Full_text.php?text_id=91titem_id=1811tneusletter_id=49theader=Poverty+%2F+welfare⟩.

Twombly, R. 1997. Urban Uprising. *Environmental Health Perspective* 105 (July): 696–701.

U.S. Bureau of the Census. 2000. Available at ⟨http://www.census.gov/⟩.

U.S. Commission on Civil Rights. 2003. *Not in My Backyard: Executive Order 12898 and Title VI as Tools for Achieving Environmental Justice.* Washington, DC: U.S. Commission on Civil Rights.

U.S. Department of Education. 2004. *Characteristics of the Hundred Largest Public and Secondary School Districts in the United States: 2000–2001.* Washington, DC: U.S. Department of Education, National Center for Education Statistics.

U.S. EPA. 1996. Review of National Ambient Air Quality Standards for Ozone, Assessment of Scientific and Technical Information. Research Triangle Park, NC: EPA.

U.S. EPA. 1998. *Guidance for Incorporating Environmental Justice in EPA's NEPA Compliance Analysis.* Washington, DC: U.S. EPA.

U.S. EPA. 2000. *The President's Task Force on Environmental Health Risks and Safety Risks to Children: Asthma and the Environment: A Strategy to Protect Children.* Washington, DC: EPA. Available at ⟨http://www.epa.gov/children/whatwe/fin.pdf⟩ (accessed December 10).

U.S. EPA. 2002. Health Assessment Document for Diesel Exhaust. Washington, DC: EPA, National Center for Environmental Assessment.

U.S. EPA. 2004. *EPA Needs to Consistently Implement the Intent of the Executive Order on Environmental Justice: Evaluation Report.* Washington, DC: EPA, Office of Inspector General.

U.S. General Accountability Office. 2005. *Environmental Justice: EPA Should Devote More Attention to Environmental Justice When Developing Clean Air Rules.* Washington, DC: GAO.

U.S. General Accounting Office. 1995. *Community Development: Reuse of Urban Industrial Sites.* Washington, DC: GAO.

van Vliet P., M. Knape, J. de Hartog, N. Janssen, H. Harssema, and B. Brunekreef. 1997. Motor Vehicle Exhaust and Chronic Respiratory Symptoms in Children Living near Freeways. *Environmental Research* 74, no. 2:122–132.

Wernett, D. R., and L. A. Nieves. 1992. Breathing Polluted Air: Minorities Are Disproportionately Exposed. *EPA Journal* 18:16–17.

Wheeler, H. 2004. Interview by Robert D. Bullard. December 17, Detroit NAACP.

White, M. C., R. Etzel, W. D. Wilcox, and C. Lloyd. 1994. Exacerbations of Childhood Asthma and Ozone Pollution in Atlanta. *Environmental Research* 65:56–68.

2

Race, Poverty, and Urban Sprawl: Access to Opportunities through Regional Strategies

john a. powell

This chapter attempts to demonstrate the need for social justice and urban civil rights advocates to focus on sprawl as well as concentrated poverty. Both are as much civil rights issues as environmental or land use concerns, and sprawl has frustrated civil rights efforts. Indeed, there is strong evidence that racialized concentrated poverty is both a cause and a product of sprawl, and that due to this interrelationship, concentrated poverty cannot be addressed without addressing sprawl. To examine this relationship, I explore how the phenomena of gentrification and the revitalization strategy of infill operate differently in rich, middle-class, and poor cities. I also argue that concentrated poverty and sprawl are regional issues that can only be addressed on a regional level; therefore, it is a mistake for social justice and urban civil rights advocates to leave the regional discussion to environmentalists and land use planners.

This chapter explores the relationship between sprawl and concentrated poverty. Although there has been inadequate attention given to this relationship, a number of scholars have recently begun to examine it more closely (Rusk 1995, 1999; Massey and Denton 1993; Orfield 1997; Jargowsky 1997; Downs 1998; Freilich and Peshoff 1997). I strongly support that effort, and will briefly set out some of the historical and current processes that clearly link sprawl and concentrated poverty.

In discussing this inattention, I will focus on two specific phenomena related to concentrated poverty and sprawl: the failure of urban civil rights and social justice advocates to target the relationship between sprawl and concentrated poverty, on the one hand, and the oftentimes confusing response to gentrification, on the other. The nexus of gentrification and concentrated poverty is possibly the most misunderstood and least explored aspect of concentrated poverty as a social phenomena. In the latter half of this chapter, I will turn my attention to that issue.

I engage these issues with a focus on racialized concentrated poverty (Galster and Hill 1992). Although I am not indifferent to sprawl per se, my primary concern is to demonstrate why it is critical for civil rights and social justice advocates to address sprawl and to better understand gentrification in the wider scope of remedying the problems associated with concentrated poverty. Sprawl is not simply a problem that warrants cursory attention by civil rights advocates; it is one of the most important structural urban dynamics that frustrates many of the broad aspirations of the civil rights movement. This chapter is written for a wide audience as these issues affect the entire country, but I am particularly concerned with engaging the civil rights community.

Urban Sprawl and Its Effects on Central City Communities

Urban sprawl, which has long been a reality of the U.S. landscape, has recently drawn attention as a serious problem that must be addressed (Purdum 1999). While there are still those who would challenge the claim that sprawl is a problem in want or need of a solution (Gordon and Richardson 1998), a number of policymakers have joined the ranks of environmentalists in the call to address and retard the proliferation of urban sprawl (*Star Tribune* 1999). Terms like planned growth, smart growth, sustainable growth, and no growth are gaining currency in popular discourse. This evolving public discourse and the problems associated with sprawl usually focus on environmental and land use issues (Purdum 1999). These issues include traffic congestion, long commutes, lost time and efficiency for businesses, depleting the habitats of endangered species, and the destruction of farmland and open space. In sprawl discourse, issues of concentrated poverty and race, if discussed at all, are too often mentioned as peripheral concerns.

Suburban residents and the environment are not the only victims of sprawl. Sprawl isolates inner-city communities from economic and educational opportunities. Concentrated poverty, defined as a poverty rate at or above 40 percent within a given area, is closely aligned with several sprawl-related trends in urban America. These trends include a decrease in population density in central cities as primarily white, middle-class people flee, and the movement of employment opportunities to the outer reaches of the region following this demographic shift away from the central city (Foster-Bey 1997). These sprawl patterns have contributed to the destructive pattern of concentrated poverty and the isolation of low-income communities and communities of color from economic opportunities. It was the concentration of middle-class whites at the periphery of the region that helped cause and made possible the concentration of low-income minorities at the center. Racial discrimination and segregation have played important roles in creating and reinforcing these sprawl patterns (Foster-Bey 1997, 29–30). Racial discrimination in housing, employment, and educational opportunities has operated to concentrate poor communities of color in the central city, while economic opportunities as well as middle- and upper-class whites have moved out to suburbia.

As mentioned above, with the suburban flight that has been occurring over the last few decades, much of the employment base has also fled the central cities. In 1970, only 25 percent of the nation's offices were located in suburbs (Peirce 1993). More recent numbers indicate that over 60 percent are now located in the suburbs (Peirce 1993). Many city residents have not been able to follow this migration of jobs. The lack of transportation choices in metropolitan areas limits options for those without cars and prevents central city residents from accessing jobs located in the suburbs (Jarkowsky 1997, 105). There are also limited housing choices for lower-income residents in the suburbs—many developing suburban communities limit or prohibit multifamily housing, and have minimum lot sizes and other restrictions that push up the cost of housing (Orfield 1997, 58–59). Racial steering and redlining have also played roles in limiting housing choices for many people of color, isolating them in central city neighborhoods and declining suburbs while denying them the opportunity to develop wealth through homeownership (Oliver and Shapiro 1995). A number of related problems have developed from this isolation of people of color and low-income people in the central cities—including chronic unemployment, increased crime, and failing schools (Orfield 1997, 2–4; Massey and Denton 1993). Solving these problems is beyond the ability of local governments, especially in light of their declining tax bases (Orfield 1997, 2–5). The deteriorating state of many cities drives still more middle-class families to the suburbs. This pattern continues today as many central cities still lose population while their suburbs grow (Wilson 1997).

There are some who claim that urban sprawl is a free market outcome and that it is actually the preferred lifestyle of most Americans, as evidenced by the tremendous growth of suburbs (Gordon and Richardson 1998). Such claims do not fully account for the federal government's role in creating sprawl as well as the lack of access to opportunities for minority communities. The federal government provided the highways that helped pave the way out for the fleeing middle class, and insured the cheap Federal Housing Administration (FHA) mortgages that helped buy many suburban homes (Jackson 1985). At the same time, this financing was not initially available to many central city residents and people of color due to official and informal policies of redlining, racial steering, and refusing loans to residents that remained in the city (Jackson 1985, 206, 217).

The costs of sprawl, including increased traffic and the increased cost of infrastructure, are becoming more evident every year. People are beginning to realize that the negative effects of hollowing out the urban core caused by sprawl cannot so easily be confined to the central city (Downs 1997). There is growing evidence that the fate of the city and suburb are inextricably linked. Studies indicate that the better the central city does, the better the suburb does (Rusk 1999; Savitch et al. 1993; Voith 1992), and during the last recession, the metropolitan areas with the greatest income differential between the central city and the suburbs suffered the most (Peirce 1993, 31). Inner-ring suburbs are now suffering many of the same problems that central cities faced a generation ago (Downs 1997; Orfield 1997, 2). In today's global economy, regions compete with each other for capital and jobs (Peirce 1993, 3). Crippled central cities and declining suburbs can serve as a drag on the whole regional economy (Peirce 1993, 19).

There are currently a number of limited antisprawl solutions. Many of them are aimed at slowing the outward spread of suburban growth— usually by buying land on the fringe of metropolitan areas. Despite or maybe because of these limited efforts, most metropolitan areas have not been effective in slowing sprawl. Even in the absence of effective government action, however, there are signs of change and a possible reorientation of middle-class residents back to the city. After years of flight, there are modest signs of people moving back to downtown areas. Cities like Houston, Cleveland, Denver, and Chicago are seeing an influx of upscale residents moving into downtown neighborhoods (Brooke 1998). Although this influx is hopeful, the numbers are usually not enough to offset the amount of people still leaving the central city.

The weak antisprawl movement and the influx of new residents to the city are, at best, only partial solutions to sprawl and concentrated poverty. Job growth and entry-level employment opportunities are projected to continue to be concentrated in the suburbs of most metropolitan regions (Peirce 1993, 19). Educational opportunities are still grossly unequal for city and suburban residents (Orfield 1997, 35–54). And housing choices continue to shrink as existing affordable housing is being demolished or upgraded out of the reach of lower- and middle-income residents without being replaced (McLeod 1998). To effectively address the issues of sprawl and concentrated poverty it is necessary to closely examine how sprawl patterns dictate the location of these opportunities denied to low-income communities of color. Regional strategies are critical to remedy these inequities in meaningful ways.

Sprawl, Concentrated Poverty, and Desegregation

The growing antisprawl movement is frequently spearheaded by those in the suburbs who have not traditionally focused on inner-city social justice issues. At the same time, social justice advocates who work on issues associated with racial segregation and concentrated poverty traditionally do not focus directly on land use policy outside their immediate neighborhood (Bullard 1993). Many antisprawl and social justice advocates have failed to recognize the important connections between these seemingly disparate issues. This is more than a small oversight.

Earlier I suggested that sprawl and fragmentation had effectively undermined the aspirations of the civil rights movement. How and when did this occur? Before the civil rights movement there was the forced segregation of blacks and whites imposed by law. We are all familiar with this racial caste system referred to as Jim Crow. The civil rights movement was an attack on that system. Yet the dynamics of sprawl and jurisdictional fragmentation largely blunted the civil rights movement. While the civil rights movement was concerned with ending segregation, the courts and policymakers adopted a different approach that distinguished intrajurisdictional segregation from interjurisdictional segregation, thus limiting desegregation efforts and remedies to segregation within local political boundaries (Ford 1994). This clever legal distinction rendered many desegregation efforts virtually meaningless and made a mockery of the goals of the civil rights movement.

In the school desegregation context, *Milliken v. Bradley* (1974), provides a forceful example of how political fragmentation curtailed the aims of the civil rights movement. In *Milliken*, the court ordered the Detroit schools to be desegregated, but prohibited an interdistrict desegregation remedy that would have included the white suburban districts along with the largely minority school district in Detroit. The narrow focus of the desegregation remedy, as limited by local municipal boundaries, did not remedy segregation on a broad scale and in fact may have entrenched racial segregation.

The increased deference to local political boundaries occurred almost exactly at the same time as the early gains of the civil rights movement. This move toward greater fragmentation in the wake of the civil rights movement was not just a coincidence; it was part of a deliberate move to compromise the idea of integration while responding to the growing demands for racial justice by blacks (Weiher 1991). Political boundaries maintained segregation despite the efforts of the civil rights movement.

The tendency of boundaries to perform this function has been increased by public policy produced from the late 1940s to the seventies and early eighties. In the presence of a persistent aversion to blacks on the part of whites, public policy has not ameliorated residential segregation. Rather, it has restructured it by presenting these whites with altered incentives and institutional forms. The result has been a change in the geographic pattern of rather than a reduction in, residential segregation. (Weiher 1991, 87–88)

Gregory Weiher (1991, 88) goes on to note that "civil rights policy has substantially dismantled neighborhood level, or 'intrajurisdictional,' mechanisms of segregation. But federal court policy has reinforced

devices which support interjurisdictional racial segregation." This resorting of whites not just to new neighborhoods but to new cities explains
the persistent racial segregation in housing markets and in non-Southern
schools despite the efforts of the civil rights movement. Indeed, one study
has shown that the more fragmented a region, the more racially and economically segregated it is (Rusk 1999). And importantly, blacks were not
simply being segregated from whites but also from opportunity.

The fragmentation associated with sprawl in the 1990s is a version of
states' rights. Support for states' rights was a strategy often used by civil
rights opponents in the early part of the civil rights movement to undermine desegregation efforts at the federal level. Opponents of civil rights
would argue that federal laws governing civil rights infringed on states'
rights to govern themselves. Thus, through states' rights they attempted
to circumvent the gains of the civil rights movement.

There is a historical connection between the push for states' rights and
the current political fragmentation at the municipal level. Both movements have used fragmentation and local control to prevent desegregation. The local control advocated by states' rights proponents was state
control to circumvent federal laws. The local control and fragmentation
associated with sprawl is a more refined version of the same localism
touted by states' rights advocates, and is used by residents of the municipalities to exclude low-income residents of color while trying to attract
high tax base resources. Sprawl, as a method of fragmentation, perpetu-
ates the dysfunctional dynamic of our regions, and is a continuation of
the sorting and local control movement that undermined civil rights desegregation efforts dating back to the 1950s.

The Reciprocal Relationship between Sprawl and Racialized Space

Concentrated poverty can be equated with racialized space at the urban
core because these isolated low-income populations are also disproportionately populations of color (Goldberg 1993; Jargowsky 1997; Calmore 1995; Rusk 1999). Economist Anthony Downs (1997) and urban
scholar David Rusk (1999, 44) have asserted that where there is a
sprawling metropolitan area with political fragmentation and a substantial presence of racial minorities, you will have concentrated poverty and

racial segregation at the urban core (see also Massey and Denton, 1993; powell 1996). This phenomenon is not simply the result of naturally occurring economic sorting or private policy over the last fifty years. Poverty in the United States is racialized and systemic; it is the product of well-documented, formal and informal, racially discriminatory federal, state, and municipal policies, including housing and transportation policies that encourage middle-class whites to flee the city for the suburbs (Massey and Denton 1993; Jackson 1985; powell 1996).

Concentrated poverty is both a substantial cause and product of sprawl. On the one hand, concentrated poverty has been a strong causative force behind sprawl. The fear of minority ghettos and barrios, along with the social problems often associated with the poverty there, is one of the causes of white and middle-class flight from the core of metropolitan areas—a flight that has created and exacerbated sprawl patterns (Massey and Denton 1993; Jackson 1985; powell 1996).

On the other hand, it is the abandonment of the urban core itself that creates and causes concentrated poverty, which is then used to justify white flight. It is not the poor concentrating themselves or moving to the center but rather upper- and middle-class residents moving out to the periphery that causes the isolation of low-income people of color. Policies that have encouraged sprawl over the last fifty years have also fostered concentrated poverty as key opportunities quickly followed middle-class whites' flight from the urban core. Urban residents were left behind with a declining tax base, shrinking employment opportunities, a failing educational system, and a shortage of decent, affordable housing (Freilich and Peshoff 1997; Orfield 1997). There is an economic incentive for middle-class suburban residents to keep out those with high needs and few resources. This, coupled with racial discrimination and whites' aversion to blacks, takes a high toll on low-income blacks (Weiher 1991, 87–99).

While it is difficult to address issues of sprawl without addressing concentrated poverty, it is virtually impossible to address issues of concentrated poverty without dealing with sprawl (Rusk 1999, 127–28; Orfield 1997, 75; Foster-Bey 1997; Bollens 1997). Strategies to alleviate concentrated poverty and racial discrimination center on gaining access to or creating economic and educational opportunities. Since sprawl patterns have largely shaped the spatial placement of these opportunities, however, sprawl itself must be challenged.

Civil Rights and Social Justice Advocates' Mistrust of the Antisprawl Movement

I have posited that sprawl and fragmentation caused concentrated poverty and undermined the civil rights movement. But if this is even modestly correct, then why is it that traditional civil rights and social justice advocates have not been more active participants in the attack on sprawl? There are a number of explanations for the failure of these communities to address sprawl as a strategy for dealing with issues of race and poverty. While the list of possible explanations I provide here is not exhaustive, it presents some of the most significant barriers to working on social justice issues in the context of sprawl discourse.

One explanation is simply proximity. Sprawl is primarily, but mistakenly, viewed as an issue at the edge of the metropolitan region, with little impact or direct relevance to the issues of the urban core. Many people involved with social justice issues in the urban core are often unaware of—and as a result, unconcerned with—what is happening so far from their neighborhoods and cities. Most of the active players addressing concentrated poverty issues are people working on a grassroots level, often through community development corporations. The focus of most community development corporations is to lift the economic level of the communities' residents (Vidal 1992). It is often not immediately apparent to these communities that the resources they need are being pushed away by the problems related to concentrated poverty and pulled away by sprawl patterns. Strategies addressing sprawl that seek to increase density and build up the tax base by drawing in the middle class and businesses to create a more stable, mixed-income community are seldom advocated by antisprawl regionalists. Additionally, these strategies frequently seem irrelevant or threatening to the present population.

A second explanation is the suspicion and resistance that urban communities have toward regional approaches (powell 1998; Goedert 1988; Choper 1984). Regionalism suggests the need to move beyond fragmented jurisdictional approaches toward cross-jurisdictional cooperation as a means to address issues that impact the entire region (Rusk 1995). Many inner-city communities of color have resisted regional strategies for fear of losing cultural control, cultural identity, and political power within their communities. Indeed, this fear is well-founded since the redrawing of political boundaries has often been used to disempower the minority community (Guinier 1994; Kousser 1999). Some theorists, however, have failed to address concerns over disempowerment by suggesting that although minority communities may currently have political control over their communities, in reality, due to their lack of resources or reisolation within the political system, this control is ineffectual (Orfield 1997; Guinier 1991a; Kousser 1999). The logic behind this position is that even if minorities have to give up control in order to participate in regional strategies, they have nothing to lose because, in effect, they have control over nothing significant.

The Hobson's choice that is apparently presented by these two assertions is that inner-city communities of color can either have insignificant self-control, or have access to resources but no voice or identity. These are untenable alternatives, which have been and should be rejected. But rejecting these choices is often seen as the same as rejecting regional or metropolitan efforts. This is a mistaken assumption as the dichotomy these options present is a false one. Regional approaches are necessary to adequately address the inextricable issues of sprawl, race, and concentrated poverty because these are regional problems, and the solutions are not found solely or even primarily within the neighborhoods or cities where concentrated poverty is located. As the mayor of Detroit, Dennis Archer (1998), recently noted, "We can't save our cities unless we save our farmland."

In an earlier work, I suggested a form of federated regionalism to mediate the concerns about disempowerment and the need for addressing concentrated poverty (powell 1998). This is a regional approach that preserves political and cultural status within communities or cities, while sharing regional resources and responsibilities, and balancing regional policymaking. Federated regionalism provides the opportunity to preserve and build on the assets of the inner-city community, while tapping into the resources and opportunities located elsewhere in the region.

Another explanation for many urban civil rights advocates' failure to enter the sprawl discourse is their suspicion of and skepticism about urban revitalization as a policy for bringing in or maintaining the number of middle-class households in the urban core. The fear is that by allowing middle- and upper-income residents into their neighborhoods through infill or gentrification, complete displacement of low-income residents will ultimately result. This concern has both class and racial underpinnings. While concentrated poverty generally depicts a method of sorting low-income racial minorities at the urban core, gentrification is a way in which middle- and upper-middle-class whites are sorted into urban areas by displacing low-income minorities (powell 1998).

Although gentrification in high-poverty cities is often a charged and contentious political issue, I believe that concerns about gentrification are more appropriately raised in rich cities, not poor ones. The issue is more nuanced in middle-class cities. This approach may seem counterintuitive given that rich cities have resources and low poverty rates, and poverty does not seem to be an issue. But when viewed in the wider context of how racial and class sorting occur in metropolitan areas, the approach takes on clarity.

By rich cities, I refer to central cities that have a median per capita income and fiscal capacity close to or above the average for the region in which they are situated. In addition, rich cities will usually have a growing or stable population base. San Francisco and Seattle are examples of rich cities. Middle-class cities are those that have 70 to 90 percent of the regional median per capita income, while poor cities have less than 70 percent of the regional median income (Rusk 1995). Rich cities may appear to have no serious concentrated poverty issues, certainly not of the magnitude of poor cities such as Detroit and Cleveland. This perception, however, obscures how rich cities sort along racial and class lines through gentrification, and how this method of sorting is related to concentrated poverty. Rich cities appear to have few problems with concentrated poverty because their sorting practices displace or keep most low-income minorities out of their cities where opportunity is concentrated, while relocating them in nearby poor cities and suburbs.

It is possible that a region is doing so well that the isolation of poor minorities associated with concentrated poverty is simply not an issue.

This situation is not likely, though, which makes it necessary to examine what is actually occurring in these rich cities and their surrounding regions. In San Francisco, the number of high-poverty census tracts has remained comparatively low and stable at twelve to thirteen since 1970, while most large U.S. cities in the Midwest and Northeast have experienced a large increase in the number of high-poverty census tracts during this same period (Jargowsky 1997). Through a closer examination of the forces behind this low number of high-poverty tracts, we find that lower-income residents, even those with modest means, are being pushed out of the city and into areas where there is concentrated poverty, such as Oakland, or in suburbs away from opportunity. This is disturbing for a number of reasons. Not only are people being pushed out of their homes and away from opportunity, they are also being pushed into areas with fewer social resources to address the needs of low-income residents. In essence, the dynamics of isolation remain the same, they are just relocated.

We find a similar sorting going on in places like Seattle. Seattle, which had only nine high-poverty census tracts in 1990, is a place where economic resources in the region are concentrated in the central city (Jargowsky 1997). At the same time, many of the low-income residents are being pushed out into southern working-class suburbs such as Renton (Conklin 1998; Modie 1998). This context of gentrification could be called extrajurisdictional gentrification in that low-income residents are not simply being pushed out of their neighborhood but also out of their city.

To exacerbate the problems of displaced residents, poor cities and marginal working-class suburbs receiving the displaced have declining resources and growing needs. In these suburbs, many of the long-term residents are white and many of the residents coming in are people of color. This is a recipe for racial tension and resentment (Lewis, Brand-Williams, and Taylor 1999; Associated Press 1999). Because both the Bay Area and the Seattle area are fragmented along jurisdictional lines, these rich cities are in a sense subsidized by this sorting process since they do not have to share their resources with the low-income residents they have displaced to nearby suburbs or cities. In so doing, these rich cities fail to take their fair share of responsibility for the social needs they have helped create in other locations within the region.

Contrast this experience of extrajurisdictional or complete gentrification with that of many high-poverty cities. In many high-poverty areas or cities, any effort to attract or build housing for middle-class households is misconstrued as gentrification. It is both a conceptual and political mistake to confuse gentrification with efforts to attract middle-class households back to poor cities, however. For example, in cities such as Cleveland and Detroit that have a large number of high-poverty census tracts populated primarily by low-income people of color (Jargowsky 1997, 224–25), as well as a large number of vacant lots and homes, there is an effort to attract middle-class residents. In 1990, Detroit had 149 high-poverty census tracts while Cleveland had 69 high-poverty census tracts. The effort to attract middle-income housing in these areas is better characterized as infill housing, and the goal is to build housing on vacant land or rehab existing housing that is not being used.

Infill housing can be built in areas where there is little or no existing housing, or in areas where some housing already exists. While infill can involve any type of housing and other nonresidential projects, it is the filling in with middle- and upper-middle-class homes that is most frequently associated or confused with gentrification. Gentrification is usually understood to mean the transition of a neighborhood caused by the in-migration of middle- and upper-middle-class residents who are most often white, and the resulting forced out-migration of low-income residents who are frequently people of color.

The term gentrification has been criticized as a misnomer since many gentrifiers are not from the highest echelons of society but are in fact middle income. Nevertheless, gentrification is the term most commonly used to describe the phenomenon of middle- and upper-income residents returning to live in the central city, and often renovating the existing housing stock (Durham and Shelton 1986). Given this understanding, an infill project is not gentrification because no one is being pushed out. Even if people are not directly displaced, it is possible that infill could still have the effect of pushing people out by driving up the property values in the area or city, thereby making it harder for people to stay in their homes. This is not a major problem in cities such as Detroit and Cleveland, though. It is important to distinguish between gentrification and other processes, such as infill, that are not likely to have the impact of displacing large numbers of people. When there is gentrification in poor cities, it is likely to be intrajurisdictional. This means that people will be able to relocate within their home city, if not their neighborhood, but it also means they remain tied to a jurisdiction with a limited taxing capacity. This does not mean that gentrification in poor cities does not occur. It can and it does, but usually on a modest scale. There may be good reasons to challenge even modest gentrification in poor cities, but this should not be confused with infill or the need to attract middle-class housing stock (Puls 1999).

Infill housing can be used as a strategy to create stable mixed-income communities. In contrast, gentrification occurs when middle- or upper-income gentrifiers move into economically depressed neighborhoods to restore older housing stock or build new housing, and in so doing, displace current residents from affordable housing. The mixed-income communities that result from gentrification are generally not stable, but transitional—transitioning from largely low-income to exclusively upper- and middle-income communities. Revitalization efforts that have the goal of creating stable mixed-income neighborhoods through infill or partial/small-scale gentrification should be distinguished from extrajurisdictional gentrification that pushes the poor out of the cities. This distinction is vital to strategizing to create stable mixed-income neighborhoods, cities, and regions.

Poor Cities Have Much to Gain by Attracting Middle-Income Housing

Poor cities tend to possess more than their share of their region's low-income housing. Among other things, this means that the city does not have the buying power or the tax base of other areas in the region. The poor city lacks the resources it needs to attract investment as well as address the greater social and infrastructure needs of its residents. Detroit, for example, is a city with an aging infrastructure that was designed for two million people, but now serves a population of just over one million residents mostly of modest means (Sugre 1996, 268–70). Given the dearth of population, especially residents in the middle- and upper-income brackets, Detroit overburdens relatively few residents with the cost of supporting this infrastructure. This places a tremendous economic strain on the city. In addition, many of the jobs and other resources associated with opportunities are more likely to be found outside of poor cities. These cities need a strategy to capture a fair share of the opportunity base, including the tax and job base of the region. Trying to attract middle-income residents and housing is a rational strategy for these cities to pursue because it brings in a much-needed boost to revenues and creates buying power, which in turn creates even more revenue for the central cities.

Despite the promise of expanding the central city's resources, such strategies are often contentious and strongly opposed by inner-city residents of color. There are a number of reasons for this opposition. The first, which has been a primary focus here, is that this method of city revitalization is mistakenly perceived as a gentrification process that will displace inner-city residents from their existing neighborhoods. Most historically white neighborhoods that experience an influx of people of color, particularly blacks, reach a tipping point—a point at which whites feel threatened by the growing minority population and flee. When this occurs, neighborhoods rapidly shift from predominantly white to predominantly black. In a related phenomenon, black neighborhoods that undergo gentrification experience a rapid shift by which middle- and upper-class whites move into and transform the neighborhood, and lower-class blacks are forced to move to other "affordable" neighborhoods. Although both phenomena point to the ephemeral nature of integrated neighborhoods, the key difference is that with tipping there is no actual squeezing out of whites, whereas with gentrification, the relocation is involuntary (Weiher 1991, 19–22).

The second reason is that in poor cities, there is still likely to be unmet low-income housing needs, causing resistance to revitalization efforts that focus on middle-income households with the least need of assistance. The third reason is that it has not been made clear to low-income communities why attracting middle-class households will benefit the city or its existing residents. Finally, revitalization efforts are perceived in racial terms. That is, they are viewed as a political ploy specifically intended to pander to white suburbanites and hurt blacks and other people of color.

Our history gives all four of these concerns credence. Consider, for example, the urban renewal of the 1960s (Halpern 1995, 64–71). This policy, which appears similar to the proposed infill strategies, often hurt minorities while it benefited whites. Another basis for these concerns is the fact that whites fled to the suburbs as blacks came to the central city. Because of this, minority communities often perceive any return by whites as an effort to retake the city (Sugre 1996). Indeed, even in Oakland today there is support for this perception as there is some indication that the new mayor is taking a public posture that uses black disenfranchisement to draw whites back to Oakland (Nieves 1999; Matier and Ross 1999). Jerry Brown, who is the white mayor of Oakland, may be engaging in "strategic racism." Strategic racism is a politically motivated effort to curry favor with whites after establishing a reputation as being supportive of pro-black policies; in other words, to demonstrate to outsiders that the politician has not been "captured" by blacks. Brown appears to be adopting this strategy by publicly attacking blacks, particularly Police Chief Joseph Samuels, to attract non-blacks and investment back into Oakland. Moreover, "wedge politics" combined with politicians playing the "race card" have been effective strategies to gain political favor (O'Reilly 1995).

There is also the concern that low-income people, often people of color, need assistance in the housing market by developing and subsidizing affordable housing. But the city simply cannot address the housing and other social needs of low-income citizens of the region by itself. If poor cities continue to import poor residents while exporting opportunities and resources—a role historically consigned to cities by the federal government and the region—the cities will cease to function.

Despite their often-justified concerns, it is a mistake for low-income communities to oppose policies that provide a better balance of mixed-income housing stock in the city. While it is conceivable that some partial/small-scale gentrification in poor cities will occur, it must be stressed that gentrification is not the central issue facing poor cities. In fact, most poor cities will continue to lose population, especially middle-class residents, even with the implementation of infill programs. The pull of sprawl and the push of concentrated poverty that already exist in these cities cannot be adequately addressed unless the sprawl and fragmentation issues are more directly confronted by inner-city communities.

Rich cities that engage in extrajurisdictional gentrification usually have small, politically marginalized low-income minority populations that cannot alone mount an effective opposition to ongoing displacement. By contrast, in cities with large numbers of low-income minorities, allegations of gentrification are used as a racial coding to oppose whites moving back to the city. The reality is, in most of these poor cities there is little, if any, gentrification occurring. If residents are displaced it is more likely to be to a nearby neighborhood in the city through what I have termed intrajurisdictional gentrification.

While any displacement raises legitimate concerns, the intrajurisdictional gentrification that may occur in modest amounts in poor cities and the extrajurisdictional gentrification in rich cities are of a different order. The concern in poor cities is less likely to be displacement in terms of housing, but rather a fear of displacement in terms of power. There is concern that the influx of whites to the city foreshadows white domination. While there may be a basis for such fear, as the experience of Oakland appears to be bearing out, cities like Detroit and Cleveland are far from being at risk of political domination by whites. Nonetheless, low-income communities of color in these poor cities evoke the same fears of displacement and disempowerment to oppose an influx of whites.

The future of middle-class cities, such as Minneapolis, is more difficult to foresee. The balance in middle-class cities is much more delicate and requires constant attention. In middle-class cities, intrajurisdictional gentrification and displacement are more likely to occur than in poor cities. Despite this influx of middle- and upper-income residents, these cities are still losing population and remain oversubscribed in terms of low-income housing. In light of this dynamic, similar to that of poor cities, it does not make sense for low-income communities to oppose active attempts to attract and keep middle-class residents. In middle-class cities, middle-class housing infill projects are valuable in low-income neighborhoods where there are many vacant lots. Instead of opposing it, middle-class cities should welcome middle-class infill, but with a vigilant eye toward the ultimate goal of access to opportunity for low-income communities.

Regional Strategizing for the Future

The common thread for understanding the housing needs and the ways in which opportunity is sorted in rich, middle-class, and poor cities is through a regional approach. In evaluating each of these types of cities, one must look at how population and opportunity are being sorted by race and class on a regional level. We must then adopt strategies that give people meaningful access to opportunities. From a regional perspective, concentrated poverty in the cities or declining suburbs is a method of isolation and containment, and thus should be opposed.

If the ultimate goal is to provide low-income people of color access to the opportunity structures from which they have been excluded, then communities should seek to build stable mixed-income, racially integrated communities with access to opportunities. There are those who believe you can alleviate concentrated poverty by bringing opportunities to poor city neighborhoods through localized revitalization efforts, thus avoiding the regional discussion. These efforts, however, have generally failed unless they have been linked to a larger metropolitan goal (Weiher 1991).

The strategies that should be pursued to provide access to opportunity differ greatly among rich, middle-class, and poor cities, because their experiences of racial and class sorting differ greatly. Poor cities must overcome their fear of displacement and recognize that their volatile resistance to the influx of middle-income residents through infill is vastly out of proportion to the actual threat posed. Poor city communities should refocus on the ultimate goal of access to opportunities and resources. By refocusing their strategies, low-income communities of color and social justice advocates will recognize that attracting middle-income residents and businesses is a logical next step to continue the civil rights movement's goal of true access to opportunities.

References

Archer, D. 1998. Remarks by Dennis Archer. Paper presented to the Farm Bureau/Clean Michigan Initiative, Ann Arbor.

Associated Press. 1999. Diversity Brings Racial Tension to Small California City: L.A. Suburb Considered among Safest Communities. *Baltimore Sun*, March 31, A12.

Bollens, S. A. 1997. Concentrated Poverty and Metropolitan Equity Strategies. *Stanford Law and Policy Review* 8:11–12.

Brooke, J. 1998. Denver Stands Out in Mini-Trend toward Downtown Living. *New York Times*, December 29, A10.

Bullard, R. D. 1993. *Confronting Environmental Racism: Voices from the Grass-roots*. Boston: South End Press.

Calmore, J. O. 1995. Racialized Space and the Culture of Segregation: Hewing a Stone of Hope from a Mountain of Despair. *University of Pennsylvania Law Review* 143:1233.

Choper, J. H. 1984. Consequences of Supreme Court Decisions Upholding Individual Constitutional Rights. *Michigan Law Review* 83:1–212.

Conklin, E. E. 1998. Many Priced Out by This Area's Housing Market. *Seattle Post-Intelligencer*, March 20, C1.

Denton, N. A., and D. S. Massey. 1988. Residential Segregation of Blacks, Hispanics, Asians by Status Generation. *Social Science Quarterly* 69, no. 4:797–817.

Downs, A. 1997. Suburban-Inner-City Ecosystem. *Journal of Property Management* 62, no. 20:60.

Downs, A. 1998. How America's Cities Are Growing: The Big Picture. *Brookings Review* 16, no. 4:8.

Durham, J. G., and D. E. Shelton III. 1986. Mitigating the Effects of Private Revitalization on Housing for the Poor. *Maryland Law Review* 70:1, 3.

Ford, R. T. 1994. The Boundaries of Race: Political Geography in Legal Analysis. *Harvard Law Review* 107:1841.

Foster-Bey, J. 1997. Bridging Communities: Making the Link between Economies and Local Community Development. *Stanford Law and Policy Review* 8:25, 29–30.

Freilich, R. H., and B. G. Peshoff. 1997. The Social Costs of Sprawl. *The Urban Lawyer* 29:183.

Galster, G. C., and E. E. Hill. 1992. *The Metropolis in Black and White: Place, Power, and Polarization*. New Brunswick, NJ: Center for Urban Policy Research.

Goedert, J. G. 1988. Jenkins v. Missouri: The Future of Interdistrict School Desegregation. *Georgia Law Journal* 76:1867–1916.

Goldberg, D. T. 1993. *Racist Culture: Philosophy and the Politics of Meaning*. Cambridge, UK: Blackwell Press.

Gordon, P., and H. W. Richardson. 1998. Prove It: The Costs and Benefits of Sprawl. *Brookings Review* 16, no. 4:23.

Guinier, L. 1991a. No Two Seats: The Elusive Quest for Political Equality. *Virginia Law Review* 77:1413–1514.

Guinier, L. 1991b. The Triumph of Tokenism: The Voting Rights Act and the Theory of Black Electoral Success. *Michigan Law Review* 89:1077–1154.

Guinier, L. 1994. *The Tyranny of the Majority: Fundamental Fairness in Representative Democracy.* New York: Free Press.

Halpern, R. 1995. *Rebuilding the Inner City: A History of Neighborhood Initiatives to Address Poverty in the United States.* New York: Columbia University Press.

Jackson, K. T. 1985. *Crabgrass Frontier: The Suburbanization of the United States.* New York: Oxford University Press.

Jargowsky, P. A. 1997. *Poverty and Place.* New York: Russell Sage.

Kousser, J. M. 1999. *Colorblind Injustice: Minority Voting and Rights and the Undoing of the Second Reconstruction.* Chapel Hill: University of North Carolina Press.

Lewis, S. C., O. Brand-Williams, and J. Taylor. 1999. Racial and Ethnic Tensions Strain Suburban Schools. *Detroit News,* March 11.

Massey, D. S., and N. A. Denton. 1993. *American Apartheid: Segregation and the Making of the Underclass.* Cambridge, MA: Harvard University Press.

Matier, P., and A. Ross. 1999. Looks like Oakland Police Chief's Heave-Ho Is Imminent. *San Francisco Chronicle,* March 17, A11.

McLeod, R. G. 1998. Rental Housing Crunch Hits Poor Hardest. *San Francisco Chronicle,* June 16, A1.

Milliken v. Bradley, 418 U.S. 717. 1974. Milliken, Governor of Michigan, et al. v. Bradley, certiorari to the United States Court of Appeals for the Sixth Circuit. No. 73–434. Argued February 27, decided July 25.

Modie, N. 1998. Give 'Em Shelter, Rich Suburbs Told. *Seattle Post-Intelligencer,* November 6, C1.

Nieves, E. 1999. A Bullish Jerry Brown Barges on, Stepping on Toes. *New York Times,* March 30, A14.

Oliver, M. L., and T. M. Shapiro. 1995. *Black Wealth/White Wealth: A New Perspective on Racial Inequality.* New York: Routledge.

O'Reilly, K. 1995. *Nixon's Piano: Presidents and Racial Politics from Washington to Clinton.* New York: Free Press.

Orfield, M. 1997. *Metropolitics: A Regional Agenda for Community and Stability.* Washington, DC: Brookings Institution Press.

Peirce, N. R. 1993. *Citistates: How Urban America Can Prosper in a Competitive World.* Washington, DC: Seven Locks Press.

powell, j. a. 1996. How Government Tax and Housing Policies Have Racially Segregated America. In *Taxing America,* ed. K. B. Brown and M. L. Fellows. New York: New York University Press.

powell, j. a. 1998. Race and Space: What Really Drives Metropolitan Growth. *Brookings Review* 16, no. 4:20.

Puls, M. 1999. Neighbors Fight to Save a Piece of Detroit's Past: City Wants to Clear Classic Homes for New Development. *Detroit News*, March 5, A1.

Purdum, T. S. 1999. Suburban Sprawl Takes Its Place on the Political Landscape. *New York Times*, February 6, A1.

Rusk, D. 1995. *Cities without Suburbs*. Washington, DC: Woodrow Wilson Center Press.

Rusk, D. 1999. *Inside Game/Outside Game*. New York: Brookings Institution Press.

Savitch, H. V., D. Collins, D. S. Sanders, and J. P. Markham. 1993. Ties That Bind: Central Cities, Suburbs, and the New Metropolitan Region. *Economic Development Quarterly* 7 (November): 341–357.

Star Tribune. 1999. Smarter Growth, Gore Plan to Contain Suburban Sprawl. January 17, A24.

Sugre, T. J. 1996. *The Origins of the Urban Crisis: Race and Inequality in Postwar Detroit*. Princeton, NJ: Princeton University Press.

Vidal, A. C. 1992. *Rebuilding Communities: A National Study of Urban Community Development Corporations*. New York: Community Development Research Center, New School for Social Research.

Voith, R. 1992. City and Suburban Growth: Substitutes or Complements? *Business Review of the Federal Reserve Bank of Philadelphia* (September–October): 31.

Weiher, G. R. 1991. *The Fractured Metropolis: Political Fragmentation and Metropolitan Segregation*. Albany, State University of New York Press.

Wilson, W. J. 1997. *When Work Disappears: The World of the New Urban Poor*. New York: Alfred A. Knopf, Inc.

3

¿Quién es Más Urbanista? Latinos and Smart Growth

Manuel Pastor, Jr.

While the current smart growth movement—a sometimes unwieldy amalgam of new urbanists, environmental activists, business regionalists, fiscal realists, and equity advocates—has many parents, surely one is Henry Cisneros. As a former mayor of San Antonio, Texas, and the secretary for Housing and Urban Development (HUD) under President Clinton, Cisneros articulated an earlier version of smart growth perhaps best captured by the title of his landmark essay, "Regionalism: The New Geography of Opportunity." In it, Cisneros (1996, 43) made an early effort at defining the essential elements of the equity argument for better connections between city and suburb, arguing in part that "political borders do not seal off the problem of concentrated poverty." Cisneros (1993) also provided the sort of rhetorical thread so often evoked by smart growth proponents—the notion of "interwoven destinies" between Americans living in different urban, suburban, and rural communities.

His coming to regionalism was perhaps not that surprising. As mayor of San Antonio, Cisneros realized the power of annexation as a way to prevent the disconnection of the metro area's suburbs from its sometimes struggling central city even as he launched a significant urban revitalization program intended to bring businesses and residents back downtown. Recognizing the contrast between his experience and that of central cities left stranded by the forces of sprawl, he brought new thinking to his position as the secretary of HUD. Under his watch (and to some degree under his successor, Andrew Cuomo), numerous connective programs took root, including efforts to provide better transportation for inner-city residents to suburban employment, strategies to undo concentrations of poverty in public housing, experiments that facilitated the movement of residents to move to more suburban locations, and efforts to stress the market potential of inner-city communities in an attempt to lure business investment.

While Cisneros's views reflected his own learning in public policy and urban design, they were consistent with his deep roots in, and concern for, Latino communities. Latinos, in general, would seem to be predisposed to many of the strategies articulated by the proponents of smart growth and what has been termed the new regionalism. After all, many Latinos live in the dense urban areas, replete with mixed-use zoning and vibrant street life, favored by the new urbanist wing of the smart growth movement. This rapidly growing population has been spilling over from traditional locations in key central cities to a series of inner-ring suburbs, many of which are the focus of the sort of strategies favored by leaders in the regional equity movement such as Myron Orfield. Thus, the spatial arrangements and distribution of this population would suggest an affinity with the ideal of smart growth efforts.

Latinos may also find special resonance in the workforce strategies associated with regional equity efforts. The degree of poverty in the Latino population rivals that confronting African Americans, but it is often of a different sort: rather than being a poverty of joblessness and disconnection from the labor market, it is a working poverty in which the hours of labor are long yet the pay is low (Melendez 1993; Pastor 2003). This suggests a lesser need to overcome the initial barriers to entering the labor market at all (although education is still a huge issue), and perhaps a better position to make use of the transportation connections, regional training, and broadened job networks many regional proponents espouse. In the same vein, Latinos are a rapidly growing part of the labor movement, and the labor movement itself has been experimenting with its own version of regionalism, one rooted in the revitalization of central labor councils as major actors in regional economic and workforce strategies.

Yet the world of smart growth presents an anomaly: despite the clear possibilities of connection (as well as the parental lineage of Cisneros, a national figure for many Latinos), there are few Latinos in prominent positions in the smart growth or regional equity movements. Local efforts in heavily Latino cities are sometimes just that: local, and not consciously connected to regionalist concerns or strategies. This is in contrast, for example, to the African American experience, a world in which there are several quite prominent public intellectuals in this general area, including Carl Anthony, Angela Glover Blackwell, Robert D. Bullard, and john a. powell, as well as major political or community actors, such as William Johnson, the mayor of Rochester, and Heaster Wheeler, the executive director of the nation's largest branch of the NAACP in Detroit.

Some of these African American leaders are pushing against the grain: the risk in regionalism is that the political power granted by a concentrated geographic location (as in a particular council district or city) will be diluted in a regional alliance, and this is one reason why a majority of African American voters in Louisville, Kentucky, opposed the successful business- and suburbia-supported consolidation of city and county governments in 2000 (Savitch and Vogel 2004). Of course, the counterargument is that "going regional" is absolutely necessary to achieve leverage for central cities, and this is precisely the perspective being offered by the leaders noted above, with full recognition that the best route for community empowerment is necessarily nuanced by local conditions.

What Is Smart Growth—and What Is the New Regionalism?

One of the most important recent developments in the field of urban affairs is the emergence of the new regionalism—a framework that stresses the significance of the region as a fundamental scale for understanding and addressing urban and national problems. The evolution of this framework—which some note is partly a revitalization of an older tradition (see Dreier, Mollenkopf, and Swanstrom 2001, 175–178)—has been driven by many factors and proponents. Some authors stress the economic concerns and rationales for regionalist work, with a crucial emphasis placed on the development of regionally rooted business clusters as well as the more classic economic irrationality of multiple jurisdictions providing what should be regionwide services, such as transportation (see Henton, Melville, and Walesh 1997; Barnes and Ledebur 1998). Others have underscored the environmental implications of our metropolitan landscapes (Cielewicz 2002), noting that the rapid suburbanization on the periphery of urban regions has led to the irre-trievable loss of thousands of square miles of open space.[1] Still others have emphasized how sprawl has tended to weaken civic infrastructure as suburbanites become increasingly detached from their central city fate, and regional neighbors become as politically and socially distant as the commutes that separate them.

These concerns about economic vitality, fiscal sanity, environmental integrity, and the restoration of a sense of community have often been grouped under the rubric of smart growth. The smart growth movement, linking together environmentalists, urban planners, and sympathetic developers, is generally united around the common goal of promoting re-gionally integrated, environmentally and pedestrian friendly, mixed-use communities. Places like Maryland have experimented with smart growth incentives, essentially connecting the economic and environmen-tal arguments by making suburbs pay a higher share of the costs associ-ated with the sewer and road demands raised by sprawl. The general thrust would seem to be friendly to inner-city communities, many of whom might benefit—but who also might be displaced—if public and private investments are redirected to struggling central cities.

Concerns about issues of concentrated poverty in inner-city commu-nities have helped prompt the development of one wing of the regionalist perspective: equity-oriented regionalism. This sort of regionalism pays attention to the economic, environmental, and civic imperatives, but is more focused on how regional strategies might contribute to new ap-proaches to tackling the problem of persistent poverty in central cities (Katz 2000). It also more clearly identifies race as one of the drivers of suburban sprawl and often takes an up-front approach to dealing with the question of racial justice (see Bullard, Johnson, and Torres 1999; powell 2000). Finally, it seeks to challenge both local advocates who may wish to look inward and external actors who may seek to ignore impoverished communities in their discussions of a regional future.

What is the intersection of this equity-oriented approach with the smart growth movement and principles? To understand this, it may be useful to first unpack the regional equity perspective itself. As I see it, there are three basic strands. The first is what might be called municipality-based regionalism. This perspective alternately stresses the possible mutual gains from city-suburb cooperation, mostly because of the complementarity of city and suburban economic growth (Voith 1992; Pastor et al. 2000), and the consequent need to build alliances between the inner cities and the lower-income inner-ring suburbs, particularly vis-à-vis outlying and more recent suburbs (Orfield 2002). The key policy strategy in the former consensual view is the formation of regional collaboratives to spur local investments; the main policy strategy in the latter conflict view is regional tax sharing to move resources from higher-wealth communities to those in more need—something Orfield himself has pushed in the Saint Paul–Minneapolis area.

Of course, a city-suburban alliance against a common high-wealth suburban neighbor can be problematic: older, problem-ridden, inner-ring suburbs are faced with a decision of whether to strike a deal with their often minority central cities or seek alliances with the whiter exurbs to which many of their residents wish to eventually escape. Orfield is optimistic that race will be downplayed in favor of economic interests, and others have suggested that the increasing presence of African Americans and Latinos in the immediately adjoining suburbs will eventually ameliorate demographic gaps and reduce that obstacle to interjurisdictional alliances (Frey 2001). There are, of course, good reasons to be less sanguine about the suburban–central city bond and genuinely concerned that suburbanites, no matter how inner-ring they may be now, will cast their lot outward rather than inward. In any case, the key issue for Latinos is considering how they fit into the municipal hierarchy—that is, how much suburbanization is going on and what sort of suburbs are seeing Latino growth?

A second broad variant of equity-oriented regionalism is rooted in the labor movement. Recent years have seen the revitalization of central labor councils (Ness and Eimer 2001), groups of unions organized at the level of regional labor markets. Traditionally focused on the building trades and often seen as mere shells for influencing local politics, central labor councils have been dormant even as the labor movement itself has been in decline. In the last decade, however, some have argued that these institutions could serve as the most effective vehicle for "metropolitan unionism," a strategy that understands it is the commute shed that defines workers' fortunes and lives as residents, and so seeks to transform both local political influence and the "stickiness" of capital in certain regions to labor's advantage (Luria and Rogers 1997).

One of the most sophisticated examples of this approach is the South Bay Labor Council and its affiliated policy research arm, Working Partnerships USA, in San Jose, California. The council rose up partly to counter the influence of several business-oriented regional initiatives to stir economic recovery, and first flexed its muscle with the passage of a living wage law in San Jose that at the time gave the city the highest wage level of any such ordinance in the country. But both the South Bay Labor Council and Working Partnerships USA quickly went well beyond living wages per se, participating in debates about smart growth, suggesting new approaches to affordable housing (see Bhargava et al. 2001), and pushing for a broad array of community benefits from redevelopment efforts (see Muller et al. 2003; Leroy 2003).

While some activists of color remain wary of labor-led efforts, partly as a result of past issues of discrimination by craft and other unions, the sort of regional equity efforts that unions propose, such as living wages, often find widespread support in minority communities. This support is even deeper when, as in San Jose, the labor council sees itself as explicitly building community-labor alliances that can benefit both in the longer run. Finally, the labor movement has increasingly recognized the growing presence of immigrants and other minorities in the labor force, and Latinos have achieved leadership in important central labor councils (for example, Los Angeles) that can serve as vehicles for regional equity.

A final strand of equity regionalism is what several colleages and I have termed community-based regionalism. This approach is often rooted in a combination of community-based organizations (CBOs) and community development corporations that have grasped the importance of understanding, challenging, and working with outside forces in the process of community development. In their view, the lack of development in inner-city minority neighborhoods is not merely the result of a failure to invest in the local neighborhood along with the consequent escape of both consumer dollars (due to a lack of retail amenities) and often the middle-class consumers themselves. It is also the result of isolation from positive regional economic trends, including the spatial mismatch induced by the suburbanization of employment (see Pastor 2001b; Wilson 1996).

As a result, locally focused organizing is key, but locally focused development is only part of the solution: as Jeremy Nowak (1997, 9) argues, "Strong neighborhoods are destination places and incubators; they are healthy, not because they are self-contained or self-sufficient but because their residents are appropriately linked to nonneighorhood opportunities."

Such community-regional links have been the subject of innovative organizing by groups working in both Latino and African American communities. In a heavily Latino section of downtown Los Angeles, for example, a multiracial progressive alliance spearheaded by various labor and community groups came together under the banner of the Figueroa Corridor Coalition. Facing the expansion of the Staples Convention Center, a regional attraction, the coalition bargained for the developer to sign a community benefits agreement that included $1 million worth of parks improvement, $100,000 in seed funding to create job training programs through community organizations, local hiring, and the construction of 160 affordable housing units. This built on a history of such regional equity efforts in Los Angeles, including an innovative attempt to secure job training from the movie industry led by a grassroots organizing project based in South Los Angeles named AGENDA, a major struggle for transportation equity led by the regionwide Bus Riders Union, and a broad set of campaigns for living wage laws in Southern California (Pastor 2001a). In each of these efforts, Latino community leaders were involved as either leading actors or important allies.

The relation of all these strands of regional equity to smart growth per se is not unproblematic. That is, the struggles for municipal equity, worker justice, and community development have different sectoral and constituency roots than those of the business collaboratives for regional economic growth, the environmental coalitions to constrain sprawl, and the urban design enthusiasts arguing for more compact development. The latter groups can help create the conditions for regional equity by elevating overall growth and steering such growth to more densely populated areas, but there is no guarantee that such efforts will produce more than gentrification and displacement. In short, the alliance between the smart growth and social justice movements is not necessarily "natural."

Indeed, Latinos, like other urban groups facing higher poverty rates, have more to gain from an infusion of regional equity than they do from a simple infusion of "good planning"—and so the key for engaging Latinos in the smart growth movement is to ensure that the issues of equity and justice remain high on the agenda. Unpacking the strands, as above, can help in determining which allies and strategies on the regional equity side make the most sense for Latino communities. I turn to the process of engagement below, but first I consider the basic patterns of suburbanization and demographic change so often lifted up by those stressing the municipal side of smart growth and the new regionalism.

Cities, Suburbs, and Latinos

One reason why some have suggested a potential Latino affinity for smart growth is that Latinos, despite the image and reality of a significant presence in rural areas and agricultural enterprises, are heavily urban in their location. Over 93 percent of the country's Latinos are in what the census defines as urban areas (a definition that includes most developed suburbs); the figure for non-Hispanic whites is 74 percent, while the figure for African Americans is slightly below 90 percent.[2] Issues of urban development and design, and the possibility that smart growth holds for reconcentrating economic growth in urban areas, would therefore seem to be of great relevance to Latinos.

It is useful, however, to unpack the nature of Latino settlement patterns in order to more appropriately assess the potential relationship to smart growth thinking. This is particularly important given the significant press attention given to rapidly increasing Latino populations in smaller states and metro areas that have not had a traditional presence of Latinos—a pattern that some may think hints at contributions to sprawl, fragmentation, and the consumption of rural land.

A recent report from the Brookings Institution (Suro and Singer 2002) offers some insights on this question. Roberto Suro and Audrey Singer explore the patterns of Latino growth in the hundred-largest metropolitan areas in the United States, offering a useful typology in which they break metropolitan areas into several types, including established Latino metropolitan areas (such as Los Angeles, Chicago, and New York), fast-growing Latino hubs (such as Austin, Orange County, and Riverside–San Bernardino), a set of newer Latino destinations (such as Atlanta, Boston, Milwaukee, and elsewhere), and a set of metro areas with small Latino populations (such as Akron, Cleveland, and Pittsburgh).

While media attention has focused on the new Latino destinations, particularly the emergence of Latinos in parts of the rural South, the real action is occurring in the established Latino areas and the fast-growing Latino hubs. Newer Latino destinations did see their share of the Latino population in the hundred-largest metro areas rise from about 14 to 19 percent over the 1990–2000 period; the areas with small Latino populations stayed at about 4.5 percent. But this just means that in 2000, over 75 percent of the Latino population was in the established metro areas and the new Latino hubs, with slightly over 51 percent of the Latino population in the former and nearly 25 percent in the latter.

There has certainly been change and some degree of national deconcentration within these two: in 1990, the established Latino areas held nearly 60 percent of the Latino population in the hundred-largest metro areas, and the share in the fast-growing hubs was around 22 percent. But clearly the interesting and significant action, particularly in terms of engagement in smart growth debates, is in the more established Latino areas and hubs. And the fact that most of the population continues to live in these areas suggests that Latinos are not contributing more than their share to the ongoing sprawl across the U.S. landscape.

While this discussion highlights Latino growth across various metro areas, smart growth questions also revolve around changes between the city and the suburb. The Suro and Singer (2002) study found that Latino growth was actually fastest in the suburbs: the 71 percent increase in the suburban Latino population over the 1990–2000 period outpaced the 47 percent growth rate of the Latino central city population. To look at this in more detail, and to compare the Latino patterns to those of other ethnic groups, I created a comparative data set, drawing on the hundred-largest central cities in the United States and considering the MSA or metro area they were in. Because some MSAs have multiple large central cities, I was eventually left with eighty-one metropolitan areas.[3] I then

Table 3.1
Population growth, 1990–2000

	All	Whites	Blacks	Asians	Latinos
All areas					
Metro growth	14.7%	1.9%	16.1%	50.9%	53.6%
City growth	9.5%	−7.7%	6.3%	39.4%	42.9%
Suburban growth	17.9%	5.9%	35.6%	61.7%	66.1%
Top twenty-five					
Metro growth	13.6%	−0.8%	14.5%	55.9%	51.5%
City growth	7.5%	−12.2%	0.8%	42.6%	38.8%
Suburban growth	17.0%	2.9%	39.5%	66.1%	65.0%
Established Latino areas					
Metro growth	12.1%	−6.7%	5.7%	43.8%	34.4%
City growth	9.3%	−11.0%	0.5%	37.6%	27.1%
Suburban growth	15.0%	−3.7%	20.0%	51.2%	44.8%
Fast-Growing Latino hubs					
Metro growth	26.5%	4.9%	24.9%	61.6%	76.4%
City growth	21.7%	−4.5%	9.4%	46.7%	72.0%
Suburban growth	29.5%	9.4%	54.2%	74.7%	80.2%
New Latino destinations					
Metro growth	18.5%	7.6%	26.2%	85.3%	143.3%
City growth	10.5%	−2.9%	12.1%	66.9%	121.2%
Suburban growth	22.4%	11.5%	48.1%	96.2%	160.4%

crosswalked the list with the categories developed by Suro and Singer, and explored the basic patterns.[4] Table 3.1 shows some data on Latino growth. While Latino suburbanization is indeed impressive, including much faster growth in the suburbs than the cities in our data set, it is appropriate to see this in the context of the experience of other ethnic groups.

Note, for example, that there is a pronounced pattern of white flight, particularly from cities in the larger metro areas. Whites posted a 3.4 percent growth in their nationwide numbers between 1990 and 2000, but grew by only 1.9 percent in the top eighty-one metro areas and actually lost numbers in the most populous twenty-five MSAs; basically, there seems to have been a modest movement of whites down the hierarchy to smaller cities, but this was more than overwhelmed by a pattern

Table 3.2
Latinos in cities and suburbs

	1990		2000	
	% of Latinos in cities	% of Latinos in suburbs	% of Latinos in cities	% of Latinos in suburbs
All areas	53.9%	46.1%	50.1%	49.9%
Top twenty-five	51.5%	48.5%	47.2%	52.8%
Top forty	53.1%	46.9%	48.8%	51.2%
Established Latino areas	58.4%	41.6%	55.2%	44.8%
Fast-growing Latino hubs	46.5%	53.5%	45.3%	54.7%
New Latino destinations	43.4%	56.6%	39.5%	60.5%

of moving to rural areas. On the other hand, African American, Latino, and Asian Pacific American growth in the larger metro areas was about their rate of growth in the general population. There were, however, sharp differences in the patterns of suburbanization. In the top twenty-five metro areas, for instance, African Americans saw virtually no growth in the cities, but experienced a 40 percent increase in their numbers in the adjoining suburbs.

While Latinos are indeed suburbanizing, they are also responsible for keeping up the numbers in central cities, filling in for the outward movement of whites and African Americans. An urban agenda is clearly a Latino one, and as I suggest below, a new urbanist agenda may be even more appropriate. A final glance at the data may be instructive about the patterns and the opportunities. In table 3.2, I show the breakdown for Latinos in our metropolitan areas who live in either cities or suburbs for the years 1990 and 2000. A few trends stand out. First, in general, the Latino population is roughly split between the city and the suburb in these eighty-one metropolitan areas; by contrast, nearly 75 percent of whites and about 40 percent of blacks live in the suburbs in 2000, with the latter suggesting why the regional equity movement has been important to some African American leaders seeking to protect the health of central cities.

Interestingly, the highest concentrations of Latinos in cities rather than in suburbs are in the established Latino areas—but this seems to be changing, with the percent of Latinos in the suburbs of the established areas rising from around 42 to about 45 percent in the 1990–2000 period. In the fast-growing Latino hubs, growth seems to be evenly occurring in cities and suburbs, with around 54 percent of Latinos considered to be suburban in both 1990 and 2000. Finally, the Latino population is nearly 61 percent suburban in the new Latino destinations, but it is important to put this in context: Latinos constitute only about 6 percent of the total population in those metro areas, making them a distinct minority. This again suggests that the crucial action is occurring in the established Latino areas and the fast-growing Latino hubs.

To see the complications and nuances when we actually consider one of these established areas, I examined Southern California, a place that hosts over 25 percent of the Latinos who are in the entire larger city set. Southern California is defined here as including the Los Angeles–Long Beach MSA, the Anaheim–Santa Ana MSA, and the Riverside–San Bernardino MSA, the first of which is considered an established Latino area and the latter two considered to be fast-growing Latino hubs.[5] Table 3.3 shows first that there has been rapid growth in the 1990–2000 period explored above. But the detailed composition between the city and the suburb over 1980 to 2000 suggests a complicated story, and also the need to consider the interrelationship of the various MSA types when they are in close proximity, as in Southern California, and so may be subject to interactions.[6]

For example, the central city proportion of the Latino population increase in the Los Angeles MSA actually grew over 1980–1990, mostly due to an influx of immigrants from both Mexico and Central America, and the growth has been steady in the city and the suburb ever since. In the Anaheim–Santa Ana area, there was also first a concentration in the central cities, and then a slow suburbanization since. Only in the Riverside–San Bernardino area—the so-called Inland Empire—do we see a solid and steady increase in suburbanization over the period, but since this is a smaller percentage of the total population in Southern California, the suburban portion of the Latino population has remained the same for the overall area.

Even this broad view can obscure important patterns. Figures 3.1 and 3.2 show the increase in the Latino population in the Southern

Table 3.3
Population growth and composition in Southern California

Population growth, 1990–2000

	All	Whites	Blacks	Asian	Latinos
Southern California					
Metro growth	12.7%	−12.2%	3.8%	35.3%	37.9%
City growth	8.6%	−17.9%	−6.3%	22.1%	31.7%
Suburban growth	14.9%	−9.8%	13.8%	43.2%	42.2%
Los Angeles, CA					
Metro growth	7.4%	−18.2%	−3.6%	26.4%	26.6%
City growth	6.2%	−17.2%	−8.3%	14.3%	26.2%
Suburban growth	8.4%	−18.9%	2.1%	35.0%	26.9%
Anaheim, CA					
Metro growth	18.1%	−6.1%	8.9%	62.8%	55.0%
City growth	20.7%	−19.7%	−3.0%	60.3%	49.3%
Suburban growth	17.1%	−2.9%	16.0%	63.8%	60.7%
Riverside, CA					
Metro growth	25.7%	−4.7%	43.4%	50.4%	79.1%
City growth	12.8%	−20.4%	16.5%	34.8%	60.4%
Suburban growth	28.0%	−2.3%	52.0%	54.0%	82.9%

City/suburb mix for Latinos and non-Latinos, 1980–2000

	1980		1990		2000	
	% in cities	% in suburbs	% in cities	% in suburbs	% in cities	% in suburbs
Latinos						
Southern California	40.0%	60.0%	41.1%	58.9%	39.2%	60.8%
Los Angeles, CA	42.0%	58.0%	44.5%	55.5%	44.4%	55.6%
Anaheim, CA	46.1%	53.9%	49.9%	50.1%	48.1%	51.9%
Riverside, CA	19.8%	80.2%	16.8%	83.2%	15.1%	84.9%
Non-Latinos						
Southern California	36.6%	63.4%	33.3%	66.7%	31.4%	68.6%
Los Angeles, CA	45.5%	54.5%	43.9%	56.1%	43.1%	56.9%
Anaheim, CA	21.4%	78.6%	21.0%	79.0%	19.7%	80.3%
Riverside, CA	18.2%	81.8%	14.5%	85.5%	12.6%	87.4%

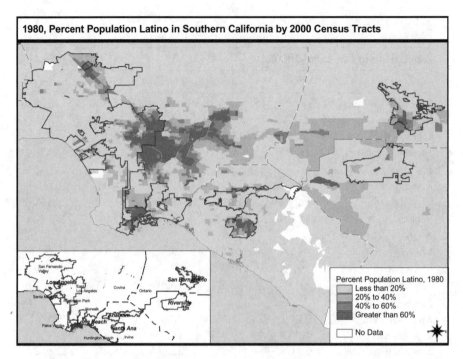

1980, Percent Population Latino in Southern California by 2000 Census Tracts

Percent Population Latino, 1980
- Less than 20%
- 20% to 40%
- 40% to 60%
- Greater than 60%

- No Data

Figure 3.1
1980, percent population Latino in Southern California by 2000 census tracts

California area between 1980 and 2000 at the tract level; the boundaries for the major cities that are the MSA anchors are overlaid to make clearer the pattern occurring at the microlevel. What can be seen is that the Latino population is indeed suburbanizing outside the main city lines, but that the growth tends to be in immediately adjoining areas—that is, the inner-ring suburbs, going beyond the traditional location in East Los Angeles to include the older industrial cities to the east of South Central Los Angeles and the Alameda Corridor that go by the name of the Gateway Cities (because they are close to the Los Angeles port and hence see a massive amount of traffic). There is also a huge growth in the Latino population in the San Fernando Valley, an area that is formally part of the city of Los Angeles, but has always followed a more suburban form in its politics and urban design. This is about as inner ring as it gets—it's actually inside the central city—and Latinos have been an important element in the changing demography there.[7]

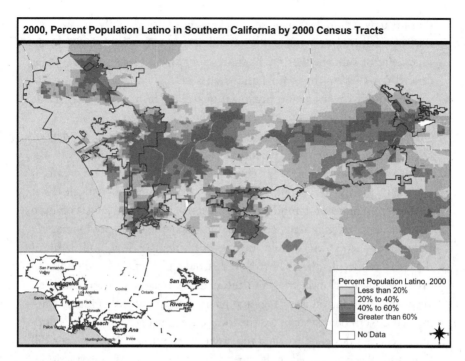

Figure 3.2
2000, percent population Latino in Southern California by 2000 census tracts

To summarize, Latinos are heavily urban in their national composition. While suburban growth is high, Latinos remain far less suburban than whites, and seem to be responsible for filling in for white flight and slow black growth in America's major metro areas. A detailed look at Southern California, a place where three metro areas come together to host about a quarter of the country's Latino population in large metro areas, shows a continued urban bias with suburbanization patterns that seem to favor the inner ring. This would appear to be exactly the stuff from which new regionalist dreams are drawn.[8]

New Regionalism, New Urbanism, and New Organizing

Latinos, particularly in the areas where they already have achieved some degree of stability and representation, constitute the sort of constituency that the new regionalists have seen as key: mostly or recently urban, with the suburbanized portion of the population having often settled in an inner ring of suburbs that might share common interests with the inner central core. Why, then, are Latinos so seemingly underrepresented in smart growth advocacy and organizations, even in the apparently fertile fields of California?

In an extensive survey of the Los Angeles area, Michael Mendez (2003) suggests that fiscal incentives are an important culprit. As the Southern California maps that comprise figures 3.1 and 3.2 indicate, it is exactly the inner-ring industrial suburbs adjoining Los Angeles that have seen significant Latino growth. These cities often have common boundaries and seemingly common interests: they are predominantly Latino, the median household income of residents is low, and many of the cities are deeply affected by the industrial and traffic-related pollution produced by local industries and the nation's busiest seaport. But their very poverty in the midst of regional plenty has, along with a highly fragmented government system, led the local governments to pursue development schemes designed to yield the highest revenues. Urban planner Bill Fulton (1997) has labeled these inner-ring areas "suburbs of extraction," reflecting the way in which traditional businesses have been able to curry favor and drive local policy to the lowest common denominator.[9] Competitive bidding for retail, especially given California's distorted tax structure in which property taxes are constrained and local governments rely on sales tax revenue, has also challenged the sort of collaboration needed for a common strategy.

While an interesting answer to the lack of collaboration, it is not a full explanation: after all, what we are really describing is a set of communities seemingly ripe for the sort of tax-sharing schemes new regionalists insist could help inner-ring areas. For the political leaders there not to be taking this up with gusto deserves a fuller examination. This is particularly so because Latino politicians, especially in the state of California, have taken significant leadership on related issues, the most prominent of which is environmental justice: of the ten successful pieces of environmental justice legislation in the state since 1999, seven have been authored by Latino and Latina legislators responding to pressing needs in their communities.

Moreover, the fact that Latinos have shown political leadership on environmental questions also indicates that this is not simply an issue of political maturation, another explanation that has been proffered in interviews with selected leaders in the smart growth movement and even with some Latino leaders actively engaged in community development questions. In this view, smart growth is a sort of "second-order" or "second-priority" issue that will take precedence after more basic questions around education, immigrant rights, higher wages, and other pressing matters have been more successfully addressed.

The issue of political maturity or aging, some have suggested, is also occurring at the municipal level: most of the Latino-run cities have seen Latinos come to power only recently and so issues more immediate than urban design, such as basic fiscal health, are at the forefront. But since many of these issues could be addressed, at least partly, through regionalist strategies, simply waiting seems to make little sense, even for the realization of a traditional Latino agenda. What's up?

Making Smart Growth *Más Inteligente*

A series of interviews with individuals active in smart growth movements suggests that they recognize that Latinos are not as involved as they might be—and the usual words about needed outreach are offered. But making smart growth more inclusive and therefore a bit smarter—más inteligente—will require more than the traditional call for diversity. In particular, both analysts and activists will need to broaden their vision of regionalism and regional equity. By this I mean that smart growth advocates need to "see" Latinos in the regional equity prism—so that Latinos can better see a place for themselves in the smart growth movement.

In an article published in *Urban Affairs Review* several years ago—appropriately titled "Looking for Regionalism in All the Wrong Places" —I examined the Los Angeles metropolitan area in detail. I contended that the failure of many analysts to find significant interjurisdictional collaboration with elected leaders and officials—the typical signal of smart growth or regionalist collaboration celebrated by many civic organizations, and the analytic framework of Orfield (2002)—did not necessarily indicate a lack of regionalist impulses in the Los Angeles area. Rather, to use our categories above, the regionalism being displayed in certain places was not primarily of a municipal nature.

Southern California was (and is), after all, an area flux with regional equity initiatives, including a vibrant labor movement organizing janitors and others in multiple cities, a set of CBOs creating pathbreaking community benefits agreements tied to regional attractions, an innovative collection of environmental justice groups bravely taking on the air quality management district, and one of the most far-reaching organizations for transit justice, the Bus Riders Union (affiliated with the Community/Labor Strategy Center), which has consistently challenged one of the country's largest transit authorities in a series of landmark legal suits and public protests. Since few of these fit into smart growth debates about land use and growth boundaries, or are the sort of discussions of municipal revenue sharing stressed by Orfield (2002), they have sometimes slipped under the radar of the new regionalists and smart growth advocates. Yet they offer a real foundation on which to build a new sort of regional effort based primarily on equity concerns.

In a similar way, smart growth advocates should recognize the impressive energy Latino communities and political officials have put into questions of environmental justice, an issue that is clearly regional in its scope and remedies. They should build on the significant presence of Latinos in regional labor markets and labor organizing in places like Los Angeles and Silicon Valley. Finally, they can build on the demonstrated willingness to take on major transit agencies in pursuit of transportation justice, as noted above. But to do this, smart growth advocates will need to see the regionalist movement as stretching far beyond the usual forums and debates, and recognize the presence of these important community movements.

Smart growth advocates also have to recognize the assets that Latinos can bring to a struggle for more compact and sustainable development. In pioneering work, Mendez (2003, 2005) has asserted that Latino lifestyles have a good fit with the new urbanist preferences for city design. He argues that the style of housing in traditional Latino immigrant entry points in California, the focus of his work, includes ample use of front porches, a tendency to maximize building on lots, and an outward orientation to the street and neighborhood. This is exactly the sort of patterns new urbanist architects seek—it is simply that these new urban areas are dotted with taquerias rather than coffee shops.

Mendez also notes the tendency of Latinos to live in more crowded housing and be more reliant on public transportation, exactly the stuff from which transit-oriented development is made. Latinos and African Americans are the most likely to carpool or use public transit—and in Southern California, Latinos are three times as likely as whites and twice as likely as African Americans to carpool or use public transit. While some of this living pattern reflects low incomes and thus the inability to purchase a larger suburban house or private cars, Mendez contends that this is an opportunity: if Latino living and transit patterns can be maintained even as families achieve economic success, then more compact and sustainable development will be the result.

Is this an opening that smart growth advocates are embracing? Mendez argues that they should, pointing out that the state of California faces a choice between Latino sprawl and Latino new urbanism—that is, a choice between allowing Latinos to follow traditional patterns of outward movement, or building on current preferences and patterns to encourage inward growth along with more compact housing and retail to accommodate the growing Latino population. The issue is definitely pressing: the state of California Demographic Research Unit is predicting that the Latino population will double between 2000 and 2030 while the Anglo population will decline over the same period by around 11 percent; the relative shares of each will shift accordingly, with Anglos falling from 47 to 29 percent, and Latinos rising from 33 to 47 percent.[10] With Latinos making a tentative entrance into the suburbs adjoining central cities, a pattern for the future is to be set—and if it is to be more sustainable, the livable, walkable, and desirable communities that smart growth advocates often discuss will have to appeal to the emerging Latino plurality in the state.

There are efforts underway to energize a smart growth response to this Latino future. In Southern California, the Transportation Land Use Coalition—based in the inner-ring suburb of Azuza, and headed by an innovative and energetic Latina urban planner named Katherine Perez—has been pushing for a Latino new urbanist agenda, and seeking to make the connections between innovative urban design and traditional Latino lifestyles. In the Pajaro Valley on the central coast of California, an effort called Action Pajaro Valley has helped begin a revitalization of the town of Watsonville, a community that is 75 percent Latino and 45 percent foreign-born, by facilitating agreement on a growth management plan that ended years of tensions between farmers, environmentalists, and an emerging Latino political leadership hungry for economic growth.

There are also good examples of Latino communities that have recognized how the principle of smart growth and good urban design can benefit their economic development dreams. The Fruitvale neighborhood of Oakland, for instance, a community that was about 63 percent Latino, 12 percent African American, 15 percent Asian Pacific, and 53 percent foreign-born as of the 2000 census, has been the site of an innovative effort at creating a transit village, one of the favorite development forms for smart growth advocates.[11]

Yet the story of how Fruitvale came to be is illustrative of the difference between how such transit-oriented development might occur in higher-income communities and how it occurs in lower-income Latino areas—and what that might mean for engaging the Latino constituency. Rather than coming to a transit village as a result of community charettes calmly conducted among constituents experienced in planning issues, the idea of the village first arose in opposition to the Bay Area's transit authority decision in 1991 to revamp the neighborhood around a local rail station to facilitate commuting into San Francisco for employment. At first blush, this might sound positive—yet the improvements were aimed not at facilitating the employment of Fruitvale residents but rather at constructing a parking garage so that suburbanites would have another place to catch the rail (called BART). Worse yet, the garage was to be located between Fruitvale's main commercial street and the station, virtually ensuring little spillover of commuter purchases for local businesses.

The community, led by a local nonprofit called the Spanish Speaking Unity Council, challenged BART in the project environment review. The initial plan for the garage was stopped and the transit authority was forced to negotiate with the community on a whole new development scheme—one that placed the garage in a different location and allowed for the creation of a walkway from the commercial district to the train station. Planning and development is, of course, a laborious process, and Fruitvale has taken years, but the plan and the emerging development include space for nonprofits, a health clinic, restaurants and stores, and both affordable and market-rate housing (Hughes 2004).

The key point is that what is now deemed a smart growth development emerged from a community struggle for environmental equity and community development. For smart growth advocates to find allies in Latino and other minority communities, they will need to take seriously the struggle for social and economic justice as the main driver for community engagement. Rather than simply inviting minorities to come to a preset table, proponents of smart growth will have to become allies in community-defined struggles.

Fortunately, smart growth advocates are becoming increasingly aware of the need for new entry points. A provocative analysis by Stolz and Ranghelli (2002), commissioned by the Funders' Network for Smart Growth and Livable Communities, points out how community organizations can become the "populist base" for smart growth provided that direct connections to local needs are made. The authors quote one organizer as saying that "Smart Growth and sprawl can be useful issues to low-income organizations, but only if these efforts pay attention to the self-interest of low-income communities" (Stolz and Ranghelli 2002, 8). A complementary work by Tony Proscio (2003) offers numerous case studies of community development groups utilizing smart growth dynamics and principles to their benefit, as in Fruitvale. Nevertheless, Proscio (2003, 1) specifically notes that none of the examples "arose as a result of some intentional good-government exercise aimed at aligning the theories of urban and suburban development. On the contrary, all arose because they solved a concrete local problem that had regional implications." It is exactly this sort of entry point that I take up below.

Bringing Latino Communities to the Table

Will Latinos come to the smart growth table? As noted above, it depends on how it is set: an agenda that includes issues of environmental justice, improvement to labor market conditions, and community development will attract leaders. But the process of inclusion and incorporation is not straightforward either.

To see this, consider the community of Mayfair in East San Jose, California. It is set in the heart of one of the most regionalist of regions—Silicon Valley has two of the country's premier regionalist business alliances, Joint Venture: Silicon Valley Network and the Silicon Valley Manufacturing Group; the city of San Jose has long employed growth boundaries to constrain sprawl and several of the surrounding suburbs have created walkable downtowns along the lines of the new urbanism; and the area is host to a central labor council that is among the most engaged in regionalist approaches in the country, complete with its own nonprofit research arm called Working Partnerships USA. Mayfair itself is predominantly Latino and immigrant, with income and other characteristics vastly different than the region in which it is situated. Site to Cesar Chavez's original urban organizing before he and others moved to work in the fields, it was long known as both an immigrant entry point and a place to leave; indeed, its historic nickname was "Sal Si Puedes" ("leave if you can").

In the mid-1990s, a foundation-sponsored neighborhood improvement initiative was launched to revitalize Mayfair. Traditionally, such efforts are inward looking, with a strong and nearly exclusive focus on internal community building, but the foundation decided early on to attempt to introduce a regional component, partly because of the regionalist buzz in the air in the surrounding Silicon Valley. An external advisory board with prominent regional actors was added, local leaders in Mayfair were afforded training and leadership opportunities outside the neighborhood, and a series of studies was conducted to afford a better understanding of how Mayfair fit into the regional economy. Still, the effort had more than an element of the artificial to it—like an invitation to a distant conversation—until a surprising local issue suggested the importance of regional levers.

One of Mayfair's early priorities was health access, particularly for children. As part of this, a *promotoras* program was launched; an emerging practice in Latino and immigrant communities, this involves "health promoters" who do outreach to families to make them aware of health care resources and issues. The stumbling block in Mayfair was a lack of documentation: many children could not access the care available for poorer children because they and their parents were not legally in the country. To address this challenge, in 2000, Mayfair leaders organized with representatives of a local PICO (People Improving Communities through Organizing) affiliate as well as the central labor council to get the city of San Jose and Santa Clara County to agree to commit dollars from tobacco settlements (with supplementary funds from foundation donors) to the creation of a local children's health insurance program that would be available to all children regardless of documentation.

This is hardly the stuff traditionally defined as regionalist or smart growth—but the fact that a coveted local goal was achieved through joining with allies to pull regional levers led to a renewed interest in the regional connection. Mayfair followed up with a conscious program of learning from others who had utilized regional equity approaches in the context of local neighborhood empowerment: the Figueroa Corridor Coalition in Los Angeles, Bethel New Life and its transit development strategy in Chicago, and immigrant rights advocates from the broader Bay Area, Texas, and Chicago (including site visits to the groups in Los Angeles and Chicago, and visits by leaders from Bethel New Life and an innovative job training program in Fort Worth, Texas). The Mayfair Neighborhood Initiative has also organized to redirect redevelopment dollars from the city to its neighborhood, joined up with organizers from around the Bay Area in a group called the Social Equity Caucus, and made building connections with regional organizations and policy tables part of its core mission.[12]

The Mayfair experiences suggest that making the link to smart growth and regional equity is possible but challenging. For Mayfair, there needed to be an immediate and clear hook, which was the role the children's health initiative played; there needed to be peer-to-peer learning, which was the role offered by site visits to Los Angeles and Chicago to learn from others who "looked like Mayfair" in terms of income, ethnic diversity, and community challenges; and there needed to a selective and strategic approach by Mayfair leaders as to which sort of regional policy tables were appropriate and would serve to elevate local issues.

This last point is important: smart growth advocates sometimes wish to invite minority community-based activists to any and all gatherings, hoping to add a bit of diversity to their efforts. But as Proscio (2003, 15) points out, many community organizations are thinly staffed and need to husband their resources for maximum effect. For Latino-based organizations taking on the issues embodied under the label of smart growth, focus is key—given other crucial issues, diverted attention must be laser focused and serve broader organizational interests.

Fortunately, there are emerging examples. In California, the Mexican American Legal Defense and Education Fund (MALDEF) cosponsored a bill to set state land use priorities favoring infill development and protecting farmlands. In Los Angeles, Latino city councillors are among those leading the charge on an inclusionary zoning ordinance that reflects many smart growth precepts (Greene 2004). The aforementioned Latino new urbanist initiative holds great promise for educating local municipal officials and allies. Environmental justice advocates, including those more rooted in Latino communities, have been raising the issue of a long-term vision of sustainable development and many participated in a Regional Equity Summit hosted by PolicyLink in Los Angeles in November 2002. There is still a long way to go, but there is much to build on.

Putting the "*Gente*" in *Crescimiento Inteligente*

I began the chapter with a dilemma: despite the seeming fit of smart growth thinking and policy with many of the needs of urban Latinos, there is a relative lack of engagement between many Latino communities and advocates of the new regionalism. The gap is all the more surprising in light of the patterns of Latino population growth, still rooted in central cities and only now spilling over to the critical inner-ring suburbs, as well as the intense involvement of Latinos in seemingly regionalist efforts like the struggles for environmental and worker justice. And closing the gap is, as Mendez (2003) argues, critical: if Latinos follow the sprawl patterns of Anglos as they achieve greater economic success in states like California, sustainability will clearly suffer.

Making the match between smart growth advocates and Latino community leaders will require movements from both sides. Smart growth proponents will need to cast a broader and move diverse net of concerns, recognizing the new urbanist potential of the Latino urban form and understanding that what will bring Latinos to the regionalist table is a series of issues that are sometimes not on the usual smart growth agenda. Latino leaders will need to recognize the tremendous opportunity offered by smart growth and new regionalist policies, and engage in the sort of training, perhaps through the National Association of Latino Elected and Appointed Officials (NALEO), that can make new urbanist and regional equity principles more familiar to new politicians and officials. Alliances will need to be built with labor and other minority groups, particularly African Americans who are already actively struggling with the balance between acting regionally and maintaining local roots and accountability.

In assessing the state of metropolitan America in the introduction to *Interwoven Destinies: Cities and the Nation*, Cisneros (1993, 26) wrote that "civic interaction within cities and metropolitan areas will determine whether our nation functions as an integrated civil society in the future, or whether class rigidities and racial and social disorder predominate." He argued, as do I, that we need "new approaches to crosscultural, crossgenerational democratic dialogue and governance." Building the *puente* that can put the gente in crescimiento inteligente—that is, building the analytic and political bridges that can put Latino peoples squarely in the midst of smart growth—will be a good bet for both the smart growth movement and the future of Latino America.

Notes

Thanks to Bob Bullard for suggesting this topic, and to Angela Glover Blackwell, Jessie Leon, Michael Mendez, Neal Peirce, and Kathy Perez for their insights and comments in the course of doing the research. Thanks also to the John D. and Catherine T. MacArthur Foundation for their support of this work and to Christian Martinez and Justin Scoggins for their research assistance along the way.

1. For more on sprawl and its causes, see the recent volumes by Bullard (1998), Fulton et al. (2001), and Wiewel and Persky (2002).

2. Data taken from national tabulation for Summary File 2, available at ⟨http://www.census.gov⟩. For a broad overview of Latinos in the United States as of 2000, see Marotta and Garcia (2003).

3. Some of these eighty-one metro areas include cities that are not among the top one hundred but are considered to be central in those MSAs, and so we included

them when dividing the population up between the city and the suburbs. The 1990 and 2000 data came from the Brookings Institution Living Cities database; we also filled in some missing data for various cities by directly accessing the data at ⟨http://www.census.gov⟩. The 1980 data used in a detailed comparison of Southern California comes from two sources. The totals for MSAs and the central city/suburban mix were calculated from summary data available at ⟨http://migration.ucdavis.edu/rmn/rural_data/hspn_census/census.htm⟩. The tract-level data used in Figures 3.3 and 3.4 differ depending on the year: the 2000 data is from the Summary File 1 and the 1980 data is from the National Change Database available from Geolytics (with data normalized to 2000 census tract shapes). The 1990 tract-level data shows a relatively smooth transition, with the data taken from the 1990 Summary File, but reshaped to 2000 shapes through a method documented in Pastor and Scoggins (2004).

4. Of Suro and Singer's two major categories of established metro areas and fast-growing Latino hubs, we are missing McAllen, Texas, in the former and Vallejo, California, in the latter.

5. Irvine is also considered a central city in the Anaheim–Santa Ana MSA.

6. For a more detailed analysis of the patterns of immigrant settlement in suburban Southern California, including a multivariate analysis of the factors driving the pattern and the implications for smart growth, see Marcelli (2004).

7. For an excellent historical account of the evolution and future of the urban Latino experience in Los Angeles, the Greater Eastside, and the new inner-ring suburbs, see Valle and Torres (2000).

8. A recent dissertation by Martha Matsuoka of the urban planning program at the University of California at Los Angeles explores Latinos in these Gateway Cities, examining when and why what she terms "community-based regionalism" finds a toehold with local political and community actors.

9. Mendez suggests, in contrast, that the city of San Fernando, which is surrounded on all sides by the city of Los Angeles, is not in as immediate a competitive situation and can leverage developers to provide more benefits.

10. African Americans are projected to increase by around 44 percent while Asian Pacifics will increase by around 65 percent. Their population shares will not change much: African Americans will stay at around 7 percent while Asian Pacifics will rise from 11 to 13 percent. The major shift is the Anglo-Latino realignment.

11. There are a variety of different definitions of the Fruitvale area. I have chosen to include a slightly tighter definition than many authors, focusing in on four census tracts including and around the Fruitvale village; the census tracts excluded are whiter and wealthier. For a longer-term history of Fruitvale, see Younis (1998).

12. For more on the experience with regionalist thinking of Mayfair and two other neighborhood initiatives in the Bay Area, see Pastor, Benner, and Matsuoka (2005).

References

Barnes, W., and L. C. Ledebur. 1998. *The New Regional Economies: The U.S. Common Market and the Global Economy.* Thousand Oaks, CA: Sage Publications.

Bhargava, S., B. Brownstein, A. Dean, and S. Zimmerman. 2001. *Everyone's Valley: Inclusion and Affordable Housing in Silicon Valley.* San Jose, CA: Working Partnerships USA.

Bullard, R. D. 1998. *Sprawl Atlanta: Social Equity Dimensions of Uneven Growth and Development.* Atlanta: Environmental Justice Resource Center, Clark Atlanta University.

Bullard, R. D., G. S. Johnson, and A. O. Torres. 1999. Race, Equity, and Smart Growth: Why People of Color Must Speak for Themselves. Available at ⟨http://www.ejrc.cau.edu/raceequitysmartgrowth.htm⟩.

Cieslewicz, D. J. 2002. The Environmental Impacts of Sprawl. In *Urban Sprawl: Causes, Consequences, and Policy Responses,* ed. G. D. Squires. Washington, DC: Brookings Institution.

Cisneros, H. G., ed. 1993. *Interwoven Destinies: Cities and the Nation.* New York: W. W. Norton.

Cisneros, H. G. 1996. Regionalism: The New Geography of Opportunity. Special edition, *Cityscape* (December): 35–53.

Dreier, P., J. Mollenkopf, and T. Swanstrom. 2001. *Place Matters: Metropolitics for the Twenty-First Century.* Lawrence: University of Kansas Press.

Frey, W. H. 2001. *Melting Pot Suburbs: A Census 2000 Study of Suburban Diversity.* Washington, DC: Brookings Institution.

Fulton, W. 1997. *The Reluctant Metropolis: The Politics of Urban Growth in Los Angeles.* Point Arena, CA: Solano Press Books.

Fulton, W., R. Pendall, M. Nguyen, and A. Harrison. 2001. *Who Sprawls Most? How Growth Patterns Differ across the U.S.* Washington, DC: Brookings Institution.

Greene, R. 2004. Rebel with a Plan. *LA Weekly,* November 19–25. Available at ⟨http://www.laweekly.com/general/features/rebel-with-a-plan/1182/⟩.

Henton, D., J. Melville, and K. Walesh. 1997. *Grassroots Leaders for a New Economy: How Civic Entrepreneurs Are Building Prosperous Communities.* San Francisco: Jossey-Bass Publishers.

Hughes, E. B. 2004. In Transit. *Ford Foundation Report* (Spring). Available at ⟨http://www.fordfound.org/publications/ff_report/view_ff_report_detail.cfm?report_index=483⟩.

Katz, B., ed. 2000. *Reflections on Regionalism.* Washington, DC: Brookings Institution.

Leroy, G. 2003. *Labor Leaders as Smart Growth Advocates: How Union Leaders See Suburban Sprawl and Work for Smart Growth Solutions.* Washington, DC: Good Jobs First.

Luria, D. D., and J. Rogers. 1997. New Urban Agenda. *Boston Review*, February–March. Available at ⟨http://bostonreview.net/BR22.1/luria.html⟩.

Marcelli, E. 2004. From the Barrio to the 'Burbs: Immigration and the Dynamics of Suburbanization. In *Up against the Sprawl: Public Policy and the Making of Southern California*, ed. J. Wolch, M. Pastor Jr., and P. Dreier. Minneapolis: University of Minnesota Press.

Marotta, S. A., and J. G. Garcia. 2003. Latinos in the United States in 2000. *Hispanic Journal of Behavioral Sciences* 25, no. 1 (February): 13–34.

Melendez, E. 1993. Understanding Latino Poverty. *Sage Race Relations Abstracts* 18, no. 2:31–42.

Mendez, M. A. 2003. Latino Lifestyle and the New Urbanism: Synergy against Sprawl. Master's thesis, MIT.

Mendez, M. A. 2005. Latino New Urbanism: Building on Cultural Preferences. *Opolis* 1, no. 1 (Winter): 33–48.

Muller, S., S. Zimmerman, B. Brownstein, A. B. Dean, and P. Ellis-Lamkins. 2003. *Shared Prosperity and Inclusion: The Future of Economic Development Strategies in Silicon Valley.* San Jose, CA: Working Partnerships USA.

Ness, I., and S. Eimer, eds. 2001. *Central Labor Councils and the Revival of American Unionism.* Armonk, NY: M. E. Sharpe.

Nowak, J. 1997. Neighborhood Initiative and the Regional Economy. *Economic Development Quarterly* 11, no. 1 (February): 3–10.

Orfield, M. 2002. *American Metropolitics: The New Suburban Reality.* Washington, DC: Brookings Institution.

Pastor, M., Jr. 2001a. Common Ground at Ground Zero? The New Economy and the New Organizing in Los Angeles. *Antipode* 33, no. 2 (March): 260–289.

Pastor, M., Jr. 2001b. Geography and Opportunity. In vol. 1 of *America Becoming: Racial Trends and Their Consequences*, ed. N. Smelser, W. J. Wilson, and F. Mitchell. Washington, DC: National Academy Press.

Pastor, M., Jr. 2003. Rising Tides and Sinking Boats: The Economic Challenge for California's Latinos. In *Latinos and Public Policy in California: An Agenda for Opportunity*, ed. D. Lopez and A. Jimenez. Berkeley, CA: Berkeley Public Policy Press.

Pastor, M., Jr., C. Benner, and M. Matsuoka. 2005. The Regional Nexus: The Promise and Risk of Community-Based Approaches to Metropolitan Equity. In *Community Economic Development in Minority Communities*, ed. P. Ong and A. Loukaitou-Sideris. Philadelphia: Temple University Press.

Pastor, M., Jr., P. Dreier, E. Grigsby, and M. L. Garza. 2000. *Regions That Work: How Cities and Suburbs Can Grow Together.* Minneapolis: University of Minnesota Press.

Pastor, M., Jr., and J. Scoggins. 2004. Income Forecasting at the Small Area Level for Southern California: Issues, Methods, and Projections: Final Report to the Southern California Association of Governments. Santa Cruz, CA: Center for Justice, Tolerance, and Community.

powell, j. a. 2000. Addressing Regional Dilemmas for Minority Communities. In *Reflections on Regionalism*, ed. Bruce Katz. Washington, DC: Brookings Institution.

Proscio, T. 2003. *Community Development and Smart Growth: Stopping Sprawl at Its Source.* Available at 〈http://www.fundersnetwork.org/usr_doc/TP_13_-_Community_Development_&_SG.pdf〉, pp. 1–20.

Savitch, H. V., and R. K. Vogel. 2004. Suburbs without a City: Power and City-County Consolidation. *Urban Affairs Review* 39, no. 6 (July): 758–790.

Stolz, R., and L. Ranghelli. 2002. Community Organizing: A Populist Base for Social Equity and Smart Growth. *Livable Communities @ Work* 1, no. 1 (November). Available at 〈http://www.fundersnetwork.org/usr_doc/LC@Work_1_-_Community_Organizing.pdf〉.

Suro, R., and A. Singer. 2002. *Latino Growth in Metropolitan America: Changing Patterns, New Locations.* Washington, DC: Brookings Institution.

Valle, V., and R. D. Torres. 2000. *Latino Metropolis.* Minneapolis: University of Minnesota Press.

Voith, R. 1992. City and Suburban Growth: Substitutes or Complements? *Business Review*, 21–33.

Wiewel, W., and J. J. Persky, eds. 2002. *Suburban Sprawl: Private Decisions and Public Policy.* Armonk, NY: M. E. Sharpe.

Wilson, W. J. 1996. *When Work Disappears: The World of the New Urban Poor.* New York: Alfred A. Knopf, Inc.

Younis, M. 1998. San Antonio and Fruitvale. *Citiscape: A Journal of Policy Development and Research* 4, no. 2:221–244.

4

Sprawl and Civil Rights: A Mayor's Reflections

William A. Johnson, Jr.

The city government of Rochester, New York, is a model of workplace diversity. Superbly qualified persons of color are generously represented at all levels of the organization. I firmly believe that Rochester's national reputation for innovation and quality service delivery is a function of the benefits that accrue when a large number of diverse people work together and exchange different life experiences. Yet at the end of the workday one observes a familiar routine. After saying good-bye to each other at an exit of city hall, white employees head for the buses that lead to the predominantly white east-side neighborhoods or the suburbs. African American employees wait for the buses that will carry them in a different direction. Rarely do blacks and whites share the same bus or bus stop, let alone the same neighborhood. For eight hours a day—at work or school—many Americans experience racial and ethnic diversity. For the balance of the day—at home—most Americans lead extremely segregated lives.

Residential segregation is not innocuous, just as decaying inner-city neighborhoods and sprawling suburbs are not innocuous. All impose social, economic, and environmental burdens. All are related to the ways our metropolitan areas are allowed to grow and develop. And all contradict the U.S. ideal of economic opportunity.

Building on other studies (Bullard, Johnson, and Torres 2000; Rusk 1999; Orfield 1998; Wilson 1987), I argue that the burdens of sprawling metropolitan growth fall disproportionately on people of color living in cities. I draw directly from my personal experiences in dealing with the effects of sprawl as the mayor of Rochester. In addition, I challenge sprawl from a civil rights perspective rooted in the African American tradition, contending that sprawl is fundamentally a civil rights issue and another hurdle in the long march toward equal opportunity for African Americans.

The modern civil rights movement, led by Martin Luther King Jr., is often misread as simply a moral crusade for social justice. Behind the King of the "I Have a Dream" speech was an astute and active critic of U.S. capitalism and individualism, both of which decimated families and communities. There is also an overlooked spatial basis to King's moral philosophy. As will be shown, King firmly believed that healthy neighborhoods were essential for positive human interactions and economic empowerment.

By addressing issues of history, social values, and law, I attempt to get to the heart of why the political system, and even the market, have fostered sprawling development in the face of overwhelming evidence that it can lead to de facto segregation.

Then I get to the crux of my argument. After a discussion of the revival of grassroots neighborhood-based development, I offer suggestions for improving equal opportunity for minorities in an era of sprawl. I maintain that while the courts are a legitimate source of relief, a lesson of the civil rights movement is that vigorous enforcement of civil rights laws will never bring an end to the fears, prejudice, pride, and irrationality that are the ultimate barriers to equal opportunity for all. I further assert that regional smart growth policies, with their promise of mixed-income neighborhoods throughout a metropolitan area, can become a powerful tool for civil rights activists concerned about the equitable organization of our living spaces. Rather than dilute hard-won minority political power, smart growth initiatives can be the foundation of a new push for equal opportunity.

Traditional Urban Lifestyle as the Basis of Modern Civil Rights

On February 1, 1960, four African American students walked nine city blocks from North Carolina A&T University to the Woolworth store in downtown Greensboro and requested service at the lunch counter. Over the following days, the students were joined by others who marched from nearby Bennett College and the Woman's College of the University of North Carolina.

The Greensboro sit-in invoked a new social order and captured the nation's conscience. It became a powerful symbol of the 1960s' civil rights movement and, indeed, remains so to this day.

The idea that everyone deserves a "seat at the lunch counter" assumes that everyone can get to the lunch counter. The original notion of civil rights, which continues to frame current discussions, was based on a traditional urban lifestyle—a compact urban form where churches, schools, jobs, stores, and homes were in close proximity, and healthy neighborhoods offered support for families and individuals at all stages of their lives.

During the famous boycott of segregated buses in Montgomery led by Reverend King, neighborhood clergy provided indigenous leadership. Churches were the focal point of African American neighborhoods, and clergy were recognized as civic leaders. They served as channels of communication and raised most of the funds that sustained a volunteer-run carpool for twelve months. The success of the boycott also depended on neighbors supporting each other, such as the black cab drivers who charged passengers the standard bus fare. It is important to note that virtually all the homes and jobs of African American workers at that time, as well as essential services, were located within a three-mile radius of downtown Montgomery.

Similarly, the famous boycotts of segregated stores in Birmingham and other Southern cities were successful because the stores had local owners and depended primarily on a local market. Black customers could, as King noted, "make the difference between profit and loss in a business" (quoted in Garrow 1986, 237). Boycotts not only undermined segregation but also supported black enterprise. Boycotts, King pointed out, could be implemented because of the existence of black businesses, which brought "economic self-help and autonomy" to the "local community" (quoted in Ansbro 1982, 143). The civil rights movement led by King achieved its greatest success wherever it could build on a solid foundation of strong neighborhoods—stable families, businesses, newspapers, colleges, churches, and enough local buying power—to make boycotts an effective weapon.

Strong families, strong neighborhoods, and economic empowerment are consistent and intertwined themes in King's work. "Nothing is so much needed as a secure family life for a people to pull themselves out of poverty and backwardness," King maintained (quoted in Garrow 1986, 718). To sustain the family, King believed that "neighborhoods had to be made more hospitable" (quoted in Carson 1998, 308).

This was the world in which the Civil Rights Act of 1964 was conceptualized and made into law—a world where Main Street was still the focus of U.S. civic life.

Sprawl, Residential Segregation, and Pressures on Livability: Public Policy's Contribution

Since the heyday of the civil rights movement, people and wealth have sprawled from traditional urban neighborhoods to the suburbs and beyond, often aided by public policy. Land use, transportation, and spending policies fuel the constant movement of housing, stores, and jobs from older urban and suburban neighborhoods. They fundamentally determine what types of housing will be built where, what kinds of people will end up living there, and how their children will be educated.

Sprawl and Residential Segregation

Two leading studies (Glaeser and Vigdor 2001; Logan 2001) analyzing the 2000 census data concluded that the nation's racial and ethnic diversity is growing, with one study even finding that there have been some gains in integration (Logan 2001). Yet as John Logan, a sociology professor at the State University of New York at Albany and author of the Lewis Mumford Center study on the 2000 data, has found, "It's a mistake to talk about a breakthrough. The only evidence of [integration] comes from places where there are few minorities to incorporate. In the other America, where 80 percent to 90 percent of minorities live, there's been very small change [in integration], if any" (quoted in Fields 2001).

Logan's finding of a persistent and pervasive racial divide is not unique to any one region. It holds across the United States. In the Northeast, for example, the city of Rochester and the county of Monroe in which it is located offer clear evidence of enduring residential segregation by race. The recent census shows that while the population of Monroe County is more diverse than it was twenty years ago, the overwhelming majority of African Americans in the county—some 84 percent—live in Rochester; the suburbs remain 82 percent white (Leingang 2001; U.S. Bureau of the Census 2000). This segregation has borne, among other things, an economic impact. As the Rochester *Democrat and Chronicle* has pointed out, "Rochester takes up only about 5 percent of the land in Monroe County, but it is home to nearly three-quarters of the county's poor, who are disproportionately African American and Hispanic" (Leingang 2001).

In the Midwest the findings are no different. As Cheryl Corley (2001) of National Public Radio's *Morning Edition* has reported, "One of Chicago's unofficial mottos is: City of Neighborhoods. In practice, it's more like: You Live in Your Neighborhood; I'll Live in Mine." Indeed, the Lewis Mumford Center study found that African American residents in Chicago are more isolated from white residents than in all other U.S. metropolitan areas except two: Detroit, another midwestern city; and Memphis, Tennessee (Logan 2001, 6).

Beyond Memphis, the South, like the rest of the nation's regions, has several segregated metropolitan areas. In fact, of the top twenty most segregated areas in the country, the South hosts eight: Birmingham, Alabama; Jackson, Mississippi; New Orleans, Louisiana; Baton Rouge, Louisiana; Shreveport–Bossier City, Louisiana; Mobile, Alabama; Atlanta, Georgia; and Richmond–Petersburg, Virginia (Logan 2001, 6).

The above examples are not exceptions but rather representative of the racial disparities in residential location prevalent in U.S. metropolitan areas. Relatively few African Americans are integrated residentially, even on an income-adjusted basis.

Sprawl and Pressures on Urban Living

Sprawl puts significant stress on urban livability as needed services become less accessible to inner-city residents and the institutional supports of healthy neighborhoods erode.

In Rochester, for instance, there are forty-five hundred licensed dogs, but just two practicing veterinarians left in the city. Each year about two thousand city residents die—about 40 percent of Monroe County's total deaths—yet only fifteen funeral homes still operate within the city limits versus sixty homes in the suburbs. There are fifteen gas stations left in the city for a quarter million registered vehicles. Suburban Monroe County has just 20 percent more vehicles registered than the city does, but has six and a half times as many gas stations. Over the past twenty years, the Catholic Diocese has closed twelve schools and seven churches in the city. Each year more new homes are built in the suburbs than new households are formed to fill them, with almost two thousand vacant homes in Rochester, according to 2002 city records.

Livability is similarly stressed by the spatial mismatch with respect to jobs. Residential segregation combined with the movement of jobs to the suburbs and the lack of adequate public transit severely restricts access to those jobs. The city of Boston, for example, contains 30 percent of the metro area's poor whites and 80 percent of the area's African American poor. Only 43 percent of the entry-level jobs in metro Boston are accessible by public transit (Lacombe 1998). The city of Cleveland contains 80 percent of the metro area's African American poor, yet 80 percent of the entry-level jobs are in the suburbs. Only one-quarter to one-third of the suburban jobs are accessible within an hour-long, one-way public transit ride (Allen and Kirby 2000).

As private-sector services and jobs are withdrawing from inner-city neighborhoods, nonprofit agencies are proliferating. While cities have become addicted to the social services these agencies provide, the needy clientele that they attract from the entire metro area adds another challenge to the economic revitalization of urban neighborhoods (Gurwitt 1997).

The stresses on the livability of inner-city neighborhoods cannot be dismissed as the unavoidable, if tragic, consequences of the free flow of capital. Rather, they represent deliberate policy choices.

Public Policy's Contribution to Sprawl

With few exceptions, U.S. metro areas are comprised of almost-autonomous units of local government, each empowered to define its own role in the broader region of which it is a part. Even if the intent is not racist, the effect is often both racially and economically discriminatory. For example, when builders attempt to construct smaller, more affordable houses in the suburbs, they run up against zoning laws designed to maximize a municipality's tax base, such as those requiring huge minimum lot sizes and large homes.

In 1973, low- and moderate-income minority residents in Rochester challenged such exclusionary zoning by bringing an action against the suburban town of Penfield. The city residents claimed that Penfield's large-lot zoning effectively excluded them from living in the town, and that this exclusion violated their constitutional rights. Despite a finding that 98 percent of Penfield's vacant land was zoned for single-family detached housing on large lots, and just 0.3 percent was zoned for multi-family dwellings, the U.S. Supreme Court in *Warth v. Seldin*, 422 U.S. 490 (1975) upheld the town's zoning provision.

The Court noted that the city residents lacked standing. It further remarked that those challenging exclusionary zoning practices must specifically demonstrate that such practices harm them, and that they would benefit personally and tangibly from the Court's intervention. Justice William Brennan's dissent in *Warth v. Seldin*, 422 U.S. 490 (1975), at 523, pointed out the irony of the Court's holding and the catch-22 situation it created for the residents of Rochester: had they been able to afford to become residents of Penfield, the plaintiffs would have been able to show that such practices harmed them—but then they would have had no grievance. Since they could not afford to become residents of Penfield, however, the plaintiffs could not demonstrate that such practices harmed them—and therefore had no standing to bring their claim.

An effect of widespread exclusionary but legal zoning is that blacks are concentrated in the poorer central sectors of U.S. metropolitan areas and whites on the wealthier edges. In Monroe County, New York, for example, an estimated seventy-two hundred people live below the poverty level—including twenty-six hundred blacks and thirty-eight hundred whites. Virtually all of the poor blacks live in forty census tracts in Rochester's inner city. Two-thirds of the poor whites are interspersed throughout the county in middle-class neighborhoods with better access to jobs and good schools (U.S. Bureau of the Census 2000).

Historically, exclusionary zoning has been buttressed by other harmful policies. Until the 1960s, mortgages backed by the FHA were limited to whites on the suburban fringe. All African American families were excluded from the FHA-subsidized suburbs. Between 1945 and 1965, the FHA insured the mortgages of 6.3 million suburban homes (Asanti 2000)—propelling an enormous wealth-creation mechanism for white suburban families. Other public and private policies—such as urban renewal, block busting by real estate agents, insurance redlining, and transportation subsidies that prioritized new roads over existing modes of transit—also damaged many of the neighborhoods and institutions that gave cities their special appeal, and pushed people outward (powell 2000).

Although civil rights laws ended such overtly discriminatory practices, what survives today is a complex—and largely hidden—structure of policies that guarantee a racial and economic divide between cities and suburbs.

Roots of the Social and Political Desirability of Sprawl

Low-density sprawl is occurring in at least 740 counties in the United States—basically anywhere physical growth is happening (Burchell et al. 2001). To understand why sprawl is often seen as socially desirable and politically acceptable, we must explore more closely the intersection of history, social values, political culture, and race in the United States. Again, King's civil rights movement provides a point of departure for an examination of the deep roots of sprawl.

King frequently quoted Ralph Waldo Emerson. He was attracted by Emerson's challenge to live on a "higher plane" than mere materialism and self-seeking. Emerson's notions of "plain living" and "high thinking" in a world in which all beings are interconnected coincided with King's independently conceived ideal of a "beloved community." Central to the philosophies of both King and Emerson was an affirmation of life in the teeth of limits on human freedom: an awareness of the danger that material comforts will extinguish a more demanding ideal of the good life; a sensibility that happiness depends on the recognition that human beings are not made for happiness; the self-forgetfulness that comes with immersion in an absorbing piece of work; and the habits of responsibility associated with property ownership. King and Emerson believed that both poverty and luxury alike eroded independence, and that spiritual and economic independence were the basis of the beloved community.[1]

King, like Emerson, wanted men and women to become more "self-reliant" precisely so that they could meet each other as equals, without deference or condescension.[2] King often urged African Americans to open family businesses, credit unions, and finance companies in order to increase personal and family independence, strengthen the local community, and join the wider economic mainstream. He preached the dignity of ordinary labor and frequently repeated Emerson's exhortation to "painstaking excellence" in the performance of even the humblest tasks: "If a man can write a better book, or preach a better sermon, or make a better mousetrap than his neighbor, even if he builds his house in the woods, the world will make a beaten path to his door" (quoted in Washington 1986, 139).

These values, which inspired King and which he used to inspire others, were deeply rooted in Protestant morality and expressed in a highly idiosyncratic form of racial and local identity in the black church service. Outside the black church, however, these populist virtues—with their unpremeditated acceptance of natural limits on freedom—were regarded by mainstream society as relics of a quaint, but unrecoverable, past.

Such American idealism essentially exhausted itself in the war against slavery. Slavery's legacy of racial antagonism confronted the nation with injustices more mountainous than even slavery itself. Our nation, though, almost immediately proved unequal to the removal of these injustices. Instead of accepting the social obligations implicit in emancipation, Northerners turned the freed people over to their former masters and threw themselves instead—with a single-minded fanaticism unprecedented in the nation's history—into the business of getting rich.

The next 140 years of mainstream U.S. history since the Civil War is largely the story of an increasingly unregulated market economy and the formation of the mass consumer. Insatiable desire came to be seen as a powerful stimulus to economic development. The more comforts people enjoyed, the more they would expect, and the more the wheels of industry would turn. A healthy economy depended on the constant creation of new demands and new discontents that could only be relieved by the consumption of new commodities. An assumption developed—indeed, an unquestioned faith—that the expansion of productive forces could continue indefinitely, thus providing satisfaction to seemingly unlimited material wants.

Rather than create a community of individuals, such a market reduces individuals to abstractions, anonymous buyers and sellers whose claims on each other are determined solely by their capacity to pay. As King (1958) succinctly noted, "Historically, capitalism failed to see the truth in collective enterprise." The family, in particular, depends on an active community life. Yet the market disrupts communities by draining off their best talent.

Such a market provides little incentive for people to stretch their minds beyond the limits of immediate experience. In 1908, barely five decades after the Civil War threatened the future survival of the United States, Georges Sorel (1986) asked, "Why worry about the fate of new generations, which are destined to have a fate that is automatically superior to ours?" Devotion to the unregulated market furnished not only a means of avoiding obligations to the future but also a justification for the abrogation of reciprocal obligations. By 1980, the *New York Times* could write that civil rights "once meant helping the Irish and Italian families who were still mired in the lower working class," but that it now meant "helping poor blacks and other racial minorities"—something the "more prosperous" beneficiaries of earlier public policies could not seem to understand (Roberts 1980).

By the 1980s, President Ronald Reagan's rhetorical defense of "family and neighborhood" could not be logically reconciled with his championship of unregulated business enterprise, which replaced neighborhoods with shopping malls and superhighways. In a society dominated by the free market, in which the American dream is defined as pure acquisitiveness and self-seeking, there is no place for family values and neighborhoods themselves become disposable.[3]

The emergence in the 1990s of a bipartisan consensus concerning the importance of low taxes and governmental thrift, together with an unspoken agreement not to raise serious questions about the distribution of wealth, means that "social issues" now continue to dominate national political debate. More precisely, it means that symbols vaguely evoked by those issues—the family, community, the flag, school prayer, small government, the American dream—will dominate national political campaigns, and that race will be a peripheral issue. Issues regarding the equitable distribution of resources across metropolitan areas will likely be relegated to the background, behind such mass media–friendly topics as racial profiling, affirmative action, hate crimes, immigration, and interracial love.

Certainly, the myths of race are part of not only U.S. history but the story of all of humanity. Consequently, the unregulated market economy cannot be made to carry the whole indictment of our cultural acceptance of suburban sprawl, urban disinvestment, and racial isolation. But neither can the market be absolved. An unregulated market, together with a boundless cultural fascination for the new, goes a long way toward explaining how wealth and law can be used to increase spatial and racial distance. It explains how policies such as traditional zoning—which gives priority to big lots, big houses, and wide roads, especially when underwritten by the state—not only reflect discriminatory attitudes but also play a significant part in creating them. It explains how fragmented systems of local governments can be defended in the face of the overwhelming evidence that they contribute to de facto segregation.

Even though the combination of race and spatial isolation is, at best, a marginal political issue, it comprises a formidable part of the national psyche.

The phenomenon of the poor, black, inner-city ghetto is burned into the U.S. consciousness. There is no direct causal relationship between race and crime, or race and school performance, or race and property values. There is little connection between individual poverty and crime, or individual poverty and school performance, or individual poverty and neighborhood property values. Studies show that high crime rates, low educational attainment, and declining property values are a function not so much of individual poverty or race but of concentrated group poverty.[4] But just try explaining that to residents of a suburb where an affordable housing project has been proposed.

In the United States, concentrated group poverty is largely a phenomenon of people of color in the inner city. The phenomenon is so overwhelming that whites cannot see past it to focus on the root causes of racial isolation, such as the legal and governmental structures that enable homogeneous neighborhoods. Homogeneous neighborhoods feed the school districts that often are supported primarily by property taxes. School quality, while determined by many influences, is almost always directly related to educational resources. In many metro areas, homogeneity ensures that suburban districts will be predominantly white, wealthy, and high performing; and that urban school districts will be black, poor, and underperforming (see, for example, Orfield and Eaton 2000; Kozol 1991).

Urban experts repeat the story of how Detroit, each year in the mid-1990s, demolished more buildings than were destroyed in Rotterdam during all of World War II (Norquist 1998, 155). There was little hope of restoring the Detroit structures that had been abandoned by their owners and had become locations of undesirable activity. The other side of the story is that enough homes were built in the suburbs of Detroit each year to house the postwar population of central Rotterdam. Sprawl is not innocuous. Malcolm X witnessed disinvestment in cities like Detroit and observed that "the white man's heaven is the black man's hell."[5]

Responding to Sprawl

Citizens are beginning to fight back against sprawl in many different ways. From the grass roots to the courts, residents are demanding attention to their neighborhoods. Many cities are enjoying an increase in infill development, mostly because some people want to live closer to their jobs. Suburbs are experimenting with "neotraditional" subdivisions that emulate pre–World War II streetscapes, and provide a more convenient lifestyle for the elderly and families with children. Downtowns large and small are being rediscovered for their uniqueness and ability to facilitate pleasurable, spontaneous social interactions.

The Resurgence of Place-Based Leadership

Over the past decade, an incipient and largely suburban movement for sustainable development has emerged. Many Americans have begun to recognize the limits of growth—a remarkable occurrence for a society that in modern times has been reluctant to acknowledge limits. For over a hundred years, Americans didn't think of long-term social, environmental, and fiscal costs. But now they are finding that vacant buildings, air pollution, clogged highways, and high taxes do represent some limits after all. At the same time, we are seeing a convergence of political ideologies that until recently, could be characterized as a struggle between the forces of participation and the forces of distribution.

The most important feature of the civil rights movement of the 1950s and early 1960s was mass participation. In Southern cities, particularly, mass protests were sustained by neighborhoods with a mutually supporting network of black institutions, a black middle class, and an influential black church.

As the 1960s wore on, the civil rights movement ventured north, but it could not be sustained in ghettos marked by weak institutions, staggering poverty, and a demoralized populace. King and others concluded that the direct participation of the masses was insufficient to address the underlying causes of inequality. Civil rights activists began advocating policies that required comprehensive federal intervention. Most subsequent urban renewal and welfare programs were concerned with the redistribution of resources. Often, such programs were in direct opposition to an indigenous, "community control" movement that briefly, if tentatively, took root in urban neighborhoods in the 1960s and 1970s. Many current local community revitalization efforts attempt to balance these ideological pressures, and thus have the support of both liberals and conservatives.

We are witnessing a potentially seismic philosophical and political change at the local level that we really can't yet understand. The immediate result is a broad-based, place-based, bottom-up approach to community development. People don't want to leave their neighborhoods to the experts. In cities throughout the country, churches, community development corporations, and other local organizations are mobilizing neighborhood residents (Grogan and Proscio 2000). Often, the goal of neighborhood empowerment is to leverage public and private investment for developments that restore the buying power and civic infrastructure of neighborhoods ravished by sprawl.

Rochester provides an example of a city government that highly prizes grassroots community participation and works hard to inculcate the values of citizen empowerment in its operations (see, for instance, Crocker 2000; Partners for Livable Communities 2000).

In 1970, there were forty-two full-service supermarkets in Rochester. By 1997, only eight were left. Many city residents faced a forty-five-minute bus ride to the suburbs to get an adequate selection of reasonably priced food. In 1995, one group, Partners through Food, mobilized against disinvestment in Rochester's northeast neighborhood, the city's most economically distressed. In partnership with city hall, the group developed a holistic plan to attract and support supermarkets, including strategies to improve public safety, property conditions, public service delivery, employment, and homeownership in the neighborhoods. In 1997, contrary to the national trend at the time, a major chain committed to build five full-service supermarkets in strategic locations throughout the city. This investment soon attracted two other national chains that subsequently opened new full-service supermarkets. It also helped attract over three hundred thousand square feet of additional retail space in neighborhoods that had been ravished by disinvestments (Hudnut 2001).

In Rochester, neighborhood residents wield significant power. Through a visioning process called Neighbors Building Neighborhoods, which began in 1994, residents develop action plans for their respective neighborhoods. Residents assume most of the responsibility for implementing the plans. They have created community development corporations, and organized politically to leverage significant resources from businesses, nonprofits, and government. The city of Rochester's budget fully supports the neighborhood plans. In fact, residents work with city hall to establish the city's spending priorities for housing, public safety, economic development, human services, land use, capital improvements, and Community Development Block Grants. Although Rochester has a tradition of powerful neighborhood groups, the Neighbors Building Neighborhoods process is rooted not just in those organizations but in the direct involvement of individuals. In this way, people from socioeconomic groups that usually don't participate become involved.

Throughout the country, urban activists are developing creative grassroots approaches to include poor and commonly disenfranchised residents in neighborhood restoration. Location-efficient mortgages, community land trusts, and urban sustainability indicators, for example, bring needed investment to urban neighborhoods, help protect residents from displacement due to gentrification, and help strengthen neighborhood cohesiveness (National Neighborhood Coalition 2000; Berry, Portney, and Thomson 1993).

Generally, however, the national spotlight is more on the physical aspects of neighborhood revitalization than on social and economic integration. Throughout the country, most urban and suburban market-rate, neotraditional developments are virtually all white. And of course, attempts to build affordable housing in the suburbs run the gauntlet of legal barriers and public resistance in the form of zoning and home rule.

In other words, in metro areas where zoning is local and communities compete with each other for development, it takes more than grassroots efforts to confront policies that drain resources from urban neighborhoods and contribute to racial isolation. The apartheid consequences of sprawl are therefore beginning to be challenged in the courts.

Laws and Litigation

The Greater Rochester Area Coalition for Education, representing a group of disadvantaged and minority students in the Rochester City School District, is suing the state of New York, alleging that concentrated inner-city poverty makes it impossible for city residents to get the sound, basic education required by the state constitution (*Paynter v. State* 2001).

A group of disabled persons in Rochester sued the regional bus company, claiming that it routinely failed to provide timely transportation to people with disabilities in compliance with the federal Americans with Disabilities Act (ADA). As people spread farther and farther out in low-density subdivisions, the bus company struggles to serve them, thus restricting the disabled from participating in the ordinary life of their community. A federal judge ruled that the bus company regularly violated the ADA and ordered it to formulate a plan to rectify the poor service (*Anderson v. Rochester-Genesee Regional Transportation Authority* 2001).

In Los Angeles, a group called the Bus Riders Union, represented by the NAACP Legal Defense and Education Fund, sued the MTA under

Title VI of the Civil Rights Act of 1964, which requires that federal funds be spent in a nondiscriminatory manner. The plaintiffs alleged that inner-city residents lacked adequate bus service because inequitable funding and operating practices in the MTA's service area disproportionately burdened inner-city neighborhoods. The citizens' group won a historic out-of-court settlement that includes major fare concessions and major new investments in the bus system (*Labor/Community Strategy Center v. Los Angeles Metropolitan Transit Authority* 2001).

As the spotlight intensifies nationally on metropolitan growth, we can reasonably expect more actions in the courts to address the negative civil rights consequences of sprawl. This does not mean an excessive reliance on legal remedies, or on the courts, to either create a new category of prescriptive rights or expand the courts' authority into the field of social engineering. Rather, it is an expectation that the courts will enforce rights already guaranteed by the Civil Rights Acts by addressing the underlying causes of spatial inequity, not just legal discrimination.

The environmental movement offers a lesson on the value of legal action backed by solid public support. Beginning in the late 1980s, about ten years after Love Canal, we began to see lawsuits alleging "environmental racism"—that environmentally poisoned communities were predominantly urban and predominantly minority. Certainly under the rhetoric of environmentalism these lawsuits pursued a broader social agenda of black economic empowerment. Lawsuits based on environmental justice helped lead to a national focus on brownfields revitalization and the reconstruction of the urban tax base. They also helped put in the national spotlight on transportation policies that effectively denied minority residents access to job centers, and exposed minority communities to health risks from poor air quality and unsafe pedestrian conditions (see Bullard and Johnson 1997; Bullard 1994).

The rhetoric of environmental justice was propelled by a broader economic agenda, which is the only way a majority of African Americans will enter the mainstream. Although the Supreme Court recently limited the scope of civil rights lawsuits in *Alexander v. Sandoval*, 531 U.S. 1049 (2001), I remain optimistic that urban activists and their attorneys will find in the courts opportunities for spatial justice and minority empowerment within the antisprawl movement.

Smart Growth

Ultimately, smart growth programs may offer the best chance to deal with our most pressing racial problems. In Portland, Oregon, for example, with its growth boundaries, there are fewer incentives for the middle class to take their wealth and run away. Property values in Albina, Portland's poorest black neighborhood, have doubled in recent years. Housing prices in Portland are rising—as they are in all booming metro areas—and affordability is an issue. To address the problem, Portland officials are discussing a Montgomery County, Maryland–style mixed-income housing policy. Unlike most of the country, there is a popularly elected regional governance structure in place in Portland to deal with the affordability issue.

Smart growth is most often viewed as a way to save open space, reduce infrastructure costs, or place more emphasis on the needs of the pedestrian. But if smart growth is to flourish, it needs to be applied to the tangled issues of where people of different races and classes live, work, and go to school. In other words, all communities within a region must come to grips with sprawl—either through reason or the force of law. When people begin to understand the implications of sprawl, they begin to understand the connection between larger regional issues and their day-to-day lives—that the economy of the region is critical to the well-being of their neighborhoods, for example. Or that what happens in one part of the metro area has serious repercussions for people living in another part.

Many African American leaders are watching the smart growth movement carefully. They fear smart growth will further restrict the choices of black homeowners or that regional efforts will dilute hard-won black political power in cities. If African Americans now enjoy many of the comforts formerly restricted to whites, it is because they have won them through their own political efforts, not because whites freely surrendered their privileges or because the market automatically assures abundance for all. As the boycotts in Greensboro and Montgomery remind us, the civil rights movement was a struggle for dignity—but it was a moral struggle that relied on the creation of a solid economic and political foundation.

Today, however, the economy is regional. The balance of political power has shifted outside of cities. The flows of both money and information do not respect political boundaries. The city can provide a spiritual and cultural home for racial solidarity, but for economic and political power, people of color must make alliances beyond city limits.

I understand the deep concerns of many African American leaders. I was born and raised in the segregated South. My adolescence coincided with the rise of the civil rights movement in the late 1950s. I vividly recall the attempts to distinguish between de jure and de facto segregation. The latter was always described as the unintended consequences of a series of lawful actions by benign Northerners. De jure segregation—the really bad form—was always considered the result of extralegal and unconstitutional actions by evil Southerners.

Before becoming mayor, I was employed by the Urban League for nearly twenty-five years. The Urban League's mission was to assimilate poor and disenfranchised blacks into the economic, social, and political mainstream. Through job training, education, and a variety of social work programs, we worked earnestly to attain that mission. But we didn't recognize the impracticality of our efforts. Quite simply, the mainstream was relentlessly relocating itself further from our reach. All of the tools we needed to achieve success—accessible neighborhoods, institutional investment, and stable families—were literally moving beyond our grasp.

As mayor of Rochester, I have come to realize that as the middle class moves out of the city, African American urban leaders have less and less to protect. As the economic power of cities diminishes, so does the political power of black urban leaders. The leader of an empire of useless, unwanted land is a paper tiger. As mayor, I have come to realize the wisdom of King when he said, "I see nothing in this world more dangerous than Negro cities ringed with white suburbs."[6] As King verified, both with his movement's success in the South and its failure in the North, creating stable, mixed-income neighborhoods throughout a metro area will do more for civil rights and economic justice than just about any other reform. This is the promise of smart growth.

Sprawl, geographic isolation by race, and highly concentrated black poverty are three constants of metropolitan growth in the United States. A predictable result is unequal access to opportunity.

Our sprawling patterns of land use cannot be dismissed as the product of an invisible hand or unintended consequences. Rather, they are the spatial result of power relationships deeply rooted in the history and philosophy of the United States. The emerging smart growth movement offers the potential to disrupt established relationships. Smart growth, moreover, appears compatible with the spatial, moral, and economic foundations of the modern civil rights movement championed by King.

The lesson that the civil rights movement holds for metropolitan America is that equity—including spatial equity—arises from a combination of grassroots leadership, shared power, new legislation, and vigorous legal action.

Notes

1. Emerson's views on the conduct of life deeply influenced King. See, particularly, Emerson's (1936) essays (and the themes they treated): "Fate" (how shall I live?), "Wealth" (higher plane), "New England Reformers" (plain living), "Spiritual Laws" (high thinking), and "Compensation" (self-reliance).

2. In "Compensation," one of King's favorite Emerson essays, Emerson (1936) wrote that the "mechanic at his bench," with his "quiet heart and assured manner," deals "on even terms with men of any condition." Those who speak through their "faithful work" can "afford not to conciliate."

3. This chapter's critique of unregulated consumer capitalism and the analysis of King's cultural critique, including much of the rhetoric, follow that of Lasch (1991).

4. For good discussions of concentrated poverty in the United States, see Rusk (1997), from which this paragraph and the next were substantially derived; Massey and Denton (1993).

5. Malcolm X quoted in Cone (1991, 151). In like spirit, King (1967, 201) said, "The suburbs are white nooses around the black necks of cities."

6. In a prescient essay published posthumously, King wrote, "the anarchy of unplanned city growth is destined to confound our confidence. What is unique to this period is our inability to arrange an order of priorities and promising solutions that are decent and just" (Garrow 1986, 507; Washington 1986, 121).

References

Allen, K., and M. Kirby. 2000. *Unfinished Business: Why Cities Matter to Welfare Reform*. Washington, DC: Brookings Institution.

Anderson v. Rochester-Genesee Regional Transportation Authority. 2001. No. 00 CV 6275 L, U.S. Dist. LEXIS 21124.

Ansbro, J. 1982. *Martin Luther King, Jr.: The Making of a Mind*. New York: Orbis Books.

Asanti, N. M. 2000. E-mail response to author's inquiry. HUD research staff. June 23.

Berry, J., K. Portney, and K. Thomson. 1993. *The Rebirth of Urban Democracy*. Washington, DC: Brookings Institution.

Bullard, R. D., ed. 1994. *Unequal Protection: Environmental Justice and Communities of Color*. San Francisco: Sierra Club Books.

Bullard, R. D., and G. S. Johnson, eds. 1997. *Just Transportation: Dismantling Race and Class Barriers to Mobility*. Gabriola Island, BC: New Society Publishers.

Bullard, R. D., G. S. Johnson, and A. O. Torres, eds. 2000. *Sprawl City: Race, Politics, and Planning Atlanta*. Washington, DC: Island Press.

Burchell, R., et al. 2001. *Costs of Sprawl—2000*. Washington, DC: National Academy Press.

Carson, C., ed. 1998. *The Autobiography of Martin Luther King, Jr*. Sydney, Australia: Warner Books.

Cone, J. H. 1991. *Martin and Malcolm and America: A Dream or a Nightmare*. Maryknoll, NY: Orbis Books.

Corley, C. 2001. Racial Segregation in the U.S. and Chicago in Particular. *Morning Edition*, National Public Radio, April 6.

Crocker, J. 2000. The Neighbors Building Initiative in Rochester, New York. *National Civic Review* 89:259.

Emerson, R. W. 1936. *The Works of Ralph Waldo Emerson*. New York: Tudor.

Fields, R. 2001. Integration Progress Unclear: Same Census Numbers Used to Say It Has Climbed, Stalled. *Dallas Morning News*, June 25.

Garrow, D. 1986. *Bearing the Cross*. New York: W. Morrow.

Glaeser, E. D., and J. L. Vigdor. 2001. *Racial Segregation in the 2000 Census: Promising News*. Washington, DC: Brookings Institution.

Grogan, P., and T. Proscio. 2000. *Comeback Cities: A Blueprint for Urban Neighborhood Revival*. Boulder, CO: Westview Press.

Gurwitt, R. 1997. Dueling with Do-Gooders. *Governing* (May).

Hudnut, W. H. 2001. Turning Communities Around. *Urban Land* (July).

King, M. L., Jr. 1958. *Stride toward Freedom*. San Francisco: Harper.

King, M. L., Jr. 1967. *Where Do We Go from Here: Chaos or Community?* New York: Harper and Row.

Kozol, J. 1991. *Savage Inequalities: Children in America's Schools*. New York: Crown Publishers.

Labor/Community Strategy Center v. Los Angeles Metropolitan Transit Authority. 2001. 263 F.3d 1041 (9th Cir.).

Lacombe, A. 1998. *Welfare Reform and Access to Jobs in Boston*. Cambridge, MA: Volpe National Transportation System Center.

Lasch, C. 1991. *The True and Only Heaven: Progress and Its Critics*. New York: W. W. Norton.

Leingang, M. 2001. Area Diverse But Not Blended. *Democrat and Chronicle*, April 7. Available at ⟨http://www.democratandcrenide.com/news/extra/census/0407diversity.shtml⟩ (accessed May 14, 2006).

Logan, J. 2001. *Ethnic Diversity Grows, Neighborhood Integration Is at a Standstill*. Albany, NY: Mumford Center.

Massey, D. S., and N. A. Denton. 1993. *American Apartheid: Segregation and the Making of the Underclass*. Cambridge, MA: Harvard University Press.

National Neighborhood Coalition. 2000. *Smart Growth, Better Neighborhoods: Communities Leading the Way*. Washington, DC: National Neighborhood Coalition.

Norquist, J. 1998. *The Wealth of Cities: Revitalizing Centers of American Life*. Boston: Addison-Wesley.

Orfield, M. 1998. *Metropolitics: A Regional Agenda for Community and Stability*. Washington, DC: Brookings Institution.

Orfield, G., and S. E. Eaton. 2000. *Dismantling Desegregation: The Quiet Reversal of Brown v. Board of Education*. New York: New Press.

Partners for Livable Communities. 2000. *The Livable City: Revitalizing Urban Communities*. New York: McGraw-Hill.

Paynter v. State. 2001. 720 N.Y.S. 2d 712 (S.C. Monroe Co.), modified No. (1288) CA 01–0057, N.Y. App. Div. LEXIS 12508 (December 21).

powell, j. a. 2000. Addressing Regional Dilemmas for Minority Communities. In *Reflections on Regionalism*, ed. Bruce Katz, 218–46. Washington, DC: Brookings Institution.

Roberts, S. 1980. Many Dreams Are Dying in Boston as Kennedy's Legend Is Tarnished. *New York Times*, March 2.

Rusk, D. 1997. How We Promote Poverty. *Washington Post*, May 18.

Rusk, D. 1999. *Inside Game/Outside Game: Winning Strategies for Saving Urban America*. Washington, DC: Brookings Institution.

Sorel, G. 1986. *The Illusions of Progress*. Trans. J. and C. Stanley. Berkeley: University of California Press. (Orig. pub. 1908.)

U.S. Bureau of the Census. 2000. *Census of Population*. Washington, DC: U.S. Department of Commerce.

Washington, J. M., ed. 1986. *A Testament of Hope: The Essential Writings of Martin Luther King, Jr.* New York: Harper and Row.

Wilson, W. J. 1987. *The Truly Disadvantaged: The Inner City, the Underclass, and Public Policy*. Chicago: University of Chicago Press.

II

Land Use and the Built Environment

5

Nashville: An Experience in Metropolitan Governance

David A. Padgett

This chapter focuses on applications of geographically and spatially based methods in assessing the impact of suburban sprawl on Nashville's black population. Population data reveals that the middle Tennessee region experienced significant population growth between 1980 and 2000. During that period, the Nashville MSA surpassed the Memphis MSA as the most populous in the state (Covington 2001).

Data from quality of life research and field investigations by the Tennessee State University (TSU) Geographic Information Sciences Laboratory GISL provides evidence of the overall impacts of urban growth on the black community. There are signs of both positive and negative changes. Most recently, Nashville was named fourth best from among the "ten best U.S. cities for African Americans" from the results of a *Black Enterprise* magazine online survey and socioeconomic analysis. The urban-related research was conducted under the direction of the GISL director.

Since its inception in 2000, the TSU GISL has graphically documented evidence of urban decay, environmental inequity, and health disparities in predominantly black communities. The GISL-produced maps, depicting the disparate impacts of sprawl, are used to support qualitative and quantitative impact assessment efforts led by local stakeholders, public officials, and nonprofit organizations.

Nashville Metropolitan Growth, 1980–2000

The Nashville MSA has experienced significant growth during the past two decades. Recent studies conducted by *USA Today* (El Nasser and

Overburg 2001) and the Brookings Institution (Fulton et al. 2001) have identified Nashville as one of the fastest-growing urban regions in the United States. Census estimates put the 1997 population at 1,134,524, an increase of over 280,000 since 1980. The MSA grew at a rate of 15.8 percent between 1980 and 1990, and continued at a 15.2 percent rate from 1990 to 1997 (U.S. Bureau of the Census 1998). Several counties within the MSA are expected to grow at exceptionally rapid rates between the years 2000 and 2020: Cheatham (63.9 percent), Williamson (57.8 percent), Rutherford (53.5 percent), Dickson (46.9 percent), Wilson (45.2 percent), Sumner (43.6 percent), and Robertson (34.2 percent) (Center for Business and Economic Research 1999).

Along with the increase in human population has come an expansion of the built environment. Building permits for new private housing units numbered 63,879 between 1990 and 1996 (U.S. Bureau of the Census 1998). An American Planning Association (2000) study estimates that the amount of land developed per capita in Tennessee increased by 45 percent between 1982 and 1997, the fourth-highest rate among all states. Thus, in middle Tennessee, green space is being replaced by human-built structures at a relatively accelerated pace.

Geographic information systems (GIS) and related geospatial analytic techniques were applied to assess the characteristics of regional urban growth between 1980 and 2000. Out-migration from Nashville and Davidson County to the surrounding counties was the primary direction of human relocation between 1995 and 2000. Rutherford, Williamson, and Sumner Counties received the greatest numbers of migrants, with Wilson County not far behind. The obvious implications herein are that not only humans but human capital as well are moving away from the central city, not to mention jobs and businesses.

The data in table 5.1 clearly indicates a "doughnut" growth pattern around Nashville. While the core city grew by less than 20 percent over the two-decade period of interest, Williamson and Rutherford Counties saw their populations more than double. Figure 5.1 shows that in 2000, while the overall population was booming in the outlying areas of the MSA, the African American population remained very much tied to the central city.

Table 5.1
Population growth in Nashville MSA counties, 1980–2000

County	1980 total	1990 total	2000 total	Growth 1980–2000 (%)
Cheatham	21,616	27,140	35,912	66.1
Davidson	477,811	510,784	569,891	19.3
Dickson	30,037	35,061	43,156	43.7
Robertson	37,021	41,494	54,433	47.0
Rutherford	84,058	118,570	182,023	116.5
Sumner	85,790	103,281	130,449	52.1
Williamson	58,108	81,021	126,638	117.9
Wilson	56,064	67,675	88,809	58.4
MSA	850,505	985,026	1,231,311	44.8

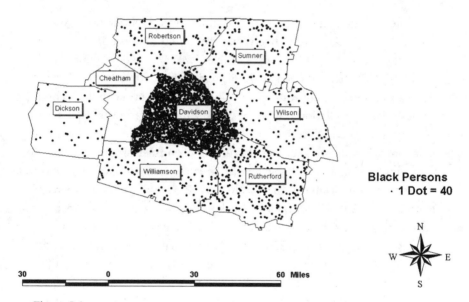

Figure 5.1
Distribution of African American population, Nashville MSA, 2000

Table 5.2
Black population change in Nashville MSA counties, 1980–2000

County	1980	1990	2000	Growth 1980–2000 (%)
Cheatham	595	570	532	−10.6
Davidson	106,369	119,412	147,696	38.9
Dickson	1,672	1,704	1,978	18.3
Robertson	4,960	4,526	4,691	−5.4
Rutherford	8,593	10,579	17,312	101.5
Sumner	5,084	5,381	7,540	48.3
Williamson	5,202	5,445	6,564	26.2
Wilson	4,873	4,685	5,563	14.2
MSA	137,348	152,302	191,876	39.7

While Cheatham and Robertson Counties' overall population grew by 66.1 and 47 percent, respectively, between 1980 and 2000, their black population percentages decreased (table 5.2). Davidson County, with over 147,000 black residents in 2000, had about 130,000 more African American residents than Rutherford County, the county with the second-highest black population (see figure 5.2). Murfreesboro, a midsize satellite city, is located in Rutherford County. Black people in the area not living in Nashville are likely drawn to this second-tier urban area.

Davidson County, with by far the greatest number and percentage of African Americans in the Nashville MSA, grew by 19.3 percent from 1980 to 2000. The county's black population grew by 38.9 percent during that same period, with blacks' percentage of the population increasing slightly from 22.3 to 25.9 percent. Comparatively, the MSA black percentage was 15.6 percent. Also from 1980 to 2000, Davidson County was the only MSA county that had African American representation above the MSA average. Nevertheless, three counties, Rutherford, Sumner, and Williamson, outpaced Davidson in the increase of black population percentage (table 5.2). Davidson's black percentage increased nearly equal to that of the MSA. The Sumner County portion grew by nearly 50 percent, while Wilson County's more than doubled. Albeit, the raw numbers of blacks in those areas' increases were signifi-

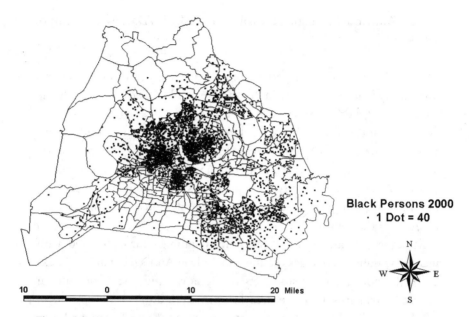

Black Persons 2000
· **1 Dot = 40**

Figure 5.2
Distribution of African American population, Nashville and Davidson County, 2000

cantly less than those of the MSA central city/county area during this time.

Public schools are probably the institution impacted the most by the population dynamics of the past two decades. New schools are built in the outlying counties only to be overcrowded the day they open. Conversely, in the Nashville/Davidson County school district, several schools are at less than 50 percent capacity. Also, a pattern of school "resegregation" has been noted (Hamburg 2003).

While Davidson County as a whole is about 26 percent black, the black percentage of nearly every public school is greater. Metro schools data reveals that approximately 58 percent of students in the district were attending "racially imbalanced" schools in 2003 (Hamburg 2003). The far-reaching effects of the loss of the tax base and population on inner-city schools is evident in that for the most part, schools in the outlying counties outperform those in the core city on various standardized exams and other achievement indicators (State of Tennessee 2004).

African American Population Dynamics in Nashville/Davidson Counties, 1980–1990

The 1980s saw a distinct pattern of movement away from Nashville's historically black community in "North Nashville." The North Nashville community generally appears as a cluster from the center toward the northwest of the county. More black residents moved to the southeastern region, an area known as Antioch. It should be noted that Antioch boasts a significant number of apartment complexes. It is primarily a working-class/middle-class community with plenty of single-family homes present, but it has a much greater number of multifamily households than the remainder of the county.

Movement away from the inner-city continued through 2000 with increasing numbers of blacks settling not only in Antioch but also in pockets to the north. The census tracts to the north and east of downtown Nashville primarily lie in an area known as Madison. Unlike Antioch, development in Madison has been much more of the single-family dwelling variety. Some area subdivisions constructed within the past ten years are predominantly black, with prices being relatively moderate, ranging from $90,000 to $110,000.

The African American pattern is not unlike that of the larger population. Until recently, local zoning regulations have favored suburban development. Thus, residential and commercial development has been and continues to be on the rise in the outlying portions of Davidson County. The primary limits to growth are physical. The karst topography dominant throughout middle Tennessee is characterized by steep slopes and unstable soils. Some areas are prone to landslides, sinkholes, and subsidence.

Recent initiatives, such as the Urban Zoning Overlay (UZO), have been implemented by the metropolitan government to stimulate growth in the inner city (Metropolitan Government of Nashville and Davidson County 2004). There has also been a relatively aggressive campaign lately to create incentives for downtown residential development. To date, there has been an increase in residential property in and around Nashville's central business district (CBD), but there is still a much greater inclination on the part of new home buyers to look to the suburbs and beyond. Only time will tell if the idea of gentrification will fully take hold in the area. At present, the traffic situation may be tenuous at times, but it has not yet hit the "pain threshold" that may push commuters to inner-city dwellings. It should be noted that of the downtown properties on the market today, few would be considered affordable. Some lofts and condominiums now under construction are advertised at $500,000 to over $1,000,000.

Following the general trend of out-migration, Nashville's predominantly black, older inner-city communities have actually lost population over the past five decades (Metropolitan Government of Nashville and Davidson County 2002). Population change in Nashville has been politically influenced. Between the years 1960 and 1970, while the number of blacks increased from about 65,000 to just over 87,000, the percentage of the black population in what was legally defined as Nashville decreased with the city-county merger in 1963 (U.S. Bureau of the Census 1961).

With the merger, Nashville's African American representation fell from 37.8 to 20 percent. The overall impact of the merger on the upward mobility of blacks is a topic of debate. While cities with similar proportions of blacks—such as Houston, Texas, and Columbus, Ohio—have elected black mayors, Nashville has not elected an African American mayor. The city/county government currently has an African American male in the position of vice mayor.

The population of the inner core was also greatly impacted by the so-called urban renewal projects of the late 1950s through the 1960s (Carry 2001). Included therein was the construction of Interstate Highway 40, which sliced through the North Nashville community, prompting a battle that went all the way to the U.S. Supreme Court. The protesting residents ultimately lost their case, and the highway construction continued from the late 1960s until completion in the early 1970s. The area lost significant numbers of residential and commercial structures. Hundreds of people were displaced. The character of the North Nashville community was changed forever, with efforts continuing to this day to return it to its former glory.

Population Change in Nashville's Black Urban Core, 1960–2000

North Nashville is the geographic and cultural heart of Nashville's African American community—generally defined as Subarea 8 (see figure 5.3). Opinions on the geographic extent of the community may vary, but for the purposes here the demographic and socioeconomic data was derived from the census tracts within Subarea 8. Few African Americans lived in the first developments of North Nashville before 1870. The newly developed area offered housing stock priced out of the range of most recently freed African American families.

After 1870, many African American residents settled the area along what is now Jefferson Street. As the large number of freed people settled in the city, education leaders assisted by the Farmers Bureau of Tennessee founded Fisk University. In addition to Fisk, North Nashville is home to two other historically black colleges and universities (HBCUs), Tennessee State University and Meharry Medical College.

In 1880, the area around Fisk was home to African American residents of all social classes. During the 1920s, the Fisk area maintained its status as a prominent neighborhood for African American residents. The Jefferson Street District, the most recognizable thoroughfare in the community, experienced a golden age during the 1940s and 1950s. Many famous musicians, including Jimi Hendrix, Aretha Franklin, and B. B. King, played in its bars and nightclubs (Gerome 2004). The strong neighborhoods of the first half of the 1900s gave way to significant change in the 1960s and the years following with the construction of Interstate Highway 40 and desegregation. The area experienced population growth until about 1960, reaching 43,705, but thereafter it decreased to 23,765 by 2000. The North Nashville community has struggled to cope with the challenges introduced by changes throughout the last thirty years.

Nashville's inner-city neighborhoods appear to be exhibiting negative impacts that may be directly or indirectly associated with urban sprawl. Abandoned buildings, illegal dump sites, and underused properties are becoming more common. Along Jefferson Street, once a bustling economic center with pharmacies, a movie theater, grocery stores, and neat residences, there are now many empty lots and buildings.

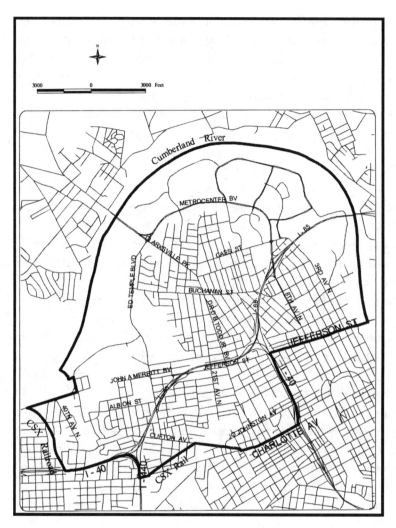

Figure 5.3
North Nashville as defined by Subarea 8
Source: Metropolitan Government of Nashville and Davidson County, 2002

The explanations for the decline of North Nashville are many. Some blame desegregation and the breaking down of racial barriers during the 1960s, resulting in blacks leaving the area to live and shop where they previously could not. Others cite the construction of the Interstate Highway 40 corridor, slicing through the community during the 1960s, as the primary factor contributing to loss of residential and commercial property. Countless debates by residents and several analyses by social scientists have not led to a consensus on the causal factors for North Nashville's present diminished status.

In an effort to stem the ill effects of urban deterioration, local grassroots organizations completed "neighborhood audits" and cited more than four thousand problems, including many abandoned buildings and overgrown vacant lots (Paine 2000). City officials have made verbal commitments to clean up the problem areas, but whether they will actually follow through remains to be seen. Unfortunately, many barriers to development currently exist in the central city. Flawed tax and zoning regulations have lessened developers' incentives to invest in downtown projects. Currently, the commercial and real estate market in the CBD and environs is sluggish, especially with serious competition coming from the Cool Springs area of Williamson County, approximately twenty miles south of downtown Nashville.

The deterioration of the Nashville MSA's inner urban core is expected to be exacerbated as businesses relocate toward the path of State Route 840, a "ring highway" that, if completed, will form a 187-mile loop around Nashville and environs. Suburban residents fear that the highway will be a harbinger for more sprawl, green space loss, and congestion, as is now the case with Interstate 285, Atlanta's ring highway (Wissner 2000). A completed section of 840, on the southeastern side of the MSA, has already attracted significant residential and commercial development.

Through legal action, a local suburban grassroots organization has successfully forced the Tennessee Department of Transportation (TDOT) to conduct an environmental assessment for a seventeen-mile portion of highway 840. As the lawsuit was being debated in local courts, construction was temporarily halted. After negotiations between the plaintiffs and TDOT officials, however, the southern loop of the project will be completed with modifications to lessen the impact on the environment. In order to alleviate future traffic congestion, plans for a regional commuter rail system have been discussed. Unfortunately, due to physical and financial constraints, it appears that no form of local rail service will be available for at least five to ten years (Peirce and Johnson 1999).

In general, the residents of the Nashville MSA face critical challenges in the near future with regard to urban sprawl. The loss of green space combined with increased automobile traffic may have negative impacts on air quality. Without continued proactive intervention with support from local government, the decline of the urban core will eventually have significantly negative effects on the quality of life of inner-city dwellers.

Community Case Studies

The idea here is to provide evidence of impacts on stakeholders' quality of life that are likely associated with the phenomenon of urban sprawl. Below are examples of maps created during various outreach initiatives. The case studies were developed in collaboration with students enrolled in the urban geography (GEOG 4850) and cartography (GEOG 3100) courses at TSU.

Case Study 1: Increasingly Disparate Access to Public Transit
Because many students do not own cars, the quality of the local public transit service has been a popular research and service-learning topic. In late 2002, the GISL partnered with the Metropolitan Government of Nashville and Davidson County, the MPO, and the MTA to assess the accessibility of the local bus system for riders with physical disabilities. The assessment had to be conducted in a relatively short amount of time, so the Global Positioning System (GPS) was selected as the most efficient way to conduct a mobile analysis.

Three GISL student researchers teamed with the MPO, the MTA, and personnel from the metro ADA to complete a GPS-based survey of the bus system. The ADA criteria questionnaire was converted into a digital format for quick and easy field evaluation. Digital photographs were shot at all of the bus stops falling under ADA guidelines. All the data was subsequently uploaded into a GIS.

A natural outgrowth of the accessibility study was curiosity about the utility of the entire MTA system. Nashville's public transit system is known to be grossly underfunded and expensive for riders. With jobs and opportunities increasingly moving to outlying areas, there was concern that the MTA was not supplying adequate services to lower-income inner-city residents wishing to find work. In fact, an analysis conducted by a local nonprofit organization found that women in a "welfare-to-work" program sometimes spent more than two hours getting to work and another two hours getting home.

African Americans rely on public transit in Nashville's inner-city communities. From casual observance it can be noted that a significantly high proportion of blacks in the area use the bus as their means of transportation to work. One only needs to ride the bus to notice the overwhelming overrepresentation of black people. Cursory interviews with public transit users brought a rash of complaints, the most important of which was the lack of outbound routes after about six o'clock in the evening. A perusal of the MTA schedule reveals that much outbound service shuts down during and after the evening rush hour. Thus, an inner-city resident wishing to work a second-shift job in the suburbs would have no chance of either getting to work or going home again.

While some improvements have been made, budget shortfalls have resulted in some cuts in the number of routes. In the city's defense, only 2 percent of Nashville residents regularly use public transit; however, in some inner-city black communities, that number is nearly 50 percent. Adding income into the mix only exacerbates the potential for "public transit apartheid."

One local leader noted that the lack of transportation alternatives may be disproportionately impacting working-class and middle-class black families by forcing them to maintain two automobiles. Having to carry two car loans may drain financial resources that might otherwise be used for health insurance, homeownership, and college savings. There has been talk of a light-rail system for Nashville, but even if it is developed, it will primarily serve to bring workers from the suburbs to their jobs downtown and then back home again.

Case Study 2: Spatial Dislocation of Public Services and Community Needs

During the past two decades, the African American population in general, and the low-income African American population in particular, has either relocated or been required to relocate to more rural regions of the city-county area. Interestingly, Nashville has been relatively successful in obtaining, implementing, and completing federal Hope VI initiatives, which have as their primary objective the replacement of old, Great Society–era public housing with less dense, mixed-use developments. There are currently four Hope VI projects in Nashville that have either been completed, are in progress, or are soon to be initiated.

One unfortunate, but unintended outcome of the Hope VI program is that many people are unable to return to the new developments due to bad credit and/or criminal records. Also, in terms of density, only about a third to one-half as many housing units usually replace the number of the former public housing structures. The dilemma faced by public and private service agencies is that of keeping up with the displaced residents, which is often difficult because many of them become unstable and transient.

The past decade has seen a growing number of black residents move to outlying Section 8 apartment complexes. Many of these housing complexes are separated from the various service institutions that African Americans were using for their basic needs. A community needs assessment, using GIS technology, was conducted by researchers at TSU in order to determine the extent of the separation between low-income residents and service providers (Tennessee State University 2003).

One question raised by the map is whether the increased numbers of African Americans in census block groups in some outlying areas has more to do with Section 8 complexes than "upward mobility." The larger question is whether public housing has "followed" blacks to middle-class suburban enclaves, or whether the "enclaves" actually represent areas where lower-income blacks reside in Section 8 housing.

Case Study 3: The Evolving Geography of Solid Waste Management and Recycling

Among the many problems discovered during the aforementioned neighborhood audits conducted in several North Nashville communities are numerous illegal dumps. The recent increase in fugitive dumping recorded by the Metropolitan Health Department is related to Nashville's shrinking options for solid waste disposal. In 1994, the local landfill, located adjacent to Bordeaux, a predominantly African American neighborhood, was closed following a heated environmental justice dispute. The former landfill took in about half of the city's garbage, approximately one thousand tons per day. Those wastes are now exported to rural disposal facilities. The other half of the city's waste was burned at the downtown Thermal Transfer Corporation facility to produce steam for heat and electricity until the facility was closed in 2003.

Thermal's steam was used to heat thirty-nine downtown buildings, with the surplus electricity sold to the Tennessee Valley Authority (TVA). Despite its seemingly environmentally friendly purpose, the Thermal plant increasingly came under scrutiny due to its toxic air releases and aesthetically unpleasing appearance. Tons of ash, a by-product of the plant, wound up in a large landfill adjacent to Salemtown, an inner-city black neighborhood. The facility also struggled to obtain the tonnage of garbage required for sufficient energy production. Local waste haulers, not required to dump at Thermal, choose to transport their loads to outlying landfills to earn higher profits. Thus, as Nashville's population grows, many questions remain regarding solid waste management. Exporting refuse to rural landfills is becoming increasingly less popular and more expensive.

In January 2001, Nashville's Mayor, Bill Purcell, introduced a new regional waste management plan that eliminated Thermal and began an aggressive local recycling program. Critics of the plan note that previous efforts at curbside recycling in Nashville have been generally unsuccessful. Anecdotal comments made by Metro Office of Solid Waste personnel indicate that the program is even less popular in black communities. One question currently being investigated is the source of this lack of enthusiasm for recycling among African Americans.

Results of a University of Michigan study reveal that on a nationwide scale, blacks are less likely to participate in recycling than whites (Mohai 2003). Interestingly, the study also found that in other aspects of environmental activity and action, blacks are about on par with whites. The dislocation of African Americans and city recycling facilities is obvious.

Could it be that the lack of participation is more a function of access than a lack of concern? The GISL is currently in the process of developing a recycling education program. The program is being used to make a case for the placement of a metro recycling center at TSU, to be managed and maintained by students.

In terms of the larger solid waste management issue, the GISL has worked in support of the efforts of several African American neighborhood associations in the Bordeaux community in their ongoing fight for environmental justice. Since there are no permanent solid waste disposal facilities in the city, plans were made to build five waste transfer stations.

The unveiling of the planned site locations elicited immediate suspicion that they would disproportionately impact black communities. A request was made from an emergent environmental organization in Bordeaux that the GISL map the proposed site locations against community demographics. The result showed that all five of the transfer station sites were planned for predominantly black neighborhoods. They were subsequently rejected.

The GISL is currently supporting the people of Bordeaux in a battle to shut down a privately owned Class III (construction and demolition) landfill. In July 2004, the landfill's operators applied for an eight-year extension that would allow them to operate until about 2018. This was after they had planned to discontinue operations several times over the past two decades. In fact, the landfill has operated for over thirty years. Bordeaux residents came out in protest against the operating permit extension. A demographic assessment was conducted using GIS that showed that indeed, Bordeaux may be defined as an environmental justice community using a method developed by the EPA, Region V.

The greatest injustice perhaps is that over the past fifty years, over 80 percent of all the city's waste, both domestic and construction, has wound up in Bordeaux. The Class III facility accepts waste from outside the county. With the local boom in new home construction, it is expected that the landfill will accept even more waste. There was mention that with the new operating permit, the facility would be open twenty-four hours per day. The adjacent community, already impacted by truck traffic, dust, and noise, would have to contend with an even greater nuisance. A public hearing was held in late July 2004 by the Metro Solid

Waste Board, during which both sides argued their cases. The board rejected the operating permit extension, but the landfill owners have appealed to the state.

At issue is not the landfill itself but the cumulative impacts of a number of LULUs in Bordeaux. In addition to the landfill, there are nearly 180 federally regulated pollution-emitting sites within a radius of approximately three miles. There is a wastewater treatment plant, a propane tank farm, several correctional facilities, high-voltage overhead power lines, a soil mine, and many other LULUs. Knowing that, the fact that the city has not followed its own solid waste management plan at the greatest expense to predominantly black Bordeaux raises a number of questions. Of particular concern is that recent studies have shown significant health disparities between African Americans and whites in Nashville (Nashville REACH 2010 2006). How closely those disparities are associated with environmental quality remains under investigation.

Case Study 4: "Food Deserts"

Among the most critical needs of any community is that of access to quality food. Unfortunately, it has become apparent in many black communities that the presence of full-service grocery stores with fresh fruits and vegetables is becoming less common. The larger chain markets tend to "chase the dollars" to the suburbs, leaving inner-city dwellers to choose between convenience stores and mom-and-pop establishments for food.

In some cases, these outlets have inflated prices. There is also a lack of inventory. In the worst cases, the food on the shelves has reached its expiration date and is potentially dangerous if consumed. A recent study on the presence or lack thereof of grocery stores in black communities concluded that there is a geographic link between access to quality foods and good health (Morland, Wing, and Roux 2002).

In fall 2003, a student enrolled in the GEOG3100 course took on the task of using GIS to map grocery stores against demographic and socioeconomic census block group data for Nashville. The initial results indicated that a food desert is present in North Nashville. When compounded with the lack of public transit and/or private vehicles, many inner-city blacks are virtually "captive" clientele for understocked and substandard food stores. The maps created by the student are currently being used in efforts to site a community grocery store in North Nashville near TSU and also to support a grocery store quality audit being conducted by a grassroots coalition organization. The audits will be used to determine the level of disparity in food quality among the city's communities.

In recognizing that the lack of access to supermarkets is more than just a matter of convenience, communities are now working to level the grocery playing field. If the current migration patterns continue, however, it will be difficult to convince major food merchants to locate in the inner city. One major chain plans to build a "neighborhood market" downtown within the next three years, but it will be located inside a luxury condominium tower.

Good News? Nashville Makes the "Best Cities for Blacks" List

While the case studies may cast a foreboding shadow on the condition of Nashville's black population, there may be a bright spot. *Black Enterprise* recently ranked Nashville fourth as the best city for blacks behind Atlanta, Washington, DC, and Dallas (Padgett and Brown 2004). The final rankings were determined via a combination of readers' answers to an online survey and a weighing of the cities' performance on a variety of critical quality of life indicators.

During spring 2004, approximately four thousand people responded to *Black Enterprise*'s twenty-one-question urban quality of life survey. The respondents expressed their level of satisfaction on a variety of issues ranging from the cost of living, to the availability of day care, to African American–police relations. In order to temper respondents' potentially biased and/or limited perspectives, the cities were weighted against each other in terms of a variety of urban factors such as crime rates, new home prices, and educational attainment.

Nashville's relatively strong economy, low cost of living, and low unemployment rate pushed it to its high position. The city did not fare as well in 2001. Could it be that things are getting better for black Nashvillians? The post–best cities discussion that the author had with various locals was mixed. Some people agreed that Nashville offers a relatively good quality of life. Others also argued that there is still much progress to be made in terms of equal opportunity, especially in the business sector. Both Nashville's cost of living and medical cost indexes are well below the national average. Respondents expressed general satisfaction with the quality of health care available in the city and environs.

The average new home price is significantly below the national average. Interestingly, despite living in an urban area with black and overall unemployment rates well below the national averages, respondents were slightly pessimistic about their job prospects. Data does indicate that recent job growth has been negative. Of note is that Nashville received high marks for the question related to children's day care center quality and availability—a question that garnered low scores in nearly every other city polled with the exception of Houston.

Of all the survey questions, Nashville respondents were least satisfied with the quality of public transit in the area and their dating prospects. The metropolitan area's miles of public transit per capita is below the national average, which is not a surprise based on what is known about the local service. Respondents were only slightly dissatisfied with Nashville's crime rate even though the city's violent crime rate is a little more than double the national average. There was also slight dissatisfaction with African Americans' relationship with local law enforcement personnel. Nashville is one of the few cities among the *Black Enterprise*'s "top ten" without a black mayor. Respondents were generally satisfied with the performance of their elected officials, but less than satisfied with the level of power and influence in the black community. It must be noted that the level of geography that survey respondents were asked to consider was the MSA. Unlike Nashville, in many urban areas, equal numbers of blacks live in the central city and the suburbs. Nashville's status as a combined city-county entity gave its residents a somewhat unique geographic perspective.

There are almost unlimited parameters one could consider in determining the impact of growth on Nashville's African American population. While on the one hand, there are indications that environmental injustice and health disparities exist on a grand scale, the overall quality of life appears to be relatively good. But this should all be taken in context. If the *Black Enterprise* survey results are any indication, the majority of blacks now living in urban areas in the United States are not happy with their situation.

There is great dissatisfaction with public school quality, the number of black-owned businesses, and police–African American relations. With the overwhelming majority of African Americans residing in cities, there is cause for concern if they are generally unhappy. And it should be noted that the demographics of those responding to the *Black Enterprise* survey are those of the well-educated upper middle class. If they are not pleased with their conditions, what does that say for those lower on the socioeconomic ladder? True, the survey cannot be considered scientific, but the opinions of over four thousand residents of U.S. cities certainly cannot be ignored.

Focusing again on Nashville, it may be said that the city has fared well economically over the past two decades. Still, while there have been many infrastructural improvements and developments in outlying areas, little has changed in the traditionally black communities. Nashville's rate of black homeownership is about 50 percent, which is above the national average for African Americans. The residential segregation dissimilarity index (66) is at about the national average. The median annual household income for blacks is relatively close to the overall average. Through further inquiry into various socioeconomic indictors, one could conclude that things are going relatively well for blacks in Nashville. Perhaps the rapid growth suggests a place where people want to be, a place where there are opportunities for anyone who perseveres.

In spatial terms, however, there is obvious inequality. A large sector of the population is being left behind in the stampede to the suburbs. In response, there have been several proactive efforts to mitigate the impacts of uneven growth and development across the city-county metropolitan area and the MSA.

Public transit must be improved in order to provide equal opportunity for economic uplift. There must be a concerted effort to support the public school system even during a time when tax-based resources are dwindling. There must be a new vision for solid waste management to lessen the burden on Nashville's black communities. There must be greater incentives for commercial and residential development in the inner city. The present "patchwork" development is not sustainable. And there must be a greater vision, involving the razing of entire areas of blight.

In a real sense, Nashville is a tale of two black communities—one having moved to the outlying areas and the suburbs, and enjoying the fruits of a booming economy along with explosive growth and opportunities; and the other facing a questionable future as it struggles to grab the attention of those leaving it behind. Perhaps looking at things spatially, as has been done here, will spark some initiatives for aggressive change. For some, the status quo of Music City USA is satisfactory, or even good. For others, just across the divide, a different tune is playing.

References

American Planning Association. 2000. *State Rankings Study of Percent Change in Developed Acres Per Capita, 1982–1997*. Washington, DC: APA.

Carry, B. 2001. A City Swept Clean: How Urban Renewal, for Better or Worse, Created the City We Know Today. *Nashville Scene* 19, no. 32:18–25.

Center for Business and Economic Research. 1999. *Population Projections for Tennessee Counties and Municipalities: 2000–2020*. Knoxville: University of Tennessee.

Covington, J. 2001. Metro Area's Rank Drops to 44; Nashville Is Bigger at 39. *Commercial Appeal* (Memphis), April 21. Available at ⟨http://www .newgomemphis.com/newgo/rememphis/census/041201/12rank.htm⟩ (accessed June 30, 2004).

Fulton, W., R. Pendall, M. Nguyen, and A. Harrison. 2001. *Who Sprawls the Most? How Growth Patterns Differ across the U.S.* Washington, DC: Brookings Institution.

Gerome, J. 2004. Nashville's Forgotten Heritage. *Athens* (Georgia) *Banner-Herald*, March 5.

Hamburg, J. 2003. Racial Imbalance Returns to Schools. *Tennessean*, June 13. ⟨http://www.tennessean.com/special/resegregation/archives/04/05/35869145 .shtml?Element_ID=35869145⟩ (accessed August 3, 2004).

Metropolitan Government of Nashville and Davidson County. Metropolitan Planning Commission. 2002. *The Plan for the North Nashville Community: Subarea 8*. Nashville: Metropolitan Government of Nashville.

Metropolitan Government of Nashville and Davidson County. 2004. Urban Zoning Overlay District Information. Available at ⟨http://www.nashville.gov/ mpc/uzod_adopt6.htm⟩ (accessed August 3).

Mohai, P. 2003. Dispelling Old Myths: African American Concern for the Environment. *Environment* 45, no. 5:11–26.

Morland, K., S. Wing, and A. D. Roux. 2002. The Contextual Effect of the Local Food Environment on Residents' Diets: The Atherosclerosis Risk in Communities Study. *American Journal of Public Health* 92, no. 11:1761–1767.

Nashville Racial and Ethnic Approaches to Community Health (REACH) 2010. 2006. Available at ⟨http://healthbehavior.psy.vanderbilt.edu/REACH/index.htm⟩ (accessed May 16, 2006).

Nasser, H. El, and P. Overburg. 2001. A Comprehensive Look at Sprawl in America. *USA Today*, February 22. Available at ⟨http://www.usatoday.com/news/sprawl/main.htm⟩ (accessed March 8, 2004).

Padgett, D. A., and M. R. Brown. 2004. Top Cities for African Americans. *Black Enterprise* 34, no. 12:78–103.

Paine, Anne. 2000. City Officials Vow to Fix Problems in Neighborhood Audit. *Tennessean*, December 5.

Peirce, N., and C. Johnson. 1999. Light Rail Gives System a Spine. *Tennessean*, October 3, D1.

State of Tennessee, Department of Education. 2004. Test Results. Available at ⟨http://www.state.tn.us/education/tsresults.htm⟩ (accessed August 3).

Tennessee State University, Office of Business and Economic Research. 2003. *Davidson County Community Needs Assessment*. Nashville: Tennessee State University.

U.S. Bureau of the Census. 1961. 1960 *Census of Population*. Vol. 1, *Characteristics of the Population: Part 44, Tennessee*. Washington, DC: U.S. Bureau of the Census.

U.S. Bureau of the Census. 1998. Table B–6: Building Permits, Cost of Living, and Poverty. In *State and Metropolitan Area Data Book, 1997–98*. Washington, DC: U.S. Bureau of the Census.

Wissner, Shelia. 2000. 840: Will It Make Us Another Atlanta? *Tennessean*, June 18, A1.

6

Smart Growth and the Legacy of Segregation in Richland County, South Carolina

Maya Wiley

Richland County, South Carolina, is growing fast in population, and faster in residential and retail strip mall construction.[1] But it is a county with a significant rural character. Like much of the South, Richland's metropolitan area has an urban core, Columbia, and rural areas. The southeastern end of the county, Lower Richland, which represents a large portion of its landmass, is rural and predominantly black. Former plantation lands are now small parcels owned by descendants of slaves, many of them low income with no other assets.

Many of these lands have remained in the same families for a hundred years (Berlau 2002, 1). These rural black communities lack many basic services, and have received few county infrastructure investments or the opportunities that come with them, in stark contrast to traditionally white parts of the county. Now the Richland County Council seeks to limit rural development, angering black landowners who see the restrictions as ending any hope of appreciation of their one real asset and threatening their tradition of subdividing property for the benefit of their children (Berlau 2002, 1).

The County Council views the situation differently. It is struggling with the crippling rise in infrastructure costs and loss of open space that come with rampant, uncontrolled growth. In 1999, at the urging and with the support of the environmental conservation community, it adopted a land use plan that it believes balances the needs for growth and conservation.

The result is a deep rift between black community leaders and conservation groups. In response to the legitimate concerns of black landowners, many conservation groups have appeared dismissive. The director of the South Carolina chapter of the Sierra Club stated publicly that the plan would not be harmful to "the true farmer," only those who wished to subdivide land (Carlisle 2000). To black landowners, this statement implies that part-time farmers or those who have not been able to sustain farming on their land are legitimately neglected by policymakers. It ignores a history of race discrimination, which denied black farmers sufficiently large tracks of land to sustain farming, as well as discrimination in access to credit and other programs to support family farming. It also ignores black landowners' desire to pass on an inheritance of their only asset to their children.

The response of black landowners has been angry and intense. One black community resident compared the Sierra Club to the Ku Klux Klan (Berlau 2002, 2). Because of the failure of policymakers and conservation advocates to consider and take seriously the concerns of black landowners, there has been a breakdown in the ability of stakeholders to discuss and negotiate policy alternatives. No policymaker can use the term smart growth or propose land use planning reforms of any kind without raising the suspicion and outright ire of many in the black community.

The anger and distrust engendered by land use planning in Richland County may not be unique in the Southern black belt. While research and policy organizations have become more effective at drawing attention to the costs of sprawl, they have largely focused on urban metropolitan regions and inner-city poverty.[2] As a result, policy responses have examined urban service growth boundaries and disincentives to suburban residential and retail construction (*Community Leader's Letter* 1995). Where low-income people of color own land and homes in rural areas, attempts to control sprawl by limiting growth and development may produce destructive results in already-impoverished communities excluded from the benefits of growth.

These complexities, as well as research demonstrating that race discrimination and racial stereotypes cause and fuel sprawl (Rusk 1998; Massey and Denton 1993), suggest a need for a more rigorous and intentional racial analysis of the causes and effects of sprawl to create policies that will stem these causes and effects. A history of government policies and programs created incentives for racially segregated suburbanization

(Jargowsky 1997; Massey and Denton 1993). Also, whites have fled school desegregation and perceived dangers of black inner-city communities by moving to the suburbs (powell 2000, 220–21). Resources for infrastructure investment and important services follow those who flee. The effect, therefore, of this white flight is both the flight of infrastructure investments and a shrinking tax base in cities (powell 2000, 221; Rusk 1995).

Because policies that create and perpetuate sprawl are not racially neutral in impact, and lead to conditions that encourage more sprawl, reinforcing racial disparities, planners, policymakers, and stakeholders must seek to ensure access to opportunities for blacks and other nonwhites and to deconcentrate racially identifiable poverty. This requires the creation of real opportunities for communities to obtain living wage jobs, quality education, adequate public services and diverse residents. Land use planning is one mechanism for controlling sprawl and increasing access to opportunities for communities excluded from the benefits of such growth (Rusk 1998).

Regional dynamics in metropolitan regions with significant rural areas may help sharpen our analysis of the problem of race and sprawl, generating planning and policy proposals that will create healthy communities. In an effort to begin such an analysis, this chapter examines the dynamics of sprawl and the policy responses to it in Richland County. It concludes that the County Council's land use vision permits sprawl to continue where it is occurring, while restricting development in poor African American communities, where development and access to opportunities within the metropolitan region are sorely needed.

Imagine Richland 2020 Comprehensive Plan

A Portrait of Richland County

To understand properly the implications of sprawl and the County Council's response to it, it is necessary to understand the characteristics of the county and its planning areas. For planning purposes, Richland County is divided into six planning areas, which represent distinguishable geographic areas within the county. These planning areas have unique characteristics. Therefore, they identify differences around the county in growth patterns, opportunity structures, and infrastructure needs. Not surprisingly, they not only show patterns of growth and places of wealth but patterns of underdevelopment, racial segregation, and poverty.

Richland County's nucleus is the city of Columbia, but the entire southern portion of that nucleus is largely rural. Lower Richland, as mentioned earlier, is predominantly black and poor with a network of floodplains and riparian corridors. It is almost half the landmass of the county (330 of 720 square miles). Relative to other parts of the county, population growth has been modest, and there has been no meaningful expansion of job or other opportunities for residents.

The North Central planning area is also rural and historically had a predominantly black population, but is now racially mixed. Like Lower Richland, it is largely rural but the southern portion along Interstate 20 (I-20) is more urbanized. Improvements in infrastructure, mining operations, and land development are occurring around the I-20 corridor.

The North Central planning area is sandwiched between wealthy and rapidly growing areas. The Northeast planning area is sprawling, characterized by large lot developments and strip malls. It is majority white, although its infrastructure has been attracting middle-class blacks in large numbers over the past decade. The black population has grown so fast that soon the planning area will reach racial parity.

The Interstate 77 (I-77) Corridor planning area borders the Northeast planning area and is the artery connecting residents to not only Columbia but also Charlotte, North Carolina (figure 6.1). Historically, this corridor has been the center of industrial development due to the interstate and public infrastructure investment. Residential growth in the Northeast is fueling commercial and industrial development in the I-77 Corridor. As a result, the population has been growing rapidly.

The Northwest planning area (figure 6.1) is predominantly low-density residential, and has been experiencing an influx of young families and retirees. It is an attractive area because of its concentration of moderately priced homes, a decent school district, and scenic Lake Murray.

The Richland County Council (1999, 3C-12) concludes that "the Northeast and Northwest are the fastest growing planning areas in Richland County in employment and population. This trend is expected

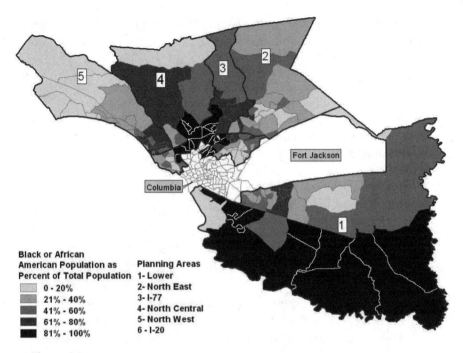

Figure 6.1
Black population as percent of total population in 2000.
Source: Based on 2000 data from the U.S. Census Bureau

to continue unless incentives can be provided to developers and employers to undertake a share of development activities in a more southernly [*sic*] direction of the County [Lower Richland], along with making it cost prohibitive to develop in the north." Unfortunately, the County Council's land use planning decisions do not appear likely to achieve this goal.

The Richland County Council Land Use Vision

The County Council's land use analysis and vision for land use planning are both contained in the 1999 *Imagine Richland 2020 Comprehensive Plan*. This represents the County Council's first significant attempt at land use planning. Because the County Council has had little planning capacity, its plan represents a patchwork of consultants' data collection and reports. The plan is nonbinding, but represents the County Council's intent with regard to land use regulation. It points to two consequences of sprawl: the consumption of green space, and runaway infrastructure costs. As a result, the County Council's vision is based on its goals of green space preservation and infrastructure cost reduction. At the same time, it seeks to support growth. The Richland County Council (1999, 1–5) states that it undertook "a comprehensive planning process to develop the plans and guidelines critical to taking advantage of the opportunities afforded by growth, while preserving the unique quality of life within the County."

Absent from the acknowledged problems caused by sprawl are the inequitable allocation of infrastructure, the inequitable allocation of the costs of new infrastructure, the lack of access to affordable housing and jobs for those who need them, and the inability of low-income property owners and homeowners to convert their assets into credit or other forms of usable capital to improve their financial security. Blacks disproportionately suffer from these sprawl-related inequities. The County Council also fails to acknowledge that whites generally have not sought to move to communities that are predominantly nonwhite. Despite the fact that the County Council collected and discussed a significant amount of useful data and information—often disaggregated by race—suggesting that these additional consequences of sprawl exist, it does not incorporate an analysis of these problems or a vision for their eradication into the plan.

Like many counties in the South, the County Council's vision is based on design elements rather than substantive opportunities for residents. It embraces a "town and country" design plan for identified unincorporated towns and the restriction of rural development to certain locations. The same design preferences would stand for existing and new "villages": they would be denser and less sprawling, and have walkable neighborhoods and mixed uses (residential, retail, and so on).

The County Council's first stated priority is the redesign of existing villages. In Lower Richland, it has prioritized two existing villages for town and country planning: Eastover and Hopkins. The residents of these two villages are almost exclusively black. These villages are both designated as "nonemployment"—a residential community with no job centers. While the plan recognizes the lack of jobs, it has no planning elements that might facilitate economic growth or job creation in or near East-over. Perhaps more disturbing, Eastover has already received new public housing development. Black public housing residents from a demolished housing project in Columbia have been relocated to Eastover. While it is unclear whether this relocation of inner-city black residents to Eastover was part of the plan's intent, it is certainly consistent with its vision—to promote new construction in designated villages.[3] Development in East-over to date has meant the greater segregation of blacks in this jobless community.

The second stated priority is the development of employment-based villages. These are villages that are located in or near job centers. There are no employment-based villages in Lower Richland or the North Central planning areas. The third priority for development is rural nonemployment-based villages. These are villages that would not contain or be located near any job centers. In Lower Richland, the plan identifies four new village locations where development would be permissible. The identified locations are former hamlets (Wateree, Acton, Kingville, and Congaree) located along railroad tracks that have long since been abandoned (Richland County Council 1999, 7.3.3).

Incentives and Disincentives

As a step in the realization of its land use vision, the County Council has developed a draft zoning ordinance. The ordinance would enact a loose system of incentives and disincentives—a carrot-and-stick approach—to direct and control land development. As a result, it would accept a market-driven strategy to reduce the occurrence of sprawl and preserve open spaces. The incentive scheme would make development easier and more profitable in designated employment- and nonemployment-based villages. The draft zoning ordinance includes a relaxation of the maximum density requirements. But to promote denser, less-sprawling developments, it would codify more stringent design guidelines (for example, zero lot line development). The disincentives for sprawling development include an increase in the minimum lot size in rural areas, outside of designated villages, from third-quarters of an acre to one acre. There would also be a small lot size increase in the low-density single-family residential zoning category.

To keep rural areas rural, the draft zoning ordinance disallows specific actions—the placement of structures or vegetation removal immediately adjacent to the water's edge. To help preserve some open space, it requires a small set-aside for open space for large developments. These incentives and disincentives do not appear to address specifically the extent of sprawl in the Northeast, the I-77 Corridor, or the Northwest. While they provide incentives to direct development to identified villages, they do not limit development to villages. As long as there is a market for sprawling development, developers are free to create subdivisions, although it might cost them more to do so. As long as the Northeast, I-77 Corridor, and Northwest planning areas are attractive to potential home buyers, they are also attractive to developers. Sprawl can and will continue with its attendant costs and inefficiencies.

As long as the Lower Richland, I-20 Corridor, and North Central planning areas are less attractive to county residents, they will see less development. According to the Richland County Council (1999, 7), most of the 211,000 acres of Lower Richland are "rural and undeveloped with occasional low-density development scattered throughout the landscape." To the extent that there have been development pressures, the County Council (1999, 2–7) states that they began in the 1950s as "large industrial firms moved into the area to take advantage of cheap lands and the existing rail line." Nonetheless, the County Council (1999, 2) describes Lower Richland as "slow growing" in both population and development.

The plan does not describe any commitments to the development of infrastructure or services, with the exception of water and sewer to make the depressed parts of the county more desirable for positive growth activity, despite the fact that the plan recognized a need to send growth southward. Nor does the draft zoning ordinance contain any significant incentives for such development in depressed areas.

Remembering that Lower Richland is predominantly black, and has few jobs and only slow development, it appears unlikely that the new villages proposed for Lower Richland will be built. If they are built, what will the impact of village development be on residential and school segregation as well as access to opportunities, such as jobs and infrastructure needs? Based on the lack of services, jobs, and transit, in addition to a poorly performing school system, there appear to be few market incentives for whites and businesses to relocate to these villages. Therefore, these villages may become new pockets of racially identifiable concentrated poverty. It is also unclear how the plan and draft zoning ordinance will impact the asset wealth of otherwise low-income black property and landowners. For example, it does not specifically analyze how the changes in minimum lot sizes or riparian corridor protections will affect poor rural landowners' asset values.

Infrastructure in County Planning Areas

One cause of sprawl in the Northeast, I-77 Corridor, and Northwest planning areas may be the infrastructure and services there. If development begets greater infrastructure and service investments, creating a growing demand for housing construction, rural parts of the county may be left out. The Lower Richland, I-20, and North Central planning areas have much less infrastructure, less desirable infrastructure, and fewer services. An examination of the County Council's description of planning area infrastructure suggests few incentives for development there.

Transportation

In its plan, the Richland County Council (1999, appendix A, 67) identified a need for "transportation connectivity" and to "provide all people with the option of using transit." Currently, only the city of Columbia and close-in areas are served by a public bus system, which is old and inadequate, and has experienced service cutbacks (Richland County Council 1999, 3G-9). Wealthier communities have resources to pay for transportation alternatives. Poor rural community residents are less able to do so.

Plans for new transit services to currently underserved areas are unformed, unfunded, and unlikely to occur, based on the information provided. While the plan locates new development—villages—on old railway lines, there is no stated commitment by the necessary state and regional authorities to produce a light-rail public transit system there. The plan notes that there may be inadequate ridership to support an expanded system (Richland County Council 1999, appendix A, 67–68). Rural areas lack transit services because the lack of population density does not justify the cost. But a discussion might then include options for the creation of affordable housing opportunities closer to job centers. The plan does not explore the relationship between transit needs, transportation infrastructure, and the need to connect areas with high unemployment rates to existing job growth centers (Richland County Council 1999, appendix A, 67).

Many of the transportation solutions in the plan relate to the creation of roadways to foster the town and country design in existing suburban towns. Most highway development is planned through the state DOT. Private developers construct the local roads that connect to those main arteries. Therefore, many transportation-planning decisions are not made locally and are generally driven by federally designated planning areas, excluding the needs of most rural areas (Richland County Council 1999, 3G-7–3G-8).

Quite often, highway expansion is viewed as a response to traffic congestion caused by sprawl, while recognizing community opposition to such expansion (Richland County Council 1999, 3G-6). Because the County Council's vision for transportation revolves around sprawl areas, it identifies highway expansion in the Northeast and Northwest portions of the county, where population growth and sprawl have been the most significant. The plan does not identify the location of populations in need of jobs and job-growth centers. Moreover, it does not consider how transportation planning might impact workforce proximity to job-growth centers. Apparently, new nonemployment villages identified for construction in Lower Richland would be quite far from any job opportunities.

Water and Sewer

Because the preservation of open space and the conservation of riparian corridors are significant themes in the plan, it is important to understand the implications for the various planning areas. The plan does not identify serious water quality issues. It states that water quality is "considerably good" (Richland County Council 1999, 3F-11). To the extent that there are water quality problems, they stem "from municipal point-source discharges and urban run-off" (Richland County Council 1999, 3F-11).

It appears that the County Council's conservation concerns may be tempered by the industrial demand for water, although this is not clearly addressed by the plan. It projects that industrial needs for water are going to increase for the Congaree subbasin, located in Lower Richland, "partially determining the suitability of other uses along the rivers" (Richland County Council 1999, 3F-11). If the County Council antici-pates permission of increased industrial uses in the Congaree basin, this might pose water quality questions for the residential population in Lower Richland and elsewhere.

The Richland County Council (1999, appendix A, 15) does identify an important sprawl-related water conservation problem. The Northeast is part of the County Council's aquifer recharge area, which supplies wells with water and keeps streams flowing. Therefore, growth in these areas could be detrimental to the water supply. The Richland County Coun-cil's (1999, appendix A, 27) response is to assume continued develop-ment characterized by detached homes on half- to one-acre lots, and suggests that development should encourage "best storm management practices." Research, however, indicates that storm water control on a site-by-site basis may fail to protect watersheds because they do not promise to reduce impervious ground cover (*Environmental Science and Technology* 2004, 2).

At the same time, the Richland County Council (1999, 3G-2) recog-nizes that Lower Richland has "several significant gaps in [water] service....As a result, a number of households are served by private water systems." Like Lower Richland, the North Central region is also underserved by water treatment systems, with homeowners relying on their own private septic tanks (Richland County Council 1999, 3G-2). The city of Columbia, which provides sewer services, has no plans to ex-pand to areas not currently served due to the small size of the customer base (Richland County Council 1999, 3G-4). Thus, as rural areas, Lower and North Central Richland will remain underserved by such municipal services, except for planned villages. It is unclear how rapid growth in the Northeast will impact the water supply for Lower Richland's wells and streams.

Education

There are two school districts wholly contained in the county—school districts one and two. A third school district straddles part of Richland County Council's Northwest planning area and neighboring Lexington County. Lower Richland, the city of Columbia, and North Central Richland share school district one. Its students have lower educational outcomes than the other school district. The Northeast is served by school district two—a district with higher per pupil expenditures and greater educational outcomes than school district one (Knight Foundation American Institutes for Research 1999, 65–85).

Emergency Services

According to the plan, outside the city of Columbia, the North Central and Lower Richland planning areas had the highest demand for emergency services. The North Central planning area had 12.2 percent of the county demand for emergency services, while Lower Richland had 11.2 percent of the demand for emergency services (Richland County Council 1999, 3G-12, table 37). It appears that North Central and Lower Richland have few emergency service facilities (Richland County Council 1999, 3G-25, map 12).

Demographic Changes between 1990 and 2000

The County Council relied largely on 1990 census data to describe the demographic character of the county in general and the planning areas in particular. This data demonstrates that sprawl continues to the north of Columbia and rural areas remain poor. While the Northeast is reaching racial parity with the influx of black residents who can afford to relocate there, rural areas are becoming increasingly segregated. To identify geographic areas for the promotion of integration as well as meaningful access to opportunities, and to advance the growth needs of black communities and rural poor communities, it is useful to examine updated census data by planning area.

Population Growth

In part, the county bases the need for future growth control on projected population growth trends to 2020. It predicts dramatically different population growth trends in the planning areas, with the greatest growth expected to occur in the Northeast planning area and I-77 Corridor (71.03 percent) and in the North Central planning area (64.05 percent) (Richland County Council 1999, 3B-11). It also predicts that by 2020, population size in the Northeast/I-77 Corridor (71,030) will be much greater than that of Lower Richland (56,131) (Richland County Council 1999, 3B-11). This would give Lower Richland the second-largest population in the county. Lower Richland is, however, the largest planning area by acreage—significantly larger than the Northeast.

As expected, according to 2000 census data, population growth in the Northeast, I-77 Corridor, and Northwest planning areas has been the most rapid, and those populations are the largest in the county. Since 1990, Northeast Richland's population increased by 71.8 percent— approximately 23,000 new residents (with 56,504 total residents in 2000). Between 1990 and 2000, population in the Northwest and I-77 planning areas grew by 28.9 and 11.9 percent, respectively. In contrast, Lower Richland's population increased by a relatively low 4.95 percent between 1990 and 2000—approximately 1,100 new residents (with 41,694 total residents in 2000). The North Central planning area grew by 2.8 percent, while the total population of the I-20 Corridor actually dropped 3.4 percent during the same time period.

Based on population growth trends, the Richland County Council (1999, 3B-12) predicts "that the racial composition of Richland County will continue to increase in diversity, with the white population remaining almost constant while the minority population continues to increase." As predicted, the population increase in the county has been racially identifiable. The black population of the county grew from 31.4 percent of the population in 1970 to 41.8 percent of the population in 1990. During this same time period, the white population decreased from 68 to 56 percent of the county population. The actual number of whites increased almost imperceptibly (from 159,092 to 160,063). Therefore, the percent change in racial makeup of the county resulted not from a net loss of white population but from the dramatic growth of the black population (Richland County Council 1999, 3B-5).

This racial demographic trend has continued, but with some notable differences when examined by planning area. The black population in both Lower Richland and the Northeast has increased dramatically over the last ten years. That increase, however, has been significantly more dramatic in the Northeast. In Lower Richland the black population grew by 20 percent, while it grew by an astounding 152 percent in the Northeast (U.S. Bureau of the Census 2000). The white population in Lower Richland, though, *decreased* by almost 19 percent, but increased by over 38 percent in the Northeast (U.S. Bureau of the Census 2000).

When the population of the county is examined by age and race, it shows that its overall black population has increased across age groups. For whites, the only age groups that experienced growth between 1990 and 2000 were five to seventeen year olds and those over sixty-five years of age. This data further illustrates the dramatic difference in population across the planning areas. It suggests that the reduction in white population in Lower Richland is the result of white out-migration. The white population decline was dramatic for people less than five years old through age sixty-four. The only increase in white population in Lower Richland was in the over sixty-five age group. Thus, it appears that whites of working age are moving, while retirees are remaining. The black population, on the other hand, experienced the largest growth in the eighteen to sixty-four age group, which suggests that black population growth in Lower Richland is due in significant part to in-migration.

Similarly, whites appear to be migrating out of the North Central planning area, while blacks are migrating in. Between 1990 and 2000, the white population of the North Central planning area decreased across almost all age groups, with the exception of a marginal increase in the five to seventeen age group. The black population, however, increased in the eighteen to sixty-four age group and increased dramatically in the over sixty-five age group, suggesting an in-migration of older blacks. There was a decrease in the young black population—those less than five years of age to seventeen years of age. The I-20 Corridor planning area has also experienced the in-migration of blacks, evidenced by a reduction in the size of the less than five age group, while the population has grown for those aged eighteen to sixty-four and over sixty-five. The picture is different in the Northeast and I-77 Corridor planning areas, where the population, both black and white, increased substantially in almost every age category.

New Construction

Not only has the population increased across the county, the number of housing units and households have also increased. Nonetheless, growth has been substantially greater in the Northeast, I-77, and Northwest planning areas than in the Lower Richland, North Central, and I-20 planning areas. The County Council predicted that between 2000 and 2020, about 11,000 housing units would be built in the Northeast/I-77 Corridor planning areas, mostly in the form of single-family detached housing. It also predicted a 50 percent increase in the number of households (Richland County Council 1999, 3D-7, tables 29 and 30). The actual growth in housing will exceed those projections.

Between 1990 and 2000, the Northeast added 10,087 new units of housing and experienced an 82 percent increase in the number of households (U.S. Bureau of the Census 2000). The I-77 Corridor added just over 1,100 units of housing and experienced a 30 percent increase in households. In the Northwest, during the same time period, the number of households increased 32.7 percent (U.S. Bureau of the Census 2000) as opposed to the 20 percent increase predicted (Richland County Council 1999, 3D-7).

Not surprisingly, housing has been built much more rapidly in the Northeast than in the rural areas of Lower and North Central Richland. In fact, the rate of new housing construction has been slowing in Lower Richland, while it has been increasing rapidly in the Northeast.

Since 1970, there has also been a steady increase in new housing units in the Northwest. While the number of new housing units increased in the North Central planning area between 1990 and March 2000, the overall number of new housing units added to that area between 1970 and March 2000 (1,724) is significantly less than that of Lower Richland (11,293), Northeast Richland (20,055), and Northwest Richland (11,019).

Table 6.1
Average household income by race and planning area, and percent of residents by type of income by planning area in 2000

	Lower Richland	Northeast	North Central
White average household income	$50,416	$79,942	$57,313
Black average household income	$40,099	$56,181	$38,173
Percent difference in household incomes	20.5	29.7	33.4
Percent households receiving public assistance income	2.6	1	2.4
Percent households receiving social security income	23.1	13.7	26.1
Percent households with no earnings	14.8	8.1	16.6

Source: Based on 2000 data from the U.S. Bureau of the Census.

Income

In Richland County, blacks have much lower incomes than their white counterparts. Based on 1990 data, the County Council stated that blacks and other minorities on average earned under $8,400 per year, while whites earned $17,032 per year (Richland County Council 1999, 3C-2). While all groups experienced an increase in per capita income between 1990 and 2000, blacks continue to earn significantly less than whites (U.S. Bureau of the Census 2000).

In 1999, countywide, white average household income was almost $25,000 higher than black average household income (table 6.1). The average household income for whites in Lower Richland was $50,416 and $40,099 for blacks—a 20.5 percent difference. Despite the growing racial integration in the Northeast and Northwest, racial disparities continue. In fact, the racial income disparity is worse among northeasterners and northwesterners. In the Northeast, whites had an average household income of $79,942, and blacks had an average household income of $56,181—a disparity close to 30 percent. The disparity between black and white households in the Northwest was even greater at 33.7 percent. Interestingly, on average the North Central planning area had an equally high racial income disparity (33.4 percent). Moreover, North Central white residents earned approximately $7,000 more per year than their white counterparts in Lower Richland.

Table 6.1
(cont.)

	North-west	I-77	I-20	All Richland
White average household income	$63,674	$54,890	$56,184	$64,297
Black average household income	$42,242	$48,205	$37,827	$39,754
Percent difference in household incomes	33.7	12.2	32.7	38.2
Percent households receiving public assistance income	1.2	1.4	2.1	2.1
Percent households receiving social security income	14.5	21.4	26.3	21
Percent households with no earnings	9.4	10	18.6	15.1

Planning areas differ greatly in terms of various poverty indicators, including the size of the population receiving public assistance, social security benefits, or with no reported earnings. Not surprisingly, the planning areas with the lowest black median household incomes are also those with the highest percentages of population on public assistance, social security, or with no reported earnings: the Lower Richland, North Central, and I-20 Corridor planning areas.

While the county's unemployment rate was relatively low in 2000 (5.1 percent), racial disparities in employment were statistically significant (U.S. Bureau of the Census 2000). Black females were unemployed at a rate of 9.3 percent, while white females were unemployed at a rate of 4.6 percent (U.S. Bureau of the Census 2000). Similarly, black men were unemployed at a rate of 10.5 percent, while their white counterparts were unemployed at a rate of 3.8 percent (U.S. Bureau of the Census 2000).

Housing, Homeownership, and Asset Accumulation

Income alone is an insufficient measure of the wealth or poverty of a particular individual or family (Oliver and Shapiro 1997, 2). For a breadwinner to adequately support one's family, they must have assets, not just income. If the breadwinner is laid off or unable to work, assets help make up for the loss of income. Blacks are more likely to be asset poor than whites (Oliver and Shapiro 1997, 86–88). According to the Center for Enterprise Development (2002), South Carolina ranked twenty-sixth in the nation in terms of the race gap in asset wealth.

While it has less of a race-based asset disparity than other states, South Carolina's rating is largely based on its high level of homeownership across the races (Center for Enterprise Development 2002, 71). This raises serious questions: What are the asset accumulation mechanisms for poor people, particularly blacks, in Richland County as they relate to land- or homeownership? What accounts for the current disparities in asset accumulation, and how might they be impacted by land use planning?

Overall, Richland County has a high level of homeownership (61.4 percent). White county residents had a significantly higher rate of ownership (63 percent) as compared to black residents (34.6 percent), however. Lower Richland and North Central residents enjoy an astounding rate of homeownership—72.4 and 76.6 percent, respectively (U.S. Bureau of the Census 2000). When the opportunity to acquire home equity is examined, South Carolina compares favorably to other states. Again according to the Center for Enterprise Development (2002, 94), it ranks second in the nation. Yet when housing values are examined, the disparities across races and planning areas are pronounced.

Housing values are significantly higher in the Northeast, with slightly more than 75 percent of the housing valued at over $90,000. In the Northwest, almost 60 percent of the housing is valued at over $90,000. In the Lower Richland and North Central planning areas, about 70 percent of the housing is valued at under $90,000 (U.S. Bureau of the Census 2000). Housing values in rural areas are much lower than suburban sprawl areas, but are meaningful. In Lower Richland, over 60 percent of the home- and landowners had property values of between $30,000 and $99,000 (U.S. Bureau of the Census 2000).

There are important differences in the types of homes being built across the planning areas. The housing trends in the rural planning areas suggest that development is not a function of large lot subdivision development but rather single-family houses ownership. It also suggests that blacks may not be able to convert their land value into real improvements, like built housing, which would increase the asset value of their property. Between 1990 and 2000, in the Lower Richland and North

Central planning areas, the number of mobile homes grew by approximately 34 and 28 percent, respectively.

The rate of mobile home growth in the Northeast and Northwest was 25.5 and 17.4 percent, respectively. When one examines the rate of single-family detached home development, the numbers are more striking. In the Lower Richland and North Central planning areas, the number of single-family detached homes grew by 11 and 8 percent, respectively. In the Northeast and Northwest, however, the number of single-family detached homes jumped by 47 and 30 percent, respectively.

Residents have complained that they have had difficulty accessing financing for housing other than mobile homes, which may account for the growth in mobile homes over single-family detached housing. Because mobile homes are considered personal and not real property, the inability to secure financing for built housing negatively impacts the asset accumulation of Lower and North Central Richland families.

Smart growth policies must be "opportunity growth" policies and equity reforms. Otherwise, reforms in the name of smart growth will be bad growth for impoverished communities, particularly in rural areas. Furthermore, proponents of sprawl control will have difficulty garnering support from black and other important constituencies. Only by fully identifying the costs and opportunities associated with growth in a particular metropolitan context, including an explicit evaluation of access to opportunities for poor communities of color, can policymakers begin to identify ways to grow smart.

Overall, the County Council identifies infrastructure needs and attractive qualities of its planning areas, including schools, water and sewer services, affordable as well as quality housing, highway construction, and roadway improvements. While these elements are related to the occurrence of sprawl and development, the County Council does not address these realities sufficiently to impact sprawl or direct development. Ignoring the policy choices that created these conditions, as well as their severity, the County Council exacerbates current racial and economic inequities, and fails to sufficiently impact sprawl.

It is unclear whether density limits will result in substantially less development in areas currently suffering from the consequences of sprawl, such as the Northeast and Northwest. If it does not, poor communities will continue to subsidize sprawl, reducing resources for infrastructure investments in their communities. Funneling growth to specific villages may improve the County Council's ability to provide some services and infrastructure to those areas. But will it be enough? It is unclear whether the conditions are sufficient to attract new development. Moreover, the plan relies heavily on private investment for implementation. Whether private investment is likely to flow to poor, predominantly black parts of the county is far from clear. Private investment is more likely in parts of the county already experiencing rapid growth. It may be that the only housing developed in poor rural areas, and the ultimate impact of such policies, is the further isolation and impoverishment of black rural and urban residents along with the continuation of sprawl.

County governments all over the South face similar challenges in land use planning and other policy choices. They have limited resources, and rural populations tend to be needy and costly to serve. Land use planning battles are contentious and important decision-making power is fragmented, requiring local, regional, and state cooperation and coordination. Nonetheless, a county government's land use planning powers are meaningful and could be used more effectively.

Municipal, county, and state governments and impoverished communities of color need research and policy support in evaluating policy alternatives to promote healthy communities. Researchers and policy institutes must engage in context-based analyses of the causes and effects of sprawl, and incorporate explicit goals of race-based disparity reduction and equity promotion in identifying policy solutions in the urban/rural context. This information must also be shared with conservation groups, developers, and other stakeholders to begin a more productive discussion of how to promote healthy, sustainable communities.

Notes

1. I would like to pay special thanks to Debra Langer and Jason Reece for their data collection and research.

2. There has been useful comparative research on sprawl in cities across the country that includes Southern cities. For example, see Rusk (1998). Few, however, have examined the unique dynamic of black landownership in rural areas near urban metropolitan centers.

3. While the plan acknowledges that Eastover has no jobs, it does mention that residents identified the economic development possibilities related to a proposed "trail system" to attract recreational users to the town.

References

Berlau, J. 2002. "Smart-Growth" Plan Riles Black Farmers. Available at ⟨http://www.mfaincorporated.com/todaysfarmer/past/940920.asp⟩ (accessed September 18, 2006).

Carlisle, J. 2000. Suburban Snob Politics Fuels "Smart Growth" Land-Use Movement. Available at ⟨http://www.nationalcenter.org/NPA312.html⟩ (accessed October 1, 2004).

Center for Enterprise Development. 2002. State Asset Development Report Card. Available at ⟨http:\www.cfed.org\publications⟩ (accessed September 15, 2004).

Community Leader's Letter. 1995. Economic Future of Some S.C. Counties Now More Tied to N.C. and Georgia Cities 6, no. 1. Available at ⟨http://www.strom.clemson.edu/teams/ced/cll/6-1Spring95.pdf⟩ (accessed October 12, 2004).

Environmental Science and Technology. 2004. Is Smart Growth Better for Water Quality? Available at ⟨http://pubs.ace.org/subscribe/journals/esthag-w/2004/aug/policy/jp_smargrowth.html⟩ (accessed October 1).

Jargowsky, P. 1997. Ghetto Poverty among Blacks in the 1980s. *Journal of Policy Analysis and Management* 13:288.

Knight Foundation American Institutes for Research. 1999. *Columbia, SC Community Profile.* Available at ⟨http://www.knightfdn.org/indicators/1999/cola/profile.pdf⟩ (accessed September 30, 2004).

Massey, D., and N. Denton. 1993. *American Apartheid: Segregation and the Making of the Underclass.* Cambridge, MA: Harvard University Press.

Oliver, M., and T. Shapiro. 1997. *Black Wealth/White Wealth: A New Perspective on Racial Inequality.* New York: Routledge.

powell, j. a. 2000. Addressing Regional Dilemmas for Minority Communities. In *Reflections on Regionalism,* ed. B. Katz, 218–46. Washington, DC: Brookings Institution Press.

Richland County Council. 1999. *Imagine Richland 2020 Comprehensive Plan.* Columbia, SC: Richland City Council.

Rusk, D. 1995. *Cities without Suburbs.* Washington, DC: Woodrow Wilson Center Press.

Rusk, D. 1998. America's Urban Problem/America's Race Problem. *Urban Geography* 19, no. 8. Available at ⟨http:www.gamaliel.org/Strategic/StrategicpartnersRuskUrbanGeographyII.htm⟩ (accessed September 28, 2004).

U.S. Bureau of the Census. 2000. *Census 2000 Summary File 3 (SF 3): Sample Data.* Washington, DC: U.S. Department of Commerce.

7

Food Justice and Health in Communities of Color

Kimberly Morland and Steve Wing

While the impact of urban sprawl on health received attention in the medical literature in the 1950s and 1960s (Urban Sprawl 1952; Woodbury 1960), more systematic explorations of the complex and interconnected relationships between neighborhoods and health is a recent phenomenon. Neighborhood environments affect residents' physical safety, exposure to pollutants, access to basic amenities like water and sewer services, social support, opportunities for routine physical activity, and a host of other factors critical to maintaining health. The environmental justice movement has brought racial and economic discrimination in waste disposal, polluting industries, access to amenities, and the impacts of transportation planning to the public's attention.

This chapter concerns racial and economic disparities in the kinds of nutrition that are available in local neighborhoods, which we refer to as the local food environment. Although nutrition has been studied almost exclusively as a matter of individual choice, and control of nutrition-related heath problems such as obesity, high blood pressure, heart disease, stroke, diabetes, and cancer has been considered a matter of health education, it is incontrovertible that what people eat depends on what is available given our agricultural and food distribution systems, including the pricing and advertising of food by retailers. We present evidence showing that neighborhood access to places where healthy foods can be obtained is related to race and wealth, and that the presence of places to obtain these foods is related to dietary intake, in particular for black Americans, who suffer disproportionately from nutrition-related diseases compared to white Americans. We begin by discussing the historical context that led to the emergence of the current structure of local food environments.

Institutionalized racism in the housing market has systematically favored homeownership for white Americans and simultaneously devalued ethnically diverse inner-city neighborhoods. Evidence pointing to these prejudices has been documented in most U.S. cities, particularly as federal government policies have enabled racial segregation across the country for the better part of the last century. These policies began as early as the 1930s when the Home Owner Loan Corporation (HOLC) was initiated. The HOLC was intended to provide government-sponsored long-term mortgages for individuals who had lost their homes due to foreclosure.

As a result, banks used the policies set forth by the HOLC, employing color-coded maps to indicate a neighborhood's risk for loan default. African Americans, in particular, became subjected to redlining (such that a majority of loans were granted to residents of white "homogeneous" neighborhoods), and disinvestments by government and corporations in central city neighborhoods that were ethnically diverse became commonplace (Massey and Denton 1993). This pattern continued as other federal housing programs such as the Veterans Administration (VA) loan program and loans through the FHA after World War II also made homeownership more accessible by lowering interest rates and decreasing down payments. These loan programs launched the construction of new homes, and renters migrated to suburbs where homes could be purchased at affordable prices.

This new tendency toward urban sprawl resulted in a further decline of the infrastructure within inner-city neighborhoods, as these loan programs encouraged the migration of middle-income whites to the suburbs in particular. Other federal policies supported, and continue to support, homeownership that includes mortgage interest deductions and tax benefits under capital gains. Federal funding for highways and other infrastructure further enhanced suburban development, and retail businesses followed the flow of middle-class consumers to these areas because industries were also able to take advantage of cheaper land (Savitch 2003; Southerland 2004).

The development of effective transportation also played a key role in the movement toward urban sprawl, primarily because federal tax policies tend to favor private transportation. Since 1980, over three trillion dollars have been spent on highways, and in 1994, four times as many of the federal dollars earmarked for transportation were spent on highway construction as compared to mass transit systems (U.S. Department of Transportation 1997). Many of the policies that encourage commuting by private automobile also include tax deductions for parking spaces, yet similar types of tax benefits and credits are not equally afforded to public transportation commuters (Blumenauer 1998).

Although these policies have benefited suburbanites over the past several decades, inner-city residents experienced high unemployment rates with deteriorating housing and increased crime. Nevertheless, much of the current medical literature on the health impact associated with urban sprawl focuses on individuals living within suburban communities. For instance, more traffic-related fatalities (Ewing, Schieber, and Zegeer 2003; Lucy 2003) as well as higher rates of sedentary behavior and obesity (Ewing et al. 2003) have been observed among people living in the suburbs.

In addition, increased traffic and air pollution in these areas has been documented (Pohanka and Fitzgerald 2004; Aucott 2001). But less empirical work has been done to document the health impact this migration has had on the people who are still living in the inner cities. For instance, changes to inner-city retail markets show residents of black neighborhoods are left with fewer food stores, and more liquor stores and check-cashing businesses (Troutt 1993). Supermarkets, in particular, have continued to migrate to the suburbs, thereby forcing residents to depend on small stores with a limited selection of foods at substantially higher prices (Curtis and McClellan 1995). In fact, a study conducted by the U.S. government showed that urban dwellers pay 3 to 37 percent more for groceries in their local community compared to the same goods purchased in large suburban supermarkets (U.S. House of Representatives Select Committee on Hunger 1990).

Besides the lower prices afforded by supermarkets, there is some suggestion that these stores have a greater variety of healthy foods as well (Sallis et al. 1986). This raises the concern that the policies that instigated urban sprawl may have also shaped the dietary choices of inner-city residents (U.S. House of Representatives Select Committee on Hunger 1987, 1992). Because these economic and land use policies have had an impact on the placement of food stores, they may work collectively to influence the diets of Americans beyond any individual choices a person might make about their food purchases or consumption. And although the impact that food choice has on health is undisputed, these factors are rarely investigated as mechanisms associated with the decisions people make about the foods they eat, nor is their impact on regional equity considered.

As an example of how the regional equity of retail businesses and food stores may influence residents' health, results from two studies are summarized in this chapter (Morland, Wing, and Diez-Roux 2002; Morland et al. 2002). First, the number of food stores and restaurants (located in four geographically different areas of the United States) are described. The neighborhoods were classified by wealth and racial segregation, and then analyzed for differences in the availability of food stores and restaurants between these neighborhood types. Second, the impact that the local availability of specific types of food stores and restaurants has on residents' dietary choices is shown.

Segregation and the Regional Equity of Food

Morland and colleagues (2002) conducted a study to compare the availability of food stores and restaurants across different types of neighborhoods. The study included 216 1990 census tracts located in Washington County, Maryland (n = 28); Forsyth County, North Carolina (n = 78); Jackson City, Mississippi (n = 56); and the following suburbs of Minneapolis: Brooklyn Center, Brooklyn Park, Crystal, Golden Valley, New Hope, Plymouth, and Robbinsdale (n = 54). The census tracts were used as proxies for neighborhoods, and these areas were analyzed for the placement of food stores and restaurants.

Housing, transportation, and the demographic characteristics of census tracts were obtained from the *Population and Housing Summary Tape Files 3A* (U.S. Bureau of the Census 1990). After exclusions, the business addresses of 2,437 businesses where people can purchase food were collected from the local Departments of Environmental Health and state Departments of Agriculture in the four study areas. The businesses were classified into five categories/industry groups of food stores (supermarket, grocery store, convenience store, convenience store with gas station, and specialty food store) and five categories of restaurants (full-service restaurant, franchised fast-food restaurant, carryout eating place, specialty carryout eating place, and bar/tavern). Descriptions and examples of the types of food stores and restaurants in each industry group are described in table 7.1.

Median house values for each census tract were used as a measure of neighborhood wealth, and the census tracts were divided equally into five levels of wealth from lowest to highest. The proportion of black residents was used as an indicator of racial segregation. The census tracts were referred to as *predominantly black* when 80 percent or more of the population were black Americans, while *predominantly white* neighborhoods were defined as having 20 percent or fewer black Americans. The remaining census tracts were classified as *racially mixed*. A full description of these classifications and further details of the methods can be found elsewhere (Morland et al. 2002).

The census tracts varied in terms of population: size; area; population density; number of single-family homes; proportion of renters; proportion of black residents; and proportion of households without an automobile or truck. Low-wealth neighborhoods had a greater population density with fewer homes and the greatest proportion of renters. Over 50 percent of the residents in the lowest-wealth neighborhoods were black Americans.

The authors analyzed the presence of the ten types of food stores and restaurants by the five levels of neighborhood wealth, and found disparities in the presence of supermarkets, small grocery stores, and bars and taverns, in particular. The presence of supermarkets was three times greater in the highest-wealth areas (n = 27) compared to the lowest-wealth neighborhoods (n = 7). Conversely, the same high-wealth neighborhoods housed a third as many bars and taverns (eleven versus thirty-five), and roughly half as many small grocery stores (twenty-six versus forty-five) than did the low-wealth areas (table 7.2).

When considering racial segregation, the authors found that the presence of supermarkets in predominantly white neighborhoods was over

Table 7.1
Description and examples of food stores and restaurants by industry group

Industry group	1997 NAICS definitions	NAICS index	Examples
Supermarkets	445110 supermarkets and other grocery (except convenience) stores	445110 supermarkets	Food Lion, Albertsons, Kroger, Piggly Wiggly, Safeway
Grocery stores	445110 supermarkets and other grocery (except convenience) stores	445110 grocery stores 445110 food stores	Beatty Street Grocery, Arkady's Market, West Side Market Potomac Grocery, JC Morris Grocery, Ken's Grocery
Convenience stores	445120 convenience stores	445120 convenience	Seven-Eleven, 4 Brothers Convenience Store
Convenience stores with gas stations	447110 gasoline stations with convenience stores	447110 gasoline stations with convenience stores	Amoco, Chevron, Shell, Texaco, Sunoco, BP, Citgo, Mobile, Conoco, Exxon, Phillips 66
Specialty food stores	4452 specialty food stores	445210 meat markets 445220 fish markets 445230 fruit/vegetable markets 445291 baked goods 445292 confectionery/nut stores 445299 all others	Davis's Meat Market, Boonsboro Produce Market, Asia Market, 66 Produce, Holsinger's Meat Market, Baron's Gourmet, Valley Street Fish

Full-service restaurants	722110 full-service restaurants	722110 restaurants, full-service 722110 steak houses 722110 pizzerias, full-service 722110 fine dining restaurants 722110 family restaurants 722110 diners, full-service 722212 cafeterias	Applebee's, Baker's, Square, Benihana, Bennigan's, Bonsai Japanese Steakhouse, The Thai House, Ruby Tuesday, View Street Diner
Fast-food restaurants	722211 limited-service restaurants	722211 fast-food restaurants 722211 pizza parlors, limited service 722211 pizza delivery shops	Arby's, Biscuitville, Bojangles, Burger King, Dominos, Blimpies, McDonald's, Wendy's, Krystal
Carryout eating places	722211 limited-service restaurants	722211 delicatessens 722211 sandwich shops 722110 bagel shops, full-service	Carla's Deli, Harle's Subs, Silver Streak Sub and Deli, Bagel-Lisious, Mr. George's Sandwich World, Country Deli
Specialty carryout places	722213 snack and non-alcoholic beverage bars	722213 beverage (e.g., coffee) bars (nonalcoholic) 722213 doughnut shops 722213 ice cream parlors 722213 pretzel shops	Baskin-Robbins, Colonial Bakery Store, Papa Vic's Gelato, Monroe's Donuts, Smoothie King, TCBY Yogurt, Dunkin Donuts, Starbucks Coffee, Gloria Jean's Coffee, Fanny Farmers Candies
Bars and taverns	72241 drinking places (Alcoholic beverages)	722410 alcoholic beverage drinking places	McBare's Pub, South End Tavern, Club City Lights, Eddie's Disco, Sportsmen's Den, Funkstown Tavern

Source: Morland et al. (2002).
Note: NAICS refer to the 1997 North America Industry Classification System codes and definitions used to define U.S. industries.

Table 7.2
Number of food stores and restaurants by neighborhood wealth

	Neighborhood wealth				
	Low	Low–medium	Medium	High–medium	High
Food stores					
Supermarkets	7	22	20	30	27
Grocery stores	45	38	24	25	26
Convenience stores	25	27	35	27	29
Convenience stores with gas stations	26	39	53	45	37
Specialty food stores	11	10	10	6	10
Restaurants					
Full-service	149	197	151	194	162
Franchised fast food	63	97	91	87	70
Carryout	26	44	24	41	24
Carryout specialty	17	29	26	36	33
Bars/taverns	35	21	22	13	11

four times greater than predominantly black neighborhoods, whereas black neighborhoods contain more small corner grocery and convenience stores.

The number of supermarkets by wealth and racial segregation is shown in figure 7.1. This figure demonstrates that the majority of supermarkets (67 percent) are located primarily in neighborhoods characterized by high wealth and a predominantly white population. Only five supermarkets are located in all of the predominantly black neighborhoods, and the wealth of the neighborhoods does not influence supermarket presence for black communities. These five supermarkets are located in thirty-five predominantly black neighborhoods to provide service to 118,000 residents, whereas there are sixty-eight supermarkets located in the predominantly white neighborhoods providing service to 259,500 people. This translates to one supermarket for every 23,582 residents of the predominantly black neighborhoods versus one supermarket for every 3,816 residents of the predominantly white neighborhoods.

Since transportation plays a key role in how far a person can travel to obtain food, investigators measured the proportion of residents without

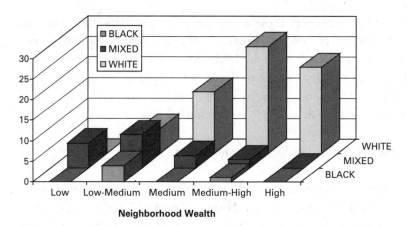

Figure 7.1
Number of supermarkets by neighborhood wealth and racial segregation

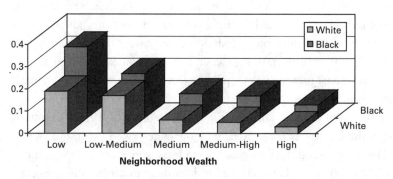

Figure 7.2
Proportion of households without an automobile or truck

access to private transportation based on 1990 census data (figure 7.2). The investigators found that neighborhood wealth was a determinant of car/truck ownership. Six percent of black households and 3 percent of white households in the highest-wealth neighborhoods were without private transportation, and a greater proportion of black households at each level of neighborhood wealth were without private transportation.

Over a third of the black households in the lowest-wealth neighborhoods were without private transportation compared to under 20 percent for the white households. In addition, public transportation was limited to bus travel in these areas, but when the association between neighborhood type and the availability of public transportation for residents was examined, it was found that most census tracts (70 percent) do not have bus transit available to them, and little variation in the proportion of neighborhoods with access to public transit was observed by neighborhood wealth or racial segregation.

Influence of the Local Food Environment on Diet

The observed disparities in local food environments, viewed within the historical context of developing housing, financing, and transportation policies in the United States, raises a number of important questions for residents. First, how are black and low-wealth neighborhoods impacted by having fewer supermarkets and more small corner grocery stores as compared to white and wealthier neighborhoods? Second, is it possible that there would be little impact on residents' diets if they were able to obtain healthier foods in other places? Third, how might factors such as transportation (access and cost) or experienced racism in white establishments lead to poorer diets among residents of black neighborhoods?

A subsequent study examined the dietary status of 10,623 residents living in the four geographic areas previously described (Morland, Wing, and Diez-Roux 2002) attempted to address some of these questions about the relationship between the local food environment and residents' reported dietary intake. A total of 8,231 white Americans and 2,392 African Americans were interviewed and asked to report how often they ate specific foods during the past year.

From this data, investigators derived four variables as indicators of meeting a healthy diet based on *Nutrition and Your Health: Dietary Guidelines for Americans* (2000). These variables included "five-a-day" of at least two servings of fruit and three servings of vegetables per day, 30 percent or less of calories from total fat, less than 10 percent of calories from saturated fat, and three hundred or fewer milligrams of dietary cholesterol per day. The associations between these dietary measures and the presence of supermarkets, small grocery stores, full-service restaurants, and franchised fast-food restaurants were analyzed.

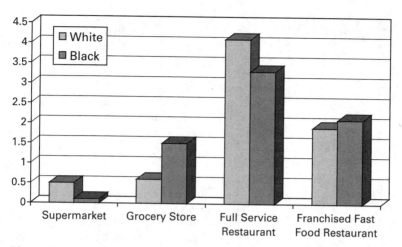

Figure 7.3
Mean number of food stores and restaurants located in census tracts of interviewed participants

Ninety-four percent of the whites interviewed in this study lived in predominantly white neighborhoods and 83 percent of the black participants lived in predominantly black neighborhoods. The white participants lived in areas with more supermarkets and full-service restaurants, whereas the blacks lived in neighborhoods with more small grocery stores and fast-food restaurants (figure 7.3). On average, a supermarket was located in every other census tract where the white participants resided and every tenth census tract populated by African Americans. In addition, there were two and a half times more small corner grocery stores in the areas where the black participants lived. The differences in the presence of full-service and fast-food restaurants for the black and white Americans sampled were not as great.

After controlling for household income and individual educational status, as well as the presence of all types of food stores and restaurants located in an individuals' census tract of residence, the presence of supermarkets was associated with healthier diets for African Americans (table 7.3). For instance, 54 percent more African Americans living in neighborhoods with at least one supermarket reported meeting the five-a-day dietary recommendation for fruits and vegetables compared to African Americans who lived in areas with no supermarkets.

Table 7.3
Adjusted prevalence ratios (PR) and 95 percent confidence intervals (CIs) of meeting dietary guidelines of foods and nutrients by presence of supermarkets, grocery stores, and full-service and franchised fast-food restaurants in the census tracts of residence for black and white Americans

	PR (95% CI)			
	Supermarkets	Grocery stores	Full service	Fast food
Black Americans (n = 2,392)				
Fruits and vegetables	1.54 (1.11, 2.12)	1.07 (0.83, 1.38)	1.06 (0.79, 1.41)	0.94 (0.74, 1.21)
Total fat	1.22 (1.03, 1.44)	1.06 (0.92, 1.21)	1.07 (0.91, 1.25)	0.98 (0.86, 1.13)
Saturated fat	1.30 (1.07, 1.56)	1.03 (0.88, 1.20)	1.21 (1.01, 1.46)	0.94 (0.81, 1.10)
Cholesterol	0.94 (0.84, 1.05)	1.01 (0.94, 1.08)	1.05 (0.96, 1.13)	0.97 (0.90, 1.04)
White Americans (n = 8,231)				
Fruits and vegetables	1.08 (0.89, 1.30)	0.93 (0.78, 1.10)	0.94 (0.75, 1.19)	1.12 (0.91, 1.37)
Total fat	1.09 (1.01, 1.18)	0.97 (0.90, 1.04)	0.95 (0.87, 1.05)	0.99 (0.91, 1.08)
Saturated fat	1.09 (0.99, 1.20)	0.92 (0.84, 1.00)	1.03 (0.91, 1.15)	0.95 (0.86, 1.05)
Cholesterol	1.00 (0.97, 1.02)	0.99 (0.97, 1.01)	1.02 (0.99, 1.04)	0.98 (0.96, 1.01)

Source: Adapted from Morland, Wing, and Diez-Roux (2002).
Note: Prevalence ratios are for meeting dietary guidelines for foods and nutrients when any of the specified type of store or restaurant is present in the respondent's census tract versus when none is present. Prevalence ratios are adjusted for income, education, and other types of food stores and food service places except convenience stores.

The benefit of the presence of supermarkets was also observed for African Americans in terms of meeting the dietary recommendations for total fat and saturated fat. In areas with at least one supermarket, 22 percent more African Americans reported consuming less than 30 percent of their calories per day from total fat compared to black residents living in neighborhoods without any supermarkets. A 30 percent greater proportion of African Americans in these neighborhoods also reported consuming less than 10 percent of their daily calories from saturated fat. Interestingly, the reported intake of fat, fruits, and vegetables among African Americans differed little according to the presence of grocery stores, full-service restaurants, and franchised fast-food restaurants.

Only moderate differences in meeting dietary recommendations were observed between black Americans who lived in areas with these types of stores and restaurants and those who did not, except for the association between the presence of full-service restaurants and saturated fat. In this instance, a 21 percent increase in meeting this recommendation was observed. In addition, the neighborhood availability of food stores and restaurants did not influence the reported adherence to dietary recommendations for cholesterol.

Furthermore, the associations between the presence of specific types of food stores and restaurants and diet were not as great among white as among African Americans. For instance, compared to white Americans living in areas with no supermarkets, the prevalence of white Americans meeting the recommendations for total fat was 9 percent greater in areas with at least one supermarket, compared to a difference of 22 percent African Americans. In general, the proportion of whites who reported meeting dietary recommendations differed little according to the presence of specific food stores or restaurants.

Summary and Direction for Future Research

These studies show that the locations of food stores and restaurants are associated with the wealth and racial makeup of neighborhoods, and that disparities in the placement of food stores are associated with residents' ability to achieve healthy diets. In a previous study conducted with the same population (although neighborhood types were defined differently), Ana V. Diez-Roux and colleagues documented that residents of low-income neighborhoods consume fewer fruits and vegetables, and residents of disadvantaged neighborhoods had a higher risk of coronary heart disease (Diez-Roux et al. 1999, 2001). These studies suggest that people's local food environments affect their dietary choices and subsequent health status, especially for black Americans.

Therefore, the changes in land use policies over the past century that have contributed to increasing urban sprawl have also resulted in racial and economic inequalities between living environments and the ensuing health disparities among residents. Racial and wealth segregation remain prominent characteristics of U.S. neighborhoods, despite efforts by the Fair Housing Act of 1968 to prohibit racial discrimination in housing (Dubofsky 1969). Although food, like housing, is an essential requirement of life, U.S. policies to maintain nondiscriminatory practices in the distribution of food do not exist, nor are there any existing policies that promote the egalitarian distribution of food stores and restaurants across neighborhoods. The result of the lack of policies in this area is that communities that are most affected by the local food environment due to racial segregation, low income, lack of transportation, and higher burdens of chronic conditions, remain at a significant disadvantage.

Research into the impacts of the local food environment on nutrition, health, and the quality of life is just beginning. Future studies could evaluate aspects of communities that may increase or decrease the negative impacts of a restricted local food environment on communities of color and low-income communities. Additional research can also attempt to answer new questions about the relationship between the local food environment and residents' food choices and health. For instance, to what extent and in what ways can smaller, locally owned and operated food stores serve communities of color in segregated urban environments where the lack of large chain supermarkets negatively impacts nutrition?

In addition, for those neighborhoods that lack both supermarkets and locally owned stores that offer a variety of healthy foods, what is the role of public and private transportation in helping residents achieve a healthy diet? And how does the impact of transportation differ across factors such as age, employment status, and health status (that is, people who are healthy versus those with chronic diseases)?

The Local Food Environment as an Environmental Justice Issue: Action for Change

The impact of the local food environment on nutrition, health, and the quality of life occur within the context of an increasingly concentrated system of food production and distribution, racial segregation, economic inequalities, loss of a food-preparation culture, health disparities, and environmental injustice. Although early U.S. farm policies supported the development of local farms that provided meat, fruits, and vegetables to a local region, since the middle of the last century food production has become more consolidated.

The industrial-scale production of grains, fruits, vegetables, meat, and dairy products is regionally concentrated, so the local food environment in most areas is disconnected from local agriculture. These agricultural and economic policies have led to a decrease in the number of farms at the same time that the size of farms has dramatically increased. This shift has directly impacted how food gets to consumers, the types of foods that get transported, and the quality of these foods (U.S. Department of Agriculture 2000). The results from this study suggest that environmental disparities exist in terms of access to food, and that these disparities ultimately influence the health of community residents. The extent to which these federal policies, combined with local land use policies that support the economic growth of suburban areas, contribute to the creation and maintenance of these regional inequities remains to be measured. Nevertheless, the remedy for low-income and people of color communities will surely require new polices at the local, state, and national levels that will promote equal access to healthy foods at affordable prices in all neighborhoods.

The massive social and economic changes that will be required to address these issues have led some public health and social science researchers to promote policy changes at the highest levels of government. Although government agencies can introduce modest policy changes, most government bodies in the United States are responsive to corporate and elite groups that benefit from injustices. For example, in the area of the food environment, stores that provide a variety of healthy foods at low prices are mostly large corporate operations whose profits are enhanced by locating in wealthier areas.

Given the inherent profit motivations of corporations, they should be expected to oppose location policies that address the health and nutrition needs of low-income populations, and they should be expected to use their political clout to prevent government bodies from taking action on behalf of communities that lack access to healthy foods. Although governments could provide additional corporate welfare to promote the location of chain supermarkets in low-income and people of color neighborhoods, these funds would compete with the other health, economic, and environmental needs of the same communities, and such policies would not achieve local control or community investment. Although large-scale policy interventions should be promoted, their prospects may be limited.

Given these challenges, another approach is local action that takes account of national and global contexts. The environmental justice movement has brought many local communities to action around threats from waste disposal sites, polluting industries, inequitable transportation planning, and other issues that connect community life to large economic and environmental forces. Environmental justice, civil rights, and other community organizations could include access to healthy food along with other issues in their portfolios, putting pressure on local governments to help bring healthier foods to their neighborhoods, create community-owned stores and food cooperatives, and establish links with local farmers.

Finally, local groups could also provide support to national organizations that work on more global food and economic policy issues. Research into the economic, nutritional, and health consequences of the local food environment will have the greatest potential for making a positive impact if it can be designed to answer questions and offer the documentation most needed by organizations that represent communities unjustly impacted by restricted local food environments.

References

Aucott, M. 2001. Comment on: Urban Sprawl Leaves Its PAH Signature. *Environmental Science Technology* 35:1889–91.

Blumenauer, Earl. 1998. The View from Capital Hill. *Brookings Review* 16:6–17.

Curtis, K. A., and S. McClellan. 1995. Falling through the Safety Net: Poverty, Food Assistance, and Shopping Constraints in an American City. *Urban Anthropology* 24:93–135.

Diez-Roux, A. V., S. S. Merkin, D. Arnett, L. Chambless, M. Massing, F. J. Nieto, P. Sorlie, M. Szklo, H. A. Tyroler, and R. L. Watson. 2001. Neighborhood of Residence and Incidence of Coronary Heart Disease. *New England Journal of Medicine* 345:99–106.

Diez-Roux, A. V., F. J. Nieto, L. Caulfield, H. A. Tyroler, R. L. Watson, and M. Szklo. 1999. Neighborhood Differences in Diet: The Atherosclerosis Risk in Communities (ARIC) Study. *Journal of Epidemiology and Community Health* 53:55–63.

Dubofsky, J. E. 1969. Fair Housing: A Legislative History and a Perspective. *Washburn Law Journal* 8:149–166.

Ewing, R., R. A. Schieber, and C. V. Zegeer. 2003. Urban Sprawl as a Risk Factor in Motor Vehicle Occupant and Pedestrian Fatalities. *American Journal of Public Health* 93:1541–1545.

Ewing, R., T. Schmid, R. Killingsworth, A. Zlot, and S. Raudenbush. 2003. Relationship between Urban Sprawl and Physical Activity, Obesity, and Morbidity. *American Journal of Public Health* 18:47–57.

Lucy, W. H. 2003. Mortality Risk Associated with Leaving Home: Recognizing the Relevance of the Built Environment. *American Journal of Public Health* 93:1564–1569.

Massey, D. S., and N. A. Denton. 1993. *American Apartheid, Segregation, and the Making of the Underclass.* Cambridge, MA: Harvard University Press.

Morland, K., S. Wing, and A. V. Diez-Roux. 2002. The Contextual Effect of the Local Food Environment on Residents' Diets: The Atherosclerosis Risk in Communities Study. *American Journal of Public Health* 92:1761–1767.

Morland, K., S. Wing, A. V. Diez-Roux, and C. Poole. 2002. Neighborhood Characteristics Associated with the Location of Food Stores and Food Service Places. *American Journal of Preventive Medicine* 22:23–29.

Nutrition and Your Health: Dietary Guidelines for Americans. 2000. Home and garden bulletin no. 232. 5th ed. Washington, DC: U.S. Department of Agriculture.

Pohanka, M., and S. Fitzgerald. 2004. Urban Sprawl and You: How Sprawl Adversely Affects Worker Health. *American Association of Occupational Health Nurses Journal* 52:242–246.

Sallis, J. F., R. Nader, J. Atkins, and L. C. Wilson. 1986. San Diego Surveyed for Heart-Healthy Foods and Exercise Facilities. *Public Health Reports* 101:216–218.

Savitch, H. V. 2003. How Suburban Sprawl Shapes Human Well-being. *Journal of Urban Health* 80:590–607.

Southerland, M. T. 2004. Environmental Impacts of Dispersed Development from Federal Infrastructure Projects. *Environmental Monitoring and Assessment* 94:63–178.

Troutt, D. D. 1993. *The Thin Red Line: How the Poor Still Pay More*. San Francisco: West Regional Office, Consumer Union of the United States Inc.

Urban Sprawl. 1952. *British Medical Journal* 22:1142–1143.

U.S. Bureau of the Census. 1990. *Population and Housing Summary Tape Files 3A*. Washington, DC: U.S. Department of Commerce.

U.S. Department of Agriculture. 2000. U.S. Farm Policy: The First 200 Years. *Agriculture Outlook* (March).

U.S. Department of Transportation, Bureau of Transportation Statistics. 1997. Federal, State, and Local Transportation Financial Statistics, Fiscal Years 1982–1994. No. BTS–97–E–02. Available at ⟨http://www.bts.gov⟩.

U.S. House of Representatives Select Committee on Hunger. 1987. *Obtaining Food: Shopping Constraints of the Poor*. Washington, DC: U.S. Government Printing Office.

U.S. House of Representatives Select Committee on Hunger. 1990. *Food Security in the United States*. Washington, DC: U.S. Government Printing Office.

U.S. House of Representatives Select Committee on Hunger. 1992. *Urban Grocery Gap*. Washington, DC: U.S. Government Printing Office.

Woodbury, C. 1960. Impact of Urban Sprawl on Housing and Community Development. *American Journal of Public Health* 50:357–363.

8

Washed Away by Hurricane Katrina: Rebuilding a "New" New Orleans

Beverly Wright and Robert D. Bullard

On August 29, 2005, Hurricane Katrina made landfall near New Orleans, leaving death and destruction across the Louisiana, Mississippi, and Alabama Gulf Coast. Katrina is likely the most destructive hurricane in U.S. history, costing over seventy billion dollars in insured damage. It was also one of the deadliest storms in decades, with a death toll of 1,325.[1] Katrina is surpassed only by the 1928 hurricane in Florida, in which the estimated deaths were between 2,500 to 3,000, and the 8,000 deaths recorded in the 1900 Galveston hurricane (Kleinberg 2003).

New Orleans before Katrina was a city in peril. In 2000, New Orleans (Orleans Parish) had population of 484,674. Of this total, 325,947 (68 percent) were African American, 135,956 (28 percent) were Caucasian American, and 22,871 (4 percent) were of other nationalities. Like many great cities, New Orleans also had its share of problems. It was the largest U.S. city without a meaningful master plan. Oil and chemical firms and land developers were so influential that local "plans" generally reflected whatever business wanted to do (Rusk 2005).

The economic structure of New Orleans made it difficult to provide jobs with wages high enough to support a family. The city's economy might fairly be described as preindustrial, in that it had never provided large numbers of heavy manufacturing jobs. Fifty-nine percent of the city's population was of traditional working age (between eighteen and sixty-four), 27.5 percent was under the age of eighteen, and 13 percent was age sixty-five or older.

The city had a median household income of only $18,477, with over 31 percent of the households having annual incomes under $10,000. Also present was an overall unemployment rate of 12.4 percent. Katrina laid bare the "dirty little secret" of poverty in the United States (Sauer 2005). Despite efforts to combat poverty that focused on housing and community development, more than 28 percent of all families lived at or below the poverty level in New Orleans. Of this, 84 percent were African American families living in the older neighborhoods of the city. Forty-four percent of the city's inhabitants occupied dwelling units that were owner occupied, and 16.6 percent of the city's housing units were vacant (U.S. Bureau of the Census 2000).

Transportation Apartheid: Why Some Residents Get Left Behind

Car ownership is almost universal in the United States, with 91.7 percent of all households owning at least one motor vehicle. Two in ten households in the Louisiana, Mississippi, and Alabama disaster area, however, had no car (Associated Press 2005b). Over one-third of African Americans in New Orleans did not own a car. Before Katrina, nearly a quarter of New Orleans residents relied on public transportation (Katz, Fellowes, and Holmes 2005). And 102,122 disabled persons lived in New Orleans at the time of the hurricane (Russell 2005).

Katrina exposed a weakness in urban mass evacuation plans. The evacuation plan failed to serve people who depend on public transit (Litman 2005). The problem is not unique to New Orleans and the Gulf Coast. The 2005 evacuation of 2.7 million people from Houston during Hurricane Rita shows that "there is no way to evacuate a large U.S. city quickly and smoothly" (Hsu and Balz 2005). Many motorists ran out of gas after spending more than fifteen hours stuck in traffic.

As in the case of Hurricane Katrina, emergency transportation planners failed the "most vulnerable" of our society—individuals without cars, nondrivers, the disabled, the homeless, sick persons, elderly people, and children. Many vulnerable people were thus left behind and may have died as a result of having no transportation. Nearly two-thirds of the Katrina victims in Louisiana were older than sixty. This data confirms what many believe: that Katrina killed the weakest residents (Riccardi 2005).

Local, state, and federal emergency planners have known for years the risks facing transit-dependent residents (State of Louisiana 2000; Bourne

2004; City of New Orleans 2005). At least "100,000 New Orleans citizens do not have means of personal transportation" to evacuate in case of a major storm (City of New Orleans 2005). An article titled "Planning for the Evacuation of New Orleans" details the risks faced by hundreds of thousands of carless people and nondrivers in the New Orleans area:

Of the 1.4 million inhabitants in the high-threat areas, it is assumed only approximately 60 percent of the population of about 850,000 people will want, or be able to leave the city. The reasons are numerous. Although the primary reasons are a lack of transportation (it is estimated that about 200,000 to 300,000 people do not have access to reliable personal transportation), an unwillingness to leave homes and property (estimated to be at least 100,000 people) and a lack of outbound roadway capacity. (Wolshon 2002, 45)

Although the various agencies had this knowledge of a large and vulnerable population, there simply was no effective plan to evacuate these New Orleanians away from rising water. This problem received national attention in 1998 during Hurricane Georges when emergency evacuation plans left behind mostly residents who did not own cars (Perlstein and Thevenot 2004). The city's emergency plan was modified to include the use of public buses to evacuate those without transportation. When Hurricane Ivan struck New Orleans in 2004, many carless New Orleanians were left to fend for themselves, while others were evacuated to the Superdome and other "shelters of last resort" (Laska 2004).

On August 28, 2005, Mayor Ray Nagin ordered New Orleans's first-ever mandatory evacuation since the city was founded in 1718 (Associated Press 2005a). Buses evacuated thousands of residents to the Superdome and other shelters within the city. It has been the policy of the Red Cross for years not to open shelters in New Orleans during hurricanes greater than category 2. As the horrific pictures flowed from the New Orleans Superdome and Morial Convention Center, Americans asked, "Where is the Red Cross?" Red Cross storm shelters were moved to higher ground north of Interstate 10 several years ago (American Red Cross 2005).

Simply put, New Orleans's emergency plan called for thousands of the city's most vulnerable population to be left behind in their homes, shelters, and hospitals (Schleifstein 2005). A *Times-Picayune* reporter, Bruce Nolan (2005), summed up the emergency transportation plan: "City, state and federal emergency officials are preparing to give the poorest of New Orleans' poor a historically blunt message: In the event of a major hurricane, you're on your own." The New Orleans Rapid Transit Authority (RTA) emergency plan designated sixty-four buses and ten lift vans to transport residents to shelters. This plan was woefully inadequate since the larger buses only hold about sixty people each.

Transporting an estimated 100,000 to 134,000 people out of harm's way is no small undertaking. Given the size of the transit-dependent population, some transportation experts estimate that at least two thousand buses would have been needed to evacuate all New Orleans residents who needed transportation (Litman 2005). Most of the city's five hundred transit and school buses were without drivers. About 190 RTA buses were lost to flooding. The thirteen hundred RTA employees were dispersed across the country and many are homeless (Eggler 2005).

A lack of car ownership and inadequate public transit services in New Orleans and most U.S. cities with a high proportion of "captive" transit-dependent residents exacerbate social, economic, and racial isolation— especially for disabled, elderly, low-income, and people of color residents who already have limited transportation options. Katrina highlighted the problem our nation's nondrivers and transit-dependent residents face every day. As jobs and opportunity flee to the distant suburbs, where public transit is inadequate or nonexistent, persons without cars are left behind. In the end, all Americans pay for the social isolation and concentrated poverty that ensue from poor urban and regional planning (Bullard, Johnson, and Torres 2004).

The bill for replacing and repairing the roads and bridges destroyed by Hurricane Katrina could exceed $2.3 billion. Repairing the damage to interstate highways and major state roads, such as I-10, alone could cost $1.5 billion, to be paid with federal funds. An estimated $77 million of repairs are needed on another nine thousand miles of "off-system roads" in the disaster area. These roads are not controlled by the local government, and are not repaired or maintained with federal dollars. The $2.3 billion price tag does not include the damage to state ports, airports, levees, or mass transit systems, or funds to relieve traffic gridlock on Baton Rouge's streets, which are now filled with vehicles from New Orleans evacuees (*Times-Picayune* 2005).

Geography of Vulnerability: Why Race and Place Matter

Race maps closely with the geography of environmental risks. Katrina's environmental devastation lies in a region that is disproportionately poor and African American. Before Katrina, New Orleans was struggling with a wide range of environmental justice and health concerns, including an older housing stock with lots of lead paint. More than 50 percent (some studies place this figure at around 70 percent) of children living in the inner-city neighborhoods of New Orleans had blood lead levels above the current guideline of ten micrograms per deciliter, which is defined as the "level of concern" by the Centers for Disease Control and Prevention (Rabito, White, and Shorter 2004). Childhood lead poisoning in some New Orleans black neighborhoods was as high as 67 percent.

Environmental health problems related to environmental exposure were hot-button issues in New Orleans long before Katrina's floodwaters emptied out the city. New Orleans's location on the Mississippi River industrial corridor increased its vulnerability to environmental threats. Dozens of toxic "time bombs" along this chemical corridor, the eighty-five-mile stretch from Baton Rouge to New Orleans, made "Cancer Alley" a major environmental justice battleground (Wright 2005).

There are questions about what a "new" New Orleans should look like. There is even talk about some "low-lying" neighborhoods, inhabited largely by African Americans, not being rebuilt, such as the sealed-off Lower Ninth Ward. It is no accident that blacks tend to live in the lowest-lying areas of the city (DeParle 2005). Residents fear that environmental reasons—location in a floodplain, environmental contamination, and new zoning codes—may be used to kill off their neighborhoods.

Black residents have deep-seated fears and resentments that they will once again be left out of the rebuilding with decisions driven more by race than by topography. Some of New Orleans's white power elites— the heads of law firms, tourist businesses, and conservation groups— have a vision and plan for the recovery, restoration, and rebuilding of New Orleans: "smaller and more upscale" (Thomas and Campo-Flores 2005).

Even the plan and color-coded maps crafted by the Urban Land Institute (ULI), a group called in to advise Mayor Nagin's Bring Back New

Orleans Commission, shrink most of eastern New Orleans East and Gen-tilly, the northern part of Lakeview, and parts of the Lower Ninth Ward, Broadmoor, Mid-City, and Hargrove areas. The ULI panel of fifty specialists also advised New Orleans leaders to concentrate city rebuild-ing efforts to those areas that occupy the "high ground" (Carr 2005). Clearly, shrinking New Orleans neighborhoods disproportionately shrinks black votes, black political power, and black wealth.

Before rebuilding and reconstruction in New Orleans can begin in earnest, mountains of debris and toxic waste must be cleaned up and dis-posed in an environmentally sound way. Katrina left behind "a complex array of environmental health problems" (Centers for Disease Control and Prevention and EPA 2005). Katrina dumped over 63 million cubic yards of debris in Louisiana and 62.5 million cubic yards of debris in Mississippi. In contrast, Hurricane Andrew in 1992 generated 20 million cubic yards of debris. Louisiana officials are faced with an enormous dis-posal challenge from Katrina. Some of the disposal methods suggested have come under fire from environmentalists, environmental justice leaders, and the EPA.

The Army Corps of Engineers is charged with cleaning up miles of sediments laced with cancer-causing chemicals, toxic metals, industrial compounds, petroleum products, and banned insecticides, all at levels that pose potential cancer risk or other long-term hazards (Loftis 2005a). This is likely to be the "mother of all toxic cleanups" (*Business Week* 2005). Much of the contaminated topsoil where 110,000 New Orleans flooded homes sit can be scooped up and replaced with clean soil. Clean-ing up the muck that seeped into houses is a major challenge, however.

Health officials are now seeing a large number of evacuees afflicted with "Katrina cough," an illness believed to be linked to mold and dust (Gold and Simmons 2005). Individuals who otherwise normally don't have allergies have been coming down with the illness. It is especially worrisome for people with health problems—such as AIDS, asthma, and other serious respiratory illnesses—who may reenter their homes. Molds are not just an irritant but can also trigger episodes and set up life-threatening infections when normal immune systems are weakened. Mold spores are known triggers of asthma attacks—an illness that dis-proportionately affects African Americans.

Generally, government air quality tests focus on toxins, such as benzene, in areas where Katrina caused oil spills. The government does not have regulatory standards for either indoor or outdoor levels of mold spores. Independent tests conducted by the Natural Resources Defense Council (NRDC) in mid-November found dangerously high mold counts in New Orleans's air (Natural Resources Defense Council 2005). The outdoor counts in most flooded neighborhoods tested by the NRDC—including New Orleans East, the Lower Ninth Ward, Chalmette, Uptown, Mid-City, and the Garden District—showed levels as high as 77,000 spores per cubic meter at one site in Chalmette, and 81,000 spores per cubic meter at another site in the Uptown area. The National Allergy Bureau of the American Academy of Allergy and Immunology considers any outdoor mold spore level of greater than 50,000 spores per cubic meter to be a serious health threat.

Katrina caused six major oil spills releasing 7.4 million gallons of oil, or 61 percent as much as the 11 million gallons that leaked into Alaska's Prince William Sound from the *Exxon Valdez* in 1989 (Cone and Powers 2005). The storm hit 60 underground storage tanks, 5 Superfund sites, and 466 industrial facilities that stored highly dangerous chemicals before the storm, and disabled more than 1,000 drinking-water systems, creating a "toxic soup" with e. *coli* in the floodwaters far exceeding EPA's safe levels (Cone 2005).

Katrina left behind an estimated 22 million tons of debris, with more than half, 12 million tons, left in Orleans Parish (Griggs 2005). Flooded homes contained over 1 million pieces of "white goods," such as refrigerators, stoves, and freezers, that require disposal. An additional 350,000 automobiles must be drained of oil and gasoline and then recycled; 60,000 boats may need to be destroyed; and 300,000 underground fuel tanks along with 42,000 tons of hazardous waste must be collected and properly disposed of at licensed facilities (Varney and Moller 2005). Government officials peg the numbers of cars lost in New Orleans alone at 145,000.

An estimated 140,000 to 160,000 homes in Louisiana may need to be demolished and disposed of (U.S. EPA and Louisiana Department of Environmental Quality 2005). More than 110,000 of New Orleans's 180,000 houses were flooded, and half sat for days or weeks in more than 6 feet of water. As many as 30,000 to 50,000 homes citywide may have to be demolished, while many others could be saved with extensive repairs.

Agricultural Street Landfill Community: A "Black Love Canal"

What gets cleaned up, where the waste is disposed, and what get rebuilt and where are all key environmental and social equity issues. Hurricane Betsy struck Louisiana and New Orleans in 1965. Betsy hit the mostly black and poor New Orleans Lower Ninth Ward especially hard (Wright 2005). A disproportionate share of Lower Ninth Ward residents did not receive sufficient post-disaster financial assistance in the form of loans and other support to revitalize the area. Betsy accelerated the decline of the neighborhood and out-migration of many of its longtime residents.

Debris from Betsy was buried in the Agricultural Street Landfill— located in a predominantly black New Orleans neighborhood.[2] Over 390 homes were built on the northern portion of the ninety-five-acre landfill site from 1976 to 1986. The Agricultural Street Landfill neighborhood was added to the National Priorities List as a Superfund site in 1994 due to toxic contaminants such as metals, polycyclic aromatic hydrocarbons (PAHs), volatile organic compounds, and pesticides.

The actual cleanup began in 1998 and was completed in 2001. The Concerned Citizens of Agricultural Street Landfill filed a class-action suit against the city of New Orleans for damages and the cost of relocation. It took nine years to bring this case to court. The case was still pending before Katrina struck. It is ironic that the environmental damage wrought by Katrina may force the cleanup and relocation of the Agricultural Street Landfill community from the dump site.

Weeks after Katrina struck, the Louisiana Department of Environmental Quality (LDEQ) allowed New Orleans to open the two-hundred-acre Old Gentilly Landfill to dump construction and demolition waste from the storm (Burdeau 2005). Federal regulators ordered the unlined landfill closed in the 1980s. LDEQ officials insist that the old landfill meets all standards. Residents and environmentalists disagree with state officials about the safety and suitability of dumping at the old landfill. Even some high-ranking elected officials have expressed fear that the reopening of the Old Gentilly Landfill could create an ecological nightmare (Russell 2005). The landfill caught fire four days after environmentalists filed a lawsuit to block the dumping (WDSU 2005).

The Color of Money and Disaster Assistance

Race plays out in natural disaster survivors' ability to rebuild, replace infrastructure, obtain loans, and locate temporary and permanent housing. Hurricanes and other natural disasters increase competition for housing in unaffected areas. Disasters place a special burden on black renters and home buyers seeking replacement housing, exposing them to housing discrimination. Disasters also expose the survivors to price gouging, home repair scams, banking and insurance redlining, and predatory lending practices.

A 2003 Association of Community Organizations for Reform Now (2003, 3) report, *The Great Divide*, found that "lower-income and minority homebuyers, primarily African Americans, have become more and more reliant on subprime loans when buying a home." Risk factors do not explain racial differences in subprime lending (Bradford 2002). African Americans in New Orleans are more than three times as likely as white borrowers to get high-interest loans.

In 2004, African Americans in New Orleans were twice as likely as their white counterparts to have their loans rejected—20.41 and 10.5 percent, respectively (Federal Financial Institutions Examination Council 2004). In December 2005, the National Fair Housing Alliance (NFHA), released a report, *No Home for the Holidays*, documenting high rates of housing discrimination against African Americans displaced by Hurricane Katrina (National Fair Housing Alliance 2005).

The NFHA conducted tests over the telephone to determine what both African American and white home seekers were told about unit availability, rent, discounts, and other terms and conditions of apartment leasing. In 66 percent of these tests—forty-three of sixty-five instances—white callers were favored over African American ones. Also, the NFHA conducted five matched pair tests in which persons visited apartment complexes. In those five tests, whites were favored over African Americans three times. The NFHA conducted an investigation of rental housing practices in five states to determine whether victims of Katrina would be treated unfairly based on their race.[3]

Based on the evidence uncovered by testing conducted in seventeen cities, the NFHA filed five race-based housing discrimination complaints against rental housing complexes located in Dallas, Texas; Birmingham, Alabama; and Gainesville, Florida (National Fair Housing Alliance 2005, 2). The NFHA will conduct further testing in 2006 to assess the treatment of displaced people based on national origin, disability, and family status.

Louisiana was slated to receive seventy-eight thousand trailers and mobile homes. Four months after the storm, only twenty-three thousand Federal Emergency Management Agency (FEMA) trailers in Louisiana were occupied (Nelson 2005). Some Louisiana parishes near New Orleans adopted "emergency ordinances" limiting the density of mobile home parks. Some small, white rural towns have adopted a NIMBY attitude to keep out "temporary housing" (Chang, Soundararajan, and Johnson 2005). No one, including FEMA (which provides the trailers and mobile homes), homeowners (who are trying to protect their property values), and Katrina victims (who must live in the tight quarters), is served well if temporary "Katrina ghettos" are created.

The NIMBY stance has also cropped up in New Orleans neighborhoods, keeping 17,777 trailers that FEMA has on hand in Louisiana from being delivered immediately (Nelson 2005). The mayor's plan to site trailers in city parks was met with stiff opposition. Opponents expressed concerns about crime, lower property values, and the need for children to have recreational space. Much of the supercharged trailer park discussions, however, bring entrenched race and class divisions to the surface. In late December 2005, FEMA had placed only 1,632 travel trailers and mobile homes in New Orleans—a small fraction of the 30,000 the agency eventually expects to provide.

Some temporary homes have not proved to be that temporary. Thousands left homeless by last year's devastating hurricanes are still waiting for new or repaired housing while living in hotels, temporary trailers, and mobile homes. Mobile homes are derisively known as "storm magnets" because of the endless reports over the years of trailer parks being demolished during bad weather. More than nine thousand families were living in temporary FEMA housing in Florida when Hurricane Dennis slammed into the Florida panhandle. That number was down from a peak of about fifteen thousand after four hurricanes hit the state in 2004 (Becker 2005).

African Americans seeking housing in the Deep South are routinely met with discrimination. Katrina worsened this problem for blacks and intensified the competition for affordable housing. For example, the East Baton Rouge Parish population surged from 425,000 to 1.2 million as a result of Katrina (Naughton and Hosenball 2005). Katrina has made Baton Rouge one of the fastest-growing region in the country (Mulligan and Fausset 2005). The influx of these new residents to the region has created traffic gridlock and crowded the schools. Many of the mostly white suburban communities and small towns are not known for their hospitality toward blacks. Thousands of black hurricane evacuees face the added burden of "closed doors" and housing discrimination, while their white counterparts are given preference based on "white privilege."

Who gets approved for loans is not always based on how much money a person makes, or their debt ratio or credit score. Race still operates in the mortgage industry. In 2004, the nation's ten-largest banks denied African American applicants twice as often as whites (Applebaum and Mellnik 2005). African Americans were four times as likely as whites to get high interest rates for mortgage loans. African Americans with incomes above $100,000 a year were charged higher interest rates than whites with incomes below $40,000.

Both FEMA and the U.S. Small Business Administration (SBA) have been swamped with requests for disaster assistance. FEMA doesn't offer small business loans but does provide emergency cash grants up to $26,200 per person for housing, medical, and other disaster-related needs (Abrams 2005). Some Katrina victims claim they were unfairly denied emergency aid (Sullivan 2005). Many accuse FEMA of leaving them behind a second time.

SBA disaster loans serve as the only salvation for companies without insurance or whose insurance didn't cover all the damage. The physical (property) disaster business loan—which provides businesses of any size with funds to repair or replace real estate, equipment, fixtures, machinery, and inventory—and the economic injury disaster loan are both available to small businesses that have suffered substantial economic injury resulting from a disaster. Both types of disaster loans are also available up to $1.5 million (Rosenberg 2005).

Yet SBA disaster loans are not just for small businesses. Homeowners and renters who suffered damage from Hurricane Katrina are also eligible for low-interest disaster loans from the SBA (Willis 2005). The SBA makes the majority of its disaster loans to homeowners and renters. The loans are for repairing or rebuilding disaster damage to private property owned by homeowners and renters. Homeowners may borrow up to $200,000 to repair or replace damaged or destroyed real estate. Homeowners and renters may borrow up to $40,000 to repair or replace damaged or destroyed personal property, including vehicles. SBA disaster home loans have low interest rates (less than 3 percent) and long terms (up to thirty years), helping to make recovery more financially affordable.

A *New York Times* study discovered that as of mid-December 2005, the SBA had processed only a third of the 276,000 home loan applications it had received (Eaton and Nixon 2005). The SBA also rejected 82 percent of the applications it received, a higher percentage than in most previous disasters. Well-off neighborhoods like Lakeview have received 47 percent of the loan approvals, while poverty-stricken neighborhoods have gotten 7 percent. The loan denial problem is not limited to poor black areas. Middle-class black neighborhoods in New Orleans East also have lower loan rates. This trend could spell doom for rebuilding black New Orleans neighborhoods.

In November 2005, several legal groups—Washington, DC–based Lawyers Committee for Civil Rights, the Public Interest Law Project of Oakland, California, and the Equal Justice Society of San Francisco—sued FEMA, claiming the agency "failed to fulfill its mandate" to provide money, housing, and other disaster assistance (Pope 2005). The class action lawsuit, filed on behalf of residents in Louisiana, Mississippi, and Alabama, is one of the first related to the agency's response to Katrina. Some Katrina victims see FEMA's slow and inept response in getting aid, loans, and grants to them as a "second disaster."

Insurance Redlining

Katrina set the stage for a monumental tug-of-war between insurers and the storm victims. Insurance adjusters have begun the arduous task of processing the mountain of insurance claims (Paul 2005). The total economic losses from the storm are expected to exceed $125 billion, with insurance companies paying an estimated $40 to $60 billion (Chu 2005). How much financial responsibility the insurance companies end up bearing will depend on how insurers handle the claims—the determination of "wind" or "flood" damage.

FEMA estimates that the majority of households and businesses in the twelve Hurricane Katrina–affected counties in Alabama, Mississippi, and Louisiana do not have flood coverage. The agency also estimates that only 12.7 percent of the households in Alabama, 15 percent in Mississippi, and 46 percent in Louisiana have flood insurance. Similarly, only 8 percent of the businesses in hurricane-affected counties in Alabama, 15 percent in Mississippi, and 30 percent in Louisiana have flood coverage (Chu 2005).

Because of the enormity of the damage in the wake of Katrina, insurance companies may try to categorize a lot of legitimate wind claims as flood related. This problem of white-collar insurance "looting" will likely hit low-income, elderly, disabled, and people of color storm victims the hardest because these groups probably have their insurance with small companies. Disaster researchers Walter G. Peacock and Chris Girard (1997, 180–81) make this point in their study of Hurricane Andrew in South Florida:

Traveling through the neighborhoods in South Dade after Hurricane Andrew was a graphic lesson in racial differences in insurance coverage. Due to the absence of street signs and even house numbers it was very difficult to find specific addresses. To aid insurance adjusters many homeowners spray painted the name of their insurance companies, along with their addresses, on the outside walls of their homes. Driving through predominately White neighborhoods, such as the famous Country Walk development, revealed a virtual *Who's Who* of insurance companies: State Farm, Allstate, and Prudential. In contrast, a drive through predominately Black areas showed names that were far from familiar, such as Utah, Delta, Ocean Casualty, and Florida Fire and Casualty. At minimum, this anecdotal evidence suggests some degree of the market segmentation reflected in the dual economy literature.

Because of the legacy of Jim Crow segregation, many African American consumers in the Louisiana, Mississippi, and Alabama Gulf Coast region may be concentrated in the secondary insurance market—smaller and less well-known insurance firms. This could prove problematic for Katrina victims. Nearly a dozen small insurance companies collapsed after Hurricane Andrew, which cost the industry about $23 billion in today's dollars (Treaster 2005). Andrew was the most expensive single hurricane until Katrina.

By September 7, 2005, State Farm Insurance (2005), the largest home and automobile insurer in the Gulf Coast region, had begun processing 223,000 Katrina-related claims. Katrina is expected to generate $40 to $60 billion in insurance loses, and it will take at least two years to process all of the claims. The insurance industry must grapple with the largest-ever loss and record number of individual claims—1.6 million from Katrina, along with another million from hurricanes Rita and Wilma (Starkman 2005). The industry's handling of the estimated $1.3 trillion in claims is shrouded in secrecy, and companies are not required to disclose their claims practices, including how quickly claims are processed, how many are denied, and for what reason. This places consumers at a sizable disadvantage when disputing settlements they perceive to be unfair and inadequate.

A New Orleans Katrina victim whose home was severely damaged by the storm filed a class action suit against American International Group and its subsidiary, Audubon, charging the companies with failure to assist their policyholders. The American International Group and Audubon are underwriters and service providers of Louisiana Citizens Fair Plan, a program that provides homeowners' policies of last resort to some four hundred thousand households that cannot get insurance elsewhere, including many low-income and black homeowners in New Orleans and the surrounding area.[4] Many Fair Plan policyholders were struggling before Katrina struck.

In late November 2005, the National Flood Insurance Program briefly ran out of money for the first time since it was founded in 1968, and some insurance companies temporarily stopped issuing checks (Thomas 2005). Congress approved an additional $18.5 billion for the National Flood Insurance Program to borrow from the U.S. Treasury each year.

The program currently covers around 4.5 million policyholders in more than 20,000 communities in floodplains and other low-lying areas (Associated Press 2005c). It received more than 204,000 claims from Katrina, 13,000 from Rita, and 12,000 from Wilma. FEMA estimates that claims from the three hurricanes could reach $23 billion.

Building Trust, Fixing Levees, and Restoring Marshes

The Army Corps of Engineers is expected to have the New Orleans levees shored up to withstand at least a category 3 storm in time for the 2006 hurricane season. The Bush administration pledged $1.5 billion for New Orleans's levee system, but stopped short of promising protection against a catastrophic category 5 hurricane (Warrick and Baker 2005). A big part of Katrina's devastation resulted from poorly designed, built, and maintained levees, and the destruction of wetlands, marshes, and barrier islands (Loftis 2005b).

Fixing the levees appears to be less controversial than restoring the coastal marshes. Before Katrina, coastal Louisiana lost about thirty-nine square miles of land per year from 1958 to 1976. The land loss rate since then has slowed to twenty-four square miles a year. Louisiana accounts for 80 percent of the nation's loss of wetlands. The costs of protection against a category 5 hurricane—involving stronger and higher levees, new drainage canals, and environmental restoration—would likely run well over $32 billion (*New York Times* 2005).

As African American residents of the hardest-hit areas struggle to return home, architects and real estate developers lick their chops at the lucrative opportunities for land use planning and construction in New Orleans. Landlords seeking to profit from rumors of gentrification and soaring land values are erecting new barriers. Rents in high and dry areas have tripled. Black renters face wholesale expulsion (Davis 2005). Ironically, green-building planning is moving forward at the same time that New Orleans and Gulf Coast tenants are being evicted from their apartments and their belongings tossed on the curb (Nossiter 2005). Evictions accelerated after the expiration of the moratorium imposed by Louisiana governor Kathleen Babineaux Blanco (Scallan 2005).

FEMA has issued revised flood elevation advisories to coastal areas in the region (Bowen 2005). Official maps are not expected for at least two years (FEMA's expedited schedule). Although the new figures are intended to guide designers and developers, they have sparked debate. Some people fear FEMA's guidelines could make some areas off-limits or prohibitively expensive to build in, pricing some people out of their current homes.

A Vision of a "New" New Orleans

Rebuilding New Orleans will be one of the largest urban reconstruction programs in the country. In a meeting held in Baton Rouge, a cross-section of black New Orleans elected officials, business and civic leaders, and educators expressed concern about "bringing people home."[5] The repopulation of New Orleans is a major challenge. Who the city is repopulated with has important social, economic, cultural, civil rights, and political implications.

Hurricane Katrina has opened the door for wholesale land speculation and redevelopment scenarios that plan "for" rather than "with" the storm victims. What gets built and redeveloped (and for whom), and who participates in the rebuilding process, are major economic justice issues. A small group of private companies, nongovernmental organizations, and members of think tanks have divided up "precompleted" no-bid contracts. Safeguards have been waived that would normally protect against fraud and waste (Drinkard 2005). For example, 80 percent of the $1.5 billion FEMA contracts for Katrina were awarded without competitive bidding.

FEMA's handling of contracts even caused the inspector general of the Department of Homeland Security some "apprehension" (Turley 2005). A predatory form of "disaster capitalism" exploits the desperation and fear created by catastrophe to engage in radical social and economic engineering. The reconstruction industry works so quickly and efficiently that privatization and landgrabs are usually completed before the local population knows what hit it.

Katrina's devastation has exposed the special vulnerability of African Americans, who for centuries have been cheated out of their land or driven from it through trickery, intimidation, violence, and even murder. In some instances, government officials approved the illegal landgrabs or took part in them. Over the past five decades, government-subsidized initiatives have cleared "blighted" neighborhoods and slums under various urban renewal or "Negro removal" programs. Urban renewal is "part of a general struggle over the control of land" (Stone 1976, 45).

Katrina emptied out black New Orleans in a way successive waves of urban renewal programs could not. Yet the process of depopulating the city's mostly black public housing, through the Hope VI program, predates Katrina. Nationally, Hope VI was responsible for a net loss of more than fifty thousand units of desperately needed low-income housing.

The Center for Community Change's (2003) report called *A HOPE Unseen: Voices from the Other Side of Hope VI* says Hope VI is used to destroy communities and deprive people of their existing affordable housing. All eyes are watching New Orleans's rebuilding efforts, especially how it addresses the repopulation of its historically African American neighborhoods and the construction of strategically sited public housing. Before Katrina, New Orleans's St. Thomas public housing development was demolished in the mostly white Uptown neighborhood to make way for upscale town houses and a Wal-Mart.

Six in ten Hurricane Katrina evacuees living in shelters in Houston said the slow response to the storm had made them feel that the government doesn't care about people like them, according to a recent poll by the *Washington Post*, the Henry J. Kaiser Family Foundation, and the Harvard School of Public Health (Morin and Rein 2005). Katrina survivors, who make up the large "African American diaspora," are dispersed all across the United States. Physically and emotionally battered (but not broken), homes, jobs, and neighborhoods destroyed, some evacuees have vowed not to return, while others have indicated that they will "do whatever it takes to return to their city."[6]

Notes

1. For an in-depth discussion of the 2005 hurricane season that ravaged the U.S. Gulf Coast, see *Atlanta Journal-Constitution* (2005).

2. For a detailed account of the dumping at the landfill, Lyttle (2004).

3. From mid-September through mid-December 2005, the NFHA conducted telephone tests of rental housing providers in seventeen cities in five states: Alabama (Birmingham, Mobile, Huntsville, and Montgomery), Florida (Gainesville, Tallahassee, and Pensacola), Georgia (Atlanta, Columbus, Macon, and Savannah), Tennessee (Nashville, Chattanooga, and Memphis), and Texas (Houston, Dallas, and Waco).

4. See "Class Action Suit Filed against AIG over Katrina Claims," October 13, 2005, available at ⟨http://www.consumeraffairs.com/news04/2005/katrina_aig .html⟩.

5. Based on the authors' notes from a meeting of black New Orleans community leaders held in the Louisiana state capitol in Baton Rouge, September 12, 2005.

6. Interviews conducted with New Orleans evacuees who were living in Atlanta. The interviews were conducted with evacuees while they waited at the American Red Cross office in Atlanta, September 12, 2005.

References

Abrams, R. 2005. Helping Small Businesses in the Wake of Katrina. *USA Today*, September 1. Available at ⟨http://www.usatoday.com/money/smallbusiness/ columnist/abrams/2005-09-01-small-business-katrina_x.htm⟩ (accessed May 14, 2006).

American Red Cross. 2005. Hurricane Katrina: Why Is the Red Cross Not in New Orleans. Available at ⟨http://www.redcross.org/faq/0,1096,0_682_4524,00 .html⟩.

Appelbaum, B., and T. Mellnik. 2005. The Hard Truth in Lending: Blacks Four Times More Likely Than Whites to Get High Rates. *Charlotte Observer*, August 28. Available at ⟨http://www.charlotte.com/mld/charlotte/business/ special_packages/lending/12496753.htm⟩ (accessed May 13, 2006).

Association of Community Organizations for Reform Now. 2003. *The Great Divide: Home Purchase Mortgage Lending Nationally and in 115 Metropolitan Areas*. Washington, DC: ACORN.

Associated Press. 2005a. Mandatory Evacuation Ordered for New Orleans. August 28. Available at ⟨http://www.letxa.com/katrina/nola-mandatory-evac-bush .html⟩ (accessed May 13, 2006).

Associated Press. 2005b. Storm's Victims Unlike Most Americans. *MSNBC.com*, September 4. Available at ⟨http://www.msnbc.msn.com/id/9207190⟩.

Associated Press. 2005c. Flood Insurance Funding to Resume. *Clarion Ledger* (Jackson), November 19. Available at ⟨http://www.clarionledger.com/apps/pbcs .dll/article?AID=/20051119/NEWS0110/511190344/0/FEAT07⟩.

Atlanta Journal-Constitution. 2005. The Worst Hurricane Season Ever. November 30, A1.

Becker, A. 2005. Storm-Resistant Homes a Long Time Coming: Left Homeless Last Year, Still Holed Up in Temporary Housing. *Dallas Morning News*, August 28, 6A.

Bourne, J. K., Jr. 2004. Gone with the Water. *National Geographic* (October). Available at ⟨http://altreligion.about.com/gi/dynamic/offsite.htm?site=http://www3.nationalgeographic.com/ngm/0410/feature5/⟩.

Bowen, T. S. 2005. Gulf Coast States Consider Code and Zoning Change. *Architectural Record*, November 18. Available at ⟨http://archrecord.construction.com/news/daily/archives/051118code.asp⟩.

Bradford, C. 2002. *Risk or Race? Racial Disparities and the Subprime Refinance Market*. Washington, DC: Neighborhood Revitalization Project.

Bullard, R. D., G. S. Johnson, and A. O. Torres. 2004. *Highway Robbery: Transportation Racism and New Routes to Equity*. Boston: South End Press.

Burdeau, C. 2005. New Orleans Area Becoming a Dumping Ground. Associated Press, October 31.

Business Week. 2005. The Mother of All Toxic Cleanups. September 26. Available at ⟨http://www.businessweek.com/magazine/content/05_39/b3952055.htm⟩.

Carr, M. 2005. Rebuilding Should Begin on High Ground, Group Says. *Times-Picayune*, November 19. Available at ⟨http://www.nola.com/news/t-p/frontpage/index.ssf?/base/news-4/113238540235800.xml⟩.

Center for Community Change. 2003. *A HOPE Unseen: Voices from the Other Side of Hope VI*. Washington, DC: CCC. Available at ⟨http://communitychange.org/shared/publications/downloads/hope_iv/00_HOPEVIfull.doc⟩.

Centers for Disease Control and Prevention and EPA. 2005. *Environmental Health Needs and Habitability Assessment*. Joint Task Force on Hurricane Katrina Response, Atlanta, September 17. Available at ⟨http://www.bt.cdc.gov/disasters/hurricanes/katrina/pdf/envassessment.pdf#search='centers%20for%20disease%20control%20katrina%20contamination'⟩.

Chang, J., T. Soundararajan, and A. Johnson. 2005. Getting Home before It's Gone. September 26. Available at ⟨http://www.alternet.org/katrina/25930⟩.

Chu, K. 2005. Wind or Flood: Fights with Insurers Loom. *USA Today*, September 20, A2.

City of New Orleans. 2005. *City of New Orleans Comprehensive Emergency Management Plan*. Available at ⟨http://www.cityofno.com⟩.

Cone, M. 2005. Floodwaters a Soup of Pathogens, EPA Finds. *Los Angeles Times*, September 8, A18.

Cone, M., and A. Powers. 2005. EPA Warns Muck Left by Floodwaters Is Highly Contaminated. *Los Angeles Times*, September 16, A16.

Davis, M. 2005. Gentrifying Diversity. *Mother Jones Online*, October 28. Available at ⟨http://www.alternet.org/katrina/27391⟩.

DeParle, J. 2005. Broken Levees, Unbroken Barriers: What Happens to a Race Deferred. *New York Times*, September 4, section 4, 1.

Drinkard, J. 2005. No-Bid Storm Contracts Prompt Warnings. *USA Today*, September 27, 2A.

Eaton, L., and R. Nixon. 2005. Loans to Homeowners Along Gulf Coast Lag. *New York Times*, December 15, 1.

Eggler, B. 2005. RTA Back on Track Slowly, Surely. *Times-Picayune*, October 14, B1.

Federal Financial Institutions Examination Council. 2004. *Home Mortgage Disclosure Act: Aggregate Report Search by State*. Washington, DC: FFIEC. Available at ⟨http://www.ffiec.gov/hmdaadwebreport/aggwelcome.aspx⟩.

Gold, S., and A. M. Simmons. 2005. Katrina Cough Floats Around. *Los Angeles Times*, November 4. Available at ⟨http://www.latimes.com/news/nationworld/nation/la-na-cough4nov04,0,7514027.story?coll=la-home-headlines⟩.

Griggs, T. 2005. Rebuilding to Be Slow, Expensive. *Advocate*, September 11, 12A.

Hsu, S. S., and D. Balz. 2005. Ins and Outs of Emergency Evacuation. *Washington Post*, September 24, A9.

Katz, B., M. Fellowes, and N. Holmes. 2005. The State of New Orleans. *New York Times*, December 7, A33.

Kleinberg, E. 2003. *Black Cloud: The Deadly Hurricane of 1928*. New York: Carroll and Graf Publishers.

Laska, S. 2004. What If Hurricane Ivan Had Not Missed New Orleans? *National Hazards Observer*, November 4. Available at ⟨http://www.colorado.edu/hazards/o/nov04/nov04c.html⟩ (accessed May 13, 2006).

Litman, T. 2005. *Lesson from Katrina and Rita: What Major Disasters Can Teach Transportation Planners*. Victoria, BC: Victoria Transport Policy Institute.

Loftis, R. L. 2005a. Extreme Cleanup on Tap in New Orleans. *Dallas Morning News*, November 6. Available at ⟨http://www.dallasnews.com/sharedcontent/dws/dn/latestnews/stories/110605dntswtoxic.c3d4a5d.html⟩.

Loftis, R. L. 2005b. New Orleans Rebirth Depends on Marshes. *Dallas Morning News*, December 10.

Lyttle, A. 2004. Agricultural Street Landfill Environmental Justice Case Study. Available at ⟨http://www.umich.edu/~snre492/Jones/agstreet.htm⟩ (accessed October 6).

Morin, R., and L. Rein. 2005. Many New Orleans Evacuees Won't Return. *Washington Post*, September 15, A1.

Mulligan, T. S., and R. Fausset. 2005. Baton Rouge a Booming Haven for the Displaced. *Los Angeles Times*, September 7, A1.

National Fair Housing Alliance. 2005. *No Home for the Holidays: Report on Housing Discrimination against Hurricane Katrina Survivors—Executive Summary*. Washington, DC: NFHA. Available at ⟨http://www.nationalfairhousing

.org/html/Press%20Releases/Katrina/Hurricane%20Katrina%20Survivors%20-%20Report.pdf〉.

Natural Resources Defense Council. 2005. New Private Testing Shows Dangerously High Mold Counts in New Orleans Air. Press release, November 16. Available at 〈http://www.nrdc.org/media/pressreleases/051116.asp〉.

Naughton, K., and M. Hosenball. 2005. Cash and "Cat 5" Chaos. *Newsweek*, September 26, 36.

Nelson, R. 2005. Not in My Backyard Cry Holding Up FEMA Trailers. *Times-Picayune*, December 26. Available at 〈http://www.nola.com/news/t-p/index.ssf?/base/news-4/1135580234129030.xml〉.

New York Times. 2005. Death of an American City. December 11, A11.

Nolan, B. 2005. In Storm, N.O. Wants No One Left Behind. *Times-Picayune*, July 24. Available at 〈http://www.mola.com/seach.ssf?/base/news-10/1122184560198030.xml?nola〉 (accessed May 13, 2006).

Nossiter, A. 2005. New Orleans Landlords Are Pitted against Tenants in Court. *New York Times*, November 4. Available at 〈http://www.nytimes.com/2005/11/04/national/nationalspecial/04evict.html?n=Top%2FNews%2FNational%2FU.S.%20States%2C%20Territories%20and%20Possessions%2Flouisiana〉.

Paul, P. C. 2005. You've Got to Make Them Feel Good about Something. *Atlanta Journal-Constitution*, September 18, Q7.

Peacock, W. G., and C. Girard. 1997. Ethnic and Racial Inequalities in Hurricane Damage and Insurance Settlements. In *Hurricane Andrew: Ethnicity, Gender, and the Sociology of Disasters*, ed. W. G. Peacock, B. H. Morrow, and H. Gladwin. New York: Routledge.

Perlstein, M., and B. Thevenot. 2004. Evacuation Isn't an Option for Many N.O. Area Residents. *Times Picayune*, September 15, A1.

Pope, J. 2005. Groups Sue FEMA on Storm Response: Suit Seeks to Unblock Certain Hindrances. *Times-Picayune*, November 11, 18.

Rabito, F. A., L. E. White, and C. Shorter. 2004. From Research to Policy: Targeting the Primary Prevention of Childhood Lead Poisoning. *Public Health Reports*, 119 (May–June): 271–278.

Riccardi, N. 2005. Many of Louisiana Dead over 60. *Atlanta Journal-Constitution*, November 6, A6.

Rosenberg, J. M. 2005. Small Business Loans Help with Rebuilding. *Houston Chronicle*, September 4.

Rusk, D. 2005. Measuring Regional Equity in the New Orleans Area: An Unsentimental Assessment. September 15. Available at 〈http://www.gamaliel.org/DavidRusk/NewOrleans/05Regional%20equity%20in%20New%20Orleans.pdf〉.

Russell, G. 2005. Landfill Reopening Is Raising New Stink. *Times-Picayune*, November 21. Available at 〈http://www.nola.com/news/t-p/frontpage/index.ssf?/base/news-4/1132559045240640.xml〉.

Russell, M. 2005. Being Disabled and Poor in New Orleans. *ZNet Daily Commentaries*, September 25. Available at ⟨http://www.zmag.org/sustainers/content/2005-09/25russell.cfm⟩ (accessed October 2).

Sauer, M. 2005. Dirty Little Secret: Disaster Laid Bare the Prevalence of Poverty in America. *San Diego Union-Tribune*, September 18. Available at ⟨http://www.signonsandiego.com/news/nation/katrina/20050918-9999-1c18poor.html⟩ (accessed June 13, 2006).

Scallan, M. 2005. After Katrina Storm, Many Tenants Are Evicted. *Times-Picayune*, October 20. Available at ⟨http://www.nola.com/news/t-/metro/index.ssf?/base/news-11/1129788228303820.xml⟩.

Schleifstein, M. 2005. Preparing for the Worst. *Times-Picayune*, May 31. Available at ⟨http://www.nola.com/news/t-p/frontpage/index.ssf?/base/news-3/1117519029150100.xml⟩ (accessed June 13, 2006).

Starkman, D. 2005. Same Insurance Claims, Different Results in La. Town. *Washington Post*, November 26, A1.

State Farm Insurance. 2005. State Farm: Hurricane Katrina Claims Top 200,000. September 8. Available at ⟨http://www.statefarm.com/media/release/hurr_katrina2.asp⟩.

State of Louisiana. 2000. *Southeast Louisiana Hurricane Evacuation and Sheltering Plan*. Baton Rouge: State of Louisiana. Available at ⟨www.ohsep.louisiana.gov/plans/EOPSupplementala.pdf⟩.

Stone, C. N. 1976. *Economic Growth and Neighborhood Discontent: System Bias in the Urban Renewal Program of Atlanta*. Chapel Hill: University of North Carolina Press.

Sullivan, B. 2005. FEMA Grants Leave Some Behind. *MSNBC*, October 19, Available at ⟨http://www.msnbc.msn.com/id/9655113⟩.

Thomas, E., and A. Campo-Flores. 2005. The Battle to Rebuild. *Newsweek*, October 3. Available at ⟨http://www.msnbc.msn.com/id/9469300/site/newsweek⟩.

Thomas, K. B. 2005. Hurricane Katrina: The Cleanup. *Time Magazine* 166, November 28, 32.

Times-Picayune. 2005. Road Damage May Exceed $2.3 Billion. September 18, C9.

Treaster, J. B. 2005. Gulf Coast Insurance Expected to Soar. *New York Times*, September 24, C1.

Turley, J. 2005. Hurricanes Bring Windfall for Lobbyists. *Atlanta Journal-Constitution*, October 3, A11.

U.S. Bureau of the Census. 2000. Orleans Parish, Louisiana. In *State and County Quick Facts*. Available at ⟨http://quickfacts.census.gov/qfd/states/22/22071.html⟩.

U.S. EPA and Louisiana Department of Environmental Quality. 2005. News Release: Top State and Federal Environmental Officials Discuss Progress and Tasks

Ahead after Katrina. September 30. Available at ⟨http://www.deq.state.la.us/news/pdf/administratorjohnson.pdf#search='katrina%20debris%20350%2C000%20automobiles'⟩.

Varney, J., and J. Moller. 2005. Huge Task of Cleaning Up Louisiana Will Take at Least a Year. *Newhouse News Service*, October 2. Available at ⟨http://www.newhousenews.com/archive/varney100305.html⟩.

Warrick, J., and P. Baker. 2005. Bush Pledges $1.5 Billion for New Orleans. *Washington Post*, December 16. Available at ⟨http://www.washingtonpost.com/wp-dyn/content/article/2005/12/15/AR2005121500874.html⟩.

WDSU. 2005. Hurricane Debris Catches Fire at Old Gentilly Landfill. November 4. Available at ⟨http://www.wdsu.com/news/4611257/detail.html?rss=no&psp=news⟩.

Willis, G. 2005. Disaster Relief: Five Tips: How to Call on the Disaster Relief Resources You Need. *CNN/Money*, September 16.

Wolshon, B. 2002. Planning for the Evacuation of New Orleans. *Institute of Transportation Engineers Journal* (February). Available at ⟨http://www.ite.org/⟩.

Wright, B. 2005. Living and Dying in Louisiana's Cancer Alley. In *The Quest for Environmental Justice: Human Rights and the Politics of Pollution*, ed. R. D. Bullard, 87–107. San Francisco: Sierra Club Books.

III

Transportation Equity

9

Confronting Transportation Sprawl in Metro Atlanta

Robert D. Bullard, Glenn S. Johnson, and Angel O. Torres

Atlanta is basically flat and landlocked, with no major bodies of water or mountains to constrain its outward growth. The city has come a long way since its humble beginning as an Indian village called Standing Peachtree, which was located at the confluence of Peachtree Creek and the Chattahoochee River (Metropolitan Planning Commission 1952, 12). Atlanta was burned to the ground by Union forces in 1864. By the 1880s, city officials were successful in promoting Atlanta as the "Gateway to the South." By 1895, Atlanta was celebrating its rebirth as the "Capital of the New South" (Rice 1983, 31).

A century later, Atlanta and its suburban neighbors are still capitalizing on the region's "growth machine" imagery. Atlanta has become the "Black Mecca" (Bullard 1991). In 2004, *Black Enterprise* hailed Atlanta as the "best" city for blacks (Padgett and Brown 2004), as mentioned in an earlier chapter. Metropolitan Atlanta has emerged as the commercial and financial center of the southeastern United States. The region is the center for federal operations as well as the center of communications and transportation.

Paying for Uneven Growth

Metropolitan Atlanta has experienced constant growth since the 1900s. The region has grown in population at an annual rate of 2.9 percent since 1950. The 1960s were considered the boom years in which Atlanta established its regional dominance. The 1970s and 1980s were characterized as a time when the city became increasingly black. During this same period, Atlanta experienced a steady decrease in its share of the metropolitan population since 1960. Metropolitan Atlanta continued to experience breakneck growth in the 1990s. An average of 71,000 people moved into the metropolitan area each year during the 1990s, compared to 61,788 in the 1980s (Atlanta Regional Commission 2003). The region gained more than 80,000 new residents each year since 2000. The ten-county metropolitan area (Cherokee, Cobb, Douglas, Clayton, Fayette, Fulton, Henry, Gwinnett, DeKalb, and Rockdale) had a population of over 3.7 million people as of April 1, 2003 (Atlanta Regional Commission 2003, 9).

The boundaries of the Atlanta metropolitan area doubled in the 1990s. The region measured 65 miles from north to south in 1990. Today, Atlanta's economic dominance reaches well beyond 110 miles from north to south (Leinberger 1998). Four counties (Fulton, DeKalb, Gwinnett, and Cobb) comprise just over half the land area in the ten-county region, but account for 77 percent of its 2004 population (Atlanta Regional Commission 2004a).

Much of the region's growth in the 1990s was characterized by suburban sprawl and economic disinvestment in Atlanta's central city (Goldberg 1997). The region added thousands of jobs during the 1990s. Most of the new jobs and newcomers settled outside the city. The city of Atlanta lagged far behind the job-rich suburbs. Atlanta captured about 40 percent of the region's jobs in 1980. By 1990, the city's share had slipped to 28.3 percent, and then 21.6 percent in 2001 (Atlanta Regional Commission 2003).

Clearly, Atlanta's northern suburbs reaped the lion's share of the jobs. From 1990 to 2000, Atlanta's northern suburbs added 273,250 jobs. This accounted for 48.3 percent of all jobs added in the region. Another 93,350 jobs or 16.5 percent were added in the southern part of the region. Only 40,425 jobs were added in the region's central core of Atlanta, representing only 7.1 percent of all jobs created during the height of the region's booming economy (Atlanta Regional Commission 2003).

In the ten-county region, nearly 47 percent of the workers commute outside their counties for work. Much of this mobility involves suburb-to-suburb commuting. Atlanta has the highest suburb-to-suburb commute among the nation's cities. Fewer than 60 percent of Atlantans

Figure 9.1
Ten-county Atlanta metropolitan region

work in the central city. The flight of jobs and white middle-income families to the suburbs has contributed to and exacerbated both economic as well as racial polarization in housing and schools.

The economic isolation of black Atlantans is complicated by inadequate public transit (limited, unaffordable, or inaccessible service and routes, and security and safety), lack of personal transportation (no privately owned car available to travel to work), and spatial mismatch (location of suitable jobs in areas that are inaccessible by public transportation). The majority of entry-level jobs in metro Atlanta are not within a quarter mile of public transportation. Only 11.3 percent of metro Atlanta's jobs are located within a three-mile radius of the CBD; 38.1 percent are located within a ten-mile radius, and 61.9 percent are located outside the ten-mile ring (Glaeser, Kahn, and Chu 2001).

Central city Atlanta has become increasingly black and poor. The region's middle-income suburbs that encircle the city are predominantly white. While suburbanization largely meant the out-migration of whites, some middle-income and poor black Atlantans also made the move to the suburbs. Middle-income blacks have found expanded homeownership opportunities in some Atlanta suburbs, while low-income blacks have found suburban rental units in the post-1996 Olympic apartment glut period.

The ten-county Atlanta metropolitan region added 180,425 housing units between 2000 and 2004—a 13.6 percent increase. The bulk of the housing was concentrated in northern Atlanta's suburbs, north of I-285. Much of the housing boom passed over the city of Atlanta. The city added only 14,732 new housing units between 2000 and 2004, or a 7.9 percent increase, compared to 41,983 units in Gwinnett (a 20 percent increase), 31,593 units in Fulton (a 9.1 percent increase), 16,658 units in Henry (a 38.6 percent increase) (Atlanta Regional Commission 2004b). These growth trends point to clear disparities between the mostly black city of Atlanta and the mostly white suburbs.

Highway Sprawl

Metropolitan Atlanta is struggling to get its roads and transit-balancing act together (Bullard, Johnson, and Torres 2000). For decades, the region has had a love affair with roads and highways (Bullard, Grisby, and Lee 1994; Bullard 2004). Because of the growing air pollution problem, the federal government placed limitations on road-building programs in the thirteen-county Atlanta nonattainment area. For many, transit was viewed as a real alternative to more roads, cars, gridlock, and air pollution. The Metropolitan Atlanta Regional Transit Authority (MARTA), however, is regional only in name, serving just two counties—Fulton and DeKalb—and the city of Atlanta.

The suburban job market is inaccessible to the predominantly African American, nondriving poor of inner-city Atlanta. Because jobs in the Atlanta area have moved to the suburbs, where public transit is minimal, they are virtually inaccessible to nondrivers. Thirty-nine percent of all black households in Atlanta do not have access to cars, and in 2000, only 34 percent of the region's jobs were within a one-hour public transit ride of low-income urban neighborhoods (Lewyn 2000). Moreover, the majority of the entry-level jobs in metropolitan Atlanta are not within a quarter mile of public transportation (Benfield, Raimi, and Chen 1999).

Race has literally stopped regional transit in its tracks. The outlying suburban counties of Cobb, Gwinnett, and Clayton opted out of MARTA and created their own "separate" bus systems. For many white suburbanites, MARTA stands for "Moving Africans Rapidly through Atlanta" and they want no part of it. MARTA is the nation's eighth-largest transit system and the only one in the country that does not receive any state-earmarked funds. In contrast, the Massachusetts Bay Transit Authority (MBTA), the nation's oldest and sixth largest, gets 20 percent of the state's five cents sales tax or about $680 million a year (Saporta 2004).

Traffic gridlock and polluted air help make Atlanta one of the "most sprawl-threatened" large cities in the United States (Sierra Club 1998, 5). The Atlanta region had more than 3.1 million registered vehicles in 2003, up from 1.9 million registered vehicles in 1986 (Atlanta Regional Commission 2003). The largest increase in registered vehicles during this period came in Gwinnett and Cobb Counties. The number of Gwinnett County vehicles jumped from 261,674 to 560,820 between 1986 and 2003. Similarly, Cobb County vehicles grew from 366,514 in 1985 to 541,465 in 2003. The two northern suburban counties alone added more than 474,097 vehicles to the region's crowded roads during this period.

The region's transportation dilemma is complicated by restricted use of the state's motor fuel tax. Georgia's motor fuel tax is one of the lowest in the nation. At 7.5 cents per gallon, the tax hardly discourages driving. The state taxing structure has no built-in incentives to support mass transportation. The Georgia motor fuel tax currently can only be used for roads and bridges. The end result is a state transportation agency that only pays lip service to mass transit. The real money goes to sprawl-driven roads.

Metropolitan Atlanta has been shortchanged in the state allocation of transportation funding for years. Much of this disparate treatment emanates from the state's rules on how motor fuel taxes can be spent. The gas tax can only be used for roads and bridges—and not a dime can go toward transit. Still, metro Atlantans do not get a fair return on the money they pay in gas taxes. For example, between 1992 and 1997, the ten-county region received back only fifty-five cents on every dollar paid out in gas taxes—resulting in a $518 million shortfall (Saporta 2003). Metro Atlanta has 42 percent of the state's population, but only 17 percent of the state's gas tax revenue actually comes back to the region—a classic case of transportation injustice (Stanford 2003). Metropolitan Atlanta has become a "donor" region for the rest of Georgia (Bullard 2004).

The majority of the entry-level jobs in metro Atlanta are not within a quarter mile of public transportation. Households in the Atlanta region pay an extra $300 per month for the lack of transportation choices. This translates to $3,600 per year that households could be using for other expenses (Center for Neighborhood Technology 2003, 34). This is not a small point since African Americans in metropolitan Atlanta earned only $703 per $1,000 earned by whites in 2000 (Mumford Center 2000).

Metro Atlanta is expected to add another two million people by 2030. To address this growth, the Atlanta Regional Commission's (ARC) *Mobility 2030* plan calls for spending $53 billion over the next twenty-five years on transportation. Yet this massive expenditure is expected to do little in terms of relieving congestion, mainly because it again shortchanges transit. The plan allocates $13.7 billion for MARTA's maintenance and operations (Frankston 2004).

Atlantans are growing weary of traffic gridlock, long commutes, and polluted air. Atlanta's smog is also hurting its image as an attractive business climate. Amid signs that federal highway dollars would be frozen, Georgia's Environmental Protection Division (EPD) helped to create the Partnership for a Smog-Free Georgia. The partnership operates from the workplace and is the beginning point for changing Atlantans' commuting habits. Since its birth in 1998, the program has recruited over 160 "partners." It also has a dozen public-sector partners, and links to eighty-five state agencies and universities and twenty-five federal agencies. Some of the large corporate partners include the Coca-Cola Company, Delta Airlines, Turner Broadcasting Systems, BellSouth, and IBM (Smith 1999).

After making some progress in reducing nitrogen oxide emissions in the early 1990s, as a result of cleaner-running cars and tighter emission inspections, the region is now experiencing reversals in air quality. In the summer of 1999, the Atlanta region had thirty-seven consecutive ozone alerts days. The region exceeded the National Ambient Air Quality Standards for ozone by 33 to 50 percent.

The ARC is the MPO responsible for land use and transportation planning in the region. In order to receive federal transportation funds, the ARC was required to develop a Transportation Improvement Plan (TIP) that would conform to federal standards. The ARC developed an interim TIP (Atlanta Regional Commission 1998b). Because of the severe ozone nonattainment, the federal government criticized the ARC's plan for concentrating too heavily on roads and failing to show how it would improve the region's poor air quality. Federal officials have also identified public participation as a major problem in the ARC's planning and decision making (U.S. Department of Transportation 1998).

In 1998, two separate coalitions of citizens' groups challenged the ARC's leadership, planning, and decision making that is tilted toward new roads. Under the Clean Air Act (CAA), a group of environmental organizations and a coalition of mainly African American environmental justice, neighborhood, and civic groups filed a notice to sue the ARC,

Georgia, and the federal government for approving sixty-one "grand-fathered" new road projects funded under the interim TIP, which they felt would add to and exacerbate the region's already severe air quality problem.[1]

In addition to challenging the illegal exemption of grandfathered road projects, the environmental justice coalition raised equity concerns with the grandfathered roads and the region's $700 million transportation spending plan.[2] The groups charged highway-dominated plans would disproportionately and adversely affect the health and safety of African Americans and other people of color.

The environmental group followed through with a lawsuit that resulted in a settlement eliminating forty-four of the sixty-one grandfathered road projects (Goldberg 1999). The seventeen other projects were allowed to proceed because the Georgia DOT had already awarded contracts to construct the roads. The settlement freed up millions of dollars for transportation alternatives that will improve air quality and mobility in the region (Southern Environmental Law Center 1999). The settlement restricts projects from proceeding until the state includes them in a regional transportation plan that meets federal clean air standards. The settlement has several requirements: that the ARC to make its computer traffic modeling public, that the Georgia DOT conduct a major study of transportation and congestion in the northern suburbs, and that the USDOT study the social equity impacts of transportation investments in the region.

Shortly after the June 1999 settlement, the environmental justice coalition entered into informal negotiations with the USDOT, state, and local agencies, including the ARC, that would begin addressing the transportation equity, environmental justice, and Title VI concerns of the groups (U.S. Department of Transportation 1999). Equity concerns revolve around three broad areas: how environmental justice issues are addressed in the planning process; how the benefits are distributed across various populations; and how the burdens of transportation investments are distributed across various populations.

Preliminary negotiations called for a two-phase analysis of transportation equity in the Atlanta region. Phase one consisted primarily of addressing the "procedural aspect of the planning process, focusing on how public participation of low-income and minority communities can be enhanced and how the concerns of these communities can be better identified and addressed in the planning process" (U.S. Department of Transportation 1999, 1). Phase two focused on the "substantive outcomes of the planning process, examining the distribution of transportation burdens and benefits to low-income and minority communities and expanding effective participation by low-income and minority communities in the planning process" (U.S. Department of Transportation 1999, 2).

Atlanta area residents are paying for sprawl with their hard-earned dollars as well as their health. A 1994 CDC-sponsored study showed that pediatric emergency department visits at Atlanta's Grady Memorial Hospital increased by one-third following peak ozone levels. The study also found that the asthma rate among African American children is 26 percent higher than the asthma rate among whites (White et al. 1994). Since children with asthma in Atlanta may not have visited the emergency department for their care, the true prevalence of asthma in the community is likely to be higher. Given the heavy dependence on the automobile in the region and the limited role of public transit, it is doubtful that emission-control technologies adopted under the 1990 CAA amendments are adequate to ensure that transportation fairly contributes to attainment of healthful air quality in the region.

Mega Airport Sprawl

Hartsfield-Jackson Atlanta International Airport (ATL) is the world's busiest airport. From its humble beginnings in 1925 as a leased 287-acre airfield, ATL now covers 4,700 acres. The airport is named for William Hartsfield, who is white and was Atlanta's longest-serving mayor, and Maynard Jackson, Atlanta's first black mayor and the person who engineered the major expansion during his first two terms (from 1974 to 1982) that helped make the Atlanta airport the world's busiest.[3] Only Chicago's O'Hare Airport rivals ATL in the number of take offs and landings. ATL handled over 75.8 million passengers in 2001,

76.9 million passengers in 2002, and 79 million passengers in 2003 (Airports Council International 2003; Atlanta Regional Commission 2003).

ATL is a major economic engine in the twenty-county Atlanta MSA. It is the largest employment center in Georgia, employing 55,300 airline, ground transportation, concessionaire, security, federal government, City of Atlanta, and airport tenants. The total ATL payroll is $2.4 billion, resulting in a direct and indirect economic impact of $5.6 billion on the local and regional economy. The total annual regional economic impact of the airport is more than $18.7 billion (Hartsfield-Jackson Atlanta International Airport 2004).

The economic benefits to the region are better known than the negative impacts that fall heaviest on the airport's South Fulton and North Clayton Counties neighbors. Although African Americans make up only 28.8 percent of the population in the twenty-county Atlanta MSA, they represent 48.2 percent of the population within a one-mile radius of ATL; and African Americans are 69.6 percent and 82.8 percent of the residents who live within a two- and three-mile radius, respectively, of the airport (figure 9.2).

Residents who live near the sprawling airport have to contend with a host of environmental problems such as noise, vibrations, pollution, lowered property values, and the displacement associated with sprawl. The Natural Resources Defense Council (1996, 7) study, *Flying Off Course*, found that "airports are significant sources of ground-level volatile organic compounds (VOC) and NOx emissions." Arriving and departing planes can create as much, if not more, ground-level VOC and NOx as many of the airport's largest industrial neighbors.

Airports present a special case since they are exempt from the federal law that requires other toxic sources to report their toxic emissions totals (that is, their Toxic Release Inventory, or TRI). The NRDC report examined the impact of this exemption: airports are not regulated in the same manner as other significant air pollution sources. Neither airports nor airlines are held accountable for the aggregate impacts of their ground-level aircraft emissions. State and local regulators remain nearly powerless to address the problem in meaningful ways, while other major industrial sources are accordingly forced to compensate on airport's be-

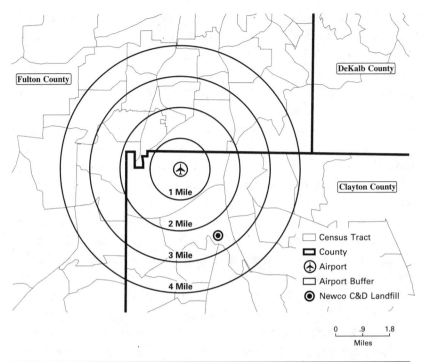

Buffer Size	Total Population	Percent Minority
1 951		48.2%
2 11,166		69.6%
3 40,948		82.8%
4 62,842		82.8%

Figure 9.2
Population near the ATL

half as states scramble to meet mandatory emissions reduction deadlines. Meanwhile, the number of commercial flights (which burn the most fuel and cause the most pollution per operation) grows higher and higher each year (Natural Resources Defense Council 1996, 8).

South Fulton County Airport Study Area

To accommodate the ever-increasing volume of air traffic, ATL embarked on a $1.3 billion, nine-thousand-foot fifth-runway expansion project.

The runway opened in May 2006 and is expected to be used primarily for landings, allowing more flights into the airport reducing delays at Atlanta, the nation's busiest airport in terms of passenger traffic. Experts predict that the world's busiest airport will serve as many as 120 million passengers each year by the end of the decade. In comparison, Hartsfield-Jackson served 85.5 million passengers in 2005. One of the largest public construction projects in Georgia history, the runway has been plagued by scandal over contracts and its cost. The runway project was financed through a mix of bonds, passenger fees and federal allotments. It is one element of Hartsfield-Jackson's overall expansion plan, which also includes a new rental car complex connected to the terminal by a monorail and a planned international terminal to the east of the existing gate concourses expected to open 2010 at the earliest (Hirschman 2006).

Because of the concerned raised by nearby southside residents, the Fulton County Commission hired its own consultants to examine the environmental justice implications of the runway expansion project.[4] Nine census tracts (CT) in South Fulton County (CTs 105.03, 105.05, 106.01, 106.02, 107, 108, 109, 110, and 113.02) were analyzed for the study area and the Atlanta MSA for the reference area. Comparative data is also presented for Fulton County, South Fulton County, and two Fulton County Superdistricts (Tri-Cities and Shannon) where the bulk of the study area CTs are found.

People of color, largely African Americans, made up over half (53.2 percent) of Fulton County in 1990 and 47.4 percent in 2000. The county's minority population is concentrated largely in the southern part of the county. The Fulton County study area is located in the southern part of the county and is heavily black. African Americans made up 71.9 percent of the population in 1990 and 80.6 percent in 2000. Much of the study area was determined to be an environmental justice community.[5] Based on the minority and low-income percentages, a combination of eight of the nine CTs in the Fulton County study area met the percent minority or percent low-income threshold. Eight tracts met the minority threshold, while only three tracts met the low-income threshold. Only one CT (108) failed to meet the minority or low-income threshold.

Table 9.1
Population trends in the Fulton County airport study area

	Population			% change	
CT	1980	1990	2000	1980–1990	1990–2000
105.03	8,823	9,385	10,339	6.4	10.2
105.05	6,805	9,061	9,562	33.2	5.5
106.01	4,593	3,536	3,299	−23.0	−6.7
106.02	12,816	10,366	9,579	−19.1	−7.6
107.00	3,193	2,464	2,326	−22.8	−5.6
108.00	6,174	5,510	5,435	−10.8	−1.4
109.00	868	716	652	−17.5	−8.9
110.00	4,483	4,039	3,940	−9.9	−2.5
113.02	15,629	14,852	14,716	−5.0	−0.9
Total	63,384	59,929	59,848	−5.5	−0.1

Source: Atlanta Regional Commission 2000; U.S. Bureau of the Census 1980.

Uneven Growth

The population in the Fulton County study area has undergone a dramatic demographic shift over the past two decades. While the population in metropolitan Atlanta experienced tremendous growth over the past twenty years, this growth has been uneven, with much of it "concentrated north of Interstate 20 (I-20) and in arc to the south some distance from the Fulton County Study Area in Fayette, Clayton, and Henry counties" (Urban Land Institute 2000, 12). The study area has steadily lost population during this same period. The population in the study area was 63,384 in 1980, 59,929 in 1990, and 59,848 in 2000. The study area population experienced a 5.5 percent decline between 1980 and 1990, and continued to lose population in the 1990s, declining by 0.1 percent between 1990 and 2000.

The economic boom of the 1980s and 1990s did not have the same effect on all communities in the Atlanta MSA. Overall, the Fulton County study area experienced a 1.6 percent increase in housing between 1980 and 1990, and a 1.4 percent increase between 1990 and 2000. Six of the CTs in the study area experienced a drop in housing units in the 1980s. Five of the nine CTs experienced a decline in housing units during

Table 9.2
Housing units in the Fulton County airport study area

CT	Housing units			% change	
	1980	1990	2000	1980–1990	1990–2000
105.03	3,426	3,725	4,166	8.7	11.8
105.05	2,552	3,927	4,280	53.9	9.0
106.01	1,972	1,797	1,716	−8.9	−4.5
106.02	5,721	5,022	4,727	−12.2	−5.9
107.00	1,475	1,184	1,137	−19.7	−4.0
108.00	2,790	2,670	2,675	−4.3	0.2
109.00	347	305	285	−12.1	−6.6
110.00	1,673	1,571	1,527	−6.1	−2.8
113.02	6,636	6,813	6,880	2.7	1.0
Total	26,592	27,014	27,393	1.6	1.4

Source: Atlanta Regional Commission 2000; U.S. Bureau of the Census 1980.

the 1990s. Clearly, airport sprawl has not stimulated a housing boom in the mostly black airport study area.

The racial and economic trends are very different for North and South Fulton. North Fulton was 3.4 percent minority in 1993 and 4.5 percent minority in 1999. South Fulton County was 65.5 percent minority in 1993 and 65.6 percent minority in 1999. Unlike the mostly white communities in the northern sector of Fulton County, the largely black communities around the ATL were left out of the region's housing boom in the 1980s and 1990s. The Atlanta Regional Commission's (1999, 8) *Atlanta Outlook* described the trends in North Fulton:

Since GA-400 opened as a limited access highway in the 1980s, North Fulton County has been one of the fastest growing areas in the Atlanta Region. The GA-400 corridor has attracted a new regional mall, North Point, many new commercial developments and some high-density housing. The southern end of this corridor continues to develop commercially thanks to its location adjacent to the densely developed Perimeter Center area of DeKalb. Housing units have increased by 53 percent in North Fulton County since 1990, with more than half of the increase occurring in the North Fulton SD [Superdistrict]. Most of the new housing in North Fulton has been decidedly upscale, enhancing its attractiveness as a location for corporate headquarters. MARTA rail serves the southern end of this SD.

Communities in South Fulton did not benefit nearly as well as their northern counterparts during the region's employment boom of the 1990s. Between 1990 and 1997, employment in North Fulton County grew from 104,601 to 179,062—a net increase of 74,461 jobs. During the same period, jobs in South Fulton increased from 65,841 to 82,236 —a net gain of 16,395 jobs. Similarly, North Fulton added 41,401 housing units between 1990 and 1999 compared to only 3,217 added in South Fulton during this same period. The Atlanta Regional Commission (1999, 8) described the growth trends in South Fulton:

The area of Fulton County south of the City of Atlanta has not seen the rapid growth found north of the City. South Fulton includes the cities of East Point, Fairburn, and Hapeville, plus most of the cities of College park and Palmetto. Shannon Mall is located in the I-85 corridor of this area. South Fulton presents a sharp contrast to the densely developed areas of central Fulton and DeKalb counties. Most of it is only lightly developed, especially it's southern tip. Because this area is adjacent to Hartsfield International Airport, much of its employment base is associated with the transportation industry. The strength of this sector may be somewhat overstated because of problems in partitioning Delta Airlines employment between the Airport in Clayton County and the adjacent Delta headquarters in Fulton.

All of the Fulton County study area CTs fall within two Fulton County SDs: Tri-Cities (CTs 106.01, 106.02, 107, 108, 109, 110, and 113.02) and Shannon (CTs 105.03 and 101.05). The Atlanta Regional Commission (1999, 17) portrayed the trends in the Tri-Cities SD as follow:

The Tri-Cities SD includes the City of Hapeville and most of the cities of College Park and East Point, hence its name. Proximity to Hartsfield International Airport has limited the attractiveness of much of this superdistrict to residential development. The net decline in housing units is largely due to the buyout by the airport of properties in high-noise areas. The large increase in Air Transportation jobs between 1995 and 1998 may overstate the true increase, because of difficulties in properly apportioning Delta Air Lines substantial employment between its headquarters facility in this SD and the airport terminal facility in the adjacent Airport SD in Clayton County. Much of the employment in this SD is directly related to the airport. One of the region's largest manufacturing facilities, a Ford Motor Co. assembly plant, is located in this SD.

The population of the Tri-Cities SD declined from 59,675 in 1990 to 58,580 in 1999. The area also lost 329 housing units between 1990 and 1999. Multifamily housing makes up 45.3 percent of the total housing units in the Tri-Cities SD. Two of the CTs in the study area fall within the Shannon SD. The Atlanta Regional Commission (1999, 16) depicts this SD as follows:

The Shannon SD lies south of the Tri-Cities SD and is bisected by I-85. The cities of Fairburn and Union City are located in this SD along with a small part of the City of College Park. The SD derives its name from the Shannon Mall, which is located north of I-85, near Union City. Population and employment have increased steadily in this SD but not nearly so rapidly as areas north of the City of Atlanta. The northern end of this SD is the Hartsfield International Airport flight path. Aircraft noise makes this part of Shannon inappropriate for residential use.

The Shannon SD added 2,039 housing units between 1990 and 1999. The Shannon SD also increased its employment from 16,130 in 1990 to 20,801 in 1998—a net gain of 4,671 jobs. The predominantly black area has had problems luring investments, commercial growth, and residential development. The Urban Land Institute's (2000, 13) *Metro Atlanta Southern Crescent* study noted this trend: "Over time, as African Americans and other minority groups moved into the area, white entrepreneurs and institutions failed to make capital or business investments in the community."

The airport study area "suffers from poor-quality development, which repels image-conscious start-up businesses desiring prestigious locations that enhance their appearance and visibility" (Urban Land Institute 2000, 13). These revelations have been known for decades. An ATL Environmental Assessment (1982) described several factors that negatively impact growth and land values around the airport:

A large number of factors affect the value of land throughout the Airport Environs Area. These factors include location, access, physical development constraints, size and shape of the property, adjacent or nearby land uses with adverse or positive impacts, existing land use, size, age and quality of existing structures and so on. Zoning and potential future use are additional factors used to appraise property values. All of these factors combine to create widely ranging property values throughout the Environs Area.

Clearly, ATL is a moneymaking machine for the region (Martin Associates 1999; Hartsfield Atlanta International Airport 1999). Yet residents who live in the shadow of the airport have had to endure its noise and pollution (Bennett 2000). The airport noise, a reduced quality of life, housing depreciation, residential displacement, and few tangible advantages of living next to the giant airport are particular sore points for nearby residents.

ATL has not been an economic magnet for high-end commercial development. Moreover, the housing and neighborhoods near the airport are "not generally attractive to corporate managers seeking business locations" (Urban Land Institute 2000, 13). Unlike its competitor, the Dallas–Forth Worth International Airport (DFW), ATL has not spurred "upscale" and major corporate growth in the airport corridor. In 2000, ATL employed 43,000 workers and DFW employed 42,000 workers. ATL pumped over $9 billion annually in the metro Atlanta economy compared to DFW's $11.2 billion. In his "Tale of Two Airports," *Atlanta Journal-Constitution* writer Gary Hendricks (2000) summed up both airports: "DFW a Magnet, Hartsfield Penned In."

DFW has attracted higher-end development such as corporate headquarters, white-collar employment, and upscale housing. The DFW area also has good schools. Schools can make or break an area. In a sense, "DFW and its environs are gold-plated" (Hendricks 2000). On the other hand, "poor schools limit desirability for housing and corporate users" in the ATL area (Urban Land Institute 2000, 13).

There are eleven public schools in the airport study area. All of them follow the same patterns as many of the public schools in the South Fulton County area: a high total enrollment, a large percentage of minority students, and a large percentage of students eligible for free or reduced lunches. All of the schools inside the study area showed over 70 percent minority students and over 60 percent of the students eligible for free lunches.

With a total enrollment of 1,189, Banneker High boasted the highest enrollment for all the schools in the area, with over 60 percent of the students eligible for free or reduced lunches. The percentage of minority students in this high school was 98.7. The schools with the highest percentage of minority students were College Park Elementary (100 percent), Brookview Elementary (99.6 percent), and Tubman Elementary (99.5 percent). College Park Elementary also had the largest percentage of students eligible for free and reduced lunches (99.7 percent).

Higher-end development has shunned the ATL area. Delta Airlines is the only major corporation that has its headquarters there. Investors, real estate planners, and business leaders' perceptions go a long way in determining the economic success or failure of a region, or a sector in a region. These are the individuals who recruit businesses and services to an area. Metro Atlanta's north-south divide has left the perception that "the airport area is all blue-collar and the northside is where the money is" (Hendricks 2000).

The Urban Land Institute (2000, 12) study reinforced the fact that most financial and real estate investors seek out "proven markets with the fewest risk factors." The study also confirmed what most Atlantans have known for years. South Fulton County and the Tri-Cities SD are unfairly stigmatized as industrial, with poor infrastructure, poor-quality development, and a high crime rate. This stigma has contributed to slow economic growth as compared to the more robust northern part of the county and region.

The airport and expansion projects over the years have done little to eradicate this stigma or enhance the residential stability of the surrounding neighborhoods. In some cases, airport expansion may have contributed to the perception of residential abandonment, property value instability, economic disinvestments, and industrial encroachment. This is especially the case as the areas surrounding the airport changed from mostly white to mostly black.

Land uses around the airport have also changed over time. The *Draft Environmental Impact Statement* (Hartsfield Atlanta International Airport 2000, 32) alludes to this trend, yet it attributes these changes to local communities rather than to airport expansion and operations:

In all cases, land use and noise impacts of airport operations are closely linked to land use decision of the surrounding local governments. Land uses compatible with airport operations include commercial, industrial, and other noise-tolerant uses. Incompatible land uses include residential, institutional, and recreational uses. The communities around ATL are slowly altering land use patterns to be more consistent with airport noise although there will likely remain some exceptions.

ATL's encroachment into residential areas along with relocations of housing have changed the character of these neighborhoods as well as accelerated shifts in land use. Local communities appear to be responding to these ATL-related pressures rather than the reverse. Generally, airport sprawl and runway expansion have come at the expense of nearby residences and businesses.

Residential Property Values and Business Development

A recent Brookings Institution (2000, 6) report found that "high housing prices on the job-rich sorthside and a desire to avoid economically declining neighborhoods on the southside cause new residents (and builders of new homes) to 'leapfrog' further out into the metropolitan fringe." Housing values tend to be higher in the northern-tier counties of the region than in the south. Moreover, average home values in South Fulton have not kept pace with those in the region.

Property values in South Fulton have been mixed. Between 1996 and 1997, new and existing home sales in the metro area increased 14.5 percent. The average home sale price was up 5.4 percent. The home sale price was up 3.6 percent in South Fulton County. In 1997, the metrowide average home sale price was $147,513 compared to an average sale price of $74,210 in South Fulton County (Banks 1998). From 1997 to 1998, average home prices climbed only slightly in the Union City area (zip code 30291) and dropped in the Palmetto (zip code 30268) area. The mostly black Union City has continued to develop almost exclusively as a commercial district. Generally, having a mega airport nearby has neither boosted South Fulton residents' property values nor improved the overall quality of life.

Airport expansion has displaced residences and businesses. Having one's home taken or having to be relocated because of an airport expansion project is not an insignificant event. A chief consideration in terms of housing displacement is the availability of replacement housing. The City of Atlanta Department of Aviation (1999, VII, B-6) alluded to this dilemma:

According to land use plans, south Fulton County is projected to experience steady single-family housing growth.... Hapeville is also involved in the redevelopment and rehabilitation of older housing areas, but is primarily built out, as is the City of East Point. Future housing growth for these cities will likely take place through infill development. Because of the extensive impacts of noise in College Park (city limits), future housing development is unlikely to occur.

Finding replacement rental housing is also complicated by residents' attitude against multifamily developments. In some cases, multifamily

Table 9.3
Average home sales in selected South Fulton County, 1996

Zip code	Homes sold	Average price (1997)	Percent change from 1996
30213	202	$91,780	2.5%
30268	70	$80,210	−6.1%
30291	77	$69,958	0.9%
30296	28	$77,246	−12.2%
30331	476	$128,033	5.2%
30337	130	$77,767	3.8%
30344	554	$65,315	5.9%
30349	471	$88,536	10.5%
30354	214	$61,817	13.9%

Source: Banks (1998).
Note: The statistics used in the *Atlanta Journal-Constitution* annual home report were compiled from sales deeds filed at courthouses in the seventeen-county metro area. The data was provided by Steve Palm of Smart Numbers, a real estate tracking firm, and analyzed by databases edition Denise Prodigo-Herrmann. Figures for new and existing home sales from 1997 were compared with data from the previous year. Mortgage assumptions, refinancing, and lot sales are not included. We divided Fulton County into two sections. For the purposes of this study, everything north of I-20 is North Fulton and everything south of I-20 is South Fulton.

housing or apartments are identified with low-income and minority households. The City of Atlanta Department of Aviation (1999, VII, B-6) states that

as of 1998, no multi-family housing developments were being constructed in the airport's vicinity, and jurisdictions such as Clayton County have placed a moratorium on new multi-family development to assess the overall impact on the County's infrastructure. The attitude against multi-family development is prominent among community residents in neighborhoods around the airport and weighs heavily at the government level when being considered. While location assistance may allow some renters to become homeowners, not all will have the financial ability to purchase homes and may face the dilemma of having to find replacement multi-family housing in the area.

The relocation dilemma outlined by the Department of Aviation is more problematic as well as traumatic for African American homeowners and renters who face housing discrimination, and generally are forced to go through more pains and sorrow than whites to acquire housing (Bullard, Grisby, and Lee 1994). When minority homeowners and renters are displaced, they often face discrimination in their search for replacement housing, unlike their white counterpart (Squires 1998). Results from fair housing "testers" reveal that African Americans are treated less favorably than whites 30 percent of the time when seeking housing in Atlanta and 67 percent of the time in Atlanta's suburbs (Bullard, Johnson, and Torres 2000). Thus, the claim that financial relocation assistance alone will mitigate the impacts of displacements is overstated.

Minority homeowners and minority businesses must also contend with insurance redlining. Moving from one location to another may negatively impact insurance rates. Insurance redlining kills neighborhoods (Squires 1997). Insurance companies routinely charge homeowners in minority urban neighborhoods higher premiums than they do their suburban customers. Insurance redlining is not isolated to an individual insurance agent. The practice is widespread among big and small companies.

A 1996 study by the *Atlanta Journal-Constitution* found that the largest insurance companies in Georgia (State Farm, Allstate, Cotton States, Cincinnati Insurance, and USAA) routinely charge consumers 40 to 90 percent more to insure homes in Atlanta's predominantly black neighborhoods than for similar or identical houses in mostly white suburbs (Emling 1996). This practice occurs even when loss ratios (the amount the company pays out per dollar collected) are higher in the suburbs. For example, a loss ratio of 75 percent means that an insurance company makes a hefty 25 percent return on its investment.

How airport officials handle relocation and other mitigation measures can be problematic, especially for low-income people and minority group members as well as individuals who may be unfamiliar with and mistrustful of government actions such as African Americans, who have had a long history of government-sanctioned discrimination such as the urban renewal of the 1950s and 1960s.

Business displacements present another challenge to airport expansion projects. Such displacement can be especially disruptive "when the community in question exhibits long-term stability, a common ethnic identity, or represents senior citizens" (City of Atlanta Department of Aviation 1999, 8). Minority and small business owners also have raised concerns about not being at the decision-making table on airport expansion projects that directly impact them. Many contend that the mere talk of airport expansion stifles commerce in the area. Because of these heightened fears, local leaders formed the Legacy Coalition to provide a forum for their views and concerns about ATL expansion (Hendricks 1998).

Minority business displacement raises some special equity and environmental justice issues. But having even one minority business, church, community center, or clinic taken is not an insignificant act given the severe underrepresentation of minority businesses.

A 2000 study from the Milken Institute and the U.S. Department of Commerce emphasized the need for removing barriers to minority business development (Yago and Pankratz 2000). African Americans make up about 12 percent of the U.S. population and 4 percent of all business owners. Similarly, Hispanics make up about 11 percent of the population and 4 percent of the business owners. Minority businesses are often undercapitalized, small, vulnerable, and sensitive to even subtle market shifts.

Moving from an established location can "kill" a small business, or severely diminish its effectiveness and sense of cohesion and community. Relocation can be especially hurtful to minority businesses. Any threat to minority businesses can have a destabilizing effect on minority communities. Involuntary relocation may also have a negative impact on minority firms' ability to stay in business. This is complicated by the fact that the minority business failure rate is higher than the failure rate of nonminority businesses. The failure rate among minority-owned businesses in 1996 (28.7 percent) was higher than that for all business (24.3 percent). Some of the reasons cited for the higher minority business failure rate are the lack of access to business or personal loans, cash flow, sales problems, and racial discrimination (National Black Business Council 1996).

Minority-owned businesses face an array of challenges. Statistically, minorities lack financial and social capital. On average, minority business owners have lower incomes, fewer assets, and diminished access to government and private contracts (Enchautegui et al. 1997). Minority entrepreneurs are significantly more likely to be denied bank credit, and when successful, receive smaller loans relative to comparable nonminority businesses (Boston and Ross 1997). Still, minority businesses are vital for community development since minority firms are more likely to employ minority workers and thus provide them with an important entry point into the labor market.

Environmental Impacts

Residents of Blair Village and nearby neighborhoods complain about the noise from airplanes as they prepare to land at ATL. These neighborhoods fall within one of the "dirtiest" zip codes (30354) in the city according to the EPA's TRI database (Bullard, Johnson, and Torres 2000; Chapman 2000). The average 1996 home sale in zip code 30354 was $61,817—the lowest of the zip code averages reported by the *Atlanta Journal-Constitution* countywide survey.

Mega airports like ATL also have to contend with motor vehicle emissions from people who drive to or park their cars at the airport. The City of Atlanta Department of Aviation (1999, 52) described this type of emissions: "Airport-attributable emissions of air pollutants and polluted precursors from motor vehicles result from local road and highway trips made by both passengers and employees traveling to and from HAIA. Emissions also result from the vehicles traveling on airport property. The vehicle mix on airport property is primarily privately-owned cars, rental cars, hotel/rental car shuttles, taxicabs, and limousines." The emissions from airplanes and motor vehicles also combine with emissions from nearby polluting industries. When examined singularly, airplane or ground-level vehicle emissions may be reported to have minimal environmental impact. An environmental justice analysis would examine these impacts along with the other toxic releases from surrounding industries on the airport study area.

Noise is a major impact associated with airports. Since 1986, Atlanta's Department of Aviation has spent over $4.3 million to make living near the airport less annoying for about nine hundred homeowners in South Fulton and North Clayton Counties. Soundproofing was conducted on homes that averaged a daily noise level of between sixty-five and seventy-five decibels.[6] Similarly, homes with noise levels higher than seventy-five decibels were bought and the families were relocated under a program administered locally by the Department of Aviation (Harvey 1998). Despite the soundproofing efforts in the past, airport noise continues to be a problem for the nearby ATL residents. According to the Urban Land Institute (2000, 13), "Airport noise is a real barrier to residential and corporate office space uses. During the first period of airport expansion, Forest Park residents sound-proofed their homes, but this effort did not help preserve the neighborhood. Owners moved from Forest Park, and a high proportion of the housing stock reverted to rental units."

Generally, noise is considered merely an annoyance, but it may actually impact health over the long run. As the Natural Resource Defense Council's (1996, 111) *Flying Off Course* reported, "The noise that people suffer near airports is, for the most part, less intense, because it is characterized by multiple short bursts of intensely loud single noise events rather than chronic levels of loud noise. Nevertheless, some studies have documented that aircraft noise can have significant impacts on the quality of health and well-being." The *Draft Environmental Impact Statement* notes that "churches and cemeteries represent almost 50 percent of the total noise sensitive land uses, followed by schools, day care facilities, and parks" in Fulton County (Hartsfield Atlanta International Airport 1999, 24). Without a doubt, persons within the 1998 noise contours are disproportionately minority and heavily low income. Of the 11,638 persons in the study area who fall within the sixty-five to seventy Day-Night Average Noise Levels (DNL), 8,860 (75.8 percent) are minorities and 3,007 are low income (25.7 percent).[7] Of the 8,764 persons in the study area who fall within the seventy to seventy-five DNL, 7,181 (81.9 percent) are minorities and 2,238 (25.5 percent) are low income. Of the 2,772 persons within the seventy-five-plus DNL, 2,556 (92.7 percent) are minorities and 693 (25.1 percent) are low income.

North Clayton County Airport Study Area

Our analysis also examined the impacts of the fifth runway expansion at ATL on the mostly black Northern Clayton County residents. The airport is located in Clayton County, one of Georgia's smallest counties in land size with an area of 146-square miles. With 251,800 residents,

Table 9.4
Persons in Fulton County airport study area within 1998 noise contours

CT	65–70 DNL			70–75 DNL			75+ DNL		
	Total persons	Minorities	Low income	Total persons	Minorities	Low income	Total persons	Minorities	Low income
105.03	23	20	4	8	8	1	0	0	0
105.05	1,317	1,049	219	0	0	0	0	0	0
106.01	1,579	1,009	670	758	484	321	6	4	3
106.02	2,063	1,933	501	4,598	4,308	1,117	2,602	2,483	632
107.00	641	273	232	368	157	133	155	66	56
108.00	1,198	405	315	748	253	197	9	3	2
109.00	55	23	23	0	0	0	0	0	0
113.02	4,807	4,148	1,043	2,284	1,971	469	0	0	0
Totals	11,683	8,860	3,007	8,764	7,181	2,238	2,772	2,556	693

Source: Draft Environmental Impact Statement (1999, 23).
Note: CT 110 was excluded from the above analysis since it does not fall within the noise-sensitive area.

Clayton County is the fifth most populous county in the Atlanta region. The county population stood at 150,000 in 1980, 184,000 in 1990, and 236,000 in 2003 (Atlanta Regional Commission 2003).

Clayton County has the highest percentage of African American residents in the Atlanta region. African Americans made up 59 percent of Clayton's population in 2004, an increase of 8 percentage points from 2000. Over the last decade, Clayton County has shifted from mainly white and rural to a popular black suburb. The 2004 elections saw the county's blacks wrest political power from whites (Associated Press 2005).

Fifth Runway Assault
The ATL fifth runway expansion is slated for completion in 2006. The increased traffic, exhaust fumes, noise, dust, and excavation of dirt for the runway project has created quite a controversy in North Clayton County (Tagami 2002). Conveyor belts, carrying dirt nearly twenty-four hours a day to the fifth runway site, snake through residents' yards and neighborhoods. Dirt from several Clayton County quarries moves along the conveyor belts at a rate of 3,200 tons an hour. Workers in twelve-person crews are slated to move 27 million cubic yards of soil, enough to fill six Georgia Domes—easily making this the largest public works project in Atlanta's history (Tagami 2003).

In some places, the dirt embankment is as tall as an eleven-story building. Nearby residents have not welcomed this recent airport encroachment. Clayton's Cherry Hill subdivision residents, who live near the nine-thousand-foot runway, complain of headaches from the clattering conveyor belts and daily blasting from rock quarries. They are also angered by the road closings and rerouting of streets that have disrupted their daily routine (Scott 2003a).

To add insult to injury, plans are underway by Newco and the French firm LaFarge, which operate a local rock quarry, to build a construction and debris landfill at the dirt site next to their rock quarry. In 2003, in a three to two vote, Clayton County commissioners approved permits and rezoning, over the objections of the nearby residents, to allow for the landfill. County commissioners took the position that a future landfill is better than the current quarry blasting at the site. The companies would be allowed to fill the quarry with nonchemical debris and dirt (Farber 2003). The landfill could grow in size to 267 acres and have a life span of decades (Duffy 2003).

Newco and LaFarge officials insist that Clayton County could reap $15 to $20 million in fees during the life of the landfill. As these officials promise Clayton County increased revenue, the Georgia General Assembly in 2005 passed legislation that could cost the county $11 million a year in tax revenues—or 8.4 percent of its $131 million annual budget. In a move to bailout the financially strapped Atlanta-based Delta Airlines, the legislature limited to $15 million the amount airlines would pay each year in sales taxes on jet fuel (Badertscher 2005). Delta Airlines, Georgia's largest employer, is the area's largest airline and the only one that pays that much in taxes on jet fuel. Delta paid $17 million in jet fuel taxes in 2004. In helping Delta, the legislature hurt the predominantly black Clayton County, where ATL is located.

Whether highway or airport sprawl is "good" or "bad" will almost always depend on where you live, and whether or not you own a car. Today, a growing number of the region's drivers are getting fed up with gridlocked traffic and polluted air—both of which are by-products of random unplanned suburban sprawl. Sprawl-driven growth has placed the health of the Atlanta metropolitan region and its residents at risk.

Although Atlanta's share of the metropolitan population has declined over the years, the health of the central city is still important to the overall metropolitan region's vitality. Atlanta as the "hole in the doughnut" does not bode well for the region. New challenges are being raised to address imbalances resulting from sprawl. What happens outside the city affects all Atlantans. Sprawl development accelerates urban-core disinvestment, infrastructure decline, and housing segregation by race and income. Moreover, these problems are not likely to go away without some renewed attention and intervention. Working together, public and private joint ventures can make a difference in the quality of life enjoyed by everyone. The future of the Atlanta region is intricately bound to how government, business, and community leaders address these quality of life issues.

Flying into, out of, and over Atlanta, one could easily overlook the airport sprawl issue. At thirty thousand feet, everything below looks green and small. Yet airport sprawl is a big issue, and unfortunately it has real consequences, many of which are negative. Hardly anyone would dispute the fact that the sprawling ATL provides tremendous economic benefits. The benefits are dispersed across the region and the state, which is largely white, while the negative impacts of the airport expansion and operations are localized in the neighborhoods surrounding the airport, which is mostly black.

No real "share the wealth" plan has gotten off the ground that would benefit those residents and businesses suffering the greatest negative impacts from past, current, and future airport expansion projects. Overall, the proximity of ATL to homes and businesses has made it an unpopular neighbor. It has also made expansion costly. ATL expansion projects have a long history of either pushing out homes and businesses that fall within their path, or making life miserable for the residents who remain in the neighborhoods near the airport.

Targeted airport investments in the South Fulton and North Clayton neighborhoods could reverse past as well as present adverse and disproportionate impacts on the minority and low-income populations that fall within the airport environs. Without an environmental justice–driven mitigation plan, residents will continue to receive less than their fair share of benefits from ATL.

Notes

1. On November 10, 1998, three environmental groups—Georgians for Transportation Alternatives, Georgia Conservancy, and the Sierra Club—filed a sixty-day notice to sue local, state, and federal transportation agencies under the CAA.

2. On December 16, 1998, a coalition of social justice and environmental groups filed a "Notice of Intent to Sue to Remedy Violations of the Clean Air Act" with local, state, and federal transportation agencies. The groups that signed on to the letter included the Environmental Defense Fund, the Southern Organizing Committee for Economic and Social Justice, Rainbow/PUSH Southern Region, Save Atlanta's Fragile Environment, the North Georgia African American Environmental Justice Network, the Southwest Atlanta Community Roundtable, the Center for Democratic Renewal, the Rebel Forest Neighborhood Task Force, and the Georgia Coalition for People's Agenda.

3. The renaming of the Hartsfield Atlanta International Airport (to include the name of former mayor Maynard Jackson) caused a split along racial lines in Atlanta. Generally, whites wanted the airport's name left alone, while blacks

wanted the airport named solely for Jackson, who died suddenly in June 2003. After much debate and heightened racial tension, Atlanta's sitting mayor Shirley Franklin pushed through a compromise to honor both mayors by renaming the airport Hartsfield-Jackson in October 2003. For details on this racial split, see Copeland (2003).

4. This analysis was conducted at the request of the Fulton County Department of Environment and Community Development. It assessed the potential impacts of the construction and operation of a nine-thousand-foot fifth runway at ATL. The runway expansion was sponsored by the City of Atlanta/Department of Aviation.

5. The 1998 EPA *National Guidance for Conducting Environmental Justice Analysis* recommends using two times the poverty threshold if an area is likely to have higher than average incomes and living expenses. Following this recommendation, our analysis utilized a multiplier of two times the national poverty threshold level to determine potential environmental justice areas of concern based on low-income status. In 1999, the national poverty level was 11.8 percent. The national poverty threshold was selected to reflect the higher cost of living in the Atlanta MSA and the study area. The environmental justice poverty threshold for low-income people in the Atlanta MSA was 23.6 percent $(2 \times 11.8 = 23.6)$. Any CT in the study area that has a percent below poverty higher than 23.6 percent will be considered an environmental justice area of concern. See Weinberg (2000, 1).

6. Seventy-five decibels is equivalent to the sound made by a lawn mower.

7. The DNL (denoted by the symbol Ldn) is a twenty-four-hour time-averaged sound exposure level with a ten decibel nighttime (10:00 p.m. to 7:00 a.m.) weighting. All federal agencies have adopted DNL as the metric of choice for airport noise analysis.

References

Airports Council International. 2003. Top Airports by Passenger Traffic. Available at ⟨http://www.sitebits.com/airports/⟩ (accessed January 30, 2005).

Associated Press. 2005. Sheriff's Firings Excite Racial Tension in Clayton County, Ga. *St. Petersburg Times*, January 16. Available at ⟨http://sptimes.com/2005/01/16/worldandnation/sheriff_s_firing_exc.shtml⟩ (accessed May 12, 2006).

Atlanta Journal-Constitution. 1997. Growing a New Atlanta. June 8, G5.

Atlanta Regional Commission. 1998a. *Atlanta Region Outlook*. December. Atlanta: ARC.

Atlanta Regional Commission. 1998b. *Proposed 1998 Amendments to the Interim Atlanta Region Transportation Improvement Program, FY 1999–FY 2001*. October. Atlanta: ARC.

Atlanta Regional Commission. 1999. *Atlanta Outlook 1999*. Atlanta: ARC.

Atlanta Regional Commission. 2000. *2000 Population and Housing*. December. Atlanta: ARC.

Atlanta Regional Commission. 2003. *Atlanta Region Transportation Planning: Fact Book 2003*. Atlanta: ARC.

Atlanta Regional Commission. 2004a. Sluggish Economy Slows Region's Growth, But Can't Stop It. News release, August 12.

Atlanta Regional Commission. 2004b. *Population and Housing*. December. Atlanta: ARC.

Badertscher, N. 2005. House Votes to Give Delta Tax Break on Fuel. *Atlanta Journal-Constitution*, March 11, F1.

Banks, B. 1998. Southside's Full Building Potential Not Yet Tapped: Throwing a Curve: Areas Affected by Airport Expansion Have Been Pinned Down. *Atlanta Journal-Constitution*, August 13, JK01.

Benfield, F. K., M. D. Raimi, and D. T. Chen. 1999. *Once There Were Greenfields: How Sprawl Is Undermining Environment, Economy, and Social Fabric*. Washington, DC: Natural Resources Defense Council and Surface Transportation Policy Project.

Bennett, D. L. 2000. Plan Aims to Share Airport's Wealth with Neighbors. *Atlanta Journal-Constitution*, July 29, A1.

Boston, T. D., and C. L. Ross. 1997. *The Inner City: Urban Poverty and Economic Development in the Next Century*. New Brunswick, NJ: Transaction.

Brookings Institution. 2000. *Moving beyond Sprawl: The Challenge for Metropolitan Atlanta*. Washington, DC: Brookings Institution.

Bullard, R. D. 1991. *In Search of the New South: The Black Urban Experience in the 1970s and 1980s*. Tuscaloosa: University of Alabama Press.

Bullard, R. D. 2004. Addressing Urban Transportation Equity in the United States. *Fordham Urban Law Journal* 31, no. 5 (October): 1183–1210.

Bullard, R. D. 2005. Transportation Policies Leave Blacks on the Side of the Road. *Crisis* 112, no. 1 (January–February): 21–22, 24.

Bullard, R. D., J. E. Grigsby, and C. Lee. 1994. *Residential Apartheid: The American Legacy*. Los Angeles: UCLA Center for African American Studies Publication.

Bullard, R. D., G. S. Johnson, and A. O. Torres. 2000. *Sprawl City: Race, Politics, and Planning in Atlanta*. Washington, DC: Island Press.

Center for Neighborhood Technology. 2004. *Making the Case for Mixed-Income and Mixed-Use Communities*. Atlanta: Atlanta Neighborhood Development Partnership, Inc.

Chapman, D. 2000. Atlanta's Most Toxic Spot. *Atlanta Journal-Constitution*, August 26, A1, A6.

City of Atlanta Department of Aviation. 1999. *Master Plan. Working Paper VIIB: Evaluation of Long-Term Alternatives—Socioeconomic and Environmental Analysis.* Atlanta: Hartsfield Atlanta International Airport.

Copeland, L. 2003. Hartsfield International Airport Renaming Splits Atlantans. *USA Today,* October 2. Available at ⟨http://www.usatoday.com/travel/news/2003/10/03-atl-name.htm⟩ (accessed June 13, 2006).

Duffy, K. 2003. Excavation Turns Up Anger; Steamed: Residents near Airport Fight Proposal to Turn Away Dirt Site into Landfill. *Atlanta Journal-Constitution,* September 29, F1.

Emling, S. 1996. Black Areas in City Pay Steep Rates. *Atlanta Journal-Constitution,* June 30, A16.

Enchautegui, M. E., M. Fix, P. Loprest, S. C. von der Lippe, and D. Wissoker. 1997. *Do Minority-Owned Businesses Get a Fair Share of Government Contracts?* Washington, DC: The Urban Institute.

Environmental Assessment. 1982. *Proposed Runway Development Project.* William B. Hartsfield Atlanta International Airport. Atlanta: City of Atlanta.

Farber, H. 2003. Mountain of Criticism Greet Landfill Approval. *Atlanta Journal-Constitution,* August 28, J11.

Frankston, J. 2004. $53 Billion OK'd to Stall Gridlock. *Atlanta Journal-Constitution,* December 2, C6.

Glaeser, E. L., M. Kahn, and C. Chu. 2001. *Job Sprawl: Employment Location in U.S. Metropolitan Areas.* Washington, DC: Brookings Institution.

Goldberg, D. 1997. Regional Growing Pains. *Atlanta Journal-Constitution,* March 10, E5.

Goldberg, D. 1999. Deal Kills Money for 44 Roads But 17 Others Get Go-ahead as Environmentalists Drop Suit. *Atlanta Journal-Constitution,* June 21, A1.

Hartsfield Atlanta International Airport. 1999. *Draft Environmental Impact Statement: 9,000-Foot Fifth Runway and Associated Projects.*

Hartsfield Atlanta International Airport. 2004. Airport Fact Sheet. Available at ⟨http://65.213.181.70/default.asp?url=http://65.213.181.70/sublevels/airport_info/operstat.htm⟩ (accessed January 31, 2005).

Harvey, S. 1998. Soundproofing Is Big Business around Hartsfield. *Atlanta Journal-Constitution,* July 29, A18.

Hendricks, G. 1998. Hartsfield City Limits: Businesses near Airport Ready to Fight for Territory; Coalition Formed: Group Wants a Say on How Expansion Will Affect Residents and Commerce. *Atlanta Journal-Constitution,* June 29, E4.

Hendricks, G. 2000. Tale of Two Airports: DFW a Magnet, Hartsfield Penned In. *Atlanta Journal-Constitution,* May 1, B1.

Hirschman, D. 2006. 5th Runway Opens with a Flourish. *Atlanta Journal-Constitution,* May 15, A1.

Leinberger, C. 1998. The Metropolis Observed. *Urban Land* 57 (October): 28–33.

Lewyn, M. 2000. Suburban Sprawl: Not Just an Environmental Issue. *Marquette Law Review* 84, no. 2 (Winter): 301–382.

Martin Associates. 2000. *The 1999 Economic Impact of Hartsfield Atlanta International Airport.*

Metropolitan Planning Commission. 1952. *Up Ahead: A Metropolitan Land Use Plan for Metropolitan Atlanta.* Atlanta: Metropolitan Planning Commission.

Mumford Center. 2000. Table 5: Neighborhood Median Income of the Average Black and White Household. In *Census 2000 Metropolitan Racial and Ethnic Change Series.* Available at ⟨http://mumford1.dyndns.org/cen2000/SepUneq/SUReport/sepunequal8.htm⟩.

National Black Business Council. 1996. *National Black Business Council Fact Sheet.* Culver City, CA: NBBC.

Natural Resources Defense Council. 1996. *Flying Off Course: Environmental Impacts of America's Airports.* New York: Natural Resources Defense Council.

Padgett, D., and C. Brown. 2004. Top Cities for African Americans. *Black Enterprise* 34, no. 12:78–103.

Rice, B. R. 1983. Atlanta: If Dixie Were Atlanta. In *Sunbelt Cities: Growth since World War II,* ed. R. M. Bernard and B. R. Rice. Austin: University of Texas Press.

Saporta, M. 2003. Transportation Funds Must Be Shared Fairly. *Atlanta Journal-Constitution,* February 24, E3.

Saporta, M. 2004. Transit Funding in Mass. Opens Eyes of Atlantans. *Atlanta Journal-Constitution,* May 17, E1.

Scott, P. 2002. Blasting for Airport's Dirt Rattles Clayton Residents. *Atlanta Journal-Constitution,* December 29, D1.

Scott, P. 2003a. Work for Runway Riles Cherry Hill Residents. *Atlanta Journal-Constitution,* April 10, J11.

Scott, P. 2003b. Foes of Blasting Say Earthquake Is Nothing New. *Atlanta Journal-Constitution,* May 8, J15.

Sierra Club. 1998. *The Dark Side of the American Dream: The Cost and Consequences of Suburban Sprawl.* College Park, MD: Sierra Club.

Smith, G. M. 1999. Atlanta's Working Solution to Smog. *Atlanta Journal-Constitution,* August 30, E1, E5.

Southern Environmental Law Center. 1999. SELC Scores Major Victory in Atlanta Lawsuit. *Southern Resources* (Summer): 1, 5.

Squires, G. 1997. *Insurance Redlining: Disinvestments and the Evolving Role of Financial Institutions.* Washington, DC: The Urban Institute.

Squires, G. 1998. Forgoing a Tradition of Redlining for a Future of Reinvestment. *Business Journal* (Milwaukee), July 24, 50.

Stanford, D. 2003. Metro Roads Shortchanged: Funding Formula Steers Cash to Rural Highways at the Expense of Gridlocked Atlanta Motorists. *Atlanta Journal-Constitution*, September 28, A1.

Tagami, K. 2002. Moving the Earth; Enough Dirt to Fill 6 Georgia Domes: Conveyor Leads to What Will Be Hartsfield's $1.3 Billion Fifth Runway. *Atlanta Journal-Constitution*, October 10, A1.

Tagami, K. 2003. Pushing Dirt: 160 Workers Like Hartsfield Runway Gig. *Atlanta Journal-Constitution*, April 20, F1.

Urban Land Institute. 2000. *Metro Atlanta Southern Crescent: Regional Economic Development for Hartsfield International Airport and Vicinity.* London: Elsevier.

U.S. Bureau of the Census. 1980. *Population and Housing Characteristics.* Washington, DC: U.S. Bureau of the Census.

U.S. Department of Transportation. 1998. *Federal Highway Administration, Certification Report for the Atlanta Transportation Management Area.* Washington, DC: Federal Highway Administration.

U.S. Department of Transportation. 1999. Assessment of Environmental Justice Issues in Atlanta Proposed Work Plan. Paper presented at meeting of the Federal Highway Administration, June 28.

Weinberg, D. H. 2000. Press Briefing on 1999 Income and Poverty Estimates. Washington, DC: U.S. Bureau of the Census.

White, M. C., R. A. Etzel, W. D. Wilcox, and C. Lloyd. 1994. Exacerbations of Childhood Asthma and Ozone Pollution in Atlanta. *Environmental Research* 65:56.

Yago, G., and A. Pankratz. 2000. *The Minority Business Challenge: Democratizing Capital for Emerging Domestic Markets.* Los Angeles: Milken Institute, U.S. Department of Commerce, Minority Business Development Agency.

10

Environmental Justice and Transportation Equity: A Review of MPOs

Thomas W. Sanchez and James F. Wolf

Surface transportation policies at the local, regional, state, and national levels have a direct impact on urban land use and development patterns. The types of transportation facilities and services in which public funds are invested provide varying levels of access to meet basic social and economic needs. The way regions develop land dictates the need for certain types of transportation, and on the other hand, the transportation options in which regions invest influence patterns of urban development.

While many lament the trend toward suburban sprawl as damaging to the environment or unaesthetic, those who support social equity should also be concerned about the associated impacts. Substantial investment in highway development and other transportation programs that encourage private automobile use has supported low-density developments that extend increasingly farther and farther from the central city, and to residential and commercial areas that are increasingly spread out, producing "edgeless cities" (Lang 2003). In addition to being costly to state and local governments, transportation policies that encourage these growth patterns play a substantial role in producing some indirect, negative social and economic effects, including perpetuating residential segregation and exacerbating the inability of minorities to access entry-level employment, which is increasingly found in suburban areas. MPOs are well suited to provide leadership in the areas of metropolitan development and civil rights.

The federal role in transportation expanded substantially during the second half of the twentieth century. The interstate highway program of the 1950s was followed by an ambitious mass transit initiative during the 1960s and 1970s. As federally supported large central city projects, federal programs included requirements for project review at the metropolitan level. MPOs were established to perform a key role in regional transportation planning, and federal transportation laws created and heavily funded these regional planning bodies to coordinate federal transportation programs. During the final decade of the twentieth century, MPOs assumed responsibilities beyond transportation planning with one of the new planning requirements being social equity, also known as environmental justice, to be included as provisions of regional plans.

Two ways to evaluate the importance that MPOs place on social or environmental equity is to examine the products of their planning activities and also the representativeness of their policymakers. This chapter discusses the extent to which large MPOs incorporate environmental justice concerns into their planning processes. Three dimensions of this issue are reviewed: efforts targeted at assessing the fairness of planning outcomes and the promotion of social equity; public participation in MPO processes; and analysis of the extent to which MPO boards underrepresent social, economic, and ethnic/racial groups. The discussion relies on existing research for background on the MPO structure and its responsibilities, and then presents the results of a survey to examine the types of equity planning conducted by MPOs, the forms of public participation efforts, and the representation of voting board members.

There is considerable potential for MPOs to efficiently and effectively confront questions of equity within metropolitan areas. The structure of MPOs is such that political and geographic fragmentation can be reduced, eroding the potential for continued housing market segregation, economic and social segregation in schools, and increasing suburban affluence at the expense of central city infrastructure and other public services (powell and Graham 2002). One challenge for MPOs is coordinating local government competition while at the same time maintaining standards of fairness and equity relative to transportation investments.

Along with acknowledging the significant impacts their decisions have on the built environment, many MPOs have attempted to evaluate their actions in light of Executive Order 12898. Now, ten years after this order was issued by President Clinton, the question is whether MPOs have undertaken actions consistent with the mandate. Environmental justice and transportation equity planning analyses are examples of such actions. While scores of equity analyses were conducted during the 1970s, the practice was relatively absent until it reemerged in the late 1990s.

Overview of MPO Structure and Responsibilities

ISTEA made MPOs primarily responsible for planning and allocating transportation funding in metropolitan areas by providing funds directly to them. Although MPOs have been in existence since the 1950s, generally operating as either a subdivision of state DOTs or a function of a regional COG, ISTEA and the USDOT's implementing regulations made them more influential, and gave them uniform functions and responsibilities. ISTEA also broadened the membership of the policy-setting boards of MPOs governing large areas, requiring that they include representatives from local governments in the region, agencies operating major transportation systems, and state officials.

ISTEA and its implementing regulations required MPOs and state planning agencies to develop twenty-year regional plans outlining in detail the priorities, policies, and strategies for the region's transportation system. MPOs were also required to prepare, with community involvement, a TIP listing the transportation projects that would be undertaken within three years.

While state DOTs control the majority of overall transportation planning decisions, MPOs play an important role in shaping urban transportation policies that affect the major concentrations of population within states that also include significant numbers of minorities and low-income individuals. Both of these organizations can play an increasingly crucial part in promoting social equity through the broad view of social inclusion.[1] Some argue that transportation service provision, the consequences of interaction between land use and transportation decisions, and issues of spatial equity are effectively addressed on a regional basis and at appropriate stages in the planning process. To be effective, this requires balancing the roles of state, regional, and local planning agencies through a coordination mechanism that does not currently exist.

ISTEA and TEA-21 established planning criteria for MPOs to consider as they review their transportation programs. These criteria went beyond specific transportation elements to include a wide range of issues where transportation projects affect other aspects of metropolitan development. The Constrained Long-Range Plan (CLRP) is expected to show compliance with EPA air quality standards, consider implications of transportation projects on air quality and land use, foster economic and community development, and be sensitive to equity issues. Except for the air quality requirement, the guidance for meeting the criteria for the remaining list of policy concerns is less defined.

Addressing Equity: Environmental Justice and Transportation Planning

The issue of equity within metropolitan transportation planning processes is primarily being addressed through the environmental justice component of MPO programs. Title VI of the Civil Rights Act of 1964 and Executive Order 12898 established environmental justice as a federal policy, with Clinton's order stating that "each Federal agency shall make achieving environmental justice part of its mission by identifying and addressing, as appropriate, disproportionately high and adverse human health or environmental effects of its programs, policies, and activities on minority populations and low-income populations."

Both the USDOT and the FHWA issued Environmental Justice Orders (USDOT Order 5610.2 and FHWA Order 6640.23) in 1997 and 1998, respectively. These orders described how environmental justice elements can be incorporated into existing federal programs. The USDOT (2000, ii) cited three core principles of environmental justice that can be used for analysis and decision making, including both procedural and substantive elements.

1. To avoid, minimize, or mitigate disproportionately high and adverse human health and environmental effects, including social and economic effects, on minority populations and low-income populations;

2. To ensure the full and fair participation by all potentially affected communities in the transportation decision-making process;

3. To prevent the denial of, reduction in, or significant delay in the receipt of benefits by minority and low-income populations.

Three issues constitute the core of equity and environmental justice concerns for MPOs. The first relates to the more formal political processes used by MPOs—specifically, the formal membership and voting processes. The second concerns the ISTEA/TEA-21 requirement for public participation in the MPO planning processes. Finally, the third equity issue concerns how the specific groups are served or underserved by transportation programs. The remainder of this chapter addresses these issues.

Fostering Public Involvement

ISTEA required greater public involvement in the MPO process, and MPOs were expected to ensure increased and formal opportunities for timely and effective public involvement in the development of the CLRP, TIP, and other planning activities. In 1995, an Advisory Commission on Intergovernmental Relations (ACIR) study reported that more MPOs were making efforts to meet this requirement, with 78 percent of MPOs reporting various efforts to encourage public involvement. The report concluded that there were more opportunities for involvement available to the public, more staff available to support these processes, the development of new involvement techniques, a sense that MPOs were listening, and a feeling that this involvement would make a difference in planning processes (U.S. ACIR 1995). A follow-on study noted improvements, but "that much work apparently remains to be done" (U.S. ACIR 1997).

In a 2000 study, Andrew Goetz and his colleagues at the University of Denver again confirmed the observation that MPOs were making progress in this area. The review of four MPOs in large metropolitan areas reported that the MPOs felt most successful about their public involvement activities. Each had extensive public involvement programs and felt that this contributed to their planning efforts. Involvement early in the process seemed particularly valuable because it surfaced potentially difficult conflicts, and provided time to head off litigation and delay (U.S. General Accounting Office 2002; McDowell 1999; Goldman and Deakin 2000). MPOs supported the public processes, but did want greater flexibility in the FHWA requirements (U.S. General Accounting Office 2002).

At the same time, it is not entirely clear that public involvement represents a deeply or enthusiastically held MPO value. On balance, Robert W. Gage and Bruce D. McDowell (1995) found that at best, the MPOs' directors rated their efforts as "slightly ineffective." The American Association of State Highway and Transportation Officials (AASHTO) and their member states have been critical of participation procedures because they seem to serve more as a "lightning rod" for controversial projects. Such procedures bring out those with strong opposition on a one-issue basis, but do not provide a more continually engaged public (Goldman and Deakin 2000).

Creating public participation places heavy demands on the capabilities of MPOs. Traditionally, they have not invested a great deal of energy in this area. They had to find new ways to engage the public when they did not have the resources or techniques to do so. MPOs needed to quickly learn how to involve diverse and hard-to-reach persons. They confronted the problem every public outreach effort faces of involving people in issues beyond the single one that they usually oppose or support intensely (U.S. Government Accounting Office 2002).

While McDowell (1999, 15) saw continuing challenges, he also found evidence of progress: "memberships of policy boards and committees have been expanded, consensus-building processes have been enhanced, non-traditional participants have been recruited, special workgroups and task forces have been established to explore new issue areas, new advisory councils have been set up, and weighted voting has been introduced." MPOs, particularly in large metropolitan areas with substantial technical capability, have taken advantage of Internet technologies to enhance contact with persons outside of normal political processes. These MPOs regularly post reports, schedules of meetings, committee membership, and other materials related to their planning activities.

MPOs are increasingly performing distributional analyses to assess the incidence of costs and benefits by location as well as demographic group. In addition to identifying and measuring direct impacts from policy interventions, these analyses are concerned with direct effects such as how individuals or groups adapt to interventions—such as transportation improvements. These adaptations can take the form of physical or psychological responses (such as health) as well as economic responses (such as residential relocation), and do not occur randomly within metropolitan regions. Distributional analyses generally identify the outcomes of decision-making processes, but unfortunately like a broader range of social impact analyses, they do not identify weaknesses or biases in the system that produced such outcomes.

MPO Political Participation and Voting Bias

Several equity issues arise from the structural arrangements of membership and voting. First, since most MPOs follow the structural format of a COG, each political jurisdiction normally receives one vote. Citing the one-person, one-vote principle, larger jurisdictions may consider themselves unfairly represented. At the same time, the smaller jurisdictions prefer the one-jurisdiction, one-vote procedure as a way to prevent larger jurisdictions, often in the urban center, from dominating planning recommendations and decisions.

Federal transportation laws do not require an organizational or vote structure that prevents bias in allocating transportation investments. Paul G. Lewis and Mary Sprague (1997) identified four major types of MPOs, each with unique voting arrangements. The most prevalent type is the COG. A COG is constituted as a cooperative organization of the local governments in a region. Typically, each participating local government in the region appoints a representative to the COG board, on which they serve as a fully voting member, regardless of the size of the local government they represent.

As most MPO boards are either COG boards or adjuncts to a COG, MPO voting is usually nonproportional or unweighted based on population. This is because many MPO governing boards, especially COG-based ones, are apportioned on a one-government, one-vote basis. This gives each jurisdiction, including small suburban municipalities, as much say in MPO policymaking and allocation as central cities. Given the new challenges facing MPOs, and especially their charge for addressing regional needs explicitly, this creates tension among competing jurisdictions (Francois 1995). As Lewis observed, however, in few cases is the MPO voting structure apportioned directly on the basis of population (Lewis and Sprague 1997; Lewis 1998). Lewis (1998, 813) argued that metropolitan bodies such as a COG and an MPO have been structured "toward consensus, with more concern toward representing all local governments on regional boards than on establishing equitable criteria for the representation of the region's population. This has led to serious problems of mal-apportionment in many regional organizations, including MPOs."

As MPOs took on more regional decision-making authority (particularly in the area of allocating funds), issues of representation emerged. Lewis and Sprague reviewed the problematic nature of various voting mechanisms in MPOs and the potential for legal challenges resulting from unequal representation embedded in these voting procedures (Lewis and Sprague 1997; Lewis 1998). They reported that MPOs employed a range of voting approaches: some used one vote per member, while others relied on variations of weighted voting. Their study of California MPOs concluded that "the average California MPO deviates from proportionate representation of its population by about one-third" (Lewis and Sprague 1997, 9).

In an approach used to lessen the impact of the disproportional representation of smaller jurisdiction, some MPOs allow for weighted voting at the request of any of the member jurisdictions. Weights for board member votes can be set in proportion to the population being represented by the board member. For example, if a metropolitan region has four member jurisdictions with one hundred thousand persons each, equally weighted votes would account for 25 percent of the overall board vote (assuming full participation). If three of the four jurisdictions had a hundred thousand persons and the fourth had two hundred thousand, however, then the voting weights would instead be 20 percent for the first three and 40 percent for the fourth. Another method gives jurisdictions additional votes in proportion to population size. In the case of the four-jurisdiction example above, the first three would have one vote each and the fourth would have two. This method is weaker in terms of producing proportionality when population sizes varying by irregular and uneven amounts. Following the practices used by many COGs, split votes are avoided whenever possible. Controversial issues are often delayed, and resorting to weighted voting is likewise avoided in order to maintain a collaborative atmosphere among COG members.

The representational issue gets even more complicated because of the hybrid character of MPOs. They are first a group of local government officials—hence the concern for the equitable representation for each jurisdiction. At the same time, they are also expected to include other transportation partners, often nonvoting, such as the state DOTs and transit providers. Structural problems abound for MPOs trying to address both the equity issue of representation implied by one-person, one-vote assumptions and the need to involve important partners in the MPO planning process. A U.S. ACIR (1997) report that examined the certification documents completed by MPOs as required by ISTEA found recurring problems associated with certain structural dimensions.

About one-third of the certification reviews identified needed improvements for MPO structural arrangements with reference to board and committee processes. The report pointed out the need for MPO boards and committees to broaden their participation on boards, and policy and technical committees, particularly with state DOTs and other providers of transportation. The ACIR report urged that MPOs allow state district offices to vote a proxy for state DOT headquarters staff and that MPOs move to weighted voting. In addition, the ACIR study identified a continuing need to define the roles and responsibilities of different partners in the MPO processes, especially in relation to the CLRPs and TIPs. Another structural recommendation of this review recognized the significance of using meetings as one of the key MPO administrative processes, and the need to move toward more regular and open meeting processes (U.S. ACIR 1997).

The ISTEA/TEA-21 emphasis on multimodalities, partnerships with nontraditional partners, and extensive public involvement has given rise to a constitutional concern over the one-person, one-vote standard for political processes. Lewis identified representation issues that would eventually involve constitutional questions of one-person, one-vote. The issue became still murkier when new partners were given varying degrees of formal status and voting power on decision-making boards. The inclusion of state DOTs, transit agencies, and other transportation providers into the voting mix only exacerbated the problem of identifying representation plans that would meet legal requirements (Lewis 1998). The problem is with both formal voting inequalities among jurisdictions as well as the more informal decision-making processes. Since most votes are unanimous, the more substantive deliberations occur in the technical committees and among members of the MPO rather than among elected political leaders (Lewis 1998).

Addressing Civil Rights and the Needs of Underserved Populations

The issues of political representation and public participation are direct examples of equity issues in the MPO process. ISTEA/TEA-21 also required MPOs to examine how traditionally underrepresented groups were engaged in MPO processes as well in the substantive issues. These policies were incorporated into ISTEA/TEA-21 and therefore MPO planning processes. Other, more specific provisions followed from these general principles. For example, transportation projects were expected to improve the mobility of the economically disadvantaged through "intermodal connections between people and jobs, goods and markets, and neighborhoods" (Bullard 1996). The Personal Responsibility and Work Opportunity Act of 1996, the welfare-to-work initiative, and the job-access/reverse-commuting program supported low-income populations to transition into the workplace (Lacombe 1998; Willis 1997). These initiatives were part of the welfare reform legislation that created job-access programs, which were designed to aid low-income populations in finding and maintaining gainful employment. Many MPOs have produced reports of various forms on reverse-commuting projects that help individuals in the welfare reform program find transportation to and from their place of employment (Blumenberg and Waller 2003; Wolf and Farquhar 2003). Most reports lack rigorous statistical analysis, but rather rely on anecdotal or descriptive summaries of service performance.

MPO Survey

A survey of fifty large MPOs assessed the level of effort put forth toward environmental justice and transportation equity issues. This included a content analysis of MPOs' "plan of work," three-year plans (TIPs), twenty-year plans, and state plans—many of which were available electronically. The objective was to determine whether transportation equity principles were integrated into transportation plans at the metropolitan scale, and whether adequate consideration was given to public participation and accountability. The review specifically looked for language codifying the enforcement or monitoring of civil rights, environmental justice, social justice, transportation equity, and public participation activities. Having addressed one or more of these issues through public reporting (that is, required plans) indicates a seriousness of intent and the degree of accountability.

Along with these planning efforts, the survey looked specifically at the racial or ethnic balance of MPO boards relative to the jurisdictions that they represent. This section addresses that issue as well as exploring trends in equity planning and concern about civil rights. In particular, we used the following general criteria to guide our data collection:

• Does the agency include specific language about civil rights issues in its long-range planning document?

• Does the agency have a separate policy document that deals specifically with civil rights issues?

• Does the agency devote staff time or positions (full-time equivalents) to civil rights affairs?

• Does the agency budget specifically allocate resources to civil rights staff, projects, or other activities?

• How has the agency involved the public in civil rights matters? This may include advisory committees, public meetings dedicated to civil rights issues, and other modes of public input.

Approach

To collect information on fifty large MPOs, we began with a search and review of individual MPO Web sites. Nearly all of the selected MPOs had Web sites, most of which included board member rosters as well as plans and other documents related to their planning activities. Follow-up telephone contacts were made in cases where certain data were not available on Web sites. Individual Web sites were examined because there were no comprehensive sources of information about MPO board members, plans, or activities other than listings of organizations and basic demographics of their constituencies. The data were collected between May and August 2004. The following is a descriptive analysis of the data collected.

Transportation Equity Planning Activities

This study examines the extent to which large MPOs incorporate transportation equity, environmental justice, and civil rights concerns into their planning processes. Most MPOs address civil rights issues in their long-range plan, and environmental justice was most commonly discussed as part of regional goals and objectives, public participation and outreach, and regional demographic trends. Several MPOs incorporated geographic analyses showing the spatial distribution of low-income households and racial minorities.[2] In addition, nearly one in four MPOs had produced a planning document specific to environmental justice or civil rights issues (a list of the eleven is shown in table 10.1). This is compared to only eight out of fifty U.S. states that reported having adopted environmental justice programs in 2000 (American Chemical Council 2000). Of the states with adopted policies, most were focused on complying with Title VI of the Civil Rights Act of 1964, which prohibits dis-

Table 10.1
Transportation equity planning documents

MPO	Plan/document
CATS (Chicago area)	Unified Work Plan
MTC (San Francisco area)	2001 RTP Equity Analysis and EJ Report
DVRPC (Philadelphia area)	"And Justice for All" Report
SEMCOG	Regional Transportation Plan
North Central Texas COG	Mobility 2025
Metropolitan Washington COG	Access for All and CLRP
Puget Sound Regional Council	Title VI Plan; Environmental Justice Demographics Profile
Boston MPO	Regional Transportation Plan
Northeast Ohio Areawide Coordinating Agency	Title VI Plan
Rhode Island Statewide Planning Program	Community Participation–Title VI
Oahu MPO (HI)	Environmental Justice in the OMPO Planning Process

crimination in any program receiving federal funds. NEPA and 23 USC 109(h) also require consideration of social impacts that may result from projects with federal support (USDOT 2003).

There were some common elements among these documents, with most being guided by either Title VI of the Civil Rights Act or Executive Order 12898. The underlying concern expressed was whether proposed transportation investments were biased toward particular demographic groups. To this end, most MPO efforts defined and quantified the proportion of metropolitan population within "targeted" or "protected" populations. In addition, the locations and concentrations of these populations were mapped along with the location of transportation improvements. The objective of such mapping efforts is to illustrate the distributional equity of MPO plans. Distributional analyses represent a subset of social impact analyses, and along with identifying and measuring direct impacts from policy interventions, social impact analysis is also concerned with direct effects such as how individuals or groups adapt to interventions. These adaptations can take the form of physical or psychological responses (such as health) as well as economic responses (such as residential relocation), and do not occur randomly within urban areas. Distributional analyses generally identify the outcomes of decision-making processes, and like a broader range of social impact analyses, do not identify weaknesses or biases in the system that produced such outcomes.

In many cases, environmental justice plans outlined specific strategies for public participation as key elements to guide and implement equity planning. Most of the efforts documented by MPOs appeared to be relatively recent, so there were few longitudinal assessments of program effectiveness. Such evaluations will be possible in the future given the types and range of indicators that were included in the plans. Indicators within planning reports include measures of regional employment accessibility, transit accessibility, traffic congestion levels, environmental impact, and transportation mobility. Few, however, concentrate on measures of outcomes such as labor participation rates, wage levels, school attendance, or overall regional accessibility.

In the United Kingdom, policymakers and social justice advocates often take a broader view of social inequity. British efforts to eradicate "social exclusion" address communities that are isolated from or marginalized by the general society. In the United States, attempts to counter spatial inequity are usually limited to improving housing and employment access—represented in some respects by residential segregation—whereas social exclusion is a much broader concept. It encompasses concerns about physical (personal) exclusion, geographic exclusion, exclusion from facilities, economic exclusion, temporal exclusion, fear-based exclusion, and space exclusion. Addressing social exclusion includes addressing problems such as the lack of access to jobs, education, and training; low levels of access to public transportation at particular times of the day, which has an impact on persons without cars who work late and early-morning shifts; and limited access to public and private spaces because of unsafe conditions and design.

Overall, it was unclear in nearly all cases how the results of MPO equity analyses could be used as feedback in the transportation planning and decision-making process. Emphasis was often placed on public involvement, where information from the analyses could be discussed and used to identify areas of potential concern. In other cases, the information generated through data analysis processes focused on social equity became inputs to regional transportation modeling (see, for example, Metropolitan Transportation Commission 2001).

In addition to planning documents, we looked at whether MPOs allocated staff or budget resources to transportation equity, public participation, and other outreach activities. Only 15 percent of the MPOs responded that they have staff specifically involved with civil rights oversight and planning. On the other hand, it is interesting to note that while the selected MPOs acknowledged that they provide little support in terms of staff positions or budget resources for civil rights, close to three-quarters reported that they conduct activities that had a civil rights focus. The selected MPOs reported that on average, they conducted three of the types of activities shown in figure 10.1—the most frequent of these being public meetings (68 percent) that were specifically for environmental justice or transportation equity purposes.

In general, it appeared that the motivation for many of these agencies to prepare plans or analyses (shown in table 10.1), or conduct planning activities (shown in figure 10.1), was a reaction to legal threats, condi-

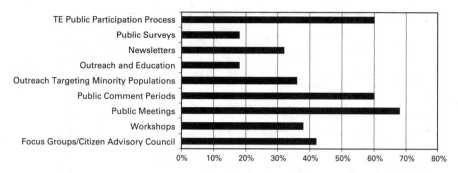

Figure 10.1
Transportation equity–related planning activities

tions of recertification, or compliance with Title VI reporting requirements. Others either directly or indirectly referred to threats of lawsuits
as a rationale for performing or preparing equity plans and policies. It
was not apparent whether any of the organizations had proactively carried out an equity plan, analysis, or other activity as a result of regional
problems identified by MPO representatives or planning staff. This is also
true when documents refer to "agency policies" as being the reason for
social equity–related planning activities. The policy could have been generated from within the organization, or could be the result of the enforcement actions mentioned above. Further research is needed to more
closely examine the quality and motivation of these studies.

Board Composition
Our survey assembled the MPO board member rosters for fifty large
MPOs based on population size. Voting members of these boards are instrumental in programming federal and state transportation funds, and
should ideally reflect the racial and ethnic diversity of their constituents.
A culturally representative board suggests that every person has an equal
chance of providing input (Nelson, Robbins, and Simonsen 1998). The
selected MPO boards averaged twenty-six voting members each, with
some having as few as seven (Greater Buffalo and Portland metro) and
others with as many as seventy-six (SCAG in Los Angeles). Board size was
not clearly correlated with the population size of the jurisdiction. This is
an artifact of the one-jurisdiction, one-vote system, where a jurisdiction's

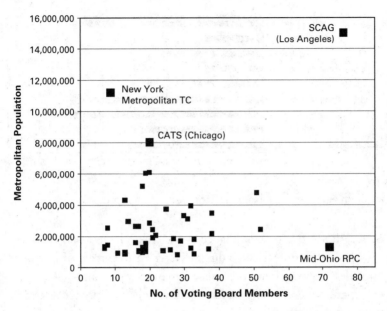

Figure 10.2
Board size and metropolitan population size

number of residents does not directly determine the number of voting board representatives per jurisdiction. In addition, participation by non-local representatives (regional, state, and federal) on each board also increased the number of voting board members. The outliers among the MPOs were the Chicago, New York, and Los Angeles ones, which had low per capita levels of board representation due to their population sizes of eight million, eleven million, and fifteen million, respectively (see figure 10.2).

Gender

Little attention has been paid to the role of gender in local or regional government decision making. While the travel patterns of women have distinct differences from those of men, decision making about transportation investments and policies ought to be informed equally by female and male perspectives (see Root and Schintler 1999). Overall, females represent about 25 percent of voting board members in the selected MPOs. No MPO boards were without female members, with an average of over six females per board. The San Diego AOG, the Denver Regional COG (DRCOG), SEMCOG, the Hillsborough County MPO, and the Metropolitan Council of Twin Cities had the highest proportion of females (each with over 40 percent). Additional research could examine whether policy emphases are affected by higher levels of female leadership, especially as they relate to the identified travel needs of women and children.

Race and Ethnicity

As expected, the voting members of the selected MPO boards were predominantly white (approximately 88 percent). African Americans represented about 7 percent of all board members, followed by Hispanics (3 percent) and Asian/Pacific Islanders (1 percent). Native Americans and "other" (combined) represented less than 1 percent of all voting board members. This compares to these MPOs' overall racial/ethnic composition, which was 61 percent non-Hispanic white, 15 percent non-Hispanic black, 6 percent Asian, and 17 percent Hispanic as of 2000.

Furthermore, thirteen of the fifty boards included in the study had all white board members. Ten of the boards surveyed had greater than 20 percent nonwhite board representatives. The most racially/ethnically diverse among these were the Oahu MPO (31 percent white) and the Miami (Florida) Urbanized Area MPO (46 percent white). The boards with the largest percentage of African American members were the MPOs in Miami (32 percent), Washington, DC (22 percent), and Philadelphia (17 percent). Overall, there was only a slight correlation between the racial/ethnic composition of MPO boards and the racial/ethnic characteristics of their jurisdictions.

Board Representation

One challenge facing MPOs is that many of their boards are overrepresented by suburban interests by virtue of a one-area, one-vote system. When district boundaries for MPO board representatives and planning units are drawn that result in approximately equal-size geographic areas, urban-core areas that have denser populations end up being underrepresented compared with suburban zones that have lower population densities. This system influences the level of public involvement and participation of persons based on residential location—and negatively so in the case of low-income neighborhoods of color in urban-core areas.

For the selected MPOs in this analysis, there was not a correlation between racially diverse MPO boards and the number of environmental justice planning activities. This suggests that board representation as previously discussed may not lead to particular planning actions—in this case, the performance of environmental justice–oriented planning analyses. Other research indicates that MPO board and voting structures have a significant effect on the outcomes of transportation investment decisions—especially those related to public transit (see Nelson et al. 2004). Arthur C. Nelson and colleagues found that the ratio of urban to suburban votes was correlated with the allocation of transportation funds between road and transit modes. In particular, they discovered that for each additional suburban voter on an MPO board, between 1 and 7 percent fewer funds were allocated to transit in MPO budgets.

Although specific information about the racial and ethnic composition of MPO boards had not previously been collected, we expected that minorities were underrepresented on MPO boards relative to the demographic characteristics of their constituents. For example, this was the situation facing SEMCOG as constituents recently challenged the representativeness of voting board members (Brooks 2004). In particular, the constituents were dissatisfied with expenditure levels for transit compared to highways in the Detroit metropolitan region, which they saw as skewing investments toward sprawl and consumption of rural land. The case has increased the visibility of board structure and procedure regarding MPO decision making.

Summary

It is difficult to gauge the level of commitment to transportation equity principles by MPOs simply by describing the types of planning activities that they undertake. In addition, while the racial and ethnic composition of voting members is an indirect measure of adequate public participation and representation, it may serve as an indicator of the degree to which minorities have a stake in regional policymaking.

While planning analyses directed at equity concerns and adequate representation are two visible factors affecting MPO planning outcomes, they certainly have both practical and symbolic importance. Data collection, analysis, and system evaluation regarding fairness at least signals an awareness of potential weaknesses and corrections. Follow-through and implementation, however, is the ultimate sign of organizational commitment. Moreover, a diverse set of representative policymakers would ideally reflect the range of constituent preferences.

An interesting question is whether planning analysis and representative boards are either substitutes or complements within an MPO structure. Is it sufficient to have thorough data collection, analysis, and monitoring of equity outcomes at the metropolitan scale despite unrepresentative board members, or do representative boards (and their consequent voting) more directly influence policy and decision making that affect distributional equity? And finally, does the combination of planning analyses and representative boards have synergistic effects that provide a greater potential for addressing the needs of traditionally underserved populations?

The Challenges Ahead

Specific challenges remain in regard to greater public participation and involvement in transportation decision making by state DOTs and MPOs (Sanchez, Stolz, and Ma 2003). Community-based groups that assist transportation agencies should be encouraged to improve outreach processes and strategies to identify culturally diverse groups and facilitate their involvement. These efforts are also greatly needed to support the information dissemination about transportation and related land use impacts. Mechanisms are needed that allow the formal recognition of coalitions of community representatives on MPO advisory committees and decision-making boards. In addition, MPOs, local governments, researchers, and CBOs need resources for more data collection and analysis about transportation access to basic needs such as health care, jobs, affordable housing, and public education (Surface Transportation Policy Project 2003).

Along with improved information, the certification of MPO compliance with the ISTEA/TEA-21 planning process is a critical area where the federal partner can play a significant role. Certification is one way that the federal agencies try to hold MPOs accountable for meeting federal requirements. MPOs and state DOTs must conduct self-certification reviews annually. They must examine major issues they face, how they undertake planning regulations and consider the seven planning criteria—involving disadvantaged business enterprises, the CCA, civil rights, and ADA provisions—and particularly how those MPOs in designated areas not meeting air conformity standards meet special requirements (McDowell 1999). The FHWA can determine that MPOs fall into one of four categories: full certification, certification subject to specific corrective actions being taken, limited certification, and withheld certification (McDowell 1999). In the first round of certification reviews in 1996, no MPO had its certification withheld.

It is in the best interest of MPOs to proactively address issues of fairness in decision making, planning, and representation, especially as it relates to allocating transportation funds. Many MPOs already have policies guided by either Title VI of the Civil Rights Act or Executive Order 12898, with several of them outlining specific strategies for public participation as key elements to guide planning. MPOs can also protect themselves against legal challenges such as those faced by SEMCOG, where as noted above, constituents recently challenged the representativeness of voting board members and were dissatisfied with expenditure levels for transit compared to highways in the Detroit metro region. Successful challenges may either be the impetus to improve MPO processes or, if ignored, could undermine MPO effectiveness.

Notes

1. The British government defines social exclusion as "a shorthand term for what can happen when people or areas suffer from a combination of linked problems such as unemployment, poor skills, low incomes, poor housing, high crime, bad health and family breakdown" (Office of the Deputy Prime Minister, Social Exclusion Unit, United Kingdom, n.d.).

2. See, for example, Maricopa Association of Governments 2003 and Mid-America Regional Council 2001.

References

American Chemistry Council. 2000. *Environmental Justice Programs: 50 State Survey.* Washington, DC: Morgan, Lewis, Bockius LLP.

Benjamin, S. B., J. Kincaid, and B. M. McDowell. 1994. MPOs and Weighted Voting. *Intergovernmental Perspective* (Spring): 31–35.

Blumenberg, E., and M. Waller. 2003. *The Long Journey to Work: A Federal Transportation Policy for Working Families.* Washington, DC: Brookings Institution.

Brooks, J. 2004. Unrest Plagues Regional Board. *Detroit News*, January 25.

Bullard, R. D. 1996. Introduction: Environmental Justice and Transportation. In *Environmental Justice and Transportation; Building Model Partnerships: Proceedings Document*, ed. R. D. Bullard. Atlanta: Clark Atlanta University.

Francois, F. B. 1995. State Perspective. Paper presented at the Institutional Aspects of Metropolitan Transportation Planning conference, Williamsburg, VA, May 21–24.

Funders' Network for Smart Growth and Livable Communities. 2002. Community Organizing: A Populist Base for Social Equity and Smart Growth. *Livable Communities@Work*. Miami, FL: FNSGLC.

Gage, R. W., and B. D. McDowell. 1995. ISTEA and the Role of MPOs in the New Transportation Environment: A Midterm Assessment. *Publius* 25, no. 3:133–154.

Goetz, A., P. S. Dempsey, and C. Larson. 2002. Metropolitan Planning Organizations: Findings and Recommendations for Improving Transportation Planning. *Publius* 32, no. 1:87–108.

Goldman, T., and E. Deakin. 2000. Regionalism through Partnerships? Metropolitan Planning since ISTEA. *Berkeley Planning Review* 14:46–75.

Lacombe, A. 1998. *Welfare Reform and Access to Jobs in Boston.* Report BTS–98–A–02. Washington, DC: U.S. Department of Transportation, Bureau of Transportation Statistics.

Lang, R. E. 2003. *Edgeless Cities: Exploring the Elusive Metropolis.* Washington, DC: Brookings Institution Press.

Lewis, P. G. 1998. Regionalism and Representation: Measuring and Assessing Representation in Metropolitan Planning Organizations. *Urban Affairs Review* 33, no. 6:839–854.

Lewis, P. G., and M. Sprague. 1997. *Federal Transportation Policy and the Role of Metropolitan Planning Organizations in California.* San Francisco: Public Policy Institute of California.

Maricopa Association of Governments. 2003. *Regional Transportation Plan.* Phoenix: MAG.

McDowell, B. D. 1999. *Improving Regional Transportation Decisions: MPOs and Certification.* Washington, DC: Brookings Center on Urban and Metropolitan Policy.

Metropolitan Transportation Commission. 2001. *The 2001 Regional Transportation Plan: Equity Analysis and Environmental Justice Report.* Oakland, CA: Metropolitan Transportation Commission.

Mid-America Regional Council. 2001. *Transportation Outlook 2030.* Kansas City, MO: MARC.

Nelson, A. C., T. W. Sanchez, J. F. Wolf, and M. B. Farquhar. 2004. Metropolitan Planning Organization Voting Structure and Transit Investment Bias: Preliminary Analysis with Social Equity Implications, Transportation Research Record (TRR). *Journal of the Transportation Research Board* 1895:1–7.

Nelson, L., M. Robbins, and B. Simonsen. 1998. Introduction to the Special Issue on Governance. *Social Science Journal* 35, no. 4:478–91.

powell, j. a., and K. M. Graham. 2002. Urban Fragmentation as a Barrier to Equal Opportunity. In *Rights at Risk: Equality in an Age of Terrorism*, ed. D. M. Piche, W. L. Taylor, and R. A. Reed. Washington, DC: Citizens Commission on Civil Rights.

Puentes, R., and L. Bailey. 2003. *Improving Metropolitan Decision Making in Transportation: Greater Funding and Devolution for Greater Accountability.* Washington, DC: Brookings Institution.

Root, A., and L. Schintler. 1999. Women, Motorization, and the Environment. *Transportation Research, Part D* 4:353–355.

Sanchez, T. W. 1998. Equity Analysis of Capital Improvement Plans Using GIS: The Case of the Des Moines Urbanized Area. *Journal of Urban Planning and Development* 124, no. 1:33–43.

Sanchez, T. W., R. Stolz, and J. S. Ma. 2003. *Moving to Equity: Addressing Inequitable Effects of Transportation Policies on Minorities.* Cambridge, MA: Civil Rights Project at Harvard University.

Surface Transportation Policy Project. 2003. *Stay the Course: How to Make TEA-21 Even Better.* Washington, DC: Surface Transportation Policy Project.

U.S. Advisory Commission on Intergovernmental Relations. 1995. *MPO Capacity: Improving the Capacity of Metropolitan Planning Organizations to Help Implement National Transportation Policies.* Washington, DC: U.S. Advisory Commission on Intergovernmental Relations.

U.S. Advisory Commission on Intergovernmental Relations. 1997. *Planning Progress: Addressing ISTEA Requirements in Metropolitan Planning Areas.* Washington, DC: U.S. Advisory Commission on Intergovernmental Relations.

U.S. Department of Transportation. 2000. *Transportation and Environmental Justice Case Studies.* Publication no. FHWA-EP-01-010. Washington, DC: U.S. Department of Transportation.

U.S. General Accounting Office. 2002. *Environmental Protection: Federal Incentives Could Help Promote Land Use That Protects Air and Water Quality.* GAO–02–12. Washington, DC: U.S. General Accounting Office.

Willis, N. 1997. Welfare to Work: Where Community and Transportation Advocates Meet. *Progress: Surface Transportation Policy Project* 7, no. 8:5–6.

Wolf, J. F., and M. Farquhar. 2003. Using Metropolitan Planning Organizations as a Test Case for the New Regionalism and the New Governance. Paper presented at the sixty-fourth American Society for Public Administration national conference, Washington, DC, March.

11

Beyond Dirty Diesels: Clean and Just Transportation in Northern Manhattan

Swati R. Prakash

The clouds of toxic black smoke that billow from the tailpipes of diesel-fueled trucks and buses are a familiar sight and smell in many low-income urban communities and communities of color. Linked to lung cancer and early death, diesel exhaust can also trigger asthma attacks, making it a special concern for people with this disorder. Ironically, diesel-fueled buses form the backbone of public transportation in many urban communities, and low-income residents are disproportionately dependent on public transportation. Rather than face a trade-off between transportation and public health, many of these communities are calling attention to the need to develop environmentally healthy public transportation systems.

This chapter reviews the health and environmental justice impacts of diesel fuel, the fuel of choice for many public bus systems in U.S. cities.[1] The efforts of WE ACT's community campaign to reduce the disproportionate impact of diesel exhaust from the New York City bus fleet on northern Manhattan neighborhoods are presented as an example of one urban community that has taken the lead in demanding cleaner buses and a meaningful role in the decision-making process regarding the city's public transportation system. Northern Manhattan is home to over six hundred thousand predominantly African American and Latino residents living in just 7.4-square miles.

The MTA currently operates seven bus depots on Manhattan; six of these are located on northern Manhattan (defined as the area of Manhattan north of Ninety-sixth Street).[2] In addition, five of the depots on northern Manhattan are in residential communities, while the sixth is in an industrial area near an elementary school. The location of these MTA diesel bus depots on northern Manhattan is an egregious instance of environmental racism, illustrating how communities of color have systematically been forced to assume a lion's share of the burdens associated with urban public transportation—in this case, the environmental health problems stemming from the siting and operations of bus depots. The public health cost of transportation-related pollution has been estimated at $1.7 billion for the New York metropolitan region (Ernst, Corless, and Greene-Roesel 2003, 36), with communities of color shouldering a disproportionate amount of that burden.

Background: Diesel Fuel

Diesel engines were invented in 1892 by Rudolph Diesel in his search to develop an engine that provided greater energy output than the gasoline-fueled one. Diesel fuel, like gasoline, is derived from oil, but because it is less refined than gasoline, it is cheaper to use (Health Effects Institute 1995, 13). Diesel engines also outlast gasoline engines, remaining on the road long after their gas-fueled counterparts have been retired. Sales of diesel trucks and buses have exploded since 1960, while the sale of diesel fuel continues to rise. In 1996, 29 billion gallons of diesel fuel was consumed in the United States; by 2000, this number was up to 35.5 billion (Weinhold 2002, A460).

The vast majority of heavy-duty trucks and buses rely on diesel fuel. These include long-haul tractor trailers, school buses, public and commercial buses, garbage trucks, and street-cleaning trucks. Heavy-duty diesel trucks are the primary means of the domestic transport of goods, outpacing trains, planes, and ships. There are other sources of diesel emissions that also introduce a significant dose of diesel into our air. Known as nonroad sources, this category includes cranes, forklifts, and other construction equipment; farming equipment such as tractors; boats and ships; and airport equipment and tarmac vehicles. Additionally, backup generators used by various institutions in case of a power outage are generally fueled with diesel.

The power advantage provided by diesel engines comes at the cost of substantially greater emissions than those generated by gas-burning engines. Although improvements in diesel engine design and emission control technology have resulted in decreased emissions from individual diesel vehicles over the years, this reduction has been offset by a trend of rising vehicle miles traveled (VMT) for diesel-fueled vehicles. The long life span of diesel engines means that there are many older and dirtier engines still on the road today. These emissions gravely affect the health and quality of life of communities of color, which disproportionately bear the burden of this nation's growing dependence on diesel fuel.

Environmental and Health Effects of Diesel Exhaust

The characteristic clouds of black smoke emitted by diesel engines are comprised of thousands of substances, including gaseous pollutants and solid PM. The gaseous pollutants include carbon monoxide, carbon dioxide, sulfur dioxide, NOx, and organic chemicals or hydrocarbons. Of these, NOx is especially problematic because it is a precursor to ground-level ozone, also known as smog. In fact, the EPA estimates that diesel trucks are responsible for one-third of the smog-forming NOx emissions coming from all vehicles in the United States (U.S. Environmental Protection Agency 2000b).

Ground-level ozone is formed when NOx reacts with VOC in the presence of sunlight. Ozone is a highly oxidizing pollutant that irritates the respiratory system, and can cause wheezing and coughing—and trigger asthma attacks—as well as damage to buildings and statues. Long-term exposure to ozone can cause lung damage, and one recent study showed that children in Los Angeles who played three or more sports had a higher risk of developing asthma later in life than children who did not play so many sports (McConnell et al. 2002). Although significant strides have been made in improving air quality overall in this country since the 1960s, ozone pollution remains a pervasive urban problem. In fact, smog-related pollution is actually getting worse in some cities, including New York, which experienced 19 percent more poor air quality days during the five-year period ending in 2002 than it did during the previous five years (Ernst, Corless, and Greene-Roesel 2003, 55).

The VOC in diesel exhaust are some of the forty-plus organic chemicals contained in diesel that have been identified by the EPA as individual hazardous air pollutants (HAPs). Also called air toxics, HAPs are chemicals that are either suspected to cause cancer or create other serious health risks. The organic chemicals that are of special concern in diesel exhaust include aldehydes, benzene, 1,3-butadiene, and PAHs. PAHs are believed to create much of the cancer risk posed by diesel exhaust, and have been recently linked to reduced birth weight and size in newborns (Perera et al. 1999). Because it contains so many different hazardous organic chemicals in varying proportions, diesel exhaust as a whole is also categorized by the EPA as a HAP.

Diesel exhaust is also made up of millions of tiny solid particles, ranging in size from 5 nanometers (a billionth of a meter) to slightly larger than 10 micrometers (μm, also known as microns, which are a millionth of a meter). The vast majority of DEP are smaller than 2.5 μm, contributing to ambient levels of fine PM, or $PM_{2.5}$. $PM_{2.5}$, defined by the EPA as particles with a diameter of 2.5 μm or less, are of special concern because they are able to bypass our respiratory defense systems and penetrate deep into the lungs. The haze that characterizes many urban skyscapes is largely a result of fine particulate pollution. PM is well-known to be associated with early mortality, largely from cardiac effects (Samet et al. 2000), hastening as many as 64,000 deaths annually (Shprentz 1996, 1). Additionally, recent studies have shown that fine PM pollution is also associated with lung cancer, and that living in the most polluted U.S. cities can increase a nonsmoker's risk of dying of lung cancer by 20 percent—about the same increase in lung cancer risk faced by a nonsmoker living with a smoker (Pope et al. 2002). $PM_{2.5}$ also exerts other chronic respiratory, immunologic, and neurological effects. In 1997, the EPA, recognizing the severe health problems created by fine PM, promulgated a National Ambient Air Quality Standard for $PM_{2.5}$ of 15 μg/m^3 annually averaged.

A National Research Council (2002, 45–47) report indicates that in cities like Denver and Los Angeles, up to 40 percent of ambient fine PM comes from motor vehicles sources, while heavy-duty diesel vehicles comprise 70 percent of the motor vehicle–related emissions of this pollutant. The toxicity of diesel fine PM is magnified by gaseous organic chemicals in diesel exhaust that can adhere to the surface of DEP. These are pollutants that could not normally get deep into our lungs because they would be "caught" by the body's natural defenses. Yet since fine diesel PM can bypass these defenses, these pollutants are essentially able to hitch a ride into the lungs, where they would not otherwise get access. Furthermore, because DEP are so small, they collectively have a lot of surface area to which other substances can adhere.

Because diesel exhaust is composed of thousands of different substances in varying proportions, exposure to this combination of multiple substances exemplifies the kind of poorly understood risk associated with exposure to multiple substances—a common phenomenon in many communities of color. In addition to each of these substances exerting its own potential health effect, they may be interacting with each other to modify their health effects in a way that remains poorly understood. Below is a brief review of other health effects of diesel exhaust, many of which are of particular concern to communities of color. The two major health effects associated with DEP, independent of its contribution to ambient $PM_{2.5}$ and smog production, are asthma attacks and lung cancer.

Diesel Exhaust and Asthma

Diesel exhaust can exacerbate asthma and contribute to respiratory symptoms. In September 2002, the EPA (2002a) released its *Health Assessment Document for Diesel Exhaust*, in which it concluded that "short-term exposures can cause irritation and inflammatory symptoms" (1), Dozens of laboratory and human studies demonstrate that diesel particles essentially act to "prime" the respiratory system for an asthma attack (Bayram et al. 1998; Boland et al. 1999). They exert an inflammatory and irritant effect on the lungs (Salvi, Frew, and Holgate 1999; Diaz-Sanchez 1997; Nel et al. 1998; Peterson and Saxon 1996; Abe et al. 2000). Recent epidemiological studies also show an association between experiencing respiratory symptoms and living near major highways and other sources of truck traffic.[3]

While diesel exhaust is fairly well characterized as contributing to asthma exacerbation, little is known about the potential impact that it might have on the development or onset of asthma. There have been cases of newly developed asthma reported in workers exposed to high levels of diesel exhaust (State of California Air Resources Board 1998, ES–16), but these levels are much higher than in community settings. Still, considering that diesel does impact the immune system, and the onset of asthma is essentially governed by alterations in immune function, it is plausible that exposure to diesel in utero (before birth) and in early childhood could contribute to the development of asthma. This is a question still being explored by researchers.

Asthma, one of the health problems associated with diesel exposure, is a major public health crisis in this nation, taking its heaviest toll on low-income communities and communities of color. Urban areas are home to both high concentrations of diesel sources, a large population, and the most rapid increase in asthma rates and morbidity. The racial/ethnic and socioeconomic groups that have the greatest prevalence of asthma are also likely to have the highest exposures to diesel exhaust.

The prevalence of asthma nationwide increased 59 percent between 1982 and 1996 (National Center for Health Statistics 1996). The burden of asthma is borne disproportionately by African Americans and persons under the age of eighteen. In 2000, the rate of asthma hospitalizations for African Americans was 35.5 per 10,000, compared to 10.4 per 10,000 for whites (American Lung Association 2002). In 1996, the estimated prevalence of asthma among African Americans was 69.6 per 1,000, compared to 53.5 per 1,000 for whites and 55.2 per 1,000 for the general population. Similarly, among all the age groups, asthma prevalence is highest in those under age eighteen: 62 per 1,000. Hispanic children were 17 percent more likely than non-Hispanic white children to have asthma in 1995–1996, while black children were 26 percent more likely to do so (President's Task Force 1999).

The greatest increase in the prevalence and severity of asthma has been among children and young adults living in poor inner-city neighborhoods (Eggleston et al. 1999). For example, in New York City the communities with the highest rates of childhood asthma hospitalization are all low-income communities of color. East Harlem heads the list at 170.2 hospitalizations per 10,000 population for newborns and children up to age fourteen in the year 2000, compared to a citywide average of 64 per 10,000 in that same year, and a national average of 31.5 childhood asthma hospitalizations per 10,000 people in 1999 (Garg et al. 2003). A study based at the Harlem Hospital Center found that 25.5 percent of children in central Harlem have asthma—three times the national average (Perez-Pena 2003).

Cancer and Other Health Effects

There is a substantial body of evidence of an association between long-term exposure to high levels of diesel exhaust (generally at the level of occupational exposure) and an increased risk of developing lung cancer (U.S. Environmental Protection Agency 2002a; Health Effects Institute 1995). A study by the South Coast Air Quality Management District (AQMD) estimates that exposure to diesel exhaust in the Los Angeles basin is responsible for 71 percent of the cancer risk from all sources of air pollution in that region (State and Territorial Air Pollution Program Administrators 2000). Based on lifetime risk, diesel PM contributes to 125,000 cancers in the United States. The EPA (2002a, 1) has concluded that "long-term inhalation exposure is likely to pose a lung cancer hazard to humans, as well as damage the lung in other ways."

In 1998, California's Air Resources Board (ARB) declared diesel exhaust to be a toxic air contaminant (TAC), defined as "an air pollutant which may cause or contribute to an increase in mortality or an increase in serious illness, or which may pose a present or potential hazard to human health" (State of California Air Resources Board 1998, 1). The state recommended a reference exposure level of five micrograms per cubic meter (five $\mu g/m^3$) as the noncancer health benchmark.

The EPA, through its National Air Toxics Assessment (NATA), has modeled and estimated ambient concentrations of thirty-two HAPs, including diesel PM. This information, available directly through the EPA Web page at ⟨http://www.epa.gov/ttn/atw/nata/⟩, estimates that ambient DEP vary as high as fifteen micrograms per cubic meter of air (fifteen $\mu g/m^3$) in some counties. The highest modeled concentrations are in Southern California, Chicago, New York City, and the northeast corridor from Washington, DC, to Boston (U.S. Environmental Protection Agency 2002b).

Existing Regulations and Pollution Control Technologies

In December 2000, the EPA announced groundbreaking regulations limiting emissions of PM, NOx, and hydrocarbons from new on-road heavy-duty diesel vehicles, and limiting the amount of sulfur in diesel fuel (U.S. Environmental Protection Agency 2000b). The emission standards, which take effect in 2007, are stated in terms of grams of a pollutant that can be emitted by an engine operating at a particular engine load, per unit of time.[4] The "Heavy-Duty Engine and Vehicle Standards and Highway Diesel Fuel Sulfur Control Requirements" rule limits particulate emissions to .01 grams per brake-horsepower per hour (g/bhp/hr), down from the previous standard of 0.1 g/bhp/hr. The rule also limits emissions of NOx to 0.20 g/bhp/hr and nonmethane hydrocarbons to 0.14 g/bhp/hr.

Heavy-duty diesel engine manufacturers will meet the 2007 emissions standards for PM by installing pollution control technologies, also known as aftertreatment technologies. The technology of choice is the diesel particulate filter, sometimes called a catalyzed diesel particulate filter, which captures 85 to 97 percent of the particles (on a mass basis) emitted from the engine. The captured soot is then "burned" or oxidized off the filter with the help of a catalyst. Particulate filters are poisoned by sulfur in fuels; therefore, their use must be paired with low-sulfur diesel fuel. Diesel particulate filters also reduce carbon monoxide and VOC emissions, but do not alter NOx emissions significantly.

Technologies for reducing emissions of NOx to meet the 2007 standards are still being evaluated by engine manufacturers. One technology familiar to U.S. manufacturers and fleet operators is exhaust gas recirculation (EGR), which has shown results in reducing emissions of NOx (Chatterjee, Conway, and Viswanathan 2003). Their impact on the performance of diesel particulate filters, however, is still being evaluated (Chatterjee, Conway, and Viswanathan 2003; Lowell 2003), with some evidence emerging that EGR can impair the effectiveness of particulate filters.[5]

The 2007 emissions limits cannot be met without the use of these sulfur-sensitive pollution control technologies; consequently, the second part of this diesel rule limits the amount of sulfur in diesel fuel. By July 15, 2006, diesel fuel for highway use cannot contain sulfur in quantities higher than fifteen parts per million, a 97 percent reduction from the current allowable levels of five hundred parts per million. This limit accomplishes two goals: it reduces the number of sulfate particles that are emitted by diesel engines, and it prevents diesel particulate filters from being "poisoned" by the sulfur in fuel.

While the Heavy-Duty Diesel Standards are a critical step in reducing harmful emissions from diesel-fueled vehicles, they are not a comprehensive solution to the environmental justice and public health problems created by diesel exhaust. One major weakness with the current diesel standards is that they do not require on-road emissions testing. Emissions testing is conducted in a lablike setting rather than on the road. Unlike most cars, trucks do not have to pass annual emissions tests; compliance with emissions standards takes place only when engines are manufactured. The effectiveness of many pollution control technologies is dependent on proper maintenance. Consequently, a major gap in the regulation of diesel vehicles that must be filled at the national level is requiring that heavy-duty trucks and buses pass annual inspection tests to ensure their emissions stay within acceptable bounds over the long life span of the engines.[6]

In sum, heavy-duty diesel engines will meet the EPA 2007 standards through three distinct changes or modifications to diesel fuel and to the engines themselves: the reduction of sulfur in diesel fuel, the installation of diesel particulate filters, and the utilization of a second, separate aftertreatment technology to reduce emissions of NOx. These aftertreatment technologies will require maintenance on the part of fleet owners, and the public must rely on the good faith effort of engine manufacturers as well as truck and fleet owners and operators to ensure that emissions remain as low as technologically possible.

This public trust is being handed over to an industry that was the target of the largest air pollution settlement—one billion dollars—ever negotiated by the EPA in an enforcement action. This consent decree was signed in 1998 with seven diesel engine manufacturers who had colluded to evade emission control standards by installing "defeat devices" in their engines. These devices enabled engines to meet emissions standards prior to the sale, and altered engine programming at higher speeds to improve fuel economy and engine performance at the expense of higher emissions (Warrick 1998).

Although this settlement means that diesel engine manufacturers are more closely watched by the EPA to ensure their compliance with the law, this precedent of collusion between diesel engine manufacturers to evade emissions standards leads critics to question how much these companies should be trusted to act in good faith. The fact remains that the only way to completely eliminate the toxic exhaust from diesel engines is to end this nation's dependence on diesel fuel altogether. Several viable fueling alternatives exist.

Alternatives to Diesel

Compressed Natural Gas (CNG)

Natural gas is a gaseous fuel, composed of 90 percent methane, found in underground deposits. Like oil, it must be mined through the drilling of surface wells, but unlike oil, natural gas requires minimal refining to produce a commercially viable product. In addition, natural gas is primarily mined domestically or in Canada or the United States, whereas oil is primarily imported from other nations.

Typically, CNG buses cost between $290,000 and $318,000, while a new diesel bus costs $250,000 to $275,000 (Cannon and Sun 2000, 30). Additionally, CNG requires an independent fueling infrastructure, including connections to natural gas pipelines and on-site fueling systems that store the natural gas and compress it under high pressure into the tanks on buses. These infrastructure requirements make CNG a natural choice for urban communities, where building and population density can allow many fleets to fuel at one fueling station.

CNG buses have traditionally demonstrated far superior emissions profiles compared to diesel buses, for both PM and NOx. Recent advances in diesel fuel technologies (both the reduction of sulfur content in the fuel and the installation of aftertreatment technologies) have narrowed this gap, however. Several studies comparing ultralow sulfur diesel fuel equipped with diesel particulate filters to engines running on CNG alone show comparable emissions profiles for PM and NOx for the two types of fuels (Ayala et al. 2003b; Lanni, Frank, and Tang 2003). Others studies, though, have compared ultralow sulfur diesel engines equipped with particulate filters to CNG engines equipped with oxidation catalysts and found the latter to be the cleanest of all the fueling options (Ayala et al. 2003a).

Natural gas is almost pure methane, with few contaminants from its source, making it the inherently cleaner fuel choice. Its primary advantage is that it starts relatively clean and remains so throughout its life cycle. In contrast, diesel fuel must go through multiple refining and extraction processes, including the removal of sulfur, to clean it up to acceptable levels. Moreover, heavy-duty vehicles will meet the 2007 engine standards only through the installation of aftertreatment technologies, adding yet another step in an already-complicated process of cleaning an inherently dirty fuel. These lifelong maintenance costs and burdens are frequently not accounted for by fleet owners, who look at the initial costs of switching to natural gas compared to the costs of using low-sulfur diesel fuel combined with aftertreatment technologies. Natural gas requires much less processing to allow it to burn relatively cleanly. Although its cleanest emissions profile occurs when it is coupled with an oxidation catalyst, these catalysts do not require regular maintenance once they are installed.

Some cities have taken the lead in creating diesel-free public transportation systems that use CNG instead. Atlanta did it almost overnight in preparation for hosting the summer Olympics in 1996. Los Angeles also has an entirely CNG-fueled bus fleet, thanks to extensive community organizing efforts that culminated in a lawsuit brought by the Bus Riders Union and the NAACP against the Los Angeles MTA. The Long Island bus system, which falls under the umbrella of New York MTA agencies, operates exclusively on natural gas as well. In India, Delhi has made the switch to natural gas–fueled buses and taxis. These cities are models of commitments to healthy and clean urban public transportation.

Hybrid Electric

Like hybrid electric gasoline cars, hybrid electric diesel engines for buses are split into two power sources: an electricity-producing battery that powers the vehicle during start-up and slow speeds, and the regular fuel-burning internal combustion engine that powers the vehicle on reaching a certain speed. Hybrid electric vehicles are often misperceived as requiring charging. In fact, the battery is automatically recharged during operation by recovery of the energy that is normally lost to heat during braking. Diesel fuel is burned only part of the time that the vehicle is operating; consequently, hybrid electric vehicles offer superior fuel efficiency and reduced emissions. Nevertheless, diesel hybrid trucks and buses are still powered by diesel, perpetuating the systematic dependence on diesel fuel that many environmental justice activists are challenging. Fleets that make the significant cost investment in purchasing hybrid buses and trucks have a disincentive to eventually make the switch to a clean, nondiesel fuel.

Pursuing or accepting diesel hybrid vehicles is an option that should only be entertained when significant, severe, and nonchangeable factors exist, and should be aggressively coupled with a conversion to biodiesel. Hybrid electric vehicles fueled by CNG with certain emissions control technologies, however, offer one of the cleanest ways to power our heavy-duty bus and truck fleets (U.S. Department of Energy 2001).

Biodiesel

Biodiesel is a fuel made from any vegetable oil—usually soybean or peanut, although any restaurant-grade vegetable oil can be used as feedstock—that has undergone a certain refining process. Emissions from burning biodiesel are significantly lower in PM, carbon monoxide, hydrocarbons, VOC, and PAHs, although with current biodiesel formulations the emissions of NOx appear to increase. This is problematic from the perspective of ozone production, particularly in urban areas.

Biodiesel is an appealing choice from several other perspectives. It produces very little PM emissions, and is primarily made from vegetable oil, a renewable resource, which can be domestically grown. It can be burned in any diesel engine with some engine modifications, precluding the need for the major infrastructure change characteristic of CNG. Biodiesel presents an interesting opportunity to stimulate sustainable development in multiple realms of our economy, including the agricultural sector (farmers supplying virgin vegetable oil) as well as small-scale restaurants recycling grease and creating a local supply in major cities.[7]

Hydrogen Fuel Cells

Hydrogen fuel cells are the state-of-the-art, emissions-free technology that generates electricity by combining hydrogen with oxygen in the air. Although this technology is still largely in the research and development stages, a few pilot programs are currently testing fuel cells in buses, including the city of Chicago, Georgetown University, and several counties in California (Cannon and Sun 2000, 52).

Case Study: WE ACT's Struggle for Clean Air and Justice

It is within this broader context of the toxicity of diesel exhaust and its impacts on communities of color, as well as the availability of cleaner fuel alternatives, that WE ACT has spearheaded efforts to challenge the disproportionate numbers and the adverse health effects of New York MTA diesel buses housed on northern Manhattan. These struggles began in 1988 with an MTA proposal to build a sixth diesel bus depot, the Manhattanville Depot, on northern Manhattan, adjacent to a middle school and a nineteen-hundred-unit residential building.

Although community organizing efforts were only successful in stopping the MTA proposal to build housing for senior citizens on top of the new depot, they sparked a wider awareness of the relationship between poor air quality, diesel exhaust, and the growing burden of asthma on northern Manhattan. Following the opening of the Manhattanville Depot, WE ACT began reaching out to physicians at the local Harlem Hospital and air quality researchers for help in understanding potential linkages between the many sources of pollution on northern Manhattan and the community's growing asthma problem.

In 1997, as a culmination of the research and community education that grew out of these efforts, WE ACT launched a massive bilingual publicity campaign called "If You Live Uptown, Breathe at Your Own Risk." This campaign placed bilingual ads in seventy-five bus shelters throughout northern Manhattan, produced a television public service announcement, made brochures, and printed mail-in postcards designed to mobilize community residents. Residents of northern Manhattan blitzed the governor of New York and the head of the MTA with thousands of postcards asking them to pursue less toxic alternatives to diesel fuel.

Conducted in collaboration with the NRDC's "Dump Dirty Diesels" campaign, this local effort helped pressure the governor (who appoints the majority of board members to the MTA) to request in the year 2000 that all new bus depots constructed in New York City would be designed to house CNG buses rather than diesel ones, and that the MTA would pursue alternative fuel options. In addition, the MTA committed to converting five bus depots citywide to CNG. The Manhattanville Depot was selected by a committee of MTA officials working with WE ACT and other environmental organizations to be one of these five depots.

Despite this gubernatorial directive, the MTA delayed the conversion of the Manhattanville Depot. Community residents of northern Manhattan continued to experience severe problems with the MTA's bus depot as well as the systematic and seemingly endless additions of parking lots and buses to existing depots. In 1998, the abrupt and unexpected closing of an MTA depot in another borough sent two hundred buses to northern Manhattan depots to be accommodated through haphazardly annexed parking lots, with minimal community notification.

In November 2000, WE ACT and several northern Manhattan community residents filed a complaint with the USDOT charging the MTA with violating the civil rights of northern Manhattan residents. This complaint, which was supplemented with additional information in June 2002, was filed under Title VI of the Civil Rights Act of 1964, which states that no entity that receives federal funding can discriminate against people on the basis of race.

The complaint included scientific, statistical, and zoning analyses making a compelling argument that the decisions the MTA made, and the way in which it made those decisions, regarding the construction, expansion, and operations of its bus depots were violating the civil rights of community residents on northern Manhattan. WE ACT contended that New York City bus depots and the adjacent parking lots are located in communities that are overwhelmingly populated by people of color, and the health threats created by these depots constitute a civil rights violation.

Despite an ongoing federal investigation of this civil rights complaint, in September 2003 the MTA closed the Hudson Depot in an industrial area downtown and opened a new twelve-story depot in a residential community of color in East Harlem. The Hudson Depot closed to make way for a park. In contrast, the Hundredth Street Depot in a residential community of East Harlem further concentrated diesel bus operations uptown, and offered those residents no similar environmental amenity such as a park. This action precisely illustrates the problematic pattern of decision making that led WE ACT to file a civil rights complaint.

In addition to pursuing this complaint, WE ACT is engaged in extensive community organizing aimed at making the MTA meet directly with a leadership council comprised of community residents living near the six uptown diesel depots. Community residents are also mobilizing to challenge recent indications by the MTA that it would attempt to cancel the planned conversion of the Manhattanville Depot to CNG.

WE ACT's experiences show just how deeply entrenched the "diesel mentality" is within one particular institution. This profound attachment to diesel fuel is seen throughout our economy, and represents a significant obstacle to efforts to accelerate a conversion to cleaner fuels in our society. As the executive director of the industry group Diesel Technology Forum notes, "There's very clearly a strong future for diesel....It's really woven into the fabric of life here" (Weinhold 2002, A464).

Broader Organizing Strategies

Organizing locally to pressure city and state fleets to switch to clean fuels is one important tactic to creating environmentally healthy public transportation. These local strategies, however, must be accompanied by concerted statewide, regional, and national strategies to address the supply of diesel fuel. In particular, commercial trucking fleets, which operate regionally and nationally, cannot only be targeted locally.

Frequently, antidiesel activists find themselves in the difficult position of being asked to choose between advocating for short-term reductions in diesel emissions through the installation of diesel emissions controls and long-term investments in the switch to cleaner fuels. Fleet owners may offer to install particulate filters on their vehicles, reducing emissions of PM—clearly a goal for environmental justice activists. Yet if this short-term reduction comes at the expense of long-term investment in clean fuels (as fleet owners later claim that the somewhat costly investment in emissions controls makes it less cost-effective to now switch to another type of fuel), we have won the battle but lost the war.

This does not mean that communities of color must continue to live with toxic and deadly diesel emissions until some vaguely defined point in the future when fleet owners make the switch to cleaner fuels. Rather, we can advocate for immediate reductions in emissions from heavy-duty vehicles through particulate filters and NOx controls, the accelerated retirement of the oldest vehicles currently on the road, state and local clean fuel vehicle purchasing policies, and financial incentives for purchasing clean fuels and clean fuel vehicles.

Understanding the life cycle of diesel helps us see how dependence on this toxic fuel is part of a larger system of environmental racism. Many oil refineries that convert oil into diesel fuel are located in low-income communities of color and thus responsible for creating severe health risks there. From the deadly wars that protect U.S. oil supplies overseas and the destructive process of oil mining, to the toxic processing of oil in dangerous refineries and the ultimate burning of diesel fuel to produce noxious fumes, this nation's dependence on dirty oil and diesel is systematically poisoning poor people and people of color all over the globe. Developing and maintaining national and international solidarity as environmental justice activists is indispensable for collectively overcoming the legacy left by this toxic, environmentally destructive form of energy.

When WE ACT launched its Breathe at Your Own Risk campaign in 1997, representatives from the Transit Workers Union (Local 100, AFL-CIO) came out to support the organization at press conferences and rallies. Additionally, community residents increasingly acknowledge that bus drivers and maintenance workers are highly exposed to diesel on the job, while workers acknowledge that they can go home at the end of their shift while the residents who live across the street from a depot can never escape those fumes. Through this relationship building, WE ACT continues the struggle to ensure that the MTA is accountable to both its workers and the communities that are home to its facilities. Considering that diesel exhaust exposure is highest among workers, this issue is ripe for community-labor collaborations. This type of collaboration can also boost efforts made by each party on its own.

In New York City, for example, the MTA often views labor organizing efforts to reduce health and safety risks with the same dismissive attitude that characterizes its response to community efforts to limit emissions from their bus fleet. One innovative approach being explored in New York City focuses on the fact that new CNG buses are manufactured in-state, whereas the primary supplier of new diesel vehicles is out-of-state. This has the potential to encourage a rare alliance between workers in the upstate facility and environmental justice activists in New York City.

Although exposure to diesel exhaust disproportionately impacts urban residents and low-income communities of color, it is important to ensure that the diesel issue does not become segregated into a ghetto of environmental concerns. Because this issue cuts across a spectrum of social, political, and environmental concerns, it is ideal for approaching through a coalitional effort. Strategically framing the problem of diesel within a broader context can lead to much broader support, sometimes from unexpected allies. For instance, the issue of reducing U.S. dependence on foreign oil cuts across a broad range of interests—critics of U.S. foreign and military policies that are increasingly based on our insatiable need for oil, conservatives who are uncomfortable with our lack of a secure energy supply, and labor communities who see opportunities to generate employment through the development of domestic sources of energy. Similarly, addressing the financial ties between powerful oil companies and elected officials presents an opportunity to build alliances with those interested in campaign finance reform, from all political walks of life.

As with the development of any alliance, collaboration with potential allies should be approached strategically, acknowledging those common points and interests, while recognizing that an ally does not necessarily share the experiences that have informed environmental justice goals. For example, many of our allies in the mainstream environmental movement are not the ones living next door to diesel bus depots. Mainstream environmental organizations frequently adopt a utilitarian approach, focusing on environmental protection for the greatest number of people. Environmental justice activists, on the other hand, concentrate our efforts on protecting the populations with the greatest exposures and health impacts. Consequently, measures that would be acceptable from a utilitarian standpoint, such as installing particulate filters in order to reduce fine PM emissions, are not acceptable permanent solutions for environmental justice goals. Nonetheless, the ability to win short-term victories through strategic participation in coalitions should not be underestimated as a powerful tool for ultimately realizing our larger vision of clean transportation and clean air.

Policies to Encourage Alternative Fuels

There are several public policy approaches to encouraging a switch away from diesel to clean alternative fuels in this country. It should be noted that the term alternative fuel is used to refer to nonpetroleum-based fuels; diesel (even so-called clean diesel) and gasoline are not considered alternative fuels.

Financial Incentives

One approach focuses on creating financial incentives for both public and privately owned fleets to make the initial investment in switching to a clean fuel. Several states currently provide tax incentives to mitigate the incremental cost of purchasing a CNG vehicle. For example, money from federal transportation dollars are available through what is known as congestion mitigation and air quality improvement (CMAQ) to offset the cost (to private fleets) of purchasing alternative fuel vehicles. Additionally, recent funding under CMAQ provides a rebate on the incremental fuel cost for alternative fuels.

Various states also offer tax incentives and write-offs to cover the incremental cost of alternative fuels and alternative fuel vehicles. New York State, for instance, provides direct funding through the Clean Air/ Clean Water Bond Act to public agencies and municipalities to cover up to 100 percent of the incremental cost of new alternative fuel buses and the needed infrastructure (National Alternative Fuels Day and Environmental Summit 2002).

Public Purchasing Policies

Another policy approach is to legislate or otherwise mandate (say, through executive orders) that public fleets incorporate a certain proportion of alternative fuels in their fleet. For example, in New York City a local law mandates that at least 20 percent of the city's new bus acquisitions must be vehicles that are ready for clean alternative fuels.

Other Policy Measures

Broader policy support for clean fuels includes increasing the research and development for emerging technologies like biodiesel and fuel cells, in order to accelerate their commercial marketability. A further need is to reduce federal subsidies of diesel fuel and other oil products that maintain their artificially low prices and inhibit competition from cleaner alternatives. The low cost of diesel fuel, like the unnaturally low cost of gasoline in our country, is a direct result of the oil industry being one of the most heavily subsidized in the nation. Direct and indirect government support of the oil industry in the form of tax incentives, lowered sales taxes, and military protection of overseas oil sources (Union of Concerned Scientists 2002) means that a gallon of diesel can cost less than a gallon of milk, or even a gallon of bottled water.

As a nation we are highly dependent on oil, almost all of which is imported, largely from the Middle East. The United States consumes 25 percent of the world's oil, while comprising only 5 percent of the world's population. This dependence on oil influences much of our foreign policy; it is also subject to the volatility of politics and economics in other nations. Consequently, natural gas is increasingly gaining appeal from an energy security perspective. The U.S. Department of Energy is increasingly investing in research and development for the commercial use of alternative fuels. Its Clean Cities program focuses on encouraging the wider use of alternative fuel vehicles and the development of alternative fuels infrastructures.[8]

From an environmental justice perspective, it is also important to push for public policy measures that prioritize the most highly exposed communities for supporting the conversion of diesel vehicles to alternative fuels. California leads the nation with its exemplary recent decision to provide funding to support the development of zero-emission vehicles (ZEV) in targeted "environmental justice communities" (State of California Air Resources Board 2002).

Another policy measure targets specific fleets, including school buses and garbage trucks, for conversion to clean fuels. Local municipalities can require that the school district only purchase clean fuel school buses, place emissions controls on existing buses, and accelerate the retirement of the oldest, dirtiest buses on the road.[9] Similarly, with their low miles traveled and centralized parking structures, city garbage trucks are an ideal fleet for fueling with CNG.

A more innovative approach to accelerating our nation's shift away from diesel dependence is to use federal transportation legislation as a means of developing nonvehicular forms of transportation in our communities. Our country's major transportation law, TEA-21, emphasizes the concept of "livable communities." This notion can be used to support urban environmental justice efforts to encourage walking and biking as essential modes of transit, potentially reducing the need for diesel-fueled public buses.

Currently under TEA-21, a gasoline tax has been established to set aside money from the sale of gasoline for supporting the development of transportation infrastructure. This bill can be expanded to create a "diesel tax" to generate revenues to support the research and development of alternative fuels and other clean transportation systems.

In summary, a crucial element of just and sustainable urban public transportation systems is the concept of the genuine participation of affected constituencies in the planning and operations of this infrastructure. A fundamental tenet of TEA-21 is that public participation is essential for equitable and locally appropriate transportation planning. The U.S. Department of Transportation's (1997, 1) *Report on Environmental Justice* specifies the goal of ensuring "full and fair participation by all potentially affected communities in the transportation decision-making process." Often public participation requirements, such as public hearings, are perfunctory, and frequently in the case of decisions around facilities and operations, these requirements are nonexistent.

The perception of who comprises "affected groups" must be expanded to include neighbors of public transportation infrastructure—those individuals who have to live with the physical, environmental, and public health costs of public transportation. In New York City, as in most U.S. cities, this group is skewed to represent communities of color, meaning that decision making regarding public transportation infrastructure in these cities is undeniably a racial justice issue.

To overcome this racially biased method of decision making, WE ACT is working on a local scale to ensure that the MTA consults with community residents living nearest to its bus depots when making decisions regarding the operations of that facility. On a broader scale, it is crucial that environmental justice activists and others interested in developing sustainable, healthy, accessible, and just urban transportation systems confront the public health realities of a continued dependence on diesel fuel, and commit to less toxic, nonpetroleum-based alternatives.

Notes

1. With thanks to Deepti K. C. and Kizzy Charles-Guzman for research support, and to Cecil Corbin Mark, Sheila Foster, Peggy Shepard, Dave Park, and Amnon Bar-Ilan for their reviews and valuable feedback.

2. One of the northern Manhattan bus depots, the Amsterdam Depot, is currently not being used to house buses and its fate is uncertain.

3. A few researchers have conducted cross-sectional studies examining the relationship between children's acute and chronic experiences of respiratory distress and their proximity to motor vehicles from highways. One study (Wjst et al. 1993) showed a small but significant decrease in peak expiratory flow among ten-year-old children in school districts in Munich with higher flows of car traffic, as well as increased self-reports of respiratory symptoms. Other analyses found that decreases in lung function and parental report of chronic respiratory symptoms were associated with truck traffic density as well as concentrations of black smoke measured in schools in the Netherlands (Van Vliet et al. 1997; Brunekreef et al. 1997). One case-control study found a linear trend between hospital admissions for asthma and traffic flow (Edwards, Walters, and Griffiths 1994), while another discovered a positive association between wheezing and symptoms of allergic rhinitis and the self-reported frequency of truck traffic (Duhme et al. 1996).

4. Hence, engines that operate with a higher power output are permitted to emit more pollution. Engine load (or power output) is stated in units of brake-horsepower.

5. EGR systems reduce exhaust temperature, which may in turn affect diesel particulate filter performance. A researcher from the New York MTA has noted that EGR engines include additional equipment that is hard to fit into tight bus engine compartments and introduces additional heat load to already-marginal engine cooling systems (Lowell 2003). Selective catalytic reduction and NOx trap systems are two other options for reducing emissions of NOx, although they remain largely in the experimental phase in the United States. Reduced NOx from EGR engines not only affects catalysts in the particulate filter; engine programming also presents challenges to balance smoke control and power acceleration.

6. Another potential weakness in the regulations as they are written deals with the issue of particle size versus particle mass. Although the vast majority of particles in diesel exhaust are nanoparticles, smaller than 1 μm, the particles that contribute the most to the total mass of diesel exhaust are those between 1 and

2.5 millimeters. Because emission standards are given in terms of mass—engines must emit no more than .01 grams of PM per hour, per bhp of the engine—it is possible to meet these standards by removing just those few larger particles. Think about a box filled with a hundred golf balls and just five bowling balls. Removing those five bowling balls will considerably reduce the total weight of the box, but all those golf balls still remain. This would not be a concern were it not for the fact that there is some evidence that nanoparticles may be exerting a disproportionate share of the health impacts caused by diesel exhaust (Kittelson 1998).

7. As the Department of Energy also notes, "There is only enough of the feed-stocks to supply 1.9 billion gallons of biodiesel (under policies designed to encourage biodiesel use). The Department of Energy is developing a new, low-cost biodiesel oil from spicy mustard seeds that could add another 5–10 billion gallons of biodiesel to the fuel supply. The mustard meal (the seed that remains once the oil is removed) is a high-value natural pesticide that helps keep the price of mustard oil low" (Alternative Fuels Data Center 2004).

8. A great deal of information on alternative fuels can be found at ⟨http://www.ccities.doe.gov/⟩.

9. See the NRDC report "No Breathing in the Aisles" for a comprehensive list of funding available to school districts to purchase clean fuel buses (Solomon et al. 2001).

References

Abe, S., H. Takizawa, I. Sugawara, and S. Kudoh. 2000. Diesel Exhaust (DE)–induced Cytokine Expression in Human Bronchial Epithelial Cells: A Study with a New Cell Exposure System to Freshly Generated DE In Vitro. *American Journal of Respiratory Cell and Molecular Biology* 22, no. 3:296–303.

Alternative Fuels Data Center, U.S. Department of Energy. 2004. Biodiesel. Available at ⟨http://www.afdc.doe.gov/altfuel/bio_general.htm⟩.

American Lung Association. *Trends in Asthma Morbidity and Mortality*. Available at ⟨http://www.lungusa.org/data/asthma/ASTHMAdt.pdf⟩.

Ayala, A., M. E. Gebel, R. A. Okamoto, P. L. Reiger, N. Y. Kado, C. Cotter, and N. Verma. 2003a. Oxidation Catalyst Effect on CNG Transit Bus Emission. *SAE Technical Paper Series*, 2003–01–1900.

Ayala, A., N. Y. Kado, R. Okamoto, M. Gebel, and P. Reiger. 2003b. CNG and Diesel Transit Bus Emission in Review. Paper presented at the ninth Diesel Engine Emissions Reduction conference, Newport, RI, August 24–28.

Bayram, H., J. L. Devalia, R. J. Sapsford, T. Ohtoshi, Y. Miyabara, M. Sagai, and R. J. Davies. 1998. The Effect of Diesel Exhaust Particles on Cell Function and Release of Inflammatory Mediators from Human Bronchial Epithelial Cells In Vitro. *American Journal of Respiratory Cell and Molecular Biology* 18, no. 3:441–448.

Boland, S., A. Baeza-Squiban, T. Fournier, and O. Houcine. 1999. Diesel Exhaust Particles Are Taken Up by Human Airway Epithelial Cells In Vitro and Alter Cytokine Production. *American Journal of Physiology—Lung Cellular and Molecular Biology* 20, no. 4:L604–L613.

Brunekreef, B., N. A. H. Jansenn, J. de Hartog, H. Harssema, M. Knape, and P. van Vliet. 1997. Air Pollution from Truck Traffic and Lung Function in Children Living near Motorways. *Epidemiology* 8:298–303.

Cannon, J. S., and C. Sun. 2000. Bus Futures: New Technologies for Cleaner Cities. New York: INFORM, Inc.

Chatterjee, S., R. Conway, and S. Viswanathan. 2003. NOx and PM Control from Heavy-duty Diesel Engines Using a Combination of Low Pressure EGR and CRPPF. *SAE Technical Paper Series*, 2003-01-0048.

Diaz-Sanchez, D. 1997. The Role of Diesel Exhaust Particles and Their Associated Polyaromatic Hydrocarbons in the Induction of Allergic Airway Disease. *Allergy* 52, no. 38:52–56.

Duhme, H., S. K. Weiland, U. Keil, B. Kraemer, M. Schmid, M. Stender, and L. Chambless. 1996. The Association between Self-Reported Symptoms of Asthma and Allergic Rhinitis and Self-Reported Traffic Density on Street of Residence in Adolescence. *Epidemiology* 7:578–582.

Edwards, J., S. Walters, and R. C. Griffiths. 1994. Hospital Admissions for Asthma in Preschool Children: Relationship to Major Roads in Birmingham, United Kingdom. *Archives of Environment Health* 49, no. 4:223–227.

Eggleston, P. A., F. J. Malveaux, A. M. Butz, K. Huss, L. Thompson, K. Kolodner, and C. S. Rand. 1998. "Medications Used by Children with Asthma in the Inner City." *Pediatrics* 101, no. 3 (March): 349–354.

Ernst, M., J. Corless, and R. Greene-Roesel. 2003. Clearing the Air: Public Health Threats from Cars and Heavy-Duty Vehicles—Why We Need to Protect Federal Clean Air Laws. Available at ⟨http://www.transact.org/library/reports_pdfs/Clean_Air/report.pdf⟩.

Garg, R., A. Karpati, J. Leighton, M. Perrin, and M. Shah. 2003. *Asthma Facts, Second Edition*. Available at ⟨http://www.ci.nyc.ny.us/html/doh/pdf/asthma/facts.pdf⟩.

Health Effects Institute. 1995. *Diesel Exhaust: A Critical Analysis of Emissions, Exposure, and Health Effects*. Cambridge, MA: Health Effects Institute.

Kittelson, D. B. 1998. Engines and Nanoparticles: A Review. *Journal of Aerosol Science* 29, no. 5/6:575–588.

Lanni, T., B. P. Frank, and S. Tang. 2003. Performance and Emission Evaluation of CNG and Clean Diesel Buses at NY City's MTA. *SAE Technical Paper Series*, 2003-01-0300.

Lowell, D. 2003. NYCT Experience with Clean Diesel Technologies. Paper presented at the World Bank Diesel Day, Washington, DC, January 17.

McConnell, R., K. Berhane, F. Gilliland, S. J. London, T. Islam, W. J. Gauderman, E. Avol, H. G. Margolis, and J. M. Peters. 2002. Asthma in Exercising Children Exposed to Ozone: A Cohort Study. *Lancet* 359:386–391.

National Alternative Fuels Day and Environmental Summit. 2002. New York City Outcomes and Recommendations for Greater Alternative Fuel Vehicle Use. Available at ⟨http://www.ccities.doe.gov/pdfs/nafd_outcomes.pdf⟩.

National Center for Health Statistics. 1996. *Current Estimates from the National Health Interview Survey.* Hyattsville, MD: Centers for Disease Control & Prevention.

National Research Council, Transportation Research Board. 2002. The Congestion Mitigation and Air Quality Improvement Program: Assessing ten Years of Experience/Committee for the Evaluation of the Congestion Mitigation and Air Quality Improvement Program. Washington, DC: National Academy Press.

Nel, A. E., D. Diaz-Sanchez, D. Ng, T. Hiura, and A. Saxon. 1998. Enhancement of Allergic Inflammation by the Interaction between Diesel Exhaust Particles and the Immune System. *Journal of Allergy and Clinical Immunology* 102:539–554.

Northeast States for Coordinated Air Use Management. 1997. Heavy-Duty Engine Emissions in the Northeast. Boston: Natural Resources Defense Council.

Peterson, B., and A. Saxon. 1996. Global Increases in Allergic Respiratory Disease: The Possible Role of Diesel Exhaust Particles. *Annals of Allergy, Asthma and Immunology* 77:263–270.

Perera, F., W. Jedrychowski, V. Rauh, and R. M. Whyatt. 1999. Molecular Epidemiologic Research on the Effects of Environmental Pollutants on the Fetus. *Environmental Health Perspectives* 107, no. 3:451–460.

Perez-Pena, R. 2003. Study Finds Asthma in 25% of Children in Central Harlem. *New York Times*, April 19. Available at ⟨http://query.nytimes.com/qst/fullpage.html?sec=health&res=9F03E6DE153AF93AA25757COA9659C8B63⟩.

Pope, C. A., R. T. Burnett, M. J. Thun, E. E. Calle, D. Krewski, K. Ito, and G. D. Thurston. 2002. Lung Cancer, Cardiopulmonary Mortality, and Long-Term Exposure to Fine Particulate Pollution. *JAMA* 287:1132–1141.

President's Task Force on Environmental Health Risks and Safety Risks to Children. 1999. Asthma and the Environment: A Strategy to Protect Children. Washington, DC. Available at ⟨http://aspe.hhs.gov/sp/asthma/appxd.pdf⟩.

Salvi, S., A. Frew, and S. Holgate. 1999. Is Diesel Exhaust a Cause for Increasing Allergies? *Clinical and Experimental Allergy* 29:4–8.

Samet, D., F. Dominici, F. C. Curriero, I. Coursac, and S. L. Zeger. 2000. Fine Particulate Air Pollution and Mortality in 20 U.S. Cities: 1987–1994. *New England Journal of Medicine* 343, no. 24:1742–1749.

Shprentz, D. S. 1996. Breath-Taking: Premature Mortality due to Particulate Air Pollution in 239 American Cities. New York: Natural Resources Defense Council Inc.

Solomon, G. M., T. R. Campbell, G. R. Feuer, J. Masters, A. Samkian, and K. A. Paul. 2001. No Breathing in the Aisles: Diesel Exhaust inside School Buses. Los Angeles: Natural Resources Defense Council, Inc., and Coalition for Clean Air.

State and Territorial Air Pollution Program Administrators and the Association of Local Air Pollution Control Officials. 2000. Cancer Risk from Diesel Particulate: National and Metropolitan Area Estimates for the United States. Available at ⟨http://www.4cleanair.org/comments/Cancerriskreport.PDF⟩.

State of California Air Resources Board. 1998. Identification of Diesel Particulate Emissions from Diesel Engines as a Toxic Air Contaminant. Resolution 98-35. Available at ⟨http://www.arb.ca.gov/regact/diesltac/res98-35.pdf⟩ (accessed August 11).

State of California Air Resources Board. 2002. ZEV Fleet Incentive Program. Available at ⟨http://www.arb.ca.gov/msprog/zevprog/fleetzip/fleetzip.htm⟩ (accessed September 7).

Union of Concerned Scientists. 2002. Energy Security: Solutions to Protect America's Power Supply and Reduce Oil Dependence. Available at ⟨http://www.ucsusa .org/documents/ACFWUAm30.pdf⟩.

U.S. Department of Energy. 2001. Heavy Vehicle and Engine Resource Guide. Office of Transportation Technologies, NREL/TP-540-31274. Available at ⟨www.afdc.doe.gov/pdfs/hvrg.pdf⟩.

U.S. Department of Transportation. 1997. *Department of Transportation Order on Environmental Justice*, April 15. Available at ⟨http://www.fhwa.dot.gov/ environment/ejustice/dot_ord.htm⟩ (accessed June 14, 2006).

U.S. Environmental Protection Agency, 1999. *National Air Quality and Emissions Trends Report*. Office of Air Quality Planning and Standards, EPA 454/ R–01–004. Research Triangle Park, NC: EPA.

U.S. Environmental Protection Agency. 2000a. Regulatory Announcement: Final Emission Standards for 2004 and Later Model Year Highway Heavy-Duty Vehicles and Engines. Office of Transportation and Air Quality, EPA420-F-00-026.

U.S. Environmental Protection Agency. 2000b. Regulatory Announcement: Heavy-Duty Engine and Vehicle Standards and Highway Diesel Fuel Sulfur Control Requirements. Office of Transportation and Air Quality, EPA420-F-00-057. Research Triangle Park, NC: EPA.

U.S. Environmental Protection Agency. 2002a. *Health Assessment Document for Diesel Exhaust*. National Center for Environmental Assessment, EPA/600/8-90/ 057E. Washington, DC: U.S. EPA. Available at ⟨http://www.dieselnet.com/news/ 2002/09epa.php⟩ (accessed June 14, 2006).

U.S. Environmental Protection Agency. 2002b. National Air Toxics Assessment. Available at ⟨http://www.epa.gov/ttn/atw/nata/⟩.

U.S. Environmental Protection Agency. 2004a. Health and Environmental Impacts of Ground-Level Ozone. Available at ⟨http://www.epa.gov/air/urbanair/ozone/hlth.html⟩.

U.S. Environmental Protection Agency. 2004b. 1996 Emissions of Diesel Particulate Matter. Technology Transfer Network, National Air Toxics Assessment. Available at ⟨http://www.epa.gov/ttn/atw/nata/pdf/dpm_emis.pdf⟩.

Van Vliet, P., M. Knape, J. de Hartog, N. Janssen, H. Harssema, and B. Brunekreef. 1997. Motor Vehicle Exhaust and Chronic Respiratory Symptoms in Children Living near Freeways. *Environmental Research* 74:122–132.

Warrick, J. 1998. Diesel Manufacturers Settle Suit with EPA; Will Pay $1.1 Billion. *Washington Post*, October 23, A3.

Weinhold, B. 2002. Fuel for the Long-Haul? Diesel in America. *Environmental Health Perspectives* 110, no. 8:A458–A464.

Weiss, K. B., and D. K. Wagener. 1990. Geographic Variations in US Asthma Mortality: Small-Area Analyses of Excess Mortality: 1881–1985. *American Journal of Epidemiology* 132:107–115.

Wjst, M., P. Reitmer, S. Dold, A. Wulff, T. Nicolai, E. F. von Loefflholz-Colberg, and E. von Mutius. 1993. Road Traffic and Adverse Effects on Respiratory Health in Children. *British Medical Journal* 307:596–600.

World Health Organization. 1996. *Diesel Fuel and Exhaust Emissions.* Environmental Health Criteria Series, no. 171. Geneva, Switzerland: International Programme on Chemical Safety.

12

Linking Transportation Equity and Environmental Justice with Smart Growth

Don Chen

For generations, coming to the United States has meant that no matter what your social standing, religion, race, ethnicity, or political beliefs, you could attain the good life if you worked hard and played by the rules. Today, equal access to opportunities and fair play continue to be cherished American values, and we all believe that opportunities such as education, health care, housing, and jobs should be within reach for everyone.

But for many people, the American dream is difficult to attain because opportunities are *literally* out of reach. Decades of runaway sprawl development have resulted in a geographically segregated society in which relatively affluent people, businesses, and economic opportunities have relocated from older areas to newer sprawling communities. PolicyLink founder Angela Blackwell (2002) illustrates this dramatically by noting that "when we finally gained access to better schools and hospitals, the good schools and hospitals moved away. When we got a shot at decent housing and jobs, the good housing and jobs went away."

How can we ensure that lower-income people—the ones who get left behind in older communities—can have an equal shot at the American dream if metropolitan sprawl continues its outward expansion, and takes jobs and wealth along with it? Despite such disturbing trends, some glimmers of hope suggest that through coalition building and smart regional policies, we can make progress toward this goal.

The Wealth and Poverty of Sprawl Development

For mainstream America during the mid-twentieth century, trading the apartment in Brooklyn for a house in Levittown *was* the American dream. Acknowledging this demand, the U.S. government has subsidized sprawl development to an enormous degree. Trillions of dollars of government subsidies for roads, guaranteed mortgages, water and sewer infrastructure, and other amenities have created a tremendous amount of economic opportunity in places that were previously farmland or natural areas. Somewhere along the way, however, it became unclear whether government subsidies were responding to consumer demand or if they were fueling it.

Whatever the cause and effect, the result has been an infusion and enabling of wealth at the fringe of metropolitan areas, and an associated draining of jobs, services, and people from central cities. Harvard sociologist William Julius Wilson (1987) contends that the forces of suburbanization "became part of a vicious cycle of metropolitan change and relocation. The flight of the more affluent families to the suburbs has meant that the central cities are becoming increasingly the domain of the poor and the stable working class." But perhaps the most alarming impact of urban out-migration was what Wilson (1996) calls the "concentration effects" that are visible in poverty-stricken neighborhoods, which do not possess the stable working-class population necessary to maintain economic opportunities, local commerce, and decent living conditions. This concentration of poverty tends to isolate residents from mainstream society, thereby making it ever more difficult for them to have access to jobs, educational opportunities, medical services, and other prerequisites for a higher standard of living.[1]

In recent years, scholars have found that the spread of sprawl development has left many older suburbs behind as well. Myron Orfield (2002) of the Institute on Race and Poverty argues that the outward march of land development has led to the spread of what previously have been perceived to be urban pathologies—poor educational performance, crime, and poverty—from central city neighborhoods to inner-ring suburbs. As upper-income and middle-class families migrate outward, many of the suburban communities they leave behind are faced with a weaker tax base and declining services—much like the predicament of many central cities. In the end, these migration patterns tend to inflict harms on regions as a whole, as infrastructure becomes more expensive to maintain, vital centers deteriorate, and jobs and opportunities get harder to reach (Voith 1996).

Catching the Bus to Opportunity

How fast can the truly disadvantaged chase after opportunities? In most places, the bus isn't fast enough, or (more likely) it doesn't even go from here to there. But chase they must. Residents of declining older neighborhoods have far fewer job opportunities to pursue. The highways that provide accessibility for drivers also represent a barrier to those who can neither drive nor take public transit. This phenomenon is called "spatial mismatch," the notion that the urban poor in the United States are increasingly incapable of reaching job opportunities in distant suburban areas because of transportation and geographic limitations. The spatial mismatch literature begins in the 1960s and by now consists of a solid empirical base of supporting research (Kain 1992; Fernandez 1994).

Most efforts to address spatial mismatch are often described as welfare-to-work or access to jobs programs, which tend to include reverse-commute public transit services to suburban job locations. These certainly have some value. Public transit is a lifeline for millions of America's poor, and roughly 40 percent of U.S. public transit riders are low-income people. Most transit systems don't get people everywhere they need to go, however. Even in places with excellent transit services, welfare recipients still face serious mobility problems because jobs are increasingly located in areas that lack the population and activity densities that justify transit routes. During the past decade, research in the Cleveland, Boston, and Atlanta regions found that a startlingly low percentage of entry-level jobs were accessible via public transportation (Coulton, Verma, and Guo 1996; Lacombe 1998; Rich 1997).

This lack of reliable mobility choices hurts people who are trying to balance job demands with family responsibilities. For adult welfare recipients, this means juggling day care, education, training, work (often shift work), and other duties, all of which require individuals to be assiduously prompt. This is especially difficult for welfare recipients in rural areas, where transit services run less frequently and are subsidized more heavily. Another dimension to the challenge of providing transit services to the working poor is the tendency for suburban transit services to be better supported and funded than those for urban low-income areas. This problem is partly the result of agencies' efforts to increase ridership among suburban commuters—measures that are designed more to address traffic congestion and boost agency revenues.[2]

So while public transit services are certainly part of the solution, they don't meet all the needs of low-income job and opportunity seekers. Other innovative programs, such as the Good News Garage in Burlington, Vermont, seek to provide low-wage workers with cars that have been donated and repaired by volunteer technicians. But these programs are also limited in their ability to cover the growing ranks of the mobility poor. Additional solutions are needed.

Toward a More Integrated Approach to Accessing Opportunities

So what needs to happen to generate more equitable access? While more funding can certainly help in the short term, a more promising alternative would be to develop a comprehensive approach that integrates transportation, land use, and access to opportunity. In particular, we should focus equally on bringing opportunities into low-income communities, not just on ensuring that low-wage workers can gain access to faraway jobs.

Unfortunately, this won't be an easy task, because those responsible for overseeing the implementation of transportation, land use, and economic development efforts have typically worked in isolation from each other. For example, since the early twentieth century, America's surface transportation policy has focused on easing mobility for motor vehicles, originally to "get farmers out of the mud" and move goods to market. But along the way, the goal of providing transportation accessibility has been eclipsed by a narrower focus on boosting vehicle speeds, which has permeated transportation policies all the way down to the neighborhood level. We have planned and built our streets and roads to function like our highways—straight, wide, and fast. As a result, our communities are heavily dependent on automobile travel, without much consideration for how highways, arterials, and streets affect community quality of life, real estate values, job accessibility, and other important factors.

All this may be changing, however. Americans appear to be making a more varied set of demands on our transportation system that have transportation professionals looking beyond their own agencies for answers. For example, in public opinion polls, growing numbers of people appear to be rejecting the notion that we can simply tax and build our way out of traffic congestion, and recent surveys indicate severe concern about traffic and runaway sprawl as intertwined issues. A 2000 poll about local problems conducted by the Pew Center for Civic Journalism found that Americans ranked sprawl and traffic as their top concerns—more than crime, education, or jobs.

Subsequent polls have also identified growing support for tighter coordination between transportation and land use, more multimodal funding, and more infrastructure maintenance in existing communities. Road construction appears to be losing public support in nearly every region in the country. A recent poll by Smart Growth America found that 60 percent of respondents indicated support for the following statement: "[Do you favor having] your state government use more of its transportation budget for improvements to public transportation, such as trains, buses and light rail, even if this means less money to build new highways?" Also, survey findings have been consistent despite the diversity of sponsoring organizations, which include the FHWA, the National Association of Realtors, and the Atlanta Regional Commission.

Advocates for transportation reform have seized on these changing preferences, and have successfully shifted agency priorities to support more maintenance of infrastructure in older communities and more multimodal funding. Recent examples are numerous:

• In New Jersey, the Tri-State Transportation Campaign convinced the legislature to enact an unprecedented "fix-it-first" transportation law, which prioritizes the maintenance of transportation infrastructure over new highway capacity projects.

• The Latino Issues Forum and the Surface Transportation Policy Project convinced the California legislature to pass the nation's first Safe Routes to School law, which provides communities with grants to make it easier and safer for kids to walk to school.

• In North Carolina, a watchdog group called Democracy South worked with local media to unmask an illicit quid pro quo system in which major state campaign contributors (mostly developers and contractors) were rewarded with a seat on the state DOT's powerful Board of Transportation—the body responsible for highway routing, construction priorities, and other factors that affect growth.

• In Austin, Texas, the environmental justice organization PODER convinced officials to invest in sidewalks, street lighting, and bus stops in low-income neighborhoods in East Austin.

• In 1999, Texas Citizen Action and the Texas Citizen Fund worked with rural transit providers to increase rural transit funding from $35 million to $80 million in just one legislative session.

• In California, the Bay Area Transportation and Land Use Coalition successfully pushed plans to boost transit funding by $375 million with a "100 Percent Funding for Transit" campaign.

• In Columbus, Ohio, a network of thirty-eight congregations called Building Responsibility, Equity, and Dignity worked with various city and regional agencies to provide better transit services for low-wage workers.

• In 1998, a broad coalition of antipoverty, transportation, and smart growth groups helped create the $750 million Jobs Access and Reverse Commute Program within the federal transportation law. It was later successfully reauthorized under the new 2005 law.

Along with these new demands, several communities are beginning to coordinate land use, housing, and commercial development to reduce the demand for expensive transportation infrastructure and service in the first place. In particular, community development groups have gotten more involved in transportation policy issues because they are making the links between high-quality transportation access and economic development projects. Recent examples of these types of efforts also abound:

• In East Saint Louis, Illinois, the Emerson Park Development Corporation convinced its regional transit authority to reroute the alignment of a new rail transit line to come to its neighborhood, generating economic development opportunities and better accessibility to the community.

• In Chicago, the Lake Street El Coalition—made up of civil rights, community development, and environmental groups—prevented the Chicago Transit Authority from closing the Lake Street transit station, instead convincing them to reinvest in the station as an anchor for economic development.

• Bethel New Life, a community development corporation that was part of the Lake Street El Coalition, is implementing a transit-oriented development plan that includes two hundred units of affordable housing. The effort has not only revitalized the neighborhood but also helped prevent the displacement of existing residents.

• In Los Angeles, the Los Angeles Neighborhood Initiative has secured a variety of local and federal funding to redevelop transit corridors in eight neighborhoods with streetscaping, pocket parks, upgraded bus shelters, and a variety of other aesthetic and infrastructure improvements.

• In the south valley of Albuquerque, a coalition of transit advocates recently secured new bus service to a local vocation-training institute after bringing the issue to the attention of local officials.

These are just a smattering of the many transportation reform campaigns that have been waged at the local, regional, and state levels. As more advocacy efforts succeed, the spread of these stories is fueling renewed hope for real change.

What's also exciting is the growing body of research indicating that the links between transit and land use can generate substantial benefits for low-income families. Reconnecting America's (2004) recent report *Hidden in Plain Sight*, for example, analyzed every rail transit station site in the United States and found a tremendous amount of housing demand at these locations. It contends that the opportunity to build affordable housing at these stations will deliver mobility benefits to transit-dependent riders as well as higher ridership levels for transit agencies.

Coalitions for Transportation Equity and Smart Growth

The success stories discussed above have been led by a wide variety of groups, including organizations that work on environmental justice issues, mainstream environmental issues, smart growth, transportation reform, community development, government watchdog functions, and social justice. As the "big tent" entity, the smart growth movement has bonds with all of these movements, and represents a coalition-building opportunity for future efforts. Smart growth advocates are well positioned to further explore the links between transportation equity and land use. Most have a broad critique about the shortcomings of conventional land use practices, and the movement's focus is now expanding to prioritize poverty, community development, and the vitality of older communities (Proscio 1993).

Significantly, traditional efforts to fight poverty as well as promote civil rights and environmental justice are also now increasingly exploring the roles of land use and geography as contributors to disparate impacts. For example, civil rights scholar Sheryll Cashin's (2004) *The Failures of Integration* looks at how the consequences of geographic segregation on access to opportunities are beginning to undermine the gains that our nation has made in fighting institutional segregation. In her search for solutions, Cashin (2004, 307) offers three "coalition and community building" opportunities that could help the civil rights movement: "(1) coalitions in metropolitan regions that are trying to bring about more equity in the allocation of resources, benefits, and social burdens; (2) organizations that are committed to physical development and building social capital in low-income, mostly minority communities; and (3) coalitions that work to foster sustainable development and counter the forces of suburban sprawl." While acknowledging potential challenges to true coalition building, she argues that "together, [these groups] could seed a movement for a transformative integration of the races and classes" (Cashin 2004, 308).

There is much promise in Cashin's proposal. Both the smart growth and environmental justice movements were originally grounded in environmental issues, and have increasingly begun to take on community development, housing, and other issues. But the paths to the present have been quite different. Many environmental justice groups have successfully beaten back landfills, incinerators, waste transfer stations, and many other types of LULUs and health hazards. Environmental justice groups that managed to protect their communities from the most egregious toxic threats have since expanded their focus to address a wider array of health and economic challenges. A tour of some of the nation's best-known environmental justice groups reveals initiatives to boost transit service in communities of color, reclaim abandoned buildings, create urban parks, build affordable housing, plan for transit-oriented development, and pursue many other community and regional planning objectives.[3]

These efforts sound like smart growth objectives, which have been developed as an alternative approach to land development that is more responsible than sprawl development. According to Clark Atlanta University sociologist Robert Bullard (one of the founders of the environmental justice movement), haphazard sprawl development is the leading threat to communities of color, low-income families, and the environmental justice movement as a whole (Bullard, Johnson, and Torres 2000b). As cofounders of Smart Growth America, Bullard, Carl Anthony, and other environmental justice leaders have strongly encouraged smart growth advocates to help support the goals of environmental justice.

Specifically, smart growth is an approach to land development that seeks outcomes that are socially equitable, environmentally sound, and economically robust through better civic engagement. Most advocates ascribe to ten principles or ways of accomplishing smart growth:

• Mixed land uses
• Take advantage of existing community assets
• Create a range of housing opportunities and choices
• Foster "walkable," close-knit neighborhoods
• Promote distinctive, attractive communities with a strong sense of place, including the rehabilitation and use of historic buildings
• Preserve open space, farmland, natural beauty, and critical environmental areas
• Strengthen and encourage growth in existing communities
• Provide a variety of transportation choices
• Make development decisions predictable, fair, and cost-effective

• Encourage citizen and stakeholder participation in development decisions

These ten principles were developed by the Smart Growth Network, a U.S. Environmental Protection–funded forum that enables members to learn more about smart growth. The principles have since been adopted by a wide range of organizations, including the National Governors' Association, the National Association of Realtors, and many other types of groups.

Smart Growth America, the movement's national advocacy coalition, embraces these methods, but also defines smart growth according to six outcomes:

• Neighborhood livability
• Better access, less traffic
• Thriving cities, suburbs, and towns
• Shared benefits, social equity
• Lower costs
• Keeping open space open

As a concept, smart growth has really caught fire. Today's advocates include not only the environmentalists, planners, and transportation reform activists one might expect but also labor unions, public health advocates, realtors, developers, and fiscal conservatives. It has enjoyed bipartisan support from governors like Parris Glendening (Maryland), Bill Richardson (New Mexico), and Mitt Romney (Massachusetts), as well as a string of EPA administrators from Carol Browner and Christie Whitman, to Mike Leavitt and Stephen Johnson. Also, many of the policy goals and best practices of smart growth are being pursued by environmental justice groups, community development corporations, and nonprofit affordable housing developers, who have described smart growth as "same mission, new opportunities and allies" (Proscio 1993, 24).

Despite these promising signs, there have been challenges—and true tensions and conflicts—in getting smart growth advocates to be helpful to environmental justice groups and vice versa. Some of these include the fact that most environmental justice groups tend to be CBOs that have the more focused agenda of serving their communities and people of color, whereas smart growth groups are almost always big tents with many different kinds of stakeholders from community advocacy to the private sector.

Despite these and other differences, it is absolutely essential for environmental justice groups to recognize the common goals and interests that they may share with smart growth advocates. These are numerous and substantial, and in some cases are ideal candidates for joint campaigns. Such campaigns might involve the following steps:

1. *Environmental justice and smart growth groups could rely on each other as resources.* Environmental justice groups have long relied on resource organizations to aid their work. This was institutionally recognized in the Environmental Justice Resource Center's *People of Color Environmental Directory*, and in the way some environmental justice networks are set up. For example, the Northeast Environmental Justice Network has "associate members" who are not from environmental justice groups but are well-known for being environmental justice supporters, and thus can provide technical, communications training, or policy assistance. Similarly, smart growth advocates could work with environmental justice groups for their expertise, skills, and community connections to advance shared goals.

2. *Advocates could develop joint projects and initiatives.* Environmental justice and smart growth groups share many of the same policy objectives, such as transit-oriented development, greater transit funding, affordable housing development, green buildings, and many others. If these groups can develop full and respectful partnerships, they should seek opportunities that make their joint advocacy stronger than the sum of their parts. Since we are all seeking a major shift in the way things are done, coalition strategies are promising ways to achieve goals.

3. *Environmental justice groups could prioritize regional equity opportunities and smart growth strategies.* Many of the harmful decisions that impact environmental justice communities come down from regional bodies, state governments, or other places that are beyond the neighborhood. Environmental justice groups should engage these broader regional processes to ensure equitable and just outcomes. Often,

smart growth advocates are already engaged in these debates, so plugging into their efforts represents a promising opportunity for collaboration.

4. *Smart growth groups should work with environmental justice and social equity values and objectives.*   Smart growth groups typically have equity and environmental justice as merely one of many priorities when pursuing their goals, cutting deals, and articulating their message. We must work harder to make equity and environmental justice a priority. Cashin (2004, 308) acknowledges this challenge, and argues that the promise of coalition building can only be realized "by infusing [the regional equity, community development, and smart growth] efforts with an explicit discussion of how a *frontal* assault on race and class segregation can advance their specific causes."

5. *Leading environmental justice and smart growth groups should meet and collaborate regularly.*   As the leading smart growth advocacy group, Smart Growth America should host meetings with leading environmental justice groups and the environmental justice networks should have regular meetings with smart growth advocates to build relationships, identify opportunities for collaboration, develop joint research projects, and build trust.

Beyond these environmental justice and smart growth opportunities for collaboration, there are tremendous opportunities to organize community groups, labor organizations, the academic community, public health officials, private-sector players, environmentalists, bicyclists, advocates for older Americans, and countless others who stand to gain from transportation reform.

The Whole Community Approach

These opportunities shine the brightest when all of the elements of smart growth, environmental justice, and other priorities (for example, mixed-use and mixed-income housing) are put together in specific projects. By setting a higher bar for how development gets done, smart growth is gaining favor among public officials, industry groups, environmental advocates, and community development groups nationwide. Its implementation goes by many names, such as sustainable development, new urbanism, green development, quality growth, and equitable development, each of which has a different emphasis. But most of these approaches adhere to a similar set of core principles (PolicyLink 2002).

One of the strongest common threads is the need for multiple transportation choices. Therefore, such efforts prioritize the creation of convenient, walkable neighborhoods that are well served by public transit. Some are being called "transit-oriented development" or "transit towns," which are high-density areas that offer a full array of services, such as affordable housing, day care centers, dry cleaning, restaurants, hair salons, and other useful destinations, within close proximity to good public transit service (Dittmar and Ohland 2003). And increasingly, the societal and environmental benefits have been quantified in innovative ways to provide more support for such projects. For instance, in Atlanta, the transit-oriented redevelopment of the abandoned 138-acre Atlantic Steel site is regarded as not just an economic development initiative but also a strategy to clean up the region's heavily polluted air.

After conducting a state-of-the-art travel modeling study, analysts convinced the EPA that the project would reduce annual automobile travel by fifty million miles because it would capture a significant amount of growth that would otherwise have gone to outlying suburbs. These environmental benefits were instrumental in winning EPA approval for the local street improvements needed to make the project viable. In fact, they formed the basis for a new EPA guidance that allows regions to gain air quality credits in their State Implementation Plans via land use projects.[4]

Other projects envision the redevelopment of different types of underutilized land. For example, one initiative launched by three South Bronx organizations (Nos Quedamos, the Point CDC, and Youth Ministries for Peace and Justice) calls for the decommissioning of the barely used Sheridan Expressway. The organizations have developed a plan to replace it with a twenty-eight-acre greenway, complete with waterfront access, bicycle and pedestrian paths, and links to other regional parks. The New York DOT currently plans to spend $245 million refurbishing the lightly traveled 1.25-mile stretch of highway. The community groups have partnered with coalitions like the New York City Environmental Justice Alliance and the Tri-State Transportation Campaign to get the authorities to consider their plan as an alternative within the project's Environmental Impact Statement.

Policy and Institutional Strategies to Increase Access to Opportunities

These demands are getting noticed. Political leaders are becoming more responsive to calls for smarter growth and less traffic. In recent years, nearly thirty governors explicitly vowed to confront these challenges.[5] National associations of public officials are also officially expressing support for more sensible growth, including the U.S. Conference of Mayors, the National League of Cities, the National Governors' Association, the International City/County Management Association, the National Association of Counties, and many others. Also, since 1997, hundreds of ballot measures supporting open-space preservation, transit funding, water quality improvements, economic development, and affordable housing have been approved by voters in communities nationwide.

Transportation policy remains the biggest lever for achieving smarter growth and increasing low-income access to opportunity, largely because it is such a well-funded area. And decision makers are just beginning to scratch the surface of what's possible. For example, thirty states are still constitutionally barred from using state gas tax revenues on anything but roads and bridges. Those places that have chosen to pursue innovation are achieving substantial gains as well as imitators. For instance, New Jersey's groundbreaking Fix-It-First legislation requires state agencies to maintain transportation infrastructure before building new road capacity. The fiscally responsible appeal of fix it first made it a popular strategy for many states during recent state budget crises, when many major transportation projects were put on hold because of a lack of funds (Lambert and Huh 2004).

Another example is the 1999 California Safe Routes to School program, which provides grants to localities to make it safer and easier for kids to walk to school. Today, there are similar programs in over a dozen other states, some focusing on education, and others on engineering and infrastructure solutions. In 2005, the federal transportation law (SAFETEA-LU) included a $612 million Safe Routes to School program—one of the few new programs in the bill.

Some new initiatives also show promise. For example, the "complete streets" initiative is a newer effort to ensure that transportation corridors plan for the inclusion of multiple modes (transit, walking, cycling, and carpooling) when construction or reconstruction plans are being drawn up. A group of bicycle, transit, disabilities, and senior citizen advocacy groups are focused on getting complete streets measures adopted by state legislatures over the next several years.

All of these innovative programs will have to be implemented by transportation professionals. In some cases, this will be a challenge, because such projects are simply very different from current practices. Steps should be taken to support practitioners in their efforts to learn new skills and expertise to tackle these new initiatives. As agency staff people are asked to do new things like transit-oriented development, traffic calming, and context-sensitive roadway design, many are poorly equipped to do a good job. The transportation reform advocates should help produce manuals on an array of new topics to support the work of transportation practitioners. In addition to addressing design standards and improved modeling, advocates could generate examples of best practices and success stories to inspire and inform practitioners who can deliver the goods.

Focusing on practitioners is a huge opportunity for transportation reform. Industry analysts contend that the transportation workforce is in crisis because so many planners and engineers are leaving the profession. In 1990, the FHWA estimated that 45 percent of its employees would be eligible for retirement by 2010. The Rockefeller Institute of Government has found similar figures for state and local governments. Within a few years, the transportation profession will look radically different from its recent ranks. And it is generally known that the next generation of transportation professionals exhibit a much higher level of interest in environmental issues, land use, community development, and nonhighway modes.

Private-Sector Champions

The private sector has a direct economic stake in having a productive labor force. Workers who spend hours a day commuting are less likely to fit that description. Therefore, companies and businesspeople have frequently been leaders for improved transportation access in their respective regions.

In many regions, business associations are developing a keen interest in smarter growth, led by groups like the Commercial Club of Chicago, the Sierra Business Council (California), the Silicon Valley Manufacturing Group, Bluegrass Tomorrow (Kentucky), Envision Utah, and Bank of America.[6] They tend to regard haphazard sprawl as a drag on the regional economy and a detriment to community livability. The real estate industry has also started to take an active role in championing smart growth. In the annual industry-leading publication *Recent Trends in Real Estate*, writers have for years advised real estate investors against putting their money behind sprawl, and have instead urged them to finance well-planned communities in or near thriving urban centers ("twenty-four-hour cities") with good public transit service and access to open space.

Advocates should engage these leaders to a greater degree to make the case to businesses that their economic future is imperiled by our current dysfunctional transportation policies. This is getting easier and easier as new evidence rolls in. But many more linkages need to be made between all of the benefits identified above and how they accrue to make our economy stronger. Unless we are able to make this important connection, transportation reform will continue to be a fringe issue that merely generates "alternatives" rather than systemic change.

The Landscape of Opportunity and the Global Economy

If we truly wish to remain the land of opportunity for all, we clearly need to address the shortcomings in our transportation, land use, and development decisions through coalition building and a wide range of other advocacy tools. The time may be ripe to make the case that the United States can simply no longer afford to shun its responsibilities with regard to poverty and segregation. After all, how much of this can we sustain? From a big picture perspective, many economists are predicting that future generations of Americans may not attain the same level of prosperity that previous ones have enjoyed. In a global economy, can the United States really compete effectively when so many of our hollowed-out cities, older suburbs, and rural areas are struggling with such deeply rooted poverty?

According to a growing body of research, the answer is an emphatic no. According to University of California at Santa Cruz professor Manuel Pastor Jr. and several of his colleagues, "Poverty ... is clearly a drain on the economic prospects of regions. Inequality and poverty breed distrust and social tension and lower the skill base, or human capital, necessary for a competitive economy. It is little wonder that studies of regional metro areas in the U.S. have found that areas with less income disparity between city and suburb tend to have faster economic growth across the entire metro region" (Pastor et al. 1998, 2). If that is valid for competition between regions in the United States, one can only imagine the implications when all U.S. regions will have to compete more intensely with the metropolitan areas of the world for economic activity and opportunity. Commuting to Shanghai will certainly be tough on the slow bus.

Notes

1. For a more recent discussion on "concentration effects," see "Appendix A: Perspectives on Poverty Concentration" in Wilson (1996).

2. For example, University of California at Los Angeles professor Brian Taylor (1992) found that California's operating subsidy allocation formulas heavily favored suburban transit services over urban ones, largely because of political factors. Sociologist David Hodge (1986) presents similar findings with regard to the Seattle METRO transit system. See also Hirschman (1991).

3. See, for example, the Web sites for Alternatives for Community and Environment (⟨http://www.ace-ej.org⟩) and West Harlem Environmental Action (⟨http://www.weact.org⟩) as well as books like Bullard, Johnson, and Torres (2000b).

4. See the guidance at ⟨http://www.epa.gov/oms/transp/traqusd.htm⟩.

5. These promises were made during governors' State of the State addresses (see U.S. Environmental Protection Agency 2000).

6. For more examples, see National Association of Local Government Environmental Professionals, *Profiles of Business Leadership on Smart Growth* (1999).

References

Alston, D. 1990. *We Speak for Ourselves: Social Justice, Race, and Environment.* Washington, DC: Panos Institute.

Benfield, K., M. Raimi, and D. Chen. 1999. *Once There Were Greenfields: How Urban Sprawl Is Undermining America's Environment, Economy, and Social Fabric.* New York: Natural Resources Defense Council.

Blackwell, A. G. 2002. Keynote address at the Promoting Regional Equity: A National Summit, Los Angeles, November 18–19.

Boarnet, M. G. 1997. Highways and Economic Productivity: Interpreting Recent Evidence. *Journal of Planning Literature* 11, no. 4.

Buffington, J., D. Schafer, and C. Bullion. (n.d.). Attitudes, Opinions, and Experiences of Business and Institutional Relocatees Displaced by Highways under the 1970 Relocation Assistance Program. College Station: Texas Transportation Institute, Texas A&M University.

Bullard, R. D. 2005. Transportation Policies Leave Blacks on the Side of the Road. *Crisis* 112, no. 1 (January–February): 21–22, 24.

Bullard, R. D., and G. S. Johnson, eds. 1997. *Just Transportation: Dismantling Race and Class Barriers to Mobility.* Stony Creek, CT: New Society Publishers.

Bullard, R. D., G. S. Johnson, and A. O. Torres. 2000a. *Race, Equity, and Smart Growth: Why People of Color Must Speak for Themselves.* Atlanta: Environmental Justice Resource Center.

Bullard, R. D., G. S. Johnson, and A. O. Torres, eds. 2000b. *Sprawl City: Race, Politics, and Planning in Atlanta.* Washington, DC: Island Press.

Bullard, R. D., G. S. Johnson, and A. O. Torres, eds. 2004. *Highway Robbery: Transportation Racism and New Routes to Equity.* Boston: South End Press.

Caro, R. A. 1975. *The Power Broker: Robert Moses and the Fall of New York.* New York: Vintage.

Cashin, S. 2004. *The Failures of Integration: How Race and Class are Undermining the American Dream.* New York: Public Affairs.

Cervero, R. 1986. *Suburban Gridlock.* New Brunswick, NJ: Center for Urban Policy Research.

Chen, D. 1996. *Getting a Fair Share: An Analysis of Federal Transportation Spending.* Washington, DC: Surface Transportation Policy Project.

Colony, D. C. 1973. Residential Relocation: The Impact of Allowances and Procedures in Effect since July 1, 1970. Toledo: University of Toledo, for the Ohio Department of Transportation and the Federal Highway Administration.

Cook, J. T., and J. L. Brown. 1994. *Two Americas: Comparisons of U.S. Child Poverty in Rural, Inner-City and Suburban Areas: A Linear Trend Analysis to the Year 2010.* Working paper CHPNP-WP no. CPP-092394. Boston: Tufts University Center on Hunger, Poverty, and Nutrition Policy.

Coulton, C., N. Verma, and S. Guo. 1996. *Time-Limited Welfare and the Employment Prospects of AFDC Recipients in Cuyahoga County.* Cleveland: Case Western Reserve University, Center on Urban Poverty and Social Change.

Cutler, D. M., E. L. Glaeser, and J. L. Vigdor. 1997. The Rise and Decline of the American Ghetto. Working paper 5881. Cambridge, MA: National Bureau of Economic Research.

De Witt, K. 1995. Older Suburbs Struggle to Compete with New: Aging Towns Gain Cities' Problems. *New York Times*, February 26.

Dittmar, H., and G. Ohland. 2003. *The New Transit Town: Best Practices in Transit-Oriented Development.* Washington, DC: Island Press.

Downs, A. 2004. *Still Stuck in Traffic: Coping with Peak-Hour Congestion.* Washington, DC: Brookings Institution.

Duany, A., E. Plater-Zyberk, and J. Speck. 2001. *Suburban Nation: The Rise of Sprawl and the Decline of the American Dream.* New York: North Point Press.

Fernandez, R. 1994. Spatial Mismatch: Housing, Transportation, and Employment in Regional Perspective. Paper presented at the Metropolitan Assembly on Urban Problems: Linking Research to Action conference, Chicago, September 30–October 2.

Foust, H. 1932. Elevated Drive Urged as Relief for Unemployed. *Chicago Tribune*, August 7.

Frey, W. H. 2000. The New Urban Demographics: Race Space and Boomer Aging. *Brookings Review* 18, no. 3 (Summer): 18–21.

Friedman, M. S., K. E. Powell, L. Hutwagner, L. M. Graham, and W. G. Teague. 2001. Impact of Changes in Transportation and Commuting Behaviors during the 1996 Olympic Games in Atlanta on Air Quality and Childhood Asthma. *Journal of the American Medical Association* 285, no. 7:897–905.

Frumkin, H. 2002. Urban Sprawl and Public Health. *Public Health Reports* 117, no. 3:201–217.

Frumkin, H., L. Frank, and R. Jackson. 2004. *Urban Sprawl and Public Health: Designing, Planning, and Building for Healthy Communities.* Washington, DC: Island Press.

Garnett, M., and B. Taylor. 1999. Reconsidering Social Equity in Public Transit. *Berkeley Planning Journal* 13:6–27.

Glendening, P. 1997. Making Maryland the Best Place to Work, to Raise a Child, and to Build a Family. Paper presented at the State of the State Address, Annapolis, MD, January 15.

Gutfreund, O. D. 2004. *Twentieth-Century Sprawl: Highways and the Reshaping of the American Landscape.* New York: Oxford University Press.

Hirschman, I. 1991. Spatial Equity and Transportation Finance: A Case Study of the New York Metropolitan Region. PhD. diss., Rutgers University.

Hodge, D. 1986. Social Impacts of Urban Transportation Decisions: Equity Issues. In *The Geography of Urban Transportation*, ed. Susan Hanson, 301–327. New York: Guilford Press.

Hughes, M. A., and J. E. Sternberg. 1992. *The New Metropolitan Reality: Where the Rubber Meets the Road in Antipoverty Policy.* Washington, DC: Urban Institute.

Ihlanfeldt, K. R., and D. L. Sjoquist. 1998. The Spatial Mismatch Hypothesis: A Review of Recent Studies and Their Implications for Welfare Reform. *Housing Policy Debate* 9, no. 4:849–892.

Kain, J. F. 1968. Housing Segregation, Negro Employment, and Metropolitan Decentralization. *Quarterly Journal of Economics* 82:175–197.

Kain, J. F. 1992. The Spatial Mismatch Hypothesis: Three Decades Later. *Housing Policy Debate* 3, no. 2:371–460.

Katz, M. B. 1993. Reframing the "Underclass Debate." In *The "Underclass" Debate: Views from History.* Princeton, NJ: Princeton University Press.

Kay, J. H. 1998. *Asphalt Nation: How the Automobile Took over America, and How We Can Take It Back.* Berkeley: University of California Press.

Koplan, J. P., and W. H. Dietz. n.d. Caloric Imbalance and Public Health Policy. *Journal of the American Medical Association* 282, no. 16:1579.

Lacombe, A. 1998. *Welfare Reform and Access to Jobs in Boston.* Washington, DC: U.S. Department of Transportation, Bureau of Transportation Statistics.

Lambert, M., and K. Huh. 2004. Fixing It First: Targeting Infrastructure Investments to Improve State Economies and Invigorate Existing Communities. Washington, DC: National Governors' Association Center for Best Practices.

Latino Issues Forum and Surface Transportation Policy Project. 2000. *Caught in the Crosswalk: Pedestrian Safety in California.* San Francisco: LIFSTPP.

Munnell, A. H., E. L. Browne, J. McEneaney, and M. B. Geoffrey. 1992. Mortgage Lending in Boston: Interpreting HMDA Data. Working paper 92-7. Boston: Federal Reserve Bank of Boston.

National Institute for Environmental Health Sciences. 2004. $2.8 Million Public-Private Partnership to Examine How Surroundings Can Encourage Active Lifestyles. Available at ⟨http://www.niehs.nih.gov/oc/news/actlife.htm⟩.

National Neighborhood Coalition. 2000. *Communities Leading the Way.* Washington, DC: National Neighborhood Coalition.

Noland, R. 2001. Traffic Fatalities and Injuries: Are Reductions the Result of "Improvements" in Highway Design Standards? Paper presented at the annual meeting of the National Research Council, January.

Orfield, Myron. 1997. *Metropolitics: A Regional Agenda for Community and Stability.* Washington, DC: Brookings Institution Press.

Orfield, Myron. 2002. *American Metropolitics: The New Suburban Reality.* Washington, DC: Brookings Institution Press.

Pastor, M., Jr., P. Dreier, E. Grigsby III, and M. López-Garza. 1998. Growing Together: Linking Regional and Community Development in a Changing Economy. *Shelterforce* (January–February). Available at ⟨http://www.nhi.org/online/issues/97/Pastor.html⟩ (accessed May 19, 2006).

Pendered, D. 2005. Atlanta's Midtown Transformation Continues as Atlantic Station Grows Upward. *Atlanta Journal Constitution*, February 28, E2.

Perfater, M., and G. Allen. 1975. Preliminary Findings of a Diachronic Analysis of Social and Economic Effects of Relocation due to Highways. Virginia Highway and Transportation Research Council.

Pilla, A. M. 1993. The Church in the City. Cleveland, OH: Diocese of Cleveland.

PolicyLink, Inc. 2002. *Promoting Regional Equity: A Framing Paper.* Oakland, CA: PolicyLink, Inc. and Funders Network for Smart Growth.

powell, john a. 2000. What We Need to Do about the Burbs. *Progress* 10, no. 1:1.

PriceWaterhouseCoopers and Lend Lease Real Estate, LLP. 2001. *Recent Trends in Real Estate.* New York: PWC.

Proscio, T. 1993. *Community Development and Smart Growth: Stopping Sprawl at Its Source.* New York: Local Initiatives Support Corporation.

Proscio, T. 2002. *Smart Communities: Curbing Sprawl at Its Core, Exploring the Relationship between Community Development and Smart Growth.* New York: Local Initiatives Support Corporation.

Pugh, M. 1998. *Barriers to Work: The Spatial Divide between Jobs and Welfare Recipients in Metropolitan Areas.* Washington, DC: Brookings Institution.

Raphael, S., and M. A. Stoll. 2002. *Modest Progress: The Narrowing Spatial Mismatch between Blacks and Jobs in the 1990s.* Washington, DC: Brookings Institution.

Reconnecting America's Center for Transit-oriented Development. 2004. *Hidden in Plain Sight: Capturing the Demand for Housing Near Transit.* Washington, D.C.: US Department of Transportation Federal Transit Administration. Available at ⟨http://www.reconnectingamerica.org/pdfs/ctod_report.pdf⟩.

Rich, M. 1997. The Reality of Welfare Reform: Employment Prospects in Metropolitan Atlanta. *Georgia Academy Journal* (Summer).

Ross, S. R., and J. Yinger. 2002. *The Color of Credit: Mortgage Discrimination, Research Methodology, and Fair-Lending Enforcement.* Cambridge, MA: MIT Press.

Sanchez, T. W., R. Stolz, and J. S. Ma. 2003. *Moving to Equity: Addressing Inequitable Effects of Transportation Policies on Minorities.* Cambridge, MA: Civil Rights Project, Harvard University.

Satcher, D. 2001. *Healthy People 2010.* McLean, VA: International Medical Publishing.

Schlar, E., and W. Hook. 1993. The Importance of Cities to the National Economy. In *Interwoven Destinies: Cities and the Nation*, ed. Henry Cisneros. New York: W. W. Norton.

Seley, J. 1970. Spatial Bias: The Kink in Nashville's I-40. *Research on Conflict in Locational Decisions.* Philadelphia: Regional Science Department, University of Pennsylvania.

Squires, G. D. 2002. Urban Sprawl: Causes, Consequences, and Policy Responses. Washington, DC: Urban Institute.

Squires, G. D., and S. O'Connor. 2001. *Color and Money: Politics and Prospects for Community Reinvestment in Urban America*. Albany: State University of New York.

Stoll, M. A. 2004. *Job Sprawl and the Spatial Mismatch between Blacks and Jobs*. Washington, DC: Brookings Institution.

Surface Transportation Policy Project. 2000a. *Changing Direction*. Washington, DC: Surface Transportation Policy Project.

Surface Transportation Policy Project. 2000b. *Mean Streets*. Washington, DC: Surface Transportation Policy Project.

Taylor, B. 1992. When Finance Leads Planning: The Influence of Public Finance on Transportation Planning and Policy in California. PhD. diss., University of California at Los Angeles.

U.S. Department of Transportation. 2000. *National Business Relocation Study*. Report no. FHWA-EP-02-030. Washington, DC: Federal Highway Administration.

U.S. Environmental Protection Agency. 2000. *A Technical Review of Transportation and Land Use Literature*. Washington, DC: Environmental Protection Agency.

Voith, R. 1996. Central City Decline: Regional or Neighborhood Solutions. *Federal Reserve Bank of Philadelphia Business Review* (March–April).

Wilson, W. J. 1996. *When Work Disappears: The World of the New Urban Poor*. New York: Vintage Books.

Wilson, W. J., and R. Aponte. 1987. Appendix: Urban Poverty: A State-of-the-Art Review of the Literature. In *The Truly Disadvantaged: The Inner City, the Underclass, and Public Policy*. Chicago: University of Chicago Press.

Wish, N. B. 1996. *The Impact of the Mt. Laurel Initiatives: An Analysis of the Characteristics of Applicants and Occupants*. Newark, NJ: Center for Public Service, Seton Hall University.

Yinger, J. 1991. *Housing Discrimination Study: Incidence and Severity of Unfavorable Treatment*. Washington, DC: U.S. Department of Housing and Urban Development.

Yinger, J. 1993. Access Denied, Access Constrained: Results and Implications of the 1989 Housing Discrimination Study. In *Clear and Convincing Evidence: Measurement of Discrimination in America*, ed. M. Fix and R. J. Struyk. Washington, DC: Urban Institute Press.

Yinger, J. 1997. *Closed Doors, Opportunities Lost: The Continuing Costs of Housing Discrimination*. New York: Russell Sage Foundation.

IV

Growing Smarter for Livable Communities

13

Building Regional Coalitions between Cities and Suburbs

Myron Orfield

Racial discrimination and regional inequality work hand in hand. Poor white children live in mixed-income communities and go to middle-income schools. Poor blacks and Latinos as well as their children, because of consistent discrimination and segregation, live in extremely poor neighborhoods and attend schools with a majority of poor schoolchildren. As an increasing share of blacks and Latinos suburbanize, they are consistent victims of illegal steering, discrimination by rental agents and sellers, and discrimination in the mortgage market. Steering—the practice of controlling or directing certain groups to move into certain neighborhoods—is actually increasing. This unfair discrimination against Americans who are playing by all the rules of the white-majority society is devastating to personal opportunity, wealth enhancement, and the communities that are also the victims of steering.

Once communities—even seemingly prosperous black or Latino suburbs—become racially identified, they are in turn discriminated against. As whites (the largest and most affluent part of the U.S. housing market) withdraw, prices fall. The black or Latino middle class still is not big enough to sustain the price by themselves inside such a huge white economy. As prices fall, the poor move in behind middle-class blacks and Latinos, and very soon they find themselves in the same situation that they left a decade before. The private market, including malls and developers, also discriminate against these communities, which frequently did not have a strong commercial tax base in the first place. As these suburbs grow poor, they are less likely to have resources in terms of tax wealth than any other type of U.S. community. In metropolitan America, blacks and Latinos, while contributing an increasing share to metropolitan wealth, are pointed by whites in the wrong metropolitan direction. This discrimination hurts them, and it hurts us all.

This chapter offers a series of concepts and strategies for building multiracial regional coalitions to reform fiscal systems, coordinate land use planning, and improve regional governance—issues that cannot be addressed adequately at the local level alone.[1] Communities face significant obstacles in attempting to create more livable, racially integrated, and fiscally equitable regions, but these hurdles can be overcome. It's a matter of convincing people who see no stake in regional reform that they do in fact have a stake in how metropolitan regions are organized and managed. The effective presentation of demographic data through maps and other means can make an enormous difference in helping people understand what is at stake for the places they care about most.

There are numerous trends at work in the largest U.S. metropolitan regions today that demand reform on a regional scale. Growing shares of minority populations are moving to the suburbs. Americans have traditionally associated suburbs with prosperity. Yet a closer look at U.S. metropolitan areas shows that large shares of suburban residents live in communities struggling with social or fiscal stress. In an analysis of the largest twenty-five metropolitan areas, five different types of suburbs were identified, only two of which fit the traditional stereotype (Orfield 2002). Indeed, the analysis revealed that more than half of suburban residents in these metropolitan areas reside in suburbs with social or fiscal challenges severe enough to be considered "at risk" (Orfield 2002, 34).

The at-risk suburban communities are a diverse group. They include older, fully developed suburbs near the regional core, satellite cities, and newer, lower-density communities struggling with the remnants of rural poverty and the high costs of rapid growth. Overall, at-risk suburbs have only about two-thirds of the tax capacity of their regions, and this capacity has been growing more slowly than average (Orfield 2002, 34).

Although each type of at-risk community shows signs of stress, the most stressed is a group of suburbs with the greatest shares of people of color (Orfield 2002, 33). These places showed minority shares as high as central cities, and had tax capacities well below average that were growing more slowly than all of the other community types (including central cities). They also had poverty in their schools (measured by eligibility for free or reduced-cost lunch) three times greater than other suburbs and nearly as great as central cities (Orfield 2002, 33). Without the cultural and economic advantages that central cities possess, these at-risk communities are in many ways worse off than the large cities they border.

Adding to these concerns, these communities are often located in the parts of regions with the least job growth. In many metropolitan areas, people of color are suburbanizing in one direction while the bulk of jobs are suburbanizing in diametrically opposed directions (Institute on Race and Poverty n.d.). In sum, development patterns in U.S. metropolitan areas have served people of color quite poorly in many ways. Large numbers remain in central cities facing significant fiscal and economic difficulties, while many others who have migrated to the suburbs have found themselves in communities facing even greater fiscal, social, and economic stress than the cities they left.

These patterns mean that many of the most important challenges facing minority communities are regional in scope, implying the need to overcome local fragmentation to address these problems on a regional scale. These deleterious trends define the emerging reality of how our regions function, and the arguments below for the reform of fiscal programs, land use, and regional governance outline the strategies most likely to succeed.

Organizing for Fiscal Equity

The effort to create more fiscal equity has begun by states ordering the equalization of school finance. This has been caused by litigation. Over twenty-five state supreme courts have found their state funding systems unconstitutional. Virtually all of these decisions and other types of adequacy lawsuits under the equal protection and educational clauses of state constitutions have provided substantial sums of money for central city schools, although suits brought by minority plaintiffs or minority-led coalitions of plaintiffs have been far more generous for communities of color than suits brought by property-poor white districts. Most minority schools districts are far too poor to operate without state aid, as they are the property-poorest places in the state. They need to be involved and lead regional fiscal equity campaigns.

Fiscal equity across the individual cities and suburbs in metropolitan regions largely determines tax rates for homeowners and businesses, housing prices, the level of municipal services, the quality of the school systems, and the overall quality of life in a given municipality. When fiscal equalization programs are absent, disparities are great from one municipality to the next within a given metropolitan region, and people avoid or flee places with rising tax rates and declining services, and flock to places that can deliver better services at a lower tax rate. Without equalization remedies in place, the disparities from one city or suburb to the next can reach as high as ten to one, meaning a low-tax capacity community would have to tax itself at ten times the rate of a high tax-capacity place in order to deliver the same level of services. This puts older, industrial cities and aging suburbs at a disadvantage, and increasingly isolates the poor and communities of color in places with a declining tax base and mediocre services. Low–tax base places can be characterized as at-risk segregated and older communities that have slow or declining population growth, meager local resources, and commercial districts that struggle to compete with stronger localities (Orfield 2002, 39).

Communities of color are more likely to live in low–tax base places than high–tax base ones (Orfield 2002, 39). The loss of the middle class from low–tax base places leads to declining housing prices and deteriorating school quality in the hardest-hit communities. As neighborhoods become racially identifiable and poor, commercial establishments close, often the tax base that supports public services in our highly fragmented regions begins to erode (Yinger 1995, 121). Private credit dwindles based both on proven racial bias and bad conditions for investment (Yinger 1995, 200). Metropolitan housing segregation and discrimination in credit reduce the housing options of the poor of color, and as the problems intensify, the resources that support public services erode.

A major part of any regional agenda is assuring that all local governments have the financial resources they need to provide important public services. To confront the issues facing low–tax base communities, equalizing fiscal resources is a crucial part of the conversation. Although sometimes an abstract notion, equity-based fiscal reform is more comprehensible when considering examples from politics and the private sector.

By playing to the self-interest of constituents, the advantages of the system will become apparent.

Fiscal equity programs are mechanisms for local governments in a region to share both the benefits and responsibilities of economic development and growth. They do this by reducing inequalities in the resources available to local governments. Among the mechanisms for creating fiscal equity are local government aid programs administered by the states, and regional tax base–sharing programs that pool a portion of a local governments' tax base and redistribute it more equitably.

The largest such program in the United States is the Fiscal Disparities Program in the Minneapolis–Saint Paul region (Hinze and Baker 2000). Since 1971, the nearly two hundred local governments in the seven-county metropolitan region have contributed 40 percent of the growth in their commercial-industrial tax bases to a regional pool each year (Luce 1998). The funds in the regional pool are then redistributed back to local governments according to the strength of their tax bases. Tax base–poor communities get back more than they paid in to the pool, while tax base–rich communities get back less. In 2000, the program reduced the tax base disparities among local governments by 20 percent (Orfield 2002, 107). Tax base sharing in the Twin Cities has helped its core cities and at-risk suburbs remain relatively healthy, and contributed to the Twin Cities' ranking as one of the nation's best places to live. A smaller program in the New Jersey Meadowlands has helped officials there guide development in an environmentally sustainable way (New Jersey Meadowlands Commission n.d.). By guaranteeing that all fourteen Meadowlands communities share the benefits of development, no matter where in the district it occurs, they have been able to reduce the competition for a good tax base—and direct development to the areas best suited for it.

Regional fiscal equity programs have several benefits. First, they allow tax base–poor places to compete on a level playing field with their more affluent neighbors (Orfield 2002, 97). Without such policies, many central cities, inner suburbs, and outlying small towns—places living with aging infrastructure, industrial pollution, and high levels of poverty—are often forced to tax themselves at a much higher rate than their better-off neighbors to compensate for high costs and relatively meager tax bases. Likewise, many fast-growing bedroom suburbs struggle to provide the public services needed to accommodate their largely residential growth. Meanwhile, the most affluent suburbs—places offering expensive new homes and plentiful commercial development—are able to rely on their significant tax bases to offer high-quality public services at relatively low rates.

Reducing inequalities among communities helps address the ongoing challenges faced by communities of color, diminishing the effects of pockets of concentrated poverty in isolated municipalities (Orfield 2002, 23–48). Policies promoting fiscal equity also help to make a region operate more efficiently by reducing the incentives for local governments to engage in costly competition for a tax base—competition that, for the most part, simply shifts a given amount of regional tax base from place to place. Every dollar of public resources devoted to this competition—for everything from business tax breaks to the public provision of new infrastructure—takes money away from other valuable uses like police, fire protection, and schools.

For the majority of suburbs, a fiscal equity program is a win-win scenario. And for those communities that pay into the program more than they receive, there is a silver lining: those places will feel less pressure to develop tax base–rich commercial and industrial projects to maintain a low-tax, high-service environment.

Fiscal equity programs thus positively affect land use. If all local governments benefit from development anywhere in the region, they feel less pressure to zone land in their borders only for industrial and commercial uses or high-end homes. Wasteful government competition that occurs when suburbs compete for new development by offering incentives can be reduced. Fights over regional malls and corporate campuses can be diminished, making the choices for those developments based less on local incentives and more on what makes sense for the region at large. Suburbs can then preserve more open space and natural areas that enhance the area's quality of life, rather than be compelled to zone all open space for the highest fiscal return.

Fiscal equity programs already exist in every state. Virtually all state governments distribute resources to local school districts to help cover the costs associated with education. On average, states provide nearly 50 percent of local school spending (Orfield 2002, 87). In addition, state funding comprises 18 percent of local municipal budgets, which cover services like police and fire protection and libraries (Orfield 2002, 87). Several regions in the country have established programs for municipalities to share a portion of their tax base with one another.[2]

Without measures in place to address regional fiscal disparities, tax resources are distributed unequally across major U.S. metros. Just about a third of metropolitan-area residents reside in middle-class communities facing little poverty or other social strains.[3] And only a fraction of those live in affluent places with large tax bases due to expensive homes and, in most cases, plenty of commercial development. But many suburban residents assume that their town would be a net loser in fiscal equity reforms, when the reality is that many suburbanites live in places that stand to gain. For example, in most metropolitan areas, anywhere from 60 to 75 percent of residents live in communities that would benefit from regionwide tax base sharing.[4] Fiscal equity efforts support a fairer distribution of basic services and help struggling suburban communities find new life with greater resources to rebuild roads, sewers, and neighborhoods.

Even suburbs with a strong commercial base and expensive homes have good reasons to participate in regional fiscal equity efforts. First, if other communities are also perceived as attractive places to live and work, it will reduce the pressure for development in the more affluent communities. That, in turn, can bolster local efforts to reduce traffic congestion and preserve open space.

If the majority of suburbs in a region are struggling to maintain services and attract economic development, the region is likely not faring well in the national competition for jobs and residents. For example, studies show that the median household incomes of suburbs and cities of a metropolitan area rise and fall together, and that metropolitan areas with the smallest gap between city and suburban incomes have greater regional job growth (Ledebur and Barnes 1993; Barnes and Ledebur 1992). In addition, in large metropolitan areas, income growth in central cities results in income growth and house-value appreciation in the suburbs (Voith 1998, 445–464). Winners in the global race will be attractive, balanced regions, not those with a declining urban core and one or two wealthy suburban enclaves.

Despite a rebirth of some downtowns and urban neighborhoods, the nation's central cities are still suffering. The reality is that they still house and educate a large percentage of the nation's poor, without much help from the surrounding communities (Orfield 2002, 23–25). In most U.S. regions, urban centers are racially segregated neighborhoods with high poverty rates.[5] Urban planners and sociologists consider neighborhoods with over 40 percent of the people in poverty as extreme poverty tracts, and those between 20 and 40 percent as transitional areas that are steadily becoming much poorer (Jargowsky 1997, 62; Institute on Race and Poverty 1999, 3; Jargowsky 2003, 1). While there are some high-poverty white neighborhoods in Appalachia and a few older Rust Belt cities, more than 75 percent of poor whites in the United States live outside of high-poverty neighborhoods, while approximately 82 percent of poor blacks and Latinos live within neighborhoods characterized by high poverty (Jargowsky 1997, 62).

Central cities benefit from fiscal equity programs as well. Regional fiscal reforms can complement existing revitalization efforts by providing cities with more money for redevelopment and to deal with the social and economic problems that continue to plague them. Reducing the incentives for tax base competition will also help cities to retain the economic activity and tax base currently located there.

An alternative to tax base–sharing programs for regions that want to implement a fiscal equity program is to reform state municipal-aid programs. These programs could be modeled after school aid programs, which are often designed to increase equity among school districts. State aid for municipalities can ensure that all places have the resources to support services that are considered essential—among them public safety, streets, and sanitation services.

Some efforts to improve the fiscal well-being of municipalities can be counterproductive. For example, some cities have been allowed to impose special taxes unavailable to other municipalities in their regions. But special taxes can actually hurt the competitiveness of these cities because they make them more expensive places to do business than nearby suburbs.

Organizing for Land Use Reform

A regional affordable housing strategy is an important piece of any regional planning effort. Such initiatives help to reduce the consequences of concentrated poverty on core communities and provide people with real choices concerning where they want to live. Regional housing plans are also intricately related to the racial integration of public schools. Research on the effect of public housing on schools shows that if state-supported housing had been located differently in metropolitan Houston and Miami, there would have been no need for court-ordered busing because subsidized housing itself could have socially and economically integrated the schools (Cummings 1981; Orfield 1981; Goering 1986).

One of the best affordable housing strategies is the one in Montgomery County, Maryland, which requires builders and developers to include a proportion of affordable units in their projects or pay into a county-wide affordable housing fund (Common Interest n.d.). The most effective programs make a concerted effort to include residents of color. Due in part to housing discrimination, communities of color are often underrepresented in such programs. This kind of program benefits affluent suburban areas. When exclusive communities don't provide enough affordable housing, employees of local businesses—retail establishments, offices, and health care facilities—have to commute from other cities, causing greater congestion on area roads and increasing costs for local businesses.

Community reinvestment can at times lead to gentrification, a real concern for the most vulnerable residents of a region. As a lower-income neighborhood starts attracting middle-class households, the families that are displaced can find it tremendously difficult to locate new housing they can afford. Inner-city revitalization projects should not be undertaken without addressing the housing needs of low-income households. But managed correctly, central cities and older suburbs can also benefit from a diversified housing base. The problems associated with concentrated poverty—everything from high crime to poor health—dramatically limit the opportunities of residents, isolating them from educational, employment, and social opportunities (Yinger 1995). They also place a significant burden on communities' fiscal resources. A regional plan can help communities preserve housing options so there are housing choices for middle-class and poor households in all communities, whether suburban or urban.

Housing discrimination, the pattern of resegregation, the racial identification of communities, disinvestment, and decline do not stop at central city borders. Indeed, they affect huge parts of suburbia. Blacks and Latinos are suburbanizing in increasing numbers; in Minneapolis in 2000, for instance, 51 percent of blacks at or above the median income lived in the suburbs, up from 44 percent a decade earlier (Ameregis n.d.). The most rapid resegregation in the nation is now occurring in the nation's older suburbs, and has been since the 1980s (Frankenberg and Lee 2002, 7).

The central idea of opportunity-based housing is that residents of metropolitan regions are situated within a complex, interconnected web of opportunity structures (or the lack thereof) that significantly shape their quality of life. Opportunity structures are the vehicles for racial and economic fairness for all residents of the region, and are tied to metropolitan space. The geographic distribution of these structures within a region is strongly linked to the degree to which residents can access them. An analysis of opportunities must therefore take into account the presence of economic and racial segregation, and how it functions for different communities of color (powell 2003).

As middle-class blacks and Latinos continue the century-long intrametropolitan migration for opportunity, many turn to the suburbs, and in the process they experience various levels of discrimination. Real estate agents show them only a small part of the housing market. They continue to experience discrimination from sellers and landlords. They cannot get the same size mortgages that whites can access. A recent study of metropolitan Boston showed that blacks moving to the suburbs had about 25 percent of the community choices of suburbanizing whites (Stuart 2000). At the same time, white suburbanites seeking homes are not shown integrated markets (Turner et al. 2002; Turner and Skidmore

1999). As a consequence, there are few stably integrated neighborhoods in the United States. The resegregation pattern in the public schools generally precedes resegregation occurring in the larger neighborhoods.

The use of land is one of the more contentious areas of metropolitan politics. Addressing the way that land use patterns develop across a region is critical because current growth patterns are unsustainable. The nation's central cities are suffering declining fortunes, and a growing number of suburbs are experiencing similar strains. Low-density development threatens valuable farmland and natural habitat on the urban edge, and strains the local budgets of suburbs struggling to provide needed schools, roads, and sewer systems. It is also important because local governments use their planning and zoning powers to compete with other communities in their region for profitable land uses that generate more in tax base than they require in public services (Fischel 1992).

The rapid development of land on the fringes of metropolitan regions has far outstripped the rate of population growth in the United States. Across the twenty-five largest metropolitan areas, the amount of urbanized land grew by 46 percent from 1970 to 1990, while the population in those urbanized areas grew by just 20 percent (Orfield 2002, 62). Regions such as Cincinnati and Milwaukee have grown dramatically in land area while gaining little population.

There is a perception that the United States has plenty of land, such that managing land use is a low priority (Tierney 2004). Yet regions do not have an endless supply of developable land. Hemmed in by mountains, marshes, lakes, bays, and the sea, some have nearly run out of buildable land. Even if there were limitless land and no boundaries, inefficient land use compounds congestion. Regions such as Atlanta and Houston, with no natural borders, are experiencing enormous problems of congestion, pollution, and decline in the urban core (Rusk 1993). With better planning, more land could be saved for high-functioning open space, and older neighborhoods could be revitalized.

In the absence of fiscal equity programs, stability for local communities comes largely from a commercial/industrial tax base. When business owners are expanding or opening new facilities, they often choose a move to the suburbs over the urban core because of the unknown costs of cleaning any contamination on industrial land in urban areas.

Cleaning up brownfields—properties where redevelopment is complicated by the presence or potential presence of contamination (U.S. Environmental Protection Agency n.d.)—is a strategy being used in many
urban and suburban communities. Brownfields often offer major locational advantages over far-flung greenfields, which are undeveloped sites
in outlying communities. Once rehabilitated, they supply new businesses
and housing with access to existing sewer and road systems. Greenfields
often require new roads and expensive hookups to regional sewer systems. They also eat up open space and create congestion. The once-rural
highways that bring employers to these outlying locations can take
years—and millions of dollars—to improve. Brownfields are not an
urban problem alone. In many regions, especially those with military or
industrial histories, older suburbs have almost as many brownfield sites
as cities.

The coordination of land use occurs most efficiently at the regional
level rather than at the local level. Local governments oversee many
important things within their borders. But the regional coordination of
local planning efforts is so crucial because individual communities can
do little on their own to confront the underlying regional forces contributing to sprawl. For example, local growth management rules that limit
development in one community may simply push it to other areas,
increasing traffic and sending sprawl even farther into the countryside.
Without a regional plan for protecting open space and farmland, the
actions of individual places to control growth can actually make the
problems of sprawl worse.

The concept of smart growth offers communities an efficient and environmentally sound development pattern that aims to preserve open space
and agricultural lands, ease traffic congestion by creating a balanced
transportation system, and make more efficient use of public investments
(American Planning Association n.d.). Smart growth is development
done in a cost-efficient, pedestrian-friendly, transportation-rich way.[6] A
real smart growth initiative also involves a strong affordable housing
component.

Smart growth has a variety of benefits. First, it creates livable, attractive neighborhoods. It can also provide housing opportunities for low-

wage earners in newer, job-rich suburbs as well as stabilize cities and older suburbs.

Smart growth saves money too. An analysis of New Jersey's State Development and Redevelopment Plan, which emphasizes smart growth, found that implementing the plan would reduce the fiscal deficits of local governments by an estimated $160 million over twenty years, and save an estimated $1.45 billion in water and sewer infrastructure statewide (Burchell, Dolphin, and Galley 2000).

Smart growth initiatives have passed in likely and unlikely places. At least sixteen states have already adopted comprehensive smart growth acts, and their ranks are growing. Regional land use planning in Wisconsin, Pennsylvania, Maryland, and other states helps officials coordinate investments in roads, highways, sewers, and utilities. Concurrency requirements like those in Florida mandate that infrastructure be online by the time development takes place. Several states have approved or are considering "fix it first" legislation requiring state agencies to focus spending on repairing existing infrastructure instead of building new facilities. Many states have embraced agricultural and open-space preservation programs.

There's a common misperception that smart growth just limits development. The goal of smart growth is not to curtail development but simply to ensure that it occurs in a sustainable, efficient, and coordinated way. In fact, places that have used smart growth in planning their region are among the most attractive and fastest growing in the country. Economic development expert Richard Florida (2002) believes the creative class of employees—those with college degrees and high-paying jobs—prefer regions with character, social amenities, and attractive communities.

A variety of growth management tools are available to regions that seek more coordinated development. One is an urban growth boundary —a border drawn around an urban area to help contain the region's growth in and near already-established cities and suburbs. Another similar strategy allows for the construction of sewer and water lines only in defined areas. This doesn't stop development outside the border, but it makes developers and cities provide those services without assistance from taxpayers elsewhere in the region. Other strategies include concurrency requirements that link development approval to the availability of infrastructure, open-space preservation programs, and state plans that offer local governments incentives to participate in regional efforts.

Policymakers may worry that restricting the supply of land available for development will simply increase the cost of housing. This is a common criticism, largely based on Portland's experience. Housing prices, however, rose just as fast in other metropolitan areas where population grew dramatically in the 1990s as they did in Portland.[7]

Building Coalitions for Coordinated Regional Governance

In every metropolitan area in the United States, there are regional governments called MPOs. They have been in charge of the largest public works program in U.S. history: the federal highway program. These highways are the skeletons of our evolving metropolitan regions. In many of the most wickedly segregated cities—places like Detroit, Cleveland, Cincinnati, and Atlanta—these regional governments have relatively few blacks and Latinos, the central cities often have less than their fair share of appointments, and the building of new highways out to the periphery of the region works with other factors such as locally restrictive zoning to intensify racial segregation.

Every metropolitan area in the country faces the problems of unbalanced growth, concentrated poverty, fiscal disparities, growing traffic congestion, and sprawl. The need for regional governance reflects this reality. With dozens and sometimes hundreds of municipalities comprising regions, addressing problems that affect entire regions is a serious challenge. Modern metropolitan problems are simply too large for any one local government to address alone. Regional governance is not a new idea, and federal law already requires that every major region in the country have an MPO to coordinate transportation spending there. The reform of existing organizations like these is one approach to improving coordination within a region. But however it is done, regional governance raises all sorts of questions. Many residents do not entirely understand precisely how a regional organization might guide and influence regional development patterns.

At some level, most regions already have some form of regional government, but the existing, unelected organizations are not accountable to the citizens they serve. Establishing responsive regional governance is vital because the physical boundaries of elected units of government do not correspond to the regional scale of many service and infrastructure needs. Many individuals and organizations working to address the effects of concentrated poverty, segregation, and sprawl—including business leaders, environmental and historic preservation organizations, and affordable housing and poverty advocates—are all beginning to recognize that this political fragmentation and lack of regional oversight is hindering their long-term success. Regional governments can oversee efforts to help direct growth into built-up areas while maintaining green space and rural character in outlying areas. They can also coordinate transportation and land use decisions, and help deal with planning mistakes of the past. A regional body could study local conditions to determine whether that land could be better used for housing, mixed-use projects, or open space.

Effective regional efforts strike a balance by allowing local control over issues best addressed by local governments, while promoting cooperation on larger issues affecting the entire region, such as highway and sewer investments, affordable housing, transit, land use planning, air and water quality, and economic development. A regional authority may also be the appropriate venue for services such as transit, water, and sewer systems—services where economies of scale can provide significant cost savings.

Regional governance benefits suburbs in different ways. It assists fast-growing, low–tax base suburbs in limiting their growth to the level that they can effectively manage and getting the infrastructure they need to support it. It can help more affluent suburbs reduce high rates of congestion and preserve open space by distributing growth more widely in the region. Those kinds of policies also help revitalize older suburbs that are struggling with population losses and aging infrastructure. In addition, many suburbs are home to business leaders who understand that their region's health is judged as much by the region's core as the enclaves in which they reside. Regional efforts to manage growth provide an alternative to no-growth moratoriums or slow-growth movements that can restrict economic growth.

Regional governance is a concept that has found proponents on both sides of the political aisle, not just from more liberal elected officials. Progressive Republicans in Portland, Minneapolis–Saint Paul, and Indianapolis led efforts to create regional government. Strong land use laws were signed by then governors Tom Ridge in Pennsylvania and Tommy Thompson in Wisconsin, both currently members of the Bush administration. Former HUD secretary Jack Kemp (currently cochair of Empower America) is a champion of fair housing laws. A Republican governor forwarded Oregon's powerful land use act. The consolidation of Indianapolis with Marion County occurred when now senator Richard Lugar was mayor of that city, and it was nurtured by successive Republican mayors William Hudnut and Steve Goldsmith.

The concept of regionalism has caused concern among communities of color. The fear is that regionalism will ultimately dilute the political power of their constituencies by, for example, potentially undermining the cultural identity that has been fostered by Black or Latino enclaves. But there are regional strategies that address this concern. Scholar john powell (2003) advocates an approach he calls "federated regionalism." Federated regionalism allows cities or communities to retain their political and cultural institutions while sharing in regional resources. Under such an arrangement, local governments cooperate on some issues and maintain local autonomy on others. Strategies like these can assure that minority groups don't lose their hard-fought political powers and community cohesiveness, while still allowing regions to address regional problems.

The most widespread form of regional governance in the country is the MPO (Solof 2001; Orfield 2002, 137). Mandated by Congress in the 1970s to address growing transportation problems, MPOs gained additional power in the 1990s with the passage of two major transportation acts: ISTEA and TEA-21 (Orfield 2002, 137). MPOs now make decisions involving millions of transportation dollars—more money than most cities in a region spend on roads and transit. But their ability to address broader land use patterns—often patterns that contribute to the very congestion they are trying to ameliorate—is limited.

MPOs are part of the government—an unelected government. With millions of dollars flowing through MPOs, many critics believe the current system represents taxation without representation. Activists face the challenge of making these sometimes-shadowy regional governments more effective on issues of growth, and more visible and accountable to the people they serve. The membership of regional bodies should be apportioned by population and, ideally, directly elected by the people.

There are other ways to achieve improved regional government without expanding the power of MPOs. Intergovernmental cooperation can be improved by strengthening other existing regional bodies—councils of government, regional planning commissions, and so forth—that help communities make land use decisions and provide specific regional services. Like MPOs, they often work in relative obscurity without much media coverage or citizen involvement. Also like MPOs, their power to enact significant regional reforms—and in some cases, their interest in doing so—is limited. Empowered with better tools, they could make greater headway on a whole host of regional issues, such as land use planning, housing and redevelopment efforts, and the protection of farmland and other open spaces.

There is also a role for states in coordinating regional cooperation among localities. State governments could assist regions with planning, and offer incentives to encourage municipalities to enact planning and zoning rules consistent with the statewide goals. Such efforts might include giving them priority for technical assistance, streamlined permitting, and an array of spending initiatives. States are taking steps in this direction. For example, Wisconsin's new smart growth law encourages communities undergoing comprehensive planning to share and seek approval from neighboring communities.

MPOs and other planning groups can be pressured to make appropriate land use and transportation decisions. Since they are generally unelected, activists have to make these organizations accountable for their actions by casting press attention in their direction and lobbying at meetings. They can also lobby the state legislature to make existing regional agencies respond to public pressure by holding elections for representatives.

In some cases, filing a lawsuit may be necessary to get the MPO's attention. That's what a coalition of Michigan organizations have done to protest the makeup of the SEMCOG board. (Brooks 2004). The city of Ferndale, MOSES (a coalition of faith-based community groups), and Transportation Riders United have jointly filed suit alleging that SEM-COG "needs to be reformed or replaced entirely with a metropolitan planning organization that reflects the actual population. Right now, Detroit (pop. 951,000) holds three seats on SEMCOG's executive board, while Monroe County (pop. 145,000) holds four" (Brooks 2004). The plaintiffs would also like to see the members be elected, not appointed. Ultimately, the lawsuit aims to amplify black and Latino voices in transportation decisions that determine regional opportunity structures.

Lessons on Regional Coalition Building

Creating an environment for reform is a challenge, but with a game plan and a strategy to involve as many organizations as possible, you can see real movement on issues. The following are ten lessons on effective coalition building gleaned from years of hashing out strategies for reform with activists, elected officials, faith-based community groups, planners, and academics across the country.

1. *Understand the region's demographics and make maps.* Develop an accurate and comprehensive picture of the region by understanding growth management, transportation planning, and the potential for state aid to help counties and suburbs. Use comparisons with other regions. Our maps of the twenty-five largest metropolitan areas are available at ⟨http://www.ameregis.com⟩. Use them with elected officials, citizens' groups, and newspaper reporters to make your case.

2. *Reach out on a personal level.* Political persuasion is selling an idea to another person or group with power. Make connections to other groups and individuals who can help your cause before announcing problems and disparities. Invite input, and share ownership of the effort.

3. *Build a broad, inclusive coalition.* The coalition should stress the themes that it's in the short-term interest of the region's residents to solve the problems of polarization and it's in their short-term interest as well. Play to suburban self-interest. Low–tax base suburbs support tax sharing because it gives them lower taxes and better services. High–tax base suburbs support it so they can protect natural places they value, and it may serve them well in managing their supply of affordable housing.

4. *"It's the suburbs, stupid!"* Regionalism has to be a suburban issue to alter the political environment. Working-class suburbs will not love you immediately, but keep talking. Bedroom communities choking on growth can see the loss of open space and continued growth as costing a great deal, and may be open to regionalism.

5. *Reach into the central cities to make sure the message is understood.* Metropolitan reforms cannot be seen as alternatives to existing programs but rather as reforms that complement those already in place. Fair housing should be seen as a strategy that allows individuals to choose where they live rather than a strategy for fracturing inner-city communities. Make the case that overwhelming inner-city problems can be ameliorated with regionalism.

6. *Seek out the region's religious community.* Is it moral to divide a region into two communities—one prosperous and the other struggling? That's a compelling moral argument. Ask the religious community if it is moral to allow cities to rot while farmland is destroyed in the name of growth. Churches understand civil rights, and they understand how to reach skeptics in the inner-ring suburbs and the inner city. And they have a role in promoting the city since the cost of shuttering inner-city churches and building new ones in the suburbs has become onerous.

7. *Seek out the philanthropic community, establish reform groups, and appeal to business leaders.* Business and philanthropic organizations are increasingly important in influencing policymakers regarding regional cooperation. The Silicon Valley Manufacturing Group, the Greater Baltimore Committee, and Chicago Metropolis 2020 are among the national leaders in regional reform.

8. *Draw in distinct but compatible issues and organizations.* Churches, communities of color, environmental organizations, women's groups, and seniors can all be drawn into the debate over land use and metropolitan governance. So can preservationists.

9. *Prepare for controversy.* Reform requires many tough battles. This is how real reform takes place. Continually emphasize the message of the common good and the benefits to individual communities in the region.

10. *Move simultaneously on several fronts and accept compromises.* Get as many issues moving as can be effectively managed, but not too

many. Keep several bills on these issues moving at once. A governor may sign one and not another, but some legislation passed is better than none.

At a time when states and municipalities are feeling significant budget pressures, the argument for regionalism only grows stronger. By consolidating power and sharing resources, communities can function better. Regionalism can deliver more efficient services, stronger transportation, and regional planning that can actually save communities money—while saving green space, creating more attractive neighborhoods, and redeveloping urban and suburban areas.

Notes

1. This chapter was adapted from a publication called *An Activist's Guide to Metropolitics: Building Coalitions for Reform in America's Metropolitan Areas*, written by Myron Orfield with editorial and research assistance from Frank Jossi, Jill Mazullo, Baris Gumus-Dawes, and Scott Crain.

2. Tax base–sharing programs exist in Minneapolis–Saint Paul, Minnesota, Dayton, Ohio, and the Meadowlands, New Jersey.

3. For a discussion of the suburban community typology, see Orfield (2002).

4. Based on calculations made by Ameregis staff for numerous "metropolitan" reports, available at ⟨http://www.ameregis.com⟩.

5. Of those living in concentrated poverty, one-half are black and one-fourth are Hispanic. As of 1990, close to twenty-eight hundred census tracts among the nation's forty-five hundred experienced concentrated poverty compared with only a thousand in 1970. Although the level of concentrated poverty declined by 24 percent in the 1990s, the recent economic downturn and the weakening state of many older suburbs underscore that the trend may reverse once again without continued efforts to promote economic and residential opportunities for low-income families.

6. "Fair growth," an emerging concept among some regional theorists, encourages a focus on the racially and socially equitable effects of land use development.

7. Based on independent analysis by Orfield and the Ameregis research staff.

References

Ameregis. n.d. U.S. Census Data 2000. Available at ⟨http://www.ameregis.com⟩.

American Planning Association. n.d. Smart Growth Reader. Available at ⟨http://www.planning.org/sgreader/⟩.

Barnes, W. R., and L. C. Ledebur. 1992. *City Distress, Metropolitan Disparities, and Economic Growth*. Washington, DC: National League of Cities.

Brooks, J. 2004. Unrest Plagues Regional Board. *Detroit News*, January 25.

Burchell, R. W., W. R. Dolphin, and C. C. Galley. 2000. The Costs and Benefits of Alternative Growth Patterns: The Impact Assessment of the New Jersey State Plan. New Brunswick, NJ: Urban Policy Research, Edward J. Bloustein School of Planning and Public Policy. Available at ⟨http://www.nj.gov/dca/osg/docs/iaexecsumm090100.pdf⟩.

Common Interest. n.d. Inclusionary Housing in Montgomery County, MD. Available at ⟨http://www.bpichicago.org/rah/pubs/ci_issue_brief4.pdf⟩.

Cummings, S. 1981. Racial Isolation in the Public Schools: The Impact of Public and Private Housing Policies.

Fischel, W. A. 1992. Property Taxation and the Tiebout Model: Evidence for the Benefit View from Zoning and Voting. *Journal of Economic Literature* 30:171–77.

Florida, R. 2002. *The Rise of the Creative Class: And How It's Transforming Work, Leisure, Community, and Everyday Life*. New York: Basic Books.

Frankenberg, E., and C. Lee. 2002. Race in American Public Schools: Rapidly Resegregating School Districts. Available at ⟨http://www.civilrightsproject .harvard.edu/research/deseg/reseg_schools02.php⟩.

Goering, John M. 1986. *Housing Desegregation and Federal Policy: Urban and Regional Policy and Development Studies*. Chapel Hill, NC: University of North Carolina Press.

Hinze, S., and K. Baker. 2000. The Minnesota Fiscal Disparities Program Report. Prepared for the Minnesota House of Representatives Research Department, Saint Paul.

Institute on Race and Poverty. 1999. Concentrated Poverty and Racial Segregation: Evaluating Programs and Policies. Minneapolis: University of Minnesota.

Institute on Race and Poverty. n.d. Minority Suburbanization and Transportation Investments in Four Metropolitan Areas. Report to the legislative Black Caucus. Minneapolis: University of Minnesota.

Jargowsky, P. A. 1997. *Poverty and Place: Ghettos, Barrios, and the American City*. New York: Russell Sage Foundation.

Jargowsky, P. A. 2003. *Stunning Progress, Hidden Problems: The Dramatic Decline of Concentrated Poverty in the 1990s*. Washington, DC: Center on Urban and Metropolitan Policy, Brookings Institution.

Ledebur, L. C., and W. R. Barnes. 1993. *All in It Together: Cities, Suburbs, and Local Economics Regions*. Washington, DC: National League of Cities.

Luce, T. 1998. Regional Tax Base Sharing: The Twin Cities Experience. In *Local Government Tax and Land Use Policies in the United States: Understanding the Links*, ed. H. F. Ladd and W. E. Oates. Northampton, MA: Edward Elgar Publishing.

New Jersey Meadowlands Commission. n.d. Tax Sharing in the Meadowlands District. Available at ⟨http://www.meadowlands.state.nj.us/commission/tax_sharing.cfm⟩.

Orfield, G. 1981. The Housing Issues in the St. Louis Case. Testimony for Liddell v. Board of Education, 491 F. Supp. 351, 357, 359–60, aff'd 667 F.2d 643 (8th cir.), cert. denied 454 U.S. 1081.

Orfield, M. 2002. *American Metropolitics: The New Suburban Reality.* Washington, DC: Brookings Institution Press.

powell, j. 2003. Opportunity-Based Housing. *Journal of Affordable Housing and Community Development* 12:188.

Rusk, D. 1993. *Cities without Suburbs.* Washington, DC: Woodrow Wilson Center Press.

Solof, M. 2001. History of MPOs. *North Jersey Transportation Planning Authority Quarterly.*

Stuart, G. 2000. Segregation in the Boston Metropolitan Area at the End of the 20th Century. Available at ⟨http://www.civilrightsproject.harvard.edu/research/metro/housing_boston.php⟩.

Tierney, J. 2004. The Autonomist Manifesto (or How I Learned to Stop Worrying and Love the Road). *New York Times,* September 26. Available at ⟨http://query.nytimes.com/gst/abstract.html?res=F30E12FA3E5D0C758EDDA00894DC404482⟩.

Turner, M. A., S. K. Ross, G. Galster, and J. Yinger. 2002. Discrimination in Metropolitan Housing Markets: National Results from Phase I of HDS2000. Available at ⟨http://www.urban.org/template.cfm?Section=ByAuthor&NavMenuID=63&AuthorID=5903&AuthorName=Margery%20Austin⟩.

Turner, M. A., and F. Skidmore. 1999. Mortgage Lending Discrimination: A Review of Existing Evidence. Available at ⟨http://www.urban.org/template.cfm?Section=ByAuthor&NavMenuID=63&AuthorID=5903&AuthorName=Margery%20Austin⟩.

U.S. Environmental Protection Agency. n.d. Brownfields Definition. Available at ⟨http://www.epa.gov/swerosps/bf/glossary.htm#brow⟩.

Voith, R. 1998. Do Suburbs Need Cities? *Journal of Regional Science* 38, no. 8:445–464.

Yinger, J. 1995. *Closed Doors, Opportunities Lost: The Continuing Costs of Housing Discrimination.* New York: Russell Sage Foundation.

14

Smart Growth Tools for Revitalizing Environmentally Challenged Urban Communities

Daniel J. Hutch

Ground zero for metropolitan sprawl is often found in forces radiating out of African American and disadvantaged communities, fueled in part by dominant groups' aversion to shopping or living in areas where there are 20 to 25 percent minorities (Leinberger 1996, 217). The black share of suburbanization exceeds 10 percent in only 24 of the 102 largest metros while the rate of black suburban population growth exceeding 2 percent was felt in only 13 metros, and for 20 metros the black share of suburban population growth actually fell (Frey 2001).

Smart growth, or efforts to provide alternative choices to unchecked metropolitan expansion or sprawl, has the potential to foster reinvestment in existing communities, spur development that is compact in form, or increase population densities in a manner that encourages transportation and housing choices for all incomes while improving environmental, economic, and fiscal performance. This corresponds with efforts to revitalize disadvantaged communities while alleviating economic, fiscal, and environmental damages to the entire region due to sprawl and rapid white urban exodus. At stake are billions, if not trillions, of investment dollars and incentives in transportation, clean water infrastructure, power utilities, and social costs related to urban decline. The erosion of equality gains for African Americans since *Brown v. Board of Education* is linked to the emergence of sprawl development patterns aided by subsidized forms of inequitable business and residential development (Hutch 2002b, 353; powell 2000b, 1).

The self-perpetuating cycle of unemployment, eroding tax base, crime, poor education, and exodus away from existing communities toward greenfields could be countered by more equitable smart growth reinvestment initiatives. The challenge for urban advocates and policy-makers is to utilize smart growth strategies and tools to rebalance metro-politan growth to benefit African American and disadvantaged communities, while appealing to broader regional priorities, including environmental, economic, and fiscal concerns.

Challenges and Benefits of Smart Growth

State and regional planning commissions, economic development offices, and transportation and environmental planning bodies exert significant influence on new developments. They can influence whether urban com-munities or exclusive newer communities along the metropolitan fringe will receive billions of dollars of capital investment, subsidies, or trans-portation improvements. Substantial funds to tackle regional and state transportation, environmental infrastructure, public works, and utility needs often bypass older disadvantaged communities and perpetuate further inequalities. For example, older cities face a twenty-year $574 billion funding gap (U.S. EPA 2002) for clean water infrastructure. Iron-ically, the cost of rehabilitating these urban systems would be lower than constructing new systems in exurban communities (McElfish and Casey-Lefkowitz 2001, 40–41).

Water infrastructure investments are key to regional development. The Clean Water State Revolving Fund (CWSRF) has the flexibility to target resources to particular environmental needs, including contami-nated runoff from urban areas (for instance, waterfront improvements), wetlands restoration, groundwater protection, brownfields remediation, estuary management, and wastewater treatment (U.S. EPA 2003b, 1). Construction along waterways to improve sewers and reduce nonpoint runoff pollution via greenways (or natural pollution buffers) can also lead to value-enhancing waterfront redevelopments for declining areas (Little 1990, 86).

Centrally located inner cities and older suburbs are key assets in the transportation planning process to improve air quality and lessen auto dependency. A significant share of the transportation funding ($286 bil-lion) is affected by MPOs, and they have a large influence on the growth patterns and shape of urban areas in recommendations to allocate lump sum federal funds among roads, bridges, and transit projects (Rusk 2000, 100). MPOs must also assure that all equity is incorporated into the planning process (U.S. DOT 2001, 20).

Smart Growth Linked to African American Communities

African American communities exhibit key attributes of smart growth communities, including areas that are walkable and compact in form with a variety of housing types, and have mixes of commercial and residential land uses, with population densities sufficient to support transit systems. These communities utilize existing public infrastructure investments, and they offer architecturally distinct and historic sites to anchor new development. Channeling development toward these communities as opposed to outlying areas can reduce both polluted water runoff from newly paved or built impervious surfaces and air emissions due to increased transportation choices.

Affluent and predominantly white exurban communities attract most of the economic growth, and suburban communities with large black populations attract less growth and heavier social service burdens, which drives taxes higher (Cashin 2004, 151–52). Black communities are discriminated against in the market for commercial investments and isolated from favored commercial markets (Cashin 2004, 150).

The 2000 decennial census shows that the trend of substantial percentages of whites leaving cities remains intact (Brookings Institution 2001, 1). Recent population surveys have corroborated this trend. African Americans also remain highly segregated in older inner-ring suburbs, and black middle-class suburbs have heavier tax and service burdens because they often attract low-income residents (Cashin 2004, 150). Less stable middle-class inner-ring black suburbs portend serious difficulties for smart growth, whose objective is to decrease the exodus of residents, jobs, and investments to the metropolitan periphery.

African Americans are highly affected by sprawl because they are more highly segregated from whites than other minorities and have greater difficulty entering white neighborhoods (Freeman 1999). According to Environmental Justice Resource Center scholars, "People of color communities have been targeted with locally undesirable land uses"—the result of the limited choices for housing, education, and social mobility—but smart growth can resolve some of these problems (Bullard, Johnson, and Torres 2000b). Other research found that metropolitan-wide forces are far more important than neighborhood-specific effects in determining concentrated poverty outcomes for regions (Persky and Wievel 2000, 126).

Efforts to forge broad coalitions are possible, since many white communities are also hurt by the fiscal strain imposed by sprawl. For example, older residents pay more in property taxes to finance exclusive residential developments along the fringe in the Chicago metropolitan region. Hence, opportunities to form coalitions across jurisdictions are possible to meet mutual challenges from sprawl (powell 2000a, 228).

The Magnitude of Sprawl Incentives

Outward development outstripped population growth by over 2.6 times—and much more in many large cities. "New construction and new gross public investment exceeded a quarter trillion dollars in 1999. How states invest over a quarter of a trillion dollars in gross public investment" is key to regional economic well being (Haughwout 2001, 1–2). "Yet nearly all absolute job growth and the vast majority of corporate relocations have occurred beyond the metro core," and far away from African Americans or minority populations (Leinberger 1996, 208). After considering costs driven by land use, including traffic congestion, shared public goods, and business and household location choices, a Federal Reserve Bank senior economist concludes that "infrastructure investment that encourages decentralization may serve to undermine growth in productivity and social welfare" (Haughwout 2001, 5).

The region can benefit from savings by directing resources to disadvantaged communities rather than to exclusive, predominantly white and low-density suburbs along the metropolitan fringe. Under the current (sprawl development) trends, the capital facility costs are 60 percent more expensive, school facilities are over 7 percent more costly, and utilities are approximately 40 percent more costly than under a smart growth scenario that focuses on older or existing communities (Burchell and Shad 1998a). Revitalizing black urban communities can help capture these cost advantages and efficiencies.

Over $286 billion in federal transportation funds serve as a tremendous subsidy to metropolitan sprawl. Commuters who drive from fringe communities to work pay only 25 percent of the true cost of their transport (Burchell and Shad 1998b, 2). In a twenty-year span, $1 trillion was invested in a vast system of highways, and suburbs received a much greater share of highway funding than cities where African Americans live (*Economist Newspaper* 1999, 3).

Federal investments in wastewater systems between 1972 and 1990 totaled more than $60 billion (Singells 1996, 1). The combined state, federal, and local contributions have totaled $250 billion since 1970 (U.S. House of Representatives 2000). This is often directed toward the fast-growing fringes of metropolitan areas, thereby serving to reduce population density (Haughwout 2001, 1, 7) as well as the competitiveness of urban areas.

Appeals to More Efficient Growth

Sprawl development is inefficient. For example, energy efficiencies—obtained from district networks of heat, cooling, and cogeneration—are better served by clustered or more densely populated urban development than other forms such as sprawling low-density development (U.S. Department of Energy 2000, 1). In addition, sprawling development patterns require expensive investments in sewer, water, and road extensions (Siegel 1998, 16–18).

Reduced travel times and an improved jobs-to-housing balance are other benefits of smart growth for depressed urban communities. Chicago Metropolis 2020, a confederation of regional business and civic leaders, encouraged relocation or expansion decisions based on zoning and land use policies that were favorable toward affordable housing, and the availability of mass transit near work sites, which resulted in efficiencies from decreased absenteeism and turnover rates (Institute on Race and Poverty 2002, 20). Tying jobs and housing to business development can improve the profits of businesses while increasing access to opportunities for disadvantaged groups.

Regressive utility pricing occurs when customers pay one uniform rate based on average costs despite the difficulties and higher costs of servicing sprawling communities (Nelson and Duncan 1995, 113). Effectively, residents of more urban, higher-density areas subsidize new low-density developments in wealthier and more sprawling areas. A recent Florida study of utility expenditures by development type found that it costs more than twice as much to service utilities in low-density developments (Burchell 1998, 30).

Over a twenty-year projected period, from 1990 to 2010, New Jersey alone could save $1.4 billion from compact development. And if these savings to schools, utilities, and roads were extrapolated out to the nation, the annual savings would be $175 billion for municipal governments and $500 billion for schools (Rami 2002, 1). Florida was projected to save $6.1 billion (Burchell 1998, 210).

Environmental Concerns Linked with Sprawl Affecting African Americans

Alliances could be fostered across communities because policies that strengthen the urban-core and inner-suburban areas can also protect the environment. Advocates for the revitalization of disadvantaged communities could focus on sprawl, which disadvantages African American inner cities/older suburbs and causes environmental damages (see table 14.1). "The New Jersey Impact Assessment concluded that the state's compact development plan would produce 40% less water pollution than more dispersed development patterns" (U.S. EPA 2003a, 42). Already, 13 percent of shorelines, 38 percent of estuaries, 36 percent of rivers, and 55 percent of lakes are impaired due to storm water or sewer runoff (U.S. EPA 2001).

New York City's Catskill Delaware Water District was compelled to consider spending $4.57 billion on a new filtration system and increasing drinking water bills by 45 percent unless a plan to change future sprawling development patterns was considered (Clark and Stoner 2001, 11; Diamond and Noonan 1996, 78).

Metropolitan sprawl has increased the number and length of trips, which increases automobile dependency, resulting in increased automobile emissions (U.S. EPA 2003a, 25–26). Transportation sources contribute roughly half of the remaining overall pollution in the air (Brenner 2001, 6). Vehicle miles traveled can increase other harmful pollutants, including air toxics and greenhouse gases. The estimated annual costs of motor vehicle–based pollution range from $28 billion to $500 billion in increased health care costs, $2.5 to $4.6 billion in crop damage, and $6 to $43.54 billion in damage due to reduced visibility (U.S. EPA 2003a, 29).

Damages from sprawl include breaking up stretches of pristine habitats, wildlife impacts, and reductions in the abundance and diversity of bird species (U.S. EPA 2003a, 29). Ground-level ozone is responsible for $1 to $2 billion in reduced crop production per year (U.S. EPA 1997). Air quality is also affected. In 2003 alone, more than a hundred million people lived in 209 counties with poor ozone air quality based on the new eight-hour ozone standard (U.S. EPA 2004). Reducing ozone levels will result in fewer hospitalizations, emergency room visits, and doctor visits for asthmatics, significantly fewer incidents of lung inflammation for at-risk populations, and significantly fewer moderate to severe respiratory symptoms in children (Brenner 2001, 6).

Smart growth is linked to affordable housing shortages by critics because it increases housing values for minorities by restricting the available land. This does not account for discriminatory housing policies (powell 2000a, 224–25). The FHA provided ethnically and racially biased guidance to banks, and guaranteed loans that excluded African Americans (Jackson 1985, 196–98). Exclusionary zoning limits housing choices to all but affluent homeowners by requiring large lots or minimum home sizes (Orfield 1997, 5–6), or by banning secondary homes (Nelson et al. 2002). This practice is also associated with educational inequities (*San Antonio Independent School District v. Rodriguez*, 411 U.S. 1 [1973]) due to the disparities in tax bases used to finance schools. Smart growth, however, can actually increase the supply of housing by offering a better mix without the burdensome zoning restrictions as well as allow low-cost housing design (Arigoni 2001, 9).

Public transit receives a lower proportion of the budget than roadway projects that fuel sprawl. According to a report on transportation equity, the poorest fifth of urban residents in Southern California receive only 4 percent of the transportation benefits. Deficiencies exist in areas such as transportation enhancements, which provide bicycling and pedestrian facilities while also increasing the physical beauty of greenway corridors,

Table 14.1
Environmental effects of sprawl
(some of these savings are captured by reinvestment in declining or African American communities)

Problem/damage	Impact	Potential costs (annual)
Storm water overflow from new construction (roads, homes, and highways)	Strains water treatment systems New York–Catskills systems had to explore the possibility of doubling rates and spend billions on new plants until land use plans were changed	Clean water infrastructure is at risk and $250 billion invested by local, state and federal sources since 1970
Greenhouse gas emissions (CO, CO_2, NO_x, and other heat-retaining gases to a lesser extent)	Increased climatic temperatures Damage to coastal areas: 31 percent of CO_2 is from oil combustion (or 460.4 mmtc); CO_2 accounts for 80 percent of greenhouse gas emissions (⟨http://www.epa.gov/globalwarming/actions/transport/index.html⟩)	50 to 86 cm rise in ocean waters $271 to $471 billion (based on 1-meter rise)
Air pollution health impacts (vehicular) (1991 data)	50–70 million restricted activity days 852 million headaches 20–46 thousand cases of respiratory illness 530 cases of cancer from air tons 40 thousand premature deaths	$28.7 to $531 billion
Air pollution	Visibility loss Crop damage	$4 to $4.54 billion $6 to $43.54 billion
Nonattainment for ambient air quality standards (NO_x, VOCs, O_3, PM-10, CO, Sox) and ozone (VOCs and Nox)	More than 100 million people lived in 209 counties with poor ozone air quality based the new 8-hour standard	Cost to regions: share of new transportation bill—SAFETEA-LU—is $286 billion

Water	Compact development plans can produce 40 percent less water pollution than more dispersed development patterns	Compact or clustered development at 52 residential sites saved $10,000 per unit and reduced water runoff pollution
Green space and habitats	1.2 million acres of farmland lost annually. Nationally, fragmentation by roads and power lines affects the diversity of species. Roads occupied 17,345 square miles, a 2 percent increase in 7 years from 1990 to 1997	$1.4 to $26 billion WTP estimate $130 billion to protect all farmland
Damage to wetlands	Fill, fragmentation, and alteration of hydrology loses to wetlands from residential growth and construction of highways. 310,000 to 510,000 acres could have been lost between 1955 to 1980	$53 million to $6 billion to restore or repair
Brownfields: Effects of not cleaning up sites	Lead and cancer exposure risks Reparatory disease illness Risk to water quality from polluted site water runoff Property value loss Uncertain risk limits investment financing	A 24 time return on federal brownfields; $100 million in government cleanup, and reuse yields $2.4 billion

Sources: EPA, *Built and Natural Environment, Air Trends*, ⟨http://www.epa.gov/airtrends/2003ozonereport/intro.html⟩; U.S. House of Representatives, Subcommittee on Water and the Environment, Background Memorandum for Hearing, March 28, 2001, note 38; American Farmland Trust Information Center, ⟨http://www.farmlandinfo.org/agricultural_statistics⟩, ⟨http://www.farmlandinfo.org/documents/27797/FN_2001-08-31.pdf⟩.

which could in turn jump-start local economies (Dittmar and Chen n.d., 1–2). The USDOT's (2000, iii, 5–7) responsibilities under Title VI of the Civil Rights Act of 1964 include improving the fairness and transparency of the distributional impacts of statewide metropolitan planning.

Expanded enforcement of the 1968 Fair Housing Act could help reverse the racial polarization in housing that likely fosters unstable communities and more sprawl. According to the 1990 census, 80 percent of whites nationwide lived outside of cities while 70 percent of African Americans lived in cities or inner-ring suburbs (Funders' Network for Smart Growth and Livable Communities 1999, 3).

The 1969 NEPA could be used as a tool to provide information to stakeholders not previously included in developmental decisions because the act requires the public disclosure of the negative environmental impacts of new developments. Disadvantaged communities can utilize the public participation and disclosure requirements of NEPA to further smart growth and environmental justice objectives.

Executive Order 12898 coordinates environmental justice activities and strategies across many departments and agencies, and focuses federal attention on the environmental and human health conditions of minority and low-income populations. Executive Order 12866 for Regulatory Review requires an agency to examine the distributive and environmental justice impacts of policies or actions on protected minority and low-income groups.

Title VI of the Civil Rights Act of 1964 provides a ban against the use of federal funds to deny or have the effect of denying the benefits of programs to people or communities due to race, religion, or creed. Collectively, these rules and policies strengthen equity protections regarding land use and would be supportive of smart growth (Hutch 2002b, 363).

Specific Tools and Strategies to Link Smart Growth to Disadvantaged Communities

Skeptics of smart growth frequently assert that nothing can overcome the pull of resources toward larger lots and sprawling communities. The abundance of cheap land—a force too powerful to oppose—drives development to outlying areas (International City/County Management Association 1998, 22; Benfield, Rami, and Chen 1999, 25). Opportunities exist to help level the playing field, however.

The New Brownfields Act

The 2002 Brownfields Act doubles the authorized funding for the environmental cleanup and redevelopment of the sites that are abundant in center cities and older suburbs. More important, it clarifies the legal liability for cleanups, exempting small contributors and prospective purchasers or innocent owners and operators from expensive Superfund liabilities. This could increase the leverage of private-sector investment when coupled with tax credits, empowerment zones, and innovative finance, resulting in the increased conversion of abandoned properties to beneficial uses (U.S. Conference of Mayors 2002). The projected impacts include the creation of over a half-million jobs and additional tax revenues of up to $2.4 billion (U.S. Conference of Mayors 2000).

Underground Storage Tanks

Many African American communities are pockmarked with the blight of abandoned corner gas stations with leaking underground storage tanks (Tarbet 2001). Better delineating liabilities and exempting small businesses and minor contributors can spur the cleanup and redevelopment of a major source of urban blight. This would heavily benefit declining local economies, depressed real estate markets, and the environment.

New Accounting Guidelines Favor Maintenance and Upkeep over New Investment

The General Accounting Standards Board Statement 34 (Maze 2000) requires greater transparency of future infrastructure expenses, and that all current and long-term infrastructure assets and liabilities including general obligation bond debt are reported on government-wide financial statements (Dornan 2000b, 1). This could decrease the cost of government debt (Maze 2000) while adding hurdles for new sprawl construction and investments with unmet long-term costs.

This rule also provides incentives to better maintain existing capital infrastructure along the urban core, since it is more cost-effective than letting infrastructure fall into disrepair or bypassing it with new infrastructure favoring sprawl (Bernstein 1999, 10). Research has shown that preventive maintenance can reduce infrastructure lifecycle costs by 75 to 90 percent (Dornan 2000a, 5–6).

Location-Efficient Mortgages

Federal mortgage subsidies could give special priority to location-efficient mortgages, which calculate the qualifying mortgage amount as a function of the savings accrued by living in a transit-oriented location such as an inner city (Smart Growth Network and International City/County Management Association 2002). A $500 per month auto and transit savings translates to a family qualifying for a mortgage loan that is $50,000.00 greater than before the incentive (Holzclaw 1994, 6–7).

Address Exodus Associated with Race That Fuels Sprawl

Surveys show that blacks prefer to live with whites, but whites do not like to live in black neighborhoods (Massey and Denton 1993, 5). Once a neighborhood reaches one-third black, 73 percent of whites would be unwilling to move into that area (Massey and Denton 1993, 93). Whites have moved still farther out as more blacks have moved into the suburbs, perpetuating an unstable race-based cycle of outward moves to the detriment of the environment.

Enterprise zones and transit-oriented developments could alleviate the jobs-to-housing imbalances and educational iniquities (Hutch 2002b, 365–66). These efforts could make disadvantaged areas more attractive to upper-income whites, who bring with them a higher tax base while improving returns to minority homeowners. Efforts that prohibit fiscal zoning or exclusionary real estate requirements while enhancing fair housing enforcement and affordable housing incentives would mitigate gentrification pressures. Also inclusionary zoning that mandator affordable housing in upscale areas could lesson class and race divisions.

Leveraging Federal Transportation Funds

Coordinating transportation and development is cost-effective. Adding transit stations or upgrading facilities can have development benefits similar to building a new system in a neighborhood (Smart Growth Network and International City/County Management Association 2002, 68). This includes taking advantage of flexibility in federal transportation law to create public-private partnerships, including brownfields redevelopment, around transportation and development investments (Smart Growth Network and International City/County Management Association 2002, 62–63). African Americans provide strong markets for transit, yet transit underserves them (Bullard 2003, 1–2). Depressed urban communities could support transit-oriented development to rectify these inequities as well as foster revitalization and smart growth.

The ARC, for example, recognized that automobile dependency to access homes and jobs played a large role in the region's failure to meet the federal air quality standards under the CAA. This failure jeopardized the metropolitan region's ability to secure the needed federal funding to build and maintain infrastructure in order to serve the projected growth (Bullard, Johnson, and Torres 2000a, 2000b). Since communities of color are disproportionately represented in CAA nonattainment regions (U.S. EPA 1992, 11), and these funds are geared to improve regional air quality, an opportunity exits to redistribute capital back to declining areas while serving broader environmental purposes.

The U.S. DOT's CMAQ program includes provisions for funding transportation control measures, stormwater improvements, and privately owned inner-city bus terminals. Billions of dollars have been allocated to the program. In addition, the U.S. DOT has created a new $602 million 6 year program for Job Access and Reverse Commute Grants to transport welfare recipients and low-income individuals to and from jobs, and to transport residents of urban areas to suburban employment opportunities. (U.S. Department of Transportation 2006, 1).

MPO Fairness
Assuring nondiscriminatory outcomes for regional MPOs is key to equitable development. One study, however, found that while center cities comprised 34 percent of the regional population, only 5 percent of MPO board members were from these communities (Bernstein 1999, 16; McDowell, 1994, 16). This disparity exists due to jurisdictional requirements for low-density suburbs, which can underrepresent African Americans, who are concentrated in center cities (Haughwout 2001, 9).

Title VI of the Civil Rights Act of 1964 has a provision that applies to ensuring more fairness in metropolitan planning processes, and this could support improved public involvement in planning decisions.

Brownfields Tax Incentive

This incentive allows environmental cleanup costs to be fully deductible in the year they are incurred, rather than having to phase in tax benefits over a longer period of time. The tax incentive will cost only $300 million, but yield $3.4 billion in private investment and return eight thousand brownfields to productive use (U.S. Environmental Protection Agency 2000a).

Reinvest in Core Communities to Preserve Environmental Infrastructure

Although this is a considerable investment, the cost of not maintaining this infrastructure may be higher due to environmental risks and damages resulting from poorly treated sewer overflows (Staff of House Subcommittee on Water Resources and Environment 2001).

Watersheds often connect to one another, so broader regional interests are at stake when an urban wastewater system fails (Orfield 1997, 10). The dual costs of providing new infrastructure for those who are moving outward, and maintaining the old infrastructure for the population and economic entities left behind cause taxes and development costs to rise throughout the region (Burchell and Shad 1998b, 9).

Aggressively Market Urban Competitive Advantages

Declining African American communities could vigorously sell their advantages due to their central locations, proximity to markets, availability of water supplies, and large pools of labor. Since population density and the proximity to markets affect investment returns, more densely populated urban markets may provide business with greater profit returns when compared to their metropolitan fringe counterparts (Porter 1995). Business clusters can benefit from shared resources and scale economies (Haughwout 2001, 7).

Efforts to reconcentrate employment in African American communities may actually increase the economic pie (or net fiscal benefits) by utilizing otherwise-unemployed labor, land, buildings, and infrastructure (Persky and Wievel 2000, 126). Business clusters can be formed in disadvantaged urban areas, and benefit from shared resources and associated scale economies (Haughwout 2001, 7).

Utilize Expanded Bond Capacities and LITC Benefits

The volume cap on tax-exempt private activity bonds has increased by 50 percent over previous levels, and since 2002, has been indexed annually to inflation (U.S. House of Representatives 2000). This adds $8 billion to the existing baseline bond capacity, and hundreds of millions of dollars in additional capacity annually due to the continual benefits of the new indexation requirements. Yet it is up to the state and local allocation authorities, economic development offices, and legislatures to make funding priorities for these bonds, including choosing between single-family versus multifamily housing, or industrial revenue projects (Hutch 2002a). Prioritizing this funding to improve older infrastructure investments would serve smart growth as well.

In addition, authorized low-income housing tax credits were increased by 40 percent. States can direct these tax credits to expand affordable housing in hot markets and avert displacement pressures.

Tax Base Sharing

Regional solutions that include tax base sharing may be a rational choice for wealthier suburbs whose image is influenced by the relative health and safety of the urban core and inner suburbs. The Twin Cities region of Minneapolis–Saint Paul reduced wealth disparities between center cities and their outlying areas from fifty to one down to twelve to one (Orfield 1997, 85).

Tax sharing could also weaken incentives to create exclusive housing markets (Orfield 1997, 85). Since regions are linked economically and environmentally, a case can be made for tax base sharing.

Increased Regional Environmental Benefits from Urban Infill

The Atlantic Steel/Station development project in Atlanta was chosen over more sprawling locations because it had transit, pedestrian, and biking access and close proximity to residents, which would reduce auto dependency and lower the levels of air and water pollution when compared to outlying sites. Vehicle miles traveled for the site were projected to be 61 percent lower, while NOx emission levels were projected to be

27 to 42 percent lower than outlying sites. Also, water conservation would be improved over more sprawling site alternatives (U.S. Environmental Protection Agency 1999a). The central site selection also helped the region, which is in nonattainment of the CAA, to preserve its share of the $217 billion transportation appropriation by reducing emissions (U.S. Environmental Protection Agency 1999a, 1–2, 5). Core urban areas should assert these infill benefits when seeking regional investment dollars.

The Community Reinvestment Act

The Community Reinvestment Act compels banks to better serve the needs of their local communities, including disadvantaged communities. The act's scrutiny of banks occurs when the government authorities evaluate applications for charters, bank mergers, acquisitions, and branch openings (U.S. Office of Comptroller of Currency 2003). This act was the impetus for the Bank of America's huge $500 million investment in the inner cities and increased funding for affordable housing projects (*Smart Growth News* 1999, 1).

New Markets Tax Credits

Community development organizations can use the recent new markets tax credits to leverage capital to reinvest in communities. The financial leverage from the credit is due to its tax-free status, which enhances the present net value by as much as 30 percent. This can help increase capital for low-income communities to assist in business development activities (Win Win Partners 2002). The Community Development Venture Capital Alliance, the Enterprise Foundation, the Local Initiatives Support Corporation, the National Community Capital Association, the National Community Investment Fund, and the National Congress for Community Economic Development serve as new markets advisers, who can help investors to access the billions of dollars available to finance almost any type of business, from manufacturing plants to charter schools (Win Win Partners 2002, 1).

Development Linkages

Often, effective linkages can be made between developers in center cities and disadvantaged communities in the form of training, jobs, and affordable housing. Community benefits agreements link the use of public subsidies for development projects to workforce development and job access for residents of poor inner-city communities. One example includes obtaining a commitment to reserve at least 10 percent of the jobs created from a proposed development for community trainees (Funders' Network for Smart Growth and Livable Communities 1999, 5).

Exactions are a requirement that a developer pay some form of impact fees in cash or in-kind concessions (say, the construction of affordable housing) to cover the public costs of infrastructure or other services directly related to the new project. According to Policylink's (n.d., 5) *Equitable Development Toolkit*, "The ability to obtain concessions derives from a local government's power to regulate through its general planning and responsibilities, zoning ordinances and governance of subdivisions."

A more generalized linkage is an "adequate facilities ordinance" or similar law that requires the existence of necessary infrastructure and services before new developments are approved (Policylink n.d., 1–2). These exactions and concessions from developers benefit existing communities, and can reduce subsidies for greenfield developments.

Tax Increment Financing (TIF)

Other tools include TIF, which allows the needed improvements to infrastructure and services required by new redevelopment to be financed through the increase in the tax revenues as a result of the project's impact in increasing property values and the tax base. The increased revenues are applied against the bond debt service used to finance the new redevelopment (U.S. EPA 1999b, 18–19). For example, "the City of Chicago's Tax Increment Financing program helped lure millions of dollars of private investments to Chicago retail areas to provide a better mix of needed commercial and retail establishments for African American Communities" (Smith 2001).

Level the Playing Field: A Call for Action

Communities benefiting from sprawl investments do not pay the full cost of development due to overlapping jurisdictions (Haughwout 2001, 5). Sometimes these costs are extracted from the very disadvantaged communities that have lost their tax bases and jobs from sprawl investments

(Orfield 1997, 74). State economic development offices, legislatures, and state planning councils can offer targeted subsidies to disadvantaged residents and communities while reducing subsidies for sprawl.

In addition, an informed yet proactive approach by African Americans in community envisioning exercises and comprehensive planning meetings are needed to ensure that their communities are competitive with outlying areas. This means block-by-block improvements to create a physical and social infrastructure to better capture infill redevelopment that is value enhancing to existing black residents. Many cities are updating zoning codes, so understanding model smart growth codes to endorse neighborhood design, commercial vibrating is also important (APA 2006).

Appealing to broader regional environmental and fiscal concerns could assist African American low-income communities in their infill redevelopment efforts. More inclusive representation of diverse communities in key metropolitan planning and investment decisions is needed. Disadvantaged communities already offer compact and mixed-use (commercial and residential) neighborhoods and districts with access to markets and population densities sufficient for effective transit-oriented development. Highlighting how the region as a whole benefits from center city and inner-suburban redevelopment is a strategy that can complement smart growth efforts for the region as well as African Americans.

The Atlantic Station example shows that infill redevelopment in center cities can bring tangible environmental benefits to regions when compared to alternative sprawling sites. Using development set-asides for affordable housing can help ensure that the smart growth objective of jobs-to-housing balance is achieved while reducing automobile dependency and the associated pollution.

Leveraging federal funds, tax credits, bond capacities, TIF, and targeted investments as well as capturing unrealized profits from urban competitive advantages are all part of a sound strategy. A better understanding of how financial reporting requirements can facilitate smart growth for African American communities, including a greater transparency of the nonmarket subsidies for greenfield development that supports disinvestment away from center cities and suburbs, is needed. Specific financial incentives and policies can help reverse this trend.

Empowering disadvantaged communities with tools to combat sprawl and disinvestments can contribute to enhancing benefits for the entire region. Protections to ensure that smart growth reinforces equitable processes and outcomes are important. Efforts to redirect investments or constrain sprawl should help rather than thwart investments in underserved communities.

Local officials, community and urban advocates, and interests representing disadvantaged urban community groups should choose to appeal to broader regional, local, and national interests that relate to increasing fiscal and economic efficiencies as well as improving environmental quality. Utilizing specific policy tools that relate to housing, transportation, and the environment can provide assistance in bringing resources back to existing low-income communities and communities of color while supporting smart growth objectives. Nevertheless, disadvantaged communities should be vigilant in making the case that unless they are included as key stakeholders in furthering the environmental and fiscal objectives of the region, smart growth objectives cannot be achieved.

Note

This chapter represents only the views of the author. It does not necessarily represent the views and policies of the EPA, or that of other agencies in the executive branch of the federal government or affiliated organizations.

References

American Planning Association. 2006. "Smart Growth Codes." Available at ⟨http://www.planning.org/smartgrowthcodes/⟩ (accessed on May 20, 2006).

Anderson, R. 2001. Urban Water Council Convenes to Discuss Municipal Water Issues; Mayors Discuss Infrastructure Needs and EPA Regulations. Available at ⟨http://www.usmayors.org/USCM/us_mayor_newspaper/documents/01_29_01/water1.asp⟩.

Angela, V., C. Doherty, and D. Hutch. 2002. Urban Competitive Advantage and Brownfields Redevelopment. Paper presented at the Brownfields Conference. Available at ⟨http://brownfields2002.org/proceedings2000/5-07v.pdf⟩.

Arigoni, D. 2001. Affordable Housing and Smart Growth: Making the Connection. Washington, DC: Environmental Protection Agency, Development, Community, and Environment Division. Available at ⟨http://smartgrowth.org/pdf/epa_ah-sg.pdf⟩.

Benfield, F. K., M. D. Rami, and D. T. Chen. 1999. *Once There Were Greenfields: How Urban Sprawl Is Undermining America's Environment, Economic, and Social Fabric.* Available at ⟨http://www.epa.gov/dced/pdf/WhySmartGrowth_bk.pdf⟩.

Bernstein, S. 1999. Using the Hidden Assets of America's Communities and Regions to Ensure Sustainable Communities. Paper presented at the Symposium on the Future of Local Government in Michigan, Midland. Available at ⟨http://www.mml.org/foundation/sustainable_communities.htm⟩.

Boston Consulting Group. 1998. The Business Case for Pursing Retail Opportunities for the Inner City. Available at ⟨http://www.icic.org/research/pdf/pdf_2_The_Business_Case.pdf⟩.

Brenner, R. 2001. Testimony before the U.S. Senate Committee on the Environment and Public Works.

Brookings Institution, Center on Urban and Metropolitan Policy. 2001. Census 2000 Matters Racial Change in the Nation's Largest Cities: Evidence from the 2000 Census. Available at ⟨http://www.brookings.org/es/urban/census/citygrowth.htm⟩.

Bullard, R. D. 2003. New Routes to Transportation Equity: Why Race Still Matters. *Transportation Equity* 6, no. 1. Available at ⟨http://www.ejrc.cau.edu/transequnewsvol6.htm⟩.

Bullard, R. D., G. S. Johnson, and A. O. Torres. 2000a. Dismantling Transportation Apartheid: The Quest for Equity. In *Sprawl City: Race, Politics, and Planning in Atlanta*, ed. R. D. Bullard, G. S. Johnson, and A. O. Torres. Washington, DC: Island Press.

Bullard, R. D., G. S. Johnson, and A. O. Torres. 2000b. Race Equity and Smart Growth: Why People of Color Must Speak for Themselves. Atlanta, GA: Clark Atlanta University, Environmental Justice Resource Center. Available at ⟨http://www.ejrc.cau.edu⟩.

Burchell, R. W. 1998. *Eastward Ho! Development Futures: Paths to More Efficient Growth in Southeast Florida.* Hollywood: South Florida Regional Planning Council.

Burchell, R. W., and D. Listofkin. 1996. Land, Infrastructure, Housing Costs, and Fiscal Impacts Associated with Growth. Paper presented at Rail-Volution 96: Building Successful Communities with Rail, Rutgers University, New Brunswick, New Jersey.

Burchell, R. W., and N. A. Shad. 1998a. Costs of Sprawl versus Compact Development. Table 1, 13. Chicago: Metropolitan Planning Council.

Burchell, R. W., and N. A. Shad. 1998b. The National Perspective on Land Use Policy Alternatives and Consequences. Oak Brook, IL: Farm Foundation.

Cashin, S. 2004. *The Failures of Integration: How Race and Class Are Undermining the American Dream.* New York: Public Affairs.

Clark, G. A., and N. Stoner. 2001. Stormwater Strategies. *Stormwater*. Available at ⟨http://www.stormh2o.com⟩.

Diamond, H. L., and P. F. Noonan. 1996. *Land Use in America: Report of the Sustainable Use of Land Project*. Washington, DC: Lincoln Institute of Policy and Island Press.

Dittmar, H., and D. Chen. n.d. Equity in Transportation Investments. Available at ⟨http://www.fta.dot.gov/library/policy/envir-just/backcf.htm#equity⟩.

Dornan, D. 2000a. Asset Management and Innovative Finance. Available at ⟨http://accounting.rutgers.edu/raw/gasb/repmodel/TRBassetmgt.pdf⟩.

Dornan, D. 2000b. GASB 34's Impacts on the Infrastructure Management, Financing, and Reporting. Available at ⟨http://www.naco.org/gasb/dornan.pdf⟩.

Downs, A. 2002. Have Housing Prices Risen Faster in Portland Than Elsewhere? *Housing Policy Debate* 13, no. 1.

Economist Newspaper. 1999. Not Quite the monster they call it. Urban Sprawl section. U.S. ed., August 21, 1999.

Environmental Law Institute. 1998. Linking Tax Law and Sustainable Urban Development: The Taxpayer Relief Act of 1997. Washington, DC: Environmental Law Institute.

Freeman, L. 1999. Minority Housing Segregation: A Test of Three Perspectives. *Journal of Urban Affairs* 22, no. 1:32.

Frey, W. 2001. The Melting Pot Suburbs: A Census 2000 Study of Suburban Diversity. In *Census 2000 Series*. Washington, DC: Brookings Institution. Available at ⟨http://www.brook.edu/metro/projects/census/freyexecsum.htm⟩.

Funders' Network for Smart Growth and Livable Communities. 1999. Opportunities for Smarter Growth: Social Equity and the Smart Growth Movement. Translation paper no. 1. Available at ⟨http://www.fundersnetwork.org/usr_doc/equity_paper.pdf⟩.

Glendening, P. 2001. Message of Governor Glendening. Publication no. 2001-07. Available at ⟨http://www.mdp.state.md.us/annual.pdf⟩.

Growth Network, International City/County Management Association. 2003. Location-Efficient Mortgages Encourage Development in Transit Accessible Infill Sites: Infill Financing Fact Sheet. Available at ⟨http://www.smartgrowth.org⟩.

Haughwout, A. 2001. Infrastructure and Social Welfare in Metropolitan America. *FRBNY Economic Policy Review* 7, no. 3:1–2, 5, 7, 9.

Holzclaw, J. 1994. Using Residential Patterns and Transit to Decrease Automobile Auto Dependence and Costs. San Francisco: Natural Resources Defense Council. Available at ⟨http://www.smartgrowth.org/library/articles.asp?art=190&res=800⟩.

Hutch, D. 2002a. Private Activity Bonds and Smart Growth. Paper presented at the Brownfields 2002 Conference, Charlotte, November 13–15. Available at ⟨http://www.brownfields2002.org/proceedings2002/PDFS/POS-28%20Hutch%20document%201.pdf⟩.

Hutch, D. J. 2002b. The Rationale for Including Disadvantaged Communities in the Smart Growth Metropolitan Development Framework. *Yale Law and Policy Review* 20, no. 2:353–368.

Hutch, D. 2005. Building New Coalitions Around Brownfields Development. *Policy Matters*, Goldman Graduate School of Public Policy, Univ. of California at Berkeley, Autumn 2005. Available at ⟨http://policymatters.net/issue/issue_3_1 .pdf⟩.

Institute on Race and Poverty and j. powell. 2002. Racism and Metropolitan Dynamics. Minneapolis, MN: Ford Foundation. Available at ⟨http://www .instituteonraceandpoverty.org/fordinfo.html⟩.

International City/County Management Association, with G. Anderson. 1998. *Why Smart Growth: A Primer*. Washington, DC: Smart Growth Network and ICMA.

Jackson, K. 1985. *Crabgrass Frontier: The Suburbanization of the United States*. New York: Oxford University Press.

Jargowsky, P. A. 1997. *Poverty and Place: Ghettoes, Barriers, and the American City*. New York: Russell Sage Foundation.

Jargowsky, P. A. 2003. Stunning Progress Hidden Problems: The Dramatic Decline of Concentrated Poverty in the 1990s. Washington, DC: Brookings Institution.

Leinberger, C. 1996. Metropolitan Development Trends of the Late 1990's: Social and Environmental Implications. In *Land Use in America*, ed. H. Diamond and P. Noonan. Washington, DC: Island Press.

Little, C. 1990. *Greenways for America*. Baltimore, MD: Johns Hopkins University Press.

Llewyn, M. 2000. Why Sprawl Is a Conservative Issue. *Bulletin of Science, Technology, and Society* 20, no. 4:308.

Massey, D., and N. Denton. 1993. *American Apartheid, Segregation, and the Making of the Underclass*. Cambridge, MA: Harvard University Press.

Maze, T. 2000. Iowa's Local Technical Assistance Program (LTAP): Providing Transportation Technology Transfer for Iowa's Cities and Counties. *Technology News* (January–February): 2. Available at ⟨http://www.ctre.iastate.edu/gasb34/ gasb341.pdf⟩.

McDowell, B. 1994. Central City Representation on Metropolitan Planning Boards. Available at ⟨http://www.mml.org/foundation/sustainable_communities .htm⟩.

McElfish, J., Jr., and S. Casey-Lefkowitz. 2001. *Smart Growth and the Clean Water Act*. Washington, DC: Northeast Midwest Institute, Smart Growth Network. Available at ⟨http://www.nemw.org/SGCleanWater.pdf⟩.

National Association of Local Government Environmental Professionals and the Smart Growth Leadership Institute. 2004. Smart Growth Is Smart

Business. Available at ⟨http://www.resourcesaver.com/file/toolmanager/ CustomO93C337F52733.pdf⟩.

National Governor's Association. 2001. How Smart Growth Can Address Environmental Justice Issues: Issue Brief. Washington, DC: NGA Center for Best Practices. Available at ⟨http://www.nga.org/center/divisions/1,1188,C_ISSUE_ BRIEF^D_2071,00.htm⟩.

Nelson, A., and J. Duncan. 1995. *Growth Management Principles and Practices.* Chicago: American Planning Association.

Nelson, A. C., R. Pendall, C. J. Dawkins, and G. J. Knaap. 2002. The Link between Growth Management and Housing Affordability: The Academic Evidence. Washington, DC: Center on Urban and Metropolitan Policy, Brookings Institution. Available at ⟨http://www.brookings.org/dybdocroot/urban/publications/ growthmanagexsum.htm⟩.

Orfield, M. 1997. *Metropolitics: A Regional Agenda for Community and Stability.* Washington, DC: Brookings Institution Press.

Persky, J. J., and W. Wievel. 2000. *When Corporations Leave Town: The Costs and Benefits of Metropolitan Job Sprawl.* Detroit, MI: Wayne State University Press.

Policylink. n.d. *Equitable Development Toolkit.* Available at ⟨http://www .policylink.org/EDTK/⟩.

Porter, M. E. 1995. The Urban Competitive Advantage of the Inner City. *Harvard Business Review,* 1–2.

powell, j. 2000a. Addressing Regional Dilemmas for Minority Communities. In *Reflections on Regionalism,* ed. B. Katz. Washington, DC: Brookings Institution Press. Available at ⟨http://www.brookings.org/es/urban/reflections/essay8.pdf⟩.

powell, j. 2000b. Race Poverty and Urban Sprawl: Opportunities through Regional Strategies. Available at ⟨http://www1.umn.edu/irp/publications/ racepovertyandurbansprawl.html⟩.

Rami, M. 2002. Sprawl Subsidies and Smart Growth. New York: Natural Resources Defense Council. Available at ⟨http://www.trasact.org/Reports/ smartgrowth/fiscal.htm⟩ (accessed February 21).

Rose, K. 2001. Beyond Gentrification: Tools for Equitable Development. Montclair, NJ: National Housing Institute. Available at ⟨http://www.nhi.org/online/ issues/117/Rose.html⟩.

Rusk, D. 2000. Growth Management: The Core Regional Issue. In *Reflections on Regionalism,* ed. B. Katz. Washington, DC: Brookings Institution Press. Available at ⟨http://www.brookings.org/dybdocroot/es/urban/reflections/essay3.pdf⟩.

Siegel, M. L. 1998. The Effects of Land Use and Utility Service Costs, and Geographically Sensitive User Rates. New York: Natural Resources Defense Council.

Singells, N. D. 1996. Financing Priority Watershed Projects with the State Revolving Fund. Paper presented at the Watershed 1996 Conference. Available at ⟨http://www.epa.gov/OWOW/watershed/Proceed/singelis.html⟩.

Smart Growth News. 1999. December 12. Available at ⟨http://www.smartgrowth.org/news/article.asp?art=390⟩.

Smart Growth Network and International City/County Management Association. n.d. Getting to Smart Growth: 100 Policies for Implementation. Available at ⟨http://www.smartgrowth.org/pdf/gettosg.pdf⟩.

Smart Growth Network and International City/County Management Association. 2003. Getting to Smart Growth II: 100 More Policies for Implementation. Available at ⟨http://www.smartgrowth.org/pdf/gettosg2.pdf⟩.

Smith, D. 2001. Non-profits Give Community a Voice in Redevelopment. Available at ⟨http://www.newstips.org/commnews/urbdev.html⟩.

Staff of House Subcommittee on Water Resources and the Environment. 2001. Water Infrastructure Needs. Available at ⟨http://www.house.gov/transportation/water/03-28-01/03-28-01memo.html3#BACKGROUND⟩.

Tarbet, V. E. 2001. Redevelopment Agency of Salt Lake City. Paper presented at the Brownfields 2001 Conference. Available at ⟨http://www.brownfields2001.org/proceedings/MOI-39-01.pdf⟩.

U.S. Conference of Mayors. 2000. City Report Shows Effects of Brownfields in America. *Recycling America's Land*, 1.

U.S. Conference of Mayors. 2002. Major Provisions of H.R. 2869: The Small Business Liability Relief and Brownfields Revitalization Act. Available at ⟨http://www.usmayors.org/uscm/us_ma...ocuments/01-14-02/brownfields2.asp⟩.

U.S. Department of Energy, Climate Change Technologies. "Combined Heat and Power," State and Local Climate Change Programs, January 2000, used in reference. Available at ⟨http://yasimite.epa.gov/OAR/globalwarming.nsf⟩.

U.S. Department of Transportation. 1998. TEA-21—Transportation Efficiency Act for the 21st Century: Moving Americans into the 21st Century. Available at ⟨http://www.fhwa.dot.gov/tea21/suminfra.htm⟩.

U.S. Department of Transportation. 2000. *Federal Transit Administration, Transportation, and Environmental Justice*. Publication no. FHWA–EP–01–010. Washington, DC: Federal Highway Administration.

U.S. Department of Transportation. 2001. Metropolitan Capacity Building Program, Federal Highway Administration, Federal Transit Administration, ASHTO, APTA, Assoc of MPOs, The Metropolitan Transportation Planning Process: Key Issues: A Briefing Notebook for Metropolitan Planning Organization Board Members. Washington, DC: U.S. DOT. Available at ⟨http://www.mcb.fhwa.dot.gov/MCBwebBrochure.pdf⟩.

U.S. Department of Transportation. 2006. SAFETEA-LU (budget details for reverse commute). Available at ⟨http://www.fta.dot.gov/documents/SAFETEA-LU_Funding_by_Program_by_Year.pdf⟩ (accessed May 20, 2006).

U.S. Environmental Protection Agency. 1992. Reducing Risks for All Communities. Vol. 2 of *Supporting Document, United States Environmental Protection Agency, Policy Planning and Evaluation*. Washington, DC: U.S. EPA.

U.S. Environmental Protection Agency. 1997. EPA Regional Approaches to Improving Air Quality. Research Triangle Park, NC: Office of Air Quality Planning and Standards.

U.S. Environmental Protection Agency. 1998. *A Guidebook of Financial Tools.* Available at ⟨http://www.epa.gov/efinpaage/guidbk98/gbk2a.htm⟩.

U.S. Environmental Protection Agency. 1999a. Project XL and Atlantic Steel: Supporting Environmental Excellence and Smart Growth. Washington, DC: Office of Policy.

U.S. Environmental Protection Agency. 1999b. *Environmental Finance Program, A Guidebook of Financial Tools,* (April), Available at ⟨http://www.epa.gov/efinpage/guidbkpdf/introduc.pdf⟩.

U.S. Environmental Protection Agency. 2000a. Brownfields Office Fact Sheet. Available at ⟨http://www.epa.gov/swerosps/bf/html-doc/hr5542sm.htm⟩.

U.S. Environmental Protection Agency. 2000b. Financing America's Drinking Water: A Report of Progress. Washington, DC: Office of Water.

U.S. Environmental Protection Agency. 2001. The Quality of Our Nation's Water. Available at ⟨http://www.epa.gov/owow/305b/⟩.

U.S. Environmental Protection Agency. 2002. The Clean Water and Drinking Water Gap Analysis. Available at ⟨http://www.epa.gov/owm/gapfact.pdf⟩.

U.S. Environmental Protection Agency. 2003a. Built and Natural Environment: Air Trends. Available at ⟨http:www.epa.gov/airtrends/2003ozonereport/intro.htm⟩.

U.S. Environmental Protection Agency. 2003b. How the CWSRF Program Works. Washington, DC: Clean Water State Revolving Fund. Available at ⟨http://www.epa.gov/owm/cwfinance/cwsrf/basics.htm⟩.

U.S. Environmental Protection Agency. 2004. Air Trends. Available at ⟨http://www.epa.gov/airtrends/2003ozonereport/lookat2003.html⟩.

U.S. Equal Employment Opportunity Commission. 2004. Available at ⟨http://www.eeoc.gov/stats/race.html⟩.

U.S. House of Representatives. 2000. Conference Report/Agreement on H.R. 5542, Department of Labor, Health, and Human Resources, and Education; and Related Agencies Appropriations Act. Sec. 151, sec. 146 of the code.

U.S. Office of Comptroller of the Currency. n.d. Community Reinvestment Act Information. Available at ⟨http://www.occ.treas.gov/crainfo.htm⟩ (accessed April 12, 2003).

Voith, R. 1999. Does the Federal Tax Treatment of Housing Affect the Pattern of Metropolitan Development. *Business Review*, March 5.

Win Win Partners. 2002. New Markets Legislation, New Markets Tax Credit. Available at ⟨http://www.winwinpartner.com/Public%20Policy/index.html⟩ (accessed December 18).

Afterword: Growing Smarter and Fairer

Robert D. Bullard

The environmental justice and smart growth movements have the potential to bring together diverse CBOs, homeowners' associations, civic clubs, academic institutions, grassroots activists, and government officials to form broad alliances to arrest the negative impact of suburban sprawl. Because of the persistent hurdles of uncertainty, uneasiness, and mistrust that must be overcome on both sides, the smart growth and environmental movements for the most part are proceeding on two separate tracks. At present, there appears to be contentment among the various groups to work in coalitions, collaborations, and alliances on those issues where there is broad agreement—such as transportation, air and water quality, waste management, housing, schools, and strategies to address concentrated poverty and joblessness.

While few, if any, smart growth or environmental justice advocates lay all of the urban and suburban ills solely at the doorstep of sprawl, there is a growing agreement, by no means a consensus, that some sprawl-driven development exacerbates environmental, health, and economic disparities between cities, suburbs, and outlying rural areas. There are some who claim "sprawl is good" for the economy. The question is "good for whom"?

When examined in the context of regional planning and metropolitan growth, sprawl has taken on more negative than positive connotations. Since the negative health effects of sprawl fall disproportionately on poor people and people of color, it is crucial that social justice and equity considerations are built into this policymaking. The emerging regionalism movement is fraught with similar equity questions of who pays and who benefits, and how public investments and political power are distributed. These questions are complicated by race and class dynamics—and in some cases, by a historical legacy of institutionalized discrimination.

Given all of the hurdles and challenges in the nation's metropolitan areas, it is possible to have planned growth that addresses the social equity concerns of smart growth and environmental justice advocates. The environmental justice framework is a useful lens through which to evaluate how regional planning and metropolitan growth decisions are made, and how the outcomes of these decisions (the costs and benefits) are distributed. Social equity is about how the costs and benefits get distributed. How social equity is addressed has important implications for building smart growth–environmental justice alliances that can inform the regional equity debate.

The environmental justice framework can also serve as a unifying theme to broaden the smart growth dialogue around race, regionalism, transportation, equitable development, and economic justice. It can serve as a bridge for framing the common themes of the environmental justice and smart growth movements—whose recent history has not been characterized by cooperation. Working together, groups in central cities, suburbs, and surrounding rural areas can band together to arrest sprawl and plan livable communities.

Getting beyond sprawl may be less of a problem than moving beyond race. Race is a social construct and has no biological basis in science. But it still matters in the United States. Race and place are interconnected. Where Americans choose to live, work, play, go to school, and worship is not accidental. Many of our choices are shaped by race. Place affects access to jobs, education and public services, culture, shopping, level of personal security, medical services, and the air we breathe.

Racism disguised as smart growth is still racism. Race and economic geography are also connected. Some businesses and employers, including banks and insurance companies, use racialized space as a "signal" associated with perceptions about race, class, worker skills, and attitudes. Using these signals, many employers often recruit white suburban workers while avoiding central city black workers. Even in an era where an increasing share of people of color now live in the suburbs, "inner city" is still code for black or Latino, while "suburban" connotes white.

Racialized space creates perpetual demarcations and disparities. Sprawl exacerbates these disparities.

Addressing social equity and improving racial and ethnic relations need to be explicit priorities of the environmental justice and smart growth movements. Racial polarization is impeding community and economic development in almost every metropolitan area with large concentrations of people of color. Given that race and class greatly influence access to economic opportunities, good schools, good-paying jobs, and high-quality neighborhoods, dismantling racial and class barriers would go a long way to boost financial incentives and reinvestment in central cities and first-ring suburbs. Like it or not, the fate of central cities and their suburbs are intricately linked. Neither cities nor suburbs can solve regional problems alone. It takes cooperation across political jurisdictions as well as across racial and ethnic boundaries.

Sprawl-driven development diverts funds away from central cities. Smart growth and environmental justice alliances can encourage investments in low-income communities and communities of color to support job creation and economic development. Improving low-income residents' mobility, particularly for those making the transition from welfare to work, may be the difference between employment and unemployment. Still, accessing jobs and other economic opportunities in the metropolitan region, not just neighborhood-based jobs, is key to an economic justice strategy for alleviating concentrated urban poverty.

For decades, zoning was a highly effective tool of exclusion. Cities from Boston to Los Angeles are beginning to use inclusionary zoning, also referred to as inclusionary housing, as a tool to address the shortage of affordable housing that threatens the economic and social well-being of their communities, meet economic development and workforce housing needs, positively impact patterns of economic and racial segregation, and help prevent sprawl and disinvestments.

Many of our zoning and land use decision making still favor development in the suburbs or greenfields rather than central cities. Some policies foster abandonment and infrastructure decline. Alternatively, existing policies such as criteria for funding water/sewer infrastructure could be modified to favor existing rather than new development. In addition, brownfields or abandoned or underutilized property or buildings, offer potential economic opportunities to be reclaimed and brought back into production. Residents in neighborhoods with brownfield sites could become an integral part of the redevelopment process.

It makes little sense to have meetings of all-white leaders in boardrooms talking to each other about implementing smart growth, arresting sprawl, cleaning up the air, solving regional transportation, and improving the overall quality of life in cities and metropolitan regions, while acting as if people of color are invisible. One needs only to turn on the television or scan the local newspaper to witness the paucity of people of color leaders and "experts" on smart growth and regionalism. On the other hand, the environmental justice movement, over the past two decades, has grown a fairly large network of grassroots leaders and CBOs that can speak and act on a range of environmental issues that impact people of color and poor people.

Generally, people of color and their institutions have not played a visible role in the smart growth and regionalism dialogue. Much of the issue framing has been carried out principally *by* and *for* white middle-class leaders and business elites. This is the case even where people of color comprise the majority of the population in the central cities whose namesakes the smart growth initiatives bear. Color matters. Smart growth and environmental justice proponents cannot afford to be color-blind if they ever hope to understand and develop complementary action strategies to address racial and class disparities in cities and metropolitan areas.

Because many regional decisions made by MPOs have long-term costs and consequences, some twenty-five to thirty years out, they are too important to leave solely to planners. Having others "speaking for" impacted communities is antithetical to the principles of environmental justice since this movement is built around people "speaking for themselves."

Smart growth and environmental justice groups can serve as a force to persuade MPOs to incorporate social equity and environmental justice into air quality conformity requirements at all stages of the transportation planning process. They can also encourage the spending of congestion-mitigation investments to benefit low-income communities and communities of color, especially if these areas exhibit disproportionately high levels of criteria pollutants.

Public transportation improvements go hand in hand with expanding job opportunities. Transit stations can become more than a place where commuters pass through on their way to somewhere else. Planners can shape land uses and development that are amenable to walking, bicycling, and transit use. One measure to combat sprawl is transportation-oriented development that promotes more dense, mixed land uses combined with location-efficient mortgages. The idea is that the money saved from lower transportation costs (thereby boosting one's disposable income) could be used to qualify a greater number of lower- and moderate-income households for home mortgages. The spillover effect is increased homeownership in inner-city neighborhoods.

Health and safety form the core of smart growth and environmental justice. Sprawled cities tend to have the highest pedestrian fatality rates, with the highest among people of color. Thus, an action agenda to get National Highway Traffic Safety Administration and other agencies to focus on neighborhood safety issues, particularly pedestrian safety, and ensure that a reasonable amount of transportation safety funds are spent on pedestrian-related projects such as sidewalks, lighting, crosswalks, and traffic calming are issues that both movements can employ.

As a rule, sprawl development is not pedestrian, bicycle, or transit friendly. Infrastructure enhancements and service improvements are needed to get people out of their homes and cars. Walking and biking are two major travel modes that produce zero pollution. In addition, sidewalks, bike lanes, and jogging paths all encourage physical activity, enhance public health, and promote social interaction and a sense of community. Sprawl development discourages walking and biking. Today, few children walk or bike to school.

Nearly every school district in our metropolitan regions will be building new schools. Before these schools are constructed, suitable land has to be found. Unfortunately, some new schools are built on contaminated land, while many others, attended largely by students of color, are located near polluting facilities. All public schools are not created equal. "Separate and unequal" schools (though legally outlawed) still operate in the real world. Disparities exist with and between urban and suburban schools. Innovative approaches need to be taken to equalize inherent funding inequities resulting from an outdated taxing system. Working together, smart growth and environmental justice groups can press for the equitable distribution of government resources; work with the business community; set high expectations for all students; make recruitment of quality teachers a top priority; encourage a culture of learning; provide a safe and secure learning environment; and adopt a philosophy that all children can learn.

Defining sprawl as a civil rights issue also brings a unifying dimension to framing smart growth. For decades, environmental justice proponents have insisted that environmental protection is a civil rights issue. They have demanded that governmental agencies, including MPOs, demonstrate that their plans, decisions, and investments (tax dollars) comply with Title VI of the Civil Rights Act of 1964, which prohibits the use of federal funds to discriminate based on race, color, and national origin. It is for this reason that in February 1994, as mentioned earlier, President Clinton issued the Executive Order 12898 on environmental justice, requiring planning agencies to conduct a regular analysis of transportation decision making, policies, investments, and impacts to determine whether decisions have been made in an equitable fashion.

Getting smart growth and equitable development concepts and principles into environmental justice, and vice versa, is largely a matter of how these messages are framed, and who is used to carry the message. For example, clean air is an issue that resonates with smart growth and environmental justice proponents. In reality, there is no white, black, or Hispanic air. There is just air that we all breathe. Defining clean air as a basic right, a civil right, and a human right (rather than industries' right to pollute) makes clear the equity arguments involved in the problem and its solution. It is unlikely, for instance, that an equitable solution to urban pollution can be achieved without addressing public transportation and land use. Inequitable land uses form the dominant theme of most environmental justice disputes.

Environmental justice is not just about fending off LULUs. It is also about equitable development and getting a fair share of the benefits of smart growth such as affordable housing, especially in redlined and underserved people of color neighborhoods. Equitable development initiatives can eliminate the "discrimination tax" that is levied on people of color homeowners and businesses. Homeownership can act as a major stabilizing force in urban-core neighborhoods. An infusion of capital through home loans offers new hope to once-decaying urban neighborhoods.

Some urban neighborhood revitalization initiatives have created and/ or exacerbate "gentrification" pressures and the displacement of incumbent residents. The key to successful mixed-use–mixed-income neighborhood revitalization is balance. Infill and higher-density development improves infrastructure efficiency by taking advantage of existing capacity; saves on expenses for roads and utilities; requires less automobile dependence; reduces automobile emissions; improves air quality; locates people closer to stores, schools, work, and other activities; and provides access to pedestrian-friendly communities with sidewalks.

Consistent with the principles of environmental justice, people of color and lower-income residents should be given opportunities to do for themselves, plan their own agendas, formulate their vision of the future, revitalize their own neighborhoods, and provide economic opportunities for wealth creation and community services for local residents, including jobs, transportation, and housing linkage programs. With an abundance of vacant land and brownfield properties, many of which are owned by cities, unlimited opportunities abound for smart growth and environmental justice alliances to work on land banking and public-private joint ventures that could be used for developments from parks to housing.

The smart growth movement is playing a crucial role as cities from New York to Los Angeles rebound from economic stagnation and decay. For decades, many of our nation's metropolitan areas experienced a series of "slow-moving" disasters that emptied central cities of people, jobs, housing, taxes, and wealth. More important, sprawl-driven development patterns moved opportunity away from the poor, the working class, and people of color. As cities rebound and rebuild, smart growth and environmental justice principles take on added significance in addressing equitable development that minimizes displacement, gentrification, and racial exclusion.

Hurricane Katrina and its aftermath exposed the nation to the dirty little secret of urban poverty and racism that had been hidden from sight for decades. The inept emergency response to the "unnatural" (human-made) disaster overshadowed the deadly storm itself. As reconstruction and rebuilding move forward in New Orleans and the Louisiana, Mississippi, and Alabama Gulf Coast region, there is a second disaster in the making—driven by racism, classism, elitism, paternalism, and old-fashion greed. Unless the issue of environmental justice is addressed squarely in the aftermath of Katrina, there won't be any black New Orleans neighborhoods to recover or redevelop. Many of the social equity concerns raised in the rebuilding of New Orleans are not new, nor are they unique to that city. They merely reflect centuries of neglect coupled with a stubborn refusal to end white racism and white privilege.

Finally, smart growth and environmental justice advocates have been successful in building their movement and getting their message in the media. It is now time to leverage these gains into action, developing model campaigns to promote legislative reforms, tools for practitioners, and alliances with private-sector groups and regional organizing. Regional health depends on the health of all sectors in a region. Metropolitan regions cannot be healthy with concentrated poverty, rampant joblessness, and environmental "sacrifice zones." Growing smarter and fairer as a nation not only achieves the goals of healthy and sustainable communities and livability but also enhances homeland security for all Americans.

Contributors

Carl Anthony is the deputy director of the Community Resources Development Program at the Ford Foundation. Prior to joining Ford, he was the founder and executive director of the Urban Habitat Program in San Francisco.

Robert D. Bullard is the Ware Distinguished Professor of Sociology and director of the Environmental Justice Resource Center at Clark Atlanta University. His most recent book is titled *The Quest for Environmental Justice: Human Rights and the Politics of Pollution* (Sierra Club Books, 2005).

Don Chen is director of Smart Growth America, a nationwide coalition of roughly fifty organizations promoting a better way to grow—one that protects open space and farmland, revitalizes neighborhoods, keeps housing affordable, provides better transportation choices, and makes communities more livable.

Daniel J. Hutch is an economist with the Office of Policy Economics and Innovation, Office of the Administrator, U.S. Environmental Protection Agency, Washington, DC.

Glenn S. Johnson is a research associate at the Environmental Justice Resource Center and an associate professor in the Department of Sociology and Criminal Justice at Clark Atlanta University.

William A. Johnson, Jr., is the former mayor of Rochester, New York State's third-largest city. He is currently a distinguished professor in the STS/Public Policy Department at Rochester Institute of Technology.

Kimberly Morland is an epidemiologist who received her PhD at the University of North Carolina School of Public Health after earning an MPH at the University of California at Berkeley.

Myron Orfield is an adjunct professor and the executive director at the Institute on Race and Poverty, which is located at the University of Minnesota Law School.

Manuel Pastor, Jr., is a professor of Latin American and Latino studies as well as the director of the Center for Justice, Tolerance, and Community at the University of California at Santa Cruz.

David A. Padgett is an assistant professor of geography and the director of the Geographic Information Sciences Laboratory at Tennessee State University in Nashville.

john a. powell is the Gregory Williams Chair of Civil Rights and Civil Liberties Law at the Ohio State University Moritz College of Law and the executive director of the Kirwan Institute for the Study of Race and Ethnicity.

Swati R. Prakash is the environmental health director for West Harlem Environmental Action in New York City, where she works to incorporate scientific tools into community organizing efforts in low-income urban communities of color.

Thomas W. Sanchez is currently an associate professor of urban affairs and planning at Virginia Tech's Alexandria Center, and a fellow with the Metropolitan Institute.

Angel O. Torres, MCP, is a GIS training specialist with the Environmental Justice Resource Center at Clark Atlanta University.

Maya Wiley is the founder and director of the Center for Social Inclusion, a New York City–based applied research and advocacy project of the Tides Center.

Steve Wing is on the faculty at the University of North Carolina, Chapel Hill School of Public Health, and works in the area of occupational and environmental epidemiology.

James F. Wolf is currently a professor at Virginia Tech's Center for Public Administration and Policy.

Beverly Wright is a sociologist and the founding director of the Deep South Center for Environmental Justice at Dillard University (formerly at Xavier University of Louisiana) in New Orleans.

Index

1,3-butadiene, 276

Abe, S., 277
Abrams, R., 199
Action Pajaro Valley, 92
Acton, 155
*Addressing Community Concerns:
How Environmental Justice Relates
to Land Use Planning and Zoning*
(National Academy of Public
Administration report), 30
Advisory Commission on Intergovernmental Relations (ACIR), 253,
257
African Americans, 4–8, 347–348. *See
also* Racial issues
asthma and, 278
Atlanta and, 226–228, 233–235 (*see
also* Atlanta, Georgia)
automobiles and, 137
black officials and, 133
boycotts and, 104–106
*Brown v. Board of Education of
Topeka* and, 34, 345
census demographics and, 83
civil rights and, 104 (*see also* Civil
rights)
food justice and, 174–176
Greensboro sit-in and, 104–105, 119
Hurricane Katrina and, 189–206
insurance companies and, 201–203,
235
intellectual leadership and, 75

King and, 104–106, 110–112, 115,
120–121
Malcolm X and, 114
Manhattan and, 273
Metropolitan Planning Organizations
(MPOs) and, 265
mortgages and, 109–110
NAACP and, 38, 40, 117–118
Nashville and, 127, 132–137, 143–
146
Negro removal programs and, 205
North Clayton County study area
and, 238–242
public transit and, 91 (*see also*
Transportation)
regionalism and, 75, 79 (*see also*
Regionalism)
religion and, 115
Richland County and, 149–169
self-reliance and, 111
slavery and, 111
small business owners and, 236–237
South Fulton County study area and,
225–238
sprawl effects on, 103–104 (*see also*
Sprawl)
steering and, 323–324
WE ACT and, 43, 273, 285–288,
292–293
zoning and, 109–110
AGENDA, 79
Agricultural Street Landfill, 196
Agriculture, 24, 52, 60, 150

Agyeman, J., 9, 28, 31
AIDS, 194
Airports
air quality and, 224–225, 237–238
Dallas–Fort Worth International
Airport, 231
Hartsfield–Jackson Atlanta International Airport (ATL), 223–242
O'Hare, Chicago, 223
Airports Council International, 224
Air quality, 24–25, 29–30, 350–351,
374–376
1,3-butadiene and, 276
airports and, 224–225, 237–238
aldehydes and, 276
alternative fuels and, 282–285
asthma and, 275, 277–279
Atlanta and, 219–225, 237–238
automobiles and, 41–43
benzene and, 276
carbon monoxide and, 284
Clean Air Act and, 221–223, 357,
360
CMAQ and, 290
diesel fuel and, 275–282
existing regulations and, 279–282
hazardous air pollutants (HAPs) and,
275–276, 279
haze and, 276
hydrocarbons and, 279–280
National Air Toxics Assessment
(NATA) and, 279
National Ambient Air Quality
Standard and, 276
new emission standards and, 279–
280
New Orleans and, 194–195
nitrous oxide and, 41, 224, 275,
279–282, 284, 288, 359–360
ozone and, 221, 275
particulate matter and, 276–284,
289
pollution control technologies and,
279–282
polycyclic aromatic hydrocarbons
(PAHs) and, 276, 284

smog and, 275
sulfur and, 280
Transit Workers Union and, 288
volatile organic compounds (VOCs)
and, 224, 275–276, 280
WE ACT and, 285–288, 292–293
zero-emission vehicles and, 291
Akron, Ohio, 81
Alabama, 38
Alaska, 195
Aldehydes, 276
Alexander v. Sandoval, 118
Allen, K., 108
Allstate, 235
Alston, D., 25
Alternative fuels, 282–285, 290–293
Ameregis, N. D., 332
American Academy of Allergy and
Immunology, 195
American Association of State
Highway and Transportation
Officials (AASHTO), 254
American Chemical Council, 260
American International Group, 202
American Lung Association, 278
American Planning Association, 128
American Red Cross, 191
Americans with Disabilities Act
(ADA), 117, 137–138, 268
Anaheim, California, 84
*Anderson v. Rochester–Genesee
Regional Transportation Authority,*
117
Ansbro, J., 105
Anthony, Carl, 1, 75, 307
Applebaum, B., 199
Archer, Dennis, 60
Asanti, N. M., 110
Associated Press, 29–30, 62, 191
Association of Community Organiza-
tions for Reform Now, 197
Asthma, 42
diesel and, 273, 275, 277–279
Hurricane Katrina and, 194
Atlanta, Georgia, 4, 14–15, 37, 81
air quality and, 219–225, 237–238

as Black Mecca, 215
as Capital of the New South, 215
coalitions and, 336
environmental issues and, 221
as Gateway to the South, 215
Georgia fuel tax and, 220
Hartsfield–Jackson Atlanta
  International Airport (ATL) and,
  223–242
health issues in, 220–223
highway sprawl of, 218–223
housing and, 218, 233–237
MARTA and, 219, 221, 228
Mobility 2030 and, 220–221
noise levels and, 238
North Clayton County study area
  and, 238–242
ozone and, 221
property values and, 233–237
schools and, 231
South Fulton County study area and,
  225–238
as Standing Peachtree, 215
uneven growth in, 215–218, 227–
  233
Union destruction of, 215
white flight and, 218
Atlanta Journal–Constitution, 37,
  231, 235, 237
Atlanta Outlook, 228
Atlanta Regional Commission, 216,
  220–222, 224, 230, 240, 357
Atlantic Steel/Station project, 359–
  360
Aucott, M., 173
Audubon, 202
Austin, Texas, 81
Automobiles, 351. *See also*
  Transportation
  African Americans and, 137
  air pollution and, 41–43
  alternative fuels and, 282–285
  Atlanta and, 219–220
  dependence on, 1
  employment access and, 35, 39–41
  hybrid electric, 283–284

New Orleans and, 192, 195
zero-emission vehicles and, 291
Ayala, A., 282

Babineaux Blanco, Kathleen, 203
Bailey, L., 36
Baker, K., 327
Baker, P., 203
Balz, D., 190
Bank of America, 314
Barnes, W. R., 75, 329
BART, 92–93
Baton Rouge, Louisiana, 199
Bay Area Transportation and Land
  Use Coalition, 304
Bayram, H., 277
BellSouth, 221
Benfield, F. K., 219, 355
Bennett, D. L., 230
Bennett College, 105
Benzene, 276
Berlau, J., 149–150
Bernstein, S., 356–357
Berry, J., 117
Bethel New Life, 95, 305
Bhargava, S., 78
Biodiesel, 284
Black Enterprise magazine, 12, 39,
  143–145, 215
Blackwell, Angela, 8, 75, 299
Bluegrass Tomorrow, 314
Blumenauer, Earl, 173
Blumenberg, E., 258
Boland, S., 277
Bollens, S. A., 58
Bollier, D., 2, 42
Bonds, 359
Boston, Massachusetts, 81
Bourne, J. K., Jr., 190–191
Boycotts, 119
Brand-Williams, O., 62
Brennan, William, 109
Brenner, R., 350–351
Bring Back New Orleans Commission,
  193–194
Brooke, J., 55

Brookings Institution, 40, 128, 233, 347
Brooks, J., 339–340
Brown v. Board of Education of Topeka, 34, 345
Brown, C. M., 39, 215
Brown, Jerry, 66
Brown, M. K., 6
Browner, Carol, 308
Brownfields, 24, 31–32, 334, 355, 358, 374
Brownfields Act, 355
Building Responsibility, Equity, and Dignity, 304
Bullard, Robert D., 75, 103, 118
Atlanta's transportation sprawl and, 215–247
environmental justice and, 23–49
equity and, 1–2, 4, 9, 14, 16, 307
future issues and, 371–378
Hurricane Katrina and, 189–211
regional strategies and, 55
revitalization tools and, 348, 357
Burchell, R. W., 110, 335, 348–350, 358
Buses, 38–39, 103, 105
alternative fuels and, 282–285
boycotts of, 34
diesel and, 273–294
food access and, 116
Hudson Depot and, 286–287
Hurricane Katrina and, 192
Manhattan and, 273–294
WE ACT and, 43, 273, 275–288, 292–293
Bush, George H. W., 29
Bush, George W., 29
Business Week, 194
Bus Riders Union, 38–39, 79, 117–118

California, 314. *See also specific city*
Demographic Research Unit and, 91
diesel fuel and, 277, 279
distorted tax structure of, 88
greenfields and, 351, 354

L.A. Metropolitan Transit Authority and, 38–39
Latinos and, 81, 84–96
Metropolitan Planning Organizations (MPOs) and, 256
schools and, 32–33
Transportation Land Use Coalition and, 91–92
California Air Resources Board (ARB), 279
California Safe Routes to School, 312
Calmore, J. O., 57
Campo-Flores, A., 193
Cancer, 42–43
diesel fuel and, 273, 276, 279
New Orleans and, 193
Capitalism, 112
Carbon monoxide, 284
Cardiac effects, 276
Carlisle, J., 150
Carr, M., 194
Carry, B., 133
Carson, C., 106
Casey-Lefkowitz, S., 346
Cashin, Sheryll, 7, 306, 310, 347
Census tracts (CTs), 226–228
Center for Business and Economic Research, 128
Center for Community Change, 205
Center for Enterprise Development, 165–166
Center for Neighborhood Technology, 40
Centers for Disease Control and Prevention, 42, 193–194, 223
Central Business Districts (CBDs), 132–133, 136, 218
Central city neighborhoods, 134–137, 372–373
asthma and, 278
community development corporations and, 116
crime and, 113
diesel effects and, 273–294
education and, 52
food justice and, 173–186

haze in, 276
influx to, 55
land-use reform and, 331–336
Latinos and, 80–87
location-efficient mortgages and, 356
middle-income housing and, 64–67
regional coalitions and, 323–342
regionalism and, 77
suburban flight and, 53–55
transportation and, 40, 117–118
urban sprawl effects and, 52–55
Chang, J., 198
Chapman, D., 237
Chen, Don, 15–16, 39, 219, 299–320,
   354–355
Chicago, Illinois, 81, 314, 361
Metropolitan Planning Organizations
   (MPOs) and, 264
regional strategies and, 55
segregation and, 107
transportation coalitions and, 305
Child Proofing Our Communities
   Campaign, 32
Choper, J. H., 59
Chu, K., 201, 218
Cieslewicz, D. J., 76
Cincinnati, Ohio, 333, 336
Cincinnati Insurance, 235
Cisneros, Henry, 73–75, 97
City of Atlanta Department of
   Aviation, 233–236
Civil rights, 9, 12, 25, 33, 376
advocates' mistrust and, 59–64
Alexander v. Sandoval and, 118
antisprawl movement and, 59–64
boycotts and, 104–106
Civil Rights Act of 1964 and, 27,
   106, 118, 252, 260–261, 268, 286,
   354, 358, 376
food justice and, 185
Greensboro sit-in and, 104–105, 119
King and, 104–106, 110–112, 115,
   120–121
legal issues and, 117–118
Malcolm X and, 114
mass protests and, 115

Metropolitan Planning Organizations
   (MPOs) and, 258, 260–261, 268
Milliken v. Bradley and, 56
New Orleans and, 200
Paynter v. State and, 117
segregation and, 55–57 (*see also*
   Segregation)
traditional urban lifestyles and, 104–
   106
transportation and, 34–41
Clean Air Act, 221–223, 357, 360
Clean Water State Revolving Fund
   (CWSRF), 346
Clear Air/Clean Water Bond Act, 290
Cleveland, Ohio, 55, 61, 63, 67, 81,
   336
Clinton, Bill, 26–27, 73, 250–251
Coalitions, 360
Bay Area Transportation and Land
   Use Coalition, 304
Figueroa Corridor Coalition, 79, 95
fiscal equity and, 325–331
Greater Rochester Area Coalition for
   Education, 117
Lake Street El Coalition, 305
land use and, 331–336
lessons on, 340–342
public services and, 330–331
reform issues and, 324–325
regional governance and, 336–340
segregation and, 375–376
steering and, 323
taxes and, 325–331, 340
transportation and, 91–92, 302–310
Transportation Land Use Coalition
   and, 91–92
Coca-Cola, 221
Cole, L., 28
Commercial Club of Chicago, 314
Commission for Racial Justice, 27
Common Interest, 331
Community-Based Organizations
   (CBOs), 90, 308–309, 371. *See also*
   Coalitions
Community Development Block
   Grants, 116

Community development corporations, 116
Community Development Venture Capital Alliance, 360
Community land trusts, 117
Community Leader's Letter, 150
Community Reinvestment Act, 360
Compressed natural gas (CNG), 282–284, 286–287, 289–290, 292
Concerned Citizens of Agricultural Street Landfill, 196
Concurrency requirements, 335
Cone, M., 195
Confronting Environmental Racism (Bullard), 9
Congestion Mitigation and Air Quality (CMAQ), 290, 357
Conklin, E. E., 62
Conservation Law Foundation, 2
Constrained Long-Range Plan (CLRP), 252
Corless, J., 275
Corley, Cheryl, 107
Cotton States, 235
Coulton, C., 301
Council of Governments (COG), 255–256, 265, 339–340
Council on Environmental Quality, 27
Coyle, M., 28
Crime, 8, 53, 113
Crocker, J., 116
Cummings, S., 331
Cuomo, Andrew, 73
Curtis, K. A., 173
Cycling, 313, 359

Dallas–Fort Worth International Airport, 231
Dallas Morning News, 32
Danziger, S., 4
Davis, M., 203
Day-Night Average Noise Levels (DNL), 238
Deakin, E., 253–254
Delta Airlines, 221, 231–232

Demand and Response Transit (DART) system, 38
Democracy South, 304
Denton, Nancy, 6, 51, 53, 58, 150–151, 172, 356
Denver, Colorado, 55
DeParle, J., 193
Desegregation. *See* Segregation
Detroit, Michigan, 40, 61, 63, 107
coalitions and, 336
demolition in, 114
middle-income housing and, 64–65, 67
Milliken v. Bradley and, 56
Diamond, H. L., l, 7
Diaz-Sanchez, D., 277
Diesel fuel
1,3-butadiene and, 276
activism and, 285–290
aldehydes and, 276
alternatives to, 282–285, 290
asthma and, 273, 275, 277–278
benzene and, 276
biodiesel and, 284
cancer and, 273, 276, 279
cardiac effects and, 276
EPA and, 275–282
existing regulations and, 279–282
greater emissions from, 274–275
hazardous air pollutants (HAPs) and, 275–276, 279
immune system, 276–278
Los Angeles and, 276, 279
new emission standards and, 279–282
New York City and, 273–274, 283–293
nitrous oxide and, 275, 279–281, 288
particulate matter and, 276–280
policies for, 290–293
pollution control technologies and, 279–282
polycyclic aromatic hydrocarbons (PAHs) and, 276
smog and, 275

source of, 274
sulfur and, 280
in utero exposure to, 278
vehicle miles traveled (VMT) and, 275
volatile organic compounds (VOCs) and, 275, 280
WE ACT and, 273, 285–288
Diet, 180–185
Diez-Roux, A. V., 174, 180
Disabled citizens, 35, 117, 137–138, 268
Disaster capitalism, 204
Dittmar, H., 311, 354
Dolphin, W. R., 335
Donor regions, 36–37
Dornan, D., 355, 356
Downs, Anthony, 51, 54, 57
Draft Environmental Impact Statement (Hartsfield–Jackson Atlanta International Airport), 232, 238
Dreier, P., 2–4, 24, 75
Drugs, 8
Dubofsky, J. E., 184
"Dump Dirty Diesels" (NRDC), 285–286
Dumping in Dixie (Bullard), 9
Duncan, Cynthia M., 5, 349
Durham, J. G., 63

Eaton, S. E., 114
Economic issues, 13–14, 371–372
American Dream and, 112–113, 299–300
Atlanta International Airport and, 223–242
boycotts and, 104–106, 119
class distinctions and, 23
deregulation and, 112–113
disaster capitalism and, 204
fiscal equity coalitions and, 325–331
food justice and, 173–186
globalization and, 314–315
Hurricane Katrina and, 189, 192, 204–205

investment and, 1, 10, (*see also* Investment)
location-efficient mortgages and, 116–117, 356
mass consumerism and, 111–112
more efficient growth and, 349–350
new accounting guidelines and, 355–356
New Orleans and, 189–190
quality of life and, 10
racial place and, 4–8
regionalism and, 75–80, 119–120 (*see also* Regionalism)
revitalization tools and, 345–363
schools and, 32–33
self-reliance and, 111, 377
Small Business Administration (SBA) loans and, 199–200
small business owners and, 236–237
sprawl and, 23
subsidies and, 2 (*see also* Subsidies)
transparency and, 355–356
urban flight and, 7
Warth v. Seldin and, 109
Economist Newspaper, 349
Education, 3, 8, 301, 351. *See also* Schools
equity and, 55
Fisk University and, 134
Paynter v. State and, 117
poverty and, 58–59
racial issues and, 113
Richland County, South Carolina, and, 160
Rochester and, 117
San Antonio Independent School District v. Rodriguez and, 351
Eggleston, P. A., 278
Eimer, S., 77
Emerson, Ralph Waldo, 110–111
Emerson Park Development Corporation, 304
Emling, S., 235
Employment, 1–3, 8–9, 299
automobiles and, 35
development linkages and, 360–361

Employment (cont.)
 entry-level opportunities and, 55
 job flight and, 39–41
 land-use reform and, 334–335
 middle-income housing and, 64–67
 new construction and, 163
 regionalism and, 77–78
 revitalization tools and, 345–363
 Richland County, South Carolina,
   and, 152–155, 163–165
 skills and, 4
 spatial mismatch and, 39–41
 suburban flight and, 53–55
 Transit Workers Union and, 288
 transportation and, 39–41, 304 (see
   also Transportation)
Enchautegui, M. E., 236
Endangered species, 52
Enterprise Foundation, 360
Environmental issues, 9, 15, 306–
  307
 1,3-butadiene and, 276
 air quality and, 350–351, 374–376
   (see also Air quality)
 aldehydes and, 276
 alternative fuels and, 282–285
 Atlanta and, 219–225, 237–238
 benzene and, 276
 brownfields and, 24, 31–32, 334,
   355, 358, 374
 Clean Air Act and, 221–223, 357,
   360
 diesel fuel and, 273–294
 endangered species and, 52
 Exxon Valdez and, 195
 filtration systems and, 350
 greenfields and, 1, 3, 25, 345–346,
   351–352, 354, 373–374
 hazardous air pollutants (HAPs) and,
   275–276, 279
 Hurricane Katrina and, 189–206
 level playing field for, 361–363
 new emission standards and, 279–
   280
 nitrous oxide and, 41, 224, 275,
   279–282, 284, 288, 359–360

 noise levels and, 238
 oil spills and, 195
 ozone and, 221, 275
 particulate matter and, 276–284, 289
 pollution control technologies and,
   279–282
 polycyclic aromatic hydrocarbons
   (PAHs) and, 276, 284
 regionalism and, 75–76
 revitalization tools and, 345–363
 Richland County, South Carolina,
   and, 149–150
 Sierra Club and, 150
 sulfur and, 280
 Transit Workers Union and, 288
 underground storage tanks and, 355
 volatile organic compounds (VOCs)
   and, 224, 275–276, 280
 WE ACT and, 285–288, 292–293
 zero-emission vehicles and, 291
Environmental justice
 air pollution and, 24, 29–30, 41–43
 Associated Press study and, 29–30
 Atlanta International Airport and,
   232–233, 237–238
 brownfields cleanup and, 24, 31–32
 burden of proof and, 26
 Bush administration and, 29
 central city neighborhoods and, 24–
   25
 civil rights and, 25, 27
 class distinctions and, 27
 defined, 26
 diesel and, 273–294
 documenting disparities and, 27–30
 enforcement and, 26
 Executive Order 12866 and, 354
 Executive Order 12898 and, 26–27,
   250–252, 261, 268, 354
 future issues for, 371–378
 hazardous substances and, 26–30
 health issues and, 26–28, 41–43
 integrationist approach and, 44
 investment and, 23–24
 land-use zoning and, 30–33
 Latinos and, 93–96

Metropolitan Planning Organizations
(MPOs) and, 249–268
NEPA and, 27
New Orleans and, 193–196
principles of, 25–27
quality food and, 171–186
sacrifice zones and, 378
smart growth compatibility and, 23–
30, 43–44
subsidies and, 26
Superfund sites and, 28, 32–33
toxic emissions and, 30, 32
transportation and, 24, 34–41, 249–
268, 309
water pollution and, 24
WE ACT and, 43, 273, 285–287
*Environmental Justice: EPA Should
Devote More Attention to
Environmental Justice When
Developing Clean Air Rule* (GAO
report), 29
Environmental Justice Resource
Center, 309, 347–348
Environmental racism, 118
*Environmental Science and Tech-
nology,* 159
Envision Utah, 314
*EPA Needs to Consistently Implement
the Intent of the Executive Order on
Environmental Justice* (EPA report),
29
Equal Justice Society, 200
Equitable Development Toolkit
(PolicyLink), 361
Equity, 11
coalitions and, 302–310, 323–342
education and, 55
environmental justice and, 23–44
food justice and, 171–186
future issues for, 371–378
gasoline tax and, 36–37
global economy and, 314–315
institutional strategies and, 312–313
integrated approach for, 302–305
Metropolitan Planning Organizations
(MPOs) and, 249–268

private sector and, 313–314
racial issues and, 3–8 (*see also* Racial
issues)
regionalism and, 8, 76–80
revitalization tools and, 345–363
self-sufficiency and, 377
transportation and, 34–41, 215–247
(*see also* Transportation)
whole community approach and,
310–312
zoning laws and, 30–33
Ernst, M., 275
Evans, B., 9, 28, 31
Ewing, R., 173
Executive Order 12866, 354
Executive Order 12898, 26–27, 250–
252, 261, 268, 354
Exxon Valdez, 195

Faber, D. R., 31
Failures of Integration, The (Cashin),
306
Fair Housing Act, 184
Farber, H., 241
Farley, R., 4
Farquhar, M. B., 258
"Federal Actions to Address
Environmental Justice in Minority
Populations and Low-Income
Populations" (Executive Order
12898), 26–27, 250–252, 261, 268,
354
Federal Emergency Management
Agency (FEMA), 198–201, 204
Federal Financial Institutions
Examination Council, 197
Federal Highway Administration
(FHWA), 35, 252–253, 268, 303,
313
Federal Housing Administration
(FHA), 54, 109–110, 172, 351
Fernandez, R., 301
Figueroa Corridor Coalition, 79, 95
Fiscal Disparities Program, 327
Fischel, W. A., 333
Fisk University, 134

Fitton, L. J., 27–28
Fitzgerald, S., 173
Fix-It-First, 312
Florida, Richard, 335
Florida, State of, 350
Flying Off Course (Natural Resource Defense Council), 238
Food justice
  access issues and, 171–188
  future research for, 183–185
  housing and, 172
  influence on diet and, 180–183
  Nutrition and Your Health: Dietary Guidelines for Americans and, 180
  placement of stores and, 173–186
  regional equity and, 174–180
  segregation and, 174–180
  survey methodology for, 174–180
  transportation and, 116, 172–173, 178–180
Ford, R. T., 56
Ford Foundation, 5
Foster, S. R., 28
Foster-Bey, J., 53, 58
Francois, F. B., 255
Frank, B. P., 3, 282
Franklin, Aretha, 134
Frazier, J. W., 4
Freedom Riders, 34
Freeman, L., 347
Freilich, R. H., 51, 58
Frew, A., 277
Fruitvale, California, 92–93
Frumkin, H., 3
Fulton, W., 128
Funders' Network for Smart Growth and Livable Communities, 93, 354, 361

Gage, Robert W., 254
Galley, C. C., 335
Galster, G. C., 52
Garrow, D., 105–106
Gasoline tax, 36–37, 220
Gender issues, 264–265

General Accounting Standards Board, 355
Gentrification, 7, 51–52, 377
  antisprawl movement and, 61–64
  land use reform and, 331–336
  Latinos and, 80
  middle-income housing and, 64–67
  misnomer of, 63–64
Geographic information systems (GIS) techniques, 128, 138, 142–143
Gerome, J., 134
Gibson, T., 24
Gillham, Oliver, 1
Girard, Chris, 201
Glaeser, E. D., 106, 218
Glendening, Parris, 308
Globalization, 314–315
Global Positioning System (GPS), 137
Goedert, J. G., 59
Goering, J. M., 331
Goetz, Andrew, 253
Gold, S., 194
Goldberg, D. T., 57, 222
Goldman, T., 27–28, 253–254
Good News Garage, 302
Gordon, P., 52, 54
Government. *See also specific department*
  Advisory Commission on Intergovernmental Relations (ACIR) and, 253
  Bring Back New Orleans Commission and, 193–194
  civil rights and, 55–57
  coalitions and, 336–340
  donor regions and, 36–37
  environmental justice and, 25–27, 29
  Executive Order 12866 and, 354
  Executive Order 12898 and, 26–27, 250–252, 261, 268, 354
  Latinos and, 88–89
  limited abilities of, 53–55
  lower taxes and, 112–113 (*see also* Taxes)
  place-based leadership and, 114–117
  political fragmentation and, 57–58

segregation and, 55–57
sprawl creation by, 54
state DOTs and, 36
subsidies and, 2, 7, 26, 300
toxic cleanup disparities and, 28
transportation and, 34–41, 249–250
  (*see also* Transportation)
zoning laws and, 30–33
Graham, K. M., 250
Great Divide, The (Association of
  Community Organizations for
  Reform Now), 197
Greater Rochester Area Coalition for
  Education, 117
Greene, R., 96
Greene-Roesel, R., 275
Greenfields, 1, 3
environmental justice and, 25
future issues for, 373–374
revitalization tools and, 345–346,
  351–352, 354
Greensboro sit-in, 104–105, 119
Griggs, T., 195
Grogan, P., 115
Guinier, L., 60
Guo, S., 301
Gurwitt, R., 108

Haar, C. M., 30
Halpern, R., 66
Hamburg, J., 131
Harlem Hospital Center, 278
Hartsfield, William, 223
Hartsfield–Jackson Atlanta International Airport (ATL), 14–15
description of, 223–224
environmental impact of, 224–225,
  237–238
fifth runway expansion of, 225–226,
  240–242
noise levels and, 238
North Clayton County study area
  and, 238–242
passenger volume of, 223–224
property values and, 233–237
small business owners and, 236–237

South Fulton County study area and,
  225–238
toxic materials and, 224–225
Harvard University, 33, 205
Harvey, S., 238
Haughwout, A., 348, 357–359, 361
Hazardous air pollutants (HAPs),
  275–276, 279
Hazardous materials, 275–280
airports and, 224–225
diesel fuel as, 273–294
environmental justice and, 26–32
lead poisoning and, 193
New Orleans and, 193–195
*Health Assessment Document for
  Diesel Exhaust* (EPA), 277
Health Effects Institute, 42, 279
Health issues, 25, 306–307, 375
AIDS, 194
air pollution and, 41–43 (*see also* Air
  quality)
asthma, 42, 194, 273, 275, 277–279
Atlanta and, 220–223
cancer and, 42–43, 193, 273, 276,
  279
cardiac effects, 276
central city neighborhoods and, 25
diesel and, 273–294
diet and, 180–185
environmental justice and, 23–44
food justice and, 171–186
Katrina cough and, 194
lead poisoning and, 193
mold and, 194–195
New Orleans and, 193–196
*Nutrition and Your Health: Dietary
  Guidelines for Americans* and, 180
ozone and, 221, 275
particulate matter and, 276–277
transportation and, 41–43
waste management and, 139–142
"Heavy-Duty Engine and Vehicle
  Standards and Highway Diesel Fuel
  Sulfur Control Requirements, The"
  (EPA), 280–281
Hendricks, Gary, 231–232, 236

Hendrix, Jimi, 134
Henry J. Kaiser Family Foundation,
  205
Henton, D., 75
Hidden in Plain Sight (America), 305
*Highway Robbery: Transportation
  Racism and New Routes to Equity*
  (Bullard, Johnson, and Torres), 9,
  34
Hill, E. W., 36–37, 52
Hinze, S., 327
Hipp, J., 31
Hirschman, D., 226
Hispanics. *See* Latinos
Holgate, S., 277
Holzer, H. J., 4
Homeland security, 204, 378
Home Owner Loan Corporation
  (HOLC), 172
*HOPE Unseen, A: Voices from the
  Other Side of Hope VI* (Center for
  Community Change), 205
Hope VI projects, 139, 205
Hosenball, M., 199
Housing, 2–3, 7–9, 58
  American Dream and, 299–300
  Atlanta and, 218, 227–228, 233–
    237
  attracting middle-income, 64–68
  central city neighborhoods and, 25
  development linkages and, 360–361
  Fair Housing Act and, 184
  Federal Housing Administration
    (FHA) and, 54, 109–110, 172, 351
  fiscal equity coalitions and, 325–331
  food justice and, 171–186
  health issues and, 194
  Home Owner Loan Corporation and,
    172
  insurance and, 201–203
  land use reform and, 331–336
  location-efficient mortgages and,
    116–117, 356
  mixed-income policy for, 119
  mold and, 194–195
  Nashville and, 132–133

National Fair Housing Alliance and,
  197–198
New Orleans and, 194–204
property values and, 119, 233–237
redlining and, 172, 201–203
relocation and, 299–300
Richland County, South Carolina,
  and, 165–168
Section 8, 139
steering and, 323–324
suburban flight and, 58
taxes and, 340 (*see also* Taxes)
trailers and, 198–199
urban renewal projects and, 133
zoning laws and, 109–110 (*see also*
  Zoning)
Housing and Urban Development
  (HUD), 73–74
Houston, Texas, 9, 55, 133
*Houston: Growth and Decline in a
  Sunbelt Boomtown* (Shelton et al.),
  9
Hsu, S. S., 190
Hudson Depot, 286–287
Hughes, M. A., 93
Hurricane Andrew, 194, 201–202
Hurricane Betsy, 196
Hurricane Georges, 191
Hurricane Ivan, 191
Hurricane Katrina, 4–5, 14, 378
  Agricultural Street Landfill and, 196
  Baton Rouge and, 199
  buses and, 192
  cleanup from, 196–197, 203–204
  cost of, 189, 192
  death toll of, 189
  debris from, 194
  disaster assistance and, 197–200
  FEMA and, 198–201, 204
  insurance redlining and, 201–203
  Katrina cough and, 194
  landfall of, 189
  levee restoration and, 203–204
  looting and, 201
  marsh restoration and, 203–204
  "New" New Orleans and, 204–205

oil spills and, 195
Old Gentilly Landfill and, 196–197
racial issues and, 193–196
Red Cross and, 191
transportation and, 190–192
water damage and, 195–196
Hurricane Rita, 202
Hurricane Wilma, 202
Hutch, Daniel J., 16, 345–369
Hybrid electric automobiles, 283–284
Hydrocarbons, 279–280
Hydrogen fuel cells, 284–285

IBM, 221
"If You Live Uptown, Breathe at Your Own Risk" (WE ACT), 285, 288
"I Have a Dream" (King), 104
Imagine Richland 2020 Comprehensive Plan, 153–155
Immigrants, 90–91, 95
In Search of the New South (Bullard), 9
Institute of Medicine (IOM), 27–28
Institute on Race and Poverty, 325, 349
Insurance, 201–203, 235
Integrationist approach, 44
Intermodal Surface Transportation Efficiency Act (ISTEA), 35, 251–253, 257–258, 268
International City/County Management Association, 312, 355–357
Interwoven Destinies: Cities and the Nation (Cisneros), 97
Investment, 1, 10, 374–375
Community Reinvestment Act and, 360
core communities and, 358
environmental justice and, 23–24
highway development and, 249–251
(*see also* Transportation)
level playing field and, 361–363
maintenance and, 355–356
new accounting guidelines and, 355–356

Oakland and, 66
Rochester and, 116
tax credits and, 360
Invisible Houston (Bullard), 9
Iron triangle, 1

Jackson, K. T., 54, 58, 351
Jackson, Maynard, 223
Jackson, R., 3
Jargowsky, P. A., 7–8, 23, 51, 53, 57, 62, 151
Jim Crow laws, 34, 56, 202
Jobs Access and Reverse Commute Program, 304, 357
Johnson, A., 198
Johnson, C., 137
Johnson, Glenn S., 76, 307, 348, 357
Atlanta's transportation sprawl and, 215–247
environmental justice and, 24–25, 34, 37–38
regional equity and, 1–2, 4, 9, 14
Johnson, Stephen, 308
Johnson, William, Jr., 12, 75, 103–123
Joint Venture: Silicon Valley Network, 94
Just Sustainabilities (Agyeman, Bullard, and Evans), 9
Just Transportation (Bullard and Johnson), 9

Kahn, M., 218
Kain, J. F., 301
Katrina cough, 194
Katz, M. B., 76
Kayden, J. S., 30
King, B. B., 134
King, Martin Luther, Jr., 104–106, 110–112, 115, 120–121
Kirby, M., 108
Korean Immigrant Workers Advocates, 38
Kousser, J. M., 60
Kozol, J., 114
Krieg, E. J., 31

Ku Klux Klan, 150
Kunstler, J. H., 33

Labor/Community Strategy Center,
   38, 118
Lacombe, A., 108, 258, 301
Lake Street El Coalition, 305
Lancet magazine, 42
Land use, 8, 14–15, 27, 51, 307, 347–
   348
   Agricultural Street Landfill and, 196
   agriculture and, 24, 52, 60, 150
   Atlanta International Airport and,
      223–242
   brownfields and, 24, 31–32, 334,
      355, 358, 374
   central city neighborhoods and, 24–
      25
   coalitions and, 331–336
   community land trusts and, 117
   concurrency requirements and, 335
   dominant growth pattern in, 1–2
   future issues for, 373–374
   greenfields and, 1, 3, 25, 345–346,
      351–352, 354, 373–374
   increased urban, 2 (*see also*
      Urbanization)
   LULUs and, 3, 142, 306, 376–377
   metropolitan fringes and, 54–55
   middle-income housing and, 64–67
      (*see also* Housing)
   mixed, 3
   MPOs and, 249–268 (*see also*
      Metropolitan Planning Organiza-
      tions [MPOs])
   Nashville and, 127–147
   Negro removal programs and, 205
   New Orleans and, 189, 193–194,
      203–204
   Old Gentilly Landfill and, 196–197
   reform and, 331–336
   Richland County, South Carolina,
      and, 149–169
   Rochester and, 116
   transportation and, 91–92, 249–268,
      307 (*see also* Transportation)
   Urban Zoning Overlay (UZO) and,
      132–133
   zoning and, 3, 30–33, 109–110 (*see
      also* Zoning)
Lang, R. E., 249
Lanni, T., 282
Laska, S., 191
Latino Issues Forum, 303
Latinos, 372–373. *See also* Racial
   issues
   asthma and, 278
   CBOs and, 90
   census demographics and, 80–87
   Cisneros and, 73–75, 97
   civic involvement and, 88–93, 96–97
   environmental justice and, 93–96
   Figueroa Corridor Coalition and, 79,
      95
   Fruitvale and, 92–93
   gentrification and, 80
   immigrants and, 90–91
   intellectual leadership and, 75
   labor movement and, 74, 77–78, 90–
      91, 94
   Manhattan and, 273
   Mayfair and, 94–95
   Metropolitan Planning Organizations
      (MPOs) and, 265
   Perez and, 91–92
   poverty and, 74, 80
   public transit and, 91
   regionalism and, 74, 75–80, 87–96
   rural South and, 81
   Spanish Speaking Unity Council and,
      92–93
   steering and, 323–324
   suburbs and, 80–87
   sustainable development and, 90–91
   transportation and, 79
   zoning and, 74
Lavelle, M., 28
Lawyers Committee for Civil Rights,
   200
Lazaroff, C., 33
Lead poisoning, 193
Leavitt, Mike, 308

Ledebur, L. C., 75, 329
Legal issues
    Alexander v. Sandoval, 118
    *Anderson v. Rochester–Genesee
    Regional Transportation Authority*,
    117
    *Brown v. Board of Education of
    Topeka*, 34, 345
    civil rights and, 117–118
    environmental racism and, 118
    Jim Crow laws and, 34, 56, 202
    *Labor/Community Strategy Center v.
    Los Angeles Metropolitan Transit
    Authority*, 118
    Milliken v. Bradley, 56
    Paynter v. State, 117
    Plessy v. Ferguson, 34
    *San Antonio Independent School
    District v. Rodriguez*, 351
    Warth v. Seldin, 109
Leinberger, C., 348
Leroy, G., 78
Levees, 203–204
Lewis, Paul G., 62, 255–258
Lewis Mumford Center, 106–107
Lewyn, M., 219
Limitless City, The (Gillham), 1
Litman, T., 192
Local Initiatives Support Corporation,
    360
Locally unwanted land uses (LULUs),
    3, 142, 306, 376–377
Logan, John, 7, 40, 44, 106–107
Long Beach, California, 84
"Looking for Regionalism in All the
    Wrong Places" (Pastor), 89
Looting, 201
Los Angeles, California, 81, 84, 86,
    377
    Bus Riders Union and, 117–118
    diesel fuel and, 276, 279
    inclusionary zoning and, 373
    Metropolitan Planning Organizations
    (MPOs) and, 263–264
Los Angeles Metropolitan Transit
    Authority, 38–39

Los Angeles Neighborhood Iniative,
    305
Louisiana Citizens Fair Plan, 202
Louisiana Department of Environ-
    mental Quality (LDEQ), 196
Love Canal, 118
Luce, T., 327
Lucy, W. H., 173
Lung cancer, 276
Luria, D. D., 78

Ma, J., 35–36, 38
Maantay, J., 30
Malcolm X, 114
Manhattan
    African Americans and, 273
    diesel effects and, 273–274, 283–
    293
    Latinos and, 273
    WE ACT and, 43, 273, 285–288,
    292–293
Margai, F. M., 4
Martin Associates, 230
Maryland, 76, 331, 335
Massey, Douglas, 6, 51, 53, 68, 150–
    151, 172, 356
Matier, P., 66
Mayfair, 94–95
Maze, T., 355
McClellan, S., 173
McConnell, R., 275
McDowell, Bruce D., 253–254, 268,
    357
McElfish, J., Jr., 346
McLeod, R. G., 55
Meharry Medical College, 134
Melendez, E., 74
Mellnik, T., 199
Melville, J., 75
Memphis, Tennessee, 107
Mendez, M. A., 90, 96
Methane, 282–283
Metro Atlanta Southern Crescent,
    230
Metropolitan Atlanta Regional Transit
    Authority (MARTA), 219, 221, 228

Metropolitan Planning Organizations
(MPOs), 15, 346–347, 374–375
  Advisory Commission on Intergov-
    ernmental Relations (ACIR) and,
    253, 257
  assessment survey of, 258–266
  board composition and, 263–266,
    357–358
  Chicago and, 264
  civil rights and, 258, 260–261, 268,
    358
  Clinton administration and, 250–251
  coalitions and, 336–340
  COG boards and, 255–256, 265
  Constrained Long-Range Plan
    (CLRP) and, 252
  Executive Order 12898 and, 268
  Federal Highway Administration
    and, 268
  future challenges for, 267–268
  gender issues and, 264–265
  ISTEA and, 35, 251–253, 257–258,
    268
  Los Angeles and, 263–264
  Manhattan and, 273–274
  NEPA and, 261
  New York and, 264
  political participation and, 255–258
  public involvement and, 253–255
  responsibilities of, 251–252
  state DOTs and, 257–258, 268
  structure of, 251–252
  TEA-21 and, 252–253, 257–258,
    268
  three-year plans (TIPs) and, 258–
    259
  transportation planning and, 35–36,
    41, 249–253, 260–263
  underserved populations and, 258
  voting bias and, 255–258
Metropolitan Statistical Areas (MSAs),
  12
  Atlanta and, 215–242
  Latinos and, 80–87
  Nashville and, 127–146
  New Orleans and, 189–206

Metropolitan Transit Authority
  (MTA), 117–118
  Manhattan and, 273–274, 285–286,
    288–293
  Nashville and, 137–138
Metropolitan Transportation
  Commission, 262
Mexican American Legal Defense and
  Education Fund (MALDEF), 96
Migration, 9, 299–301
Milken Institute, 236
Milliken v. Bradley, 56
Milwaukee, Wisconsin, 81, 333
Minnesota, 327
Mississippi River, 193
Mobility 2030 (Atlanta Regional
  Commission), 220–221
Modie, N., 62
Mold, 194–195
Mollenkopf, J., 24, 75
Moller, J., 195
Molotch, H. L., 7
Monroe County, 106–109
More Blacks Live with Pollution
  (Associated Press study), 29
Morin, R., 205
Morland, Kimberly, 13–14, 142, 171–
  188
Morning Edition (NPR program), 107
Muller, S., 78
Music City USA. See Nashville,
  Tennessee

NAACP, 38, 40, 117–118
Nagin, Ray, 191, 193–194, 198
Nashville, Tennessee, 12–13
  African Americans and, 127, 132–
    137, 143–146
  central city neighborhoods of, 134–
    137
  fast growth of, 127–131
  Fisk University and, 134
  food quality and, 142–143
  geographic information systems (GIS)
    techniques and, 128
  Hope VI projects and, 139

housing and, 132–133
Jefferson Street and, 134
population growth in, 127
public transit access and, 137–138
Purcell and, 140
schools and, 131
spatial dislocation of public services
and, 139
State Route 840 and, 136
transportation and, 136–138
urban renewal projects and, 133
Urban Zoning Overlay (UZO) and,
132–133
waste management and, 139–142
Nasser, H. El, 127–128
National Academy of Public
Administration, 28, 30
National Air Toxics Assessment
(NATA), 279
National Allergy Bureau, 195
National Alternative Fuels Day and
Environmental Summit, 290
National Ambient Air Quality
Standards, 221, 276
National Argonne Laboratory, 41
National Association of Latino Elected
and Appointed Officials (NALEO),
97
National Association of Counties,
312
National Association of Realtors, 308
National Black Business Council, 236
National Center for Health Statistics,
278
National Community Capital
Association, 360
National Community Investment
Fund, 360
National Congress for Community
Economic Development, 360
National Environmental Policy Act
(NEPA), 27, 261, 354
National Fair Housing Alliance
(NFHA), 197–198
National Flood Insurance Program,
202–203

National Governors' Association, 308,
312
National Highway Traffic Safety
Administration, 375
National Law Journal, 28
National League of Cities, 312
National Neighborhood Coalition,
117
National Public Radio, 107
National Research Council, 276
Natural gas, 282–283
Natural Resource Defense Council
(NRDC), 195, 224–225, 238, 285–
286
Naughton, K., 199
Negro removal programs, 205
Neighbors Building Neighborhoods,
116
Nel, A. E., 277
Nelson, A., 198, 263, 349, 351
Ness, I., 77
New Jersey, 312, 327, 335, 350
New Orleans, Louisiana, 4–5, 14
Agricultural Street Landfill and, 196
air quality and, 194–195
Army Corps of Engineers and, 194
automobiles and, 192, 195
Babineaux Blanco and, 203
Bring Back New Orleans Commission
and, 193–194
buses and, 192
cancer and, 193
cleanup and, 194, 196–197, 203–
204
economic structure of, 189–190
environmental justice and, 193–196
evacuation plan weaknesses and,
190–192
FEMA and, 198–201, 204
hazardous materials and, 193–195
housing and, 194–204
Hurricane Betsy and, 196
Hurricane Katrina and, 189–206, 378
insurance claims and, 201–203
land use and, 189, 193–194, 203–
204

New Orleans, Louisiana (cont.)
   lead poisoning and, 193
   looting and, 201
   mold and, 194–195
   Morial Convention Center and, 191
   Nagin and, 191, 193–194, 198
   Old Gentilly Landfill and, 196–197
   poverty and, 189–192
   Rapid Transit Authority and, 192
   Red Cross and, 191
   Small Business Administration (SBA)
      loans and, 199–200
   Superdome and, 191
   trailers and, 198–199
   transportation and, 190–192
   zoning and, 193
New York City, 43, 81, 377
   asthma and, 278
   diesel effects and, 273–274, 283–293
   Hudson Depot and, 286–287
   Metropolitan Planning Organizations
      (MPOs) and, 264
   public purchasing policies and, 290
   water filtration and, 350
   WE ACT and, 43, 273, 285–288,
      292–293
New York City Environmental Justice
   Alliance, 311–312
New York Times, 112, 200, 203
Niagara Frontier Transportation
   Authority, 39
Nieves, L. A., 41, 66
Nitrous oxide, 41, 224, 359–360
   alternative fuels and, 282, 284
   diesel fuel and, 275, 279–281, 288
   EPA and, 279–280
No Home for the Holidays (National
   Fair Housing Alliance), 197
Noise levels, 238
Nolan, Bruce, 191–192
Noonan, P. F., 7
North Carolina A&T University, 104
Northeast Environmental Justice
   Network, 309
Nos Quedamos, 311
Nossiter, A., 203

Not in my backyard (NIMBY), 31,
   198
Not in My Backyard (USCCR report),
   28–29
Nowak, Jeremy, 79
Nutrition. See Food justice
Nutrition and Your Health: Dietary
   Guidelines for Americans, 180

Oakland, California, 62, 66–67, 92
Office Sprawl: The Evolving
   Geography of Business (Brookings
   Institution), 40
O'Hare Airport, 223
Ohland, G., 311
Oil spills, 195
Old Gentilly Landfill, 196–197
Oliver, M. L., 53, 165
Orange County, 81
Orfield, Myron, 2, 16, 103, 114, 300
   equity and, 25, 33
   Latinos and, 74, 77, 890
   regional strategies and, 51, 53–55,
      58, 60, 323–344
   revitalization tools and, 351, 359,
      362
Overburg, P., 128
Ozkaynk, H., 42
Ozone, 221, 275

Pace, D., 30
Padgett, David A., 12, 39, 127–147,
   215
Paine, Anne, 136
Pajaro Valley, 92
Pankratz, A., 236
Parks, Rosa, 34, 38
Particulate matter (PM), 276–284, 289
Partners for Livable Communities, 116
Partners through Food, 116
Pastor, Manuel, Jr., 2–3, 8, 11, 31,
   73–101, 315
Paynter v. State, 117
Peachtree Creek, 215
Peacock, Walter G., 201
Pedestrians, 307, 313, 359

Peirce, N. R., 53–55, 137
Penfield, New York, 109
Pennsylvania, 335
People Improving Communities
  through Organizing (PICO), 95
*People of Color Environmental
  Directory* (Environmental Justice
  Resource Center), 309
Perera, F., 276
Perez, Katherine, 91–92
Perez-Pena, R., 278
Perlstein, M., 191
Persky, J. J., 348, 358
Peshoff, B. G., 51, 58
Peterson, B., 277
Pew Center for Civic Journalism, 303
Pittsburgh, Pennsylvania, 81
Planned growth, 52. *See also* Metro-
  politan Planning Organizations
  (MPOs)
  Atlanta International Airport and,
    223–242
  Richland County, South Carolina,
    and, 149–169
Plessy v. Ferguson, 34
PODER, 304
Pohanka, M., 173
Point CDC, 311
Policy
  alternative fuels and, 290–293
  antisprawl movement and, 59–64
  Bring Back New Orleans Commission
    and, 193–194
  Brownfields Act and, 355
  Cisneros and, 73–75
  Civil Rights Act of 1964 and, 27,
    106, 118, 252, 260–261, 268, 286,
    354, 358, 376
  Clean Air Act and, 221–223, 357, 360
  Clean Water State Revolving Fund
    (CWSRF) and, 346
  Community Reinvestment Act and,
    360
  diesel fuel and, 290–293
  environmental justice and, 23–44 (*see
    also* Environmental justice)

Executive Order 12866, 354
Executive Order 12898 and, 26–27,
    250–252, 261, 268, 354
  food justice and, 173–186
  future issues for, 371–378
  land use, 331–336 (*see also* Land
    use)
  level playing field for, 361–363
  mixed-income housing, 119
  MPOs and, 249–268 (*see also*
    Metropolitan Planning Organi-
    zations [MPOs])
  Red Cross and, 191
  Richland County, South Carolina,
    and, 149–169
  sprawl contribution by, 108–110
  transportation, 249–268, 312–313
    (*see also* Transportation)
PolicyLink, Inc., 6, 8, 299, 361
Polycyclic aromatic hydrocarbons
  (PAHs), 276, 284
Pope, J., 200, 276
*Population and Housing Summary
  Tape Files*, 174
Porter, M. E., 358
Portland, Oregon, 119
Portney, K., 117
Poverty, 3, 8, 10, 14
  American Dream and, 299–300
  central city neighborhoods and, 24–
    25, 52–55 (*see also* Central city
    neighborhoods)
  coalitions and, 302–310, 323–342
  concentrated, 51–68
  crime and, 113
  desegregation and, 55–57
  education and, 58–59, 117
  gentrification and, 51–52, 61–64 (*see
    also* Gentrification)
  Good News Garage and, 302
  Latinos and, 74, 80
  middle-income housing and, 64–67
  migration and, 299–301
  Monroe County and, 109
  New Orleans and, 189–192
  political fragmentation and, 57–58

Poverty (cont.)
  self-sufficiency and, 111, 377
  systemic, 58
  transportation and, 34–41, 190–192
    (*see also* Transportation)
  welfare and, 301–302
  zoning laws and, 30–33
powell, john a., 75, 110, 345, 348,
    351
  Metropolitan Planning Organizations
    (MPOs) and, 250
  regional strategies and, 4, 6, 8, 11,
    51–71, 332, 338
  Richland County, South Carolina,
    and, 151
Powers, A., 195
Prakash, Swati R., 15, 273–298
Precautionary principle, 25–26
President's Task Force, 278
Pribitkin, A. E., 41, 43
Prince William Sound, 195
Proscio, Tony, 93, 96, 115, 306, 308
Protestantism, 111
Public Interest Law Project, 200
Public services, 1, 7
  Anderson v. Rochester–Genesee
    Regional Transportation Authority
    and, 117
  coalitions and, 330–331
  cost of, 349–350
  Nashville and, 139
  Richland County, South Carolina,
    and, 158–160
  Rochester and, 103
Public transit, 1–2. *See also*
    Transportation
  African Americans and, 91
  Detroit and, 40
  diesel effects and, 273–294
  gasoline tax and, 36–37
  Latinos and, 91
  Manhattan and, 273–294
  Nashville and, 137–138
  reduction of, 38
Pucher, J., 35
Puentes, R., 36

Puls, M., 64
Purcell, Bill, 140
Purdum, T. S., 52

Quest for Environmental Justice, The
  (Bullard), 9

Rabin, Y., 30
Rabito, F. A., 193
Race in American Public Schools:
  Rapidly Resegregating School
  Districts (Harvard Civil Rights
  Project), 33
Racial issues
  antisprawl movement and, 59–64
  automobile ownership and, 35
  Brown v. Board of Education of
  Topeka and, 34
  central city neighborhoods and, 24–
  25
  civil rights and, 9, 12, 27, 33 (*see also*
  Civil rights)
  crime and, 113
  educational performance and, 113
  environmental justice and, 23–44, 118
  equity and, 3–8 (*see also* Equity)
  food justice and, 171–186
  future issues for, 371–378
  insurance companies and, 201–203,
  235
  Jim Crow laws and, 34, 56, 202
  land use reform and, 331–336
  Latinos and, 73–98
  middle-income housing and, 64–67
  MPO boards and, 265–266
  Negro removal programs and, 205
  Plessy v. Ferguson and, 34
  racialized space and, 57–59
  redlining and, 9, 25, 172, 201–203
  Richland County, South Carolina,
  and, 149–169
  schools and, 32–33 (*see also* Schools)
  segregation tax and, 4 (*see also*
  Segregation)
  slavery and, 111
  small business owners and, 236–237

sprawl patterns and, 53
steering and, 323–324
suburban flight and, 58
toxic cleanup disparities and, 28
transportation and, 34–41, 252 (*see also* Transportation)
zoning laws and, 30–33 (*see also* Zoning)
Racism and Metropolitan Dynamics (powell), 8
Rami, M. D., 219, 350, 355
Ranghelli, L., 93
Raphael, S., 39
Rapid Transit Authorities (RTAs), 192
Reagan, Ronald, 112
Real estate markets. *See* Housing
Recent Trends in Real Estate journal, 314
Recycling, 139–142
Red Cross, 191
Redlining, 9, 25, 172, 201–203
Regionalism, 8, 10, 55, 374
agriculture and, 60
antisprawl movement and, 59–64
Cisneros and, 73–75
coalitions and, 323–342
community-based, 78–79
cross-jurisdictional cooperation and, 59–60
environmental issues and, 75–76
equity and, 76–80
food justice and, 174–180
future strategies and, 68
labor movement and, 77–78
Latinos and, 74, 87–97
new regionalism and, 75–80, 87–89
new urbanism and, 87–89
smart growth and, 119–121
"Regionalism: The New Geography of Opportunity" (Cisneros), 73
Rein, L., 205
Religion, 105, 111, 115
Renne, J. L., 35
Report on Environmental Justice (USDOT), 292

Residential Apartheid (Bullard, Grigsby, and Lee), 9
Restaurants, 13–14
food justice and, 174–186
Nutrition and Your Health: Dietary Guidelines for Americans and, 180
Riccardi, N., 190
Rich, M., 301
Richards, L., 2–3
Richardson, Bill, 308
Richardson, H. W., 52, 54
Richland County, South Carolina, 13
Columbia and, 149, 152, 155
community leader rift in, 149–150
conservation groups and, 149–150
County Council of, 151–160, 163, 167–168
demographic changes in, 160–168
description of, 151–153
development vision for, 153–157
education and, 157, 160
emergency services and, 160
employment and, 152–155, 163
housing and, 165–168
income in, 164–165
infrastructure costs of, 149
Interstate 77 and, 152, 156–157, 163
new construction in, 163
population growth in, 149, 161–163
sewer management and, 158–160
Sierra Club and, 150
transportation and, 152, 157–158
water and, 158–160
zoning in, 155–156
Riverside, California, 81, 84
Robbins, M., 263
Rochester, New York, 12, 120
community development corporations and, 116
education and, 117
grassroots projects and, 115–116
housing and, 109
Paynter v. State and, 117
segregation and, 103, 106–107
supermarkets in, 116
urban pressures and, 107–108

Rockefeller Institute of Government, 313
Rogers, J., 78
Romney, Mitt, 308
Root, A., 264
Rosenberg, J. M., 200
Ross, C. L., 66
Roux, A. D., 142
Rusk, David, 4–5, 103, 347
    New Orleans and, 189
    regional strategies and, 51, 54, 57–61, 333
    segregation and, 150–151
Russell, G., 197

Sacrifice zones, 378
Sadd, J., 31
Saint Paul, Minnesota, 77, 327
Salvi, S., 277
Samet, D., 276
Samuels, Joseph, 66
San Antonio, Texas, 73, 351
San Antonio Independent School District v. Rodriguez, 351
San Bernardino, California, 81, 84
Sanchez, Thomas W., 15, 25–26, 38, 249–271
San Francisco, California, 61–62
San Jose, California, 78, 94–95
Santa Ana, California, 84
Santa Clara County, California, 95
Sauer, M., 190
Savitch, H. V., 54, 75, 172
Saxon, A., 277
Scallan, M., 203
Schieber, R. A., 173
Schintler, L., 264
Schleifstein, M., 191
Schmidt, C. W., 2
Schools, 1–2, 7, 24, 312, 324–325, 372
    Atlanta and, 231
    crowding of, 23
    health issues and, 43
    Nashville and, 131
    prayer and, 112

Richland County, South Carolina, and, 157
Rochester and, 117
San Antonio Independent School District v. Rodriguez and, 351
Superfund sites and, 28, 32–33
zoning and, 32–33
Scott, P., 240
Seattle, Washington, 61–62
Section 8 housing, 139
Segregation, 3–9, 375–376
    boycotts and, 104–106
    Brown v. Board of Education of Topeka and, 34, 345
    Chicago and, 107
    civil rights and, 55–57
    coalitions and, 302–310, 323–342
    desegregation and, 55–57, 103
    food justice and, 174–180
    Jim Crow laws and, 56, 202
    King and, 104–106
    land use reform and, 331–336
    Milliken v. Bradley and, 56
    Monroe County and, 106–107
    Plessy v. Ferguson and, 34
    public services and, 103
    residential, 103, 106–107
    Richland County, South Carolina, and, 149–169
    Rochester and, 103, 106–107
    schools and, 32–33
    South and, 107
    sprawl patterns and, 53
    steering and, 323–324
    transportation and, 34–41
    zoning and, 109–110
Segregation tax, 4
Self-reliance, 111, 377
Sewage treatment, 2, 158–160
Shad, N. A., 348–349, 358
Shapiro, T. M., 53, 165
Shelton, B. A., 63
Sheridan Expressway, 311
Shorter, C., 193
Shprentz, D. S., 276
Sierra Business Council, 314

Sierra Club, 32, 150
Silicon Valley Manufacturing Group, 94, 314
Simmons, A. M., 194
Simonsen, B., 263
Singer, Audrey, 80–82
Skidmore, F., 332–333
Slavery, 111
Small Business Administration (SBA) loans, 199–200
Smart growth, 1, 9
  benefits of, 346–347
  challenges of, 346–347
  environmental justice and, 23–44, 23–49
  equity and, 76–77 (*see also* Equity)
  future issues for, 371–378
  Latinos and, 73–98
  more efficient growth and, 349–350
  new regionalism and, 75–80
  purpose of, 2–3, 75–80
  racial issues and, 119–121
  reform and, 331–336
  regionalism and, 119–121
  revitalization tools and, 345–363
  segregation and, 149–169
  transportation and, 299–315 (*see also* Transportation)
Smart Growth America, 303, 307, 310
Smart Growth Network, 308, 356–357
Smart Growth News, 360
Smith, D., 361
Smith, G. M., 221
Smith, N., 7
Smog, 275
Social justice, 308. *See also* Equity
  antisprawl movement and, 59–64
  civil rights and, 104
  urban sprawl movement and, 59–64
Solof, M., 338
Sorel, Georges, 112
Soundararajan, T., 198
South Bay Labor Council, 78
South Coast Air Quality Management District (AQMD), 279

Southeast Michigan Council of Governments (SEMCOG), 339–340
Southerland, M. T., 172
Southern Christian Leadership Conference, 38
Southern Environmental Law Center, 222
Spanish Speaking Unity Council, 92–93
Sprague, Mary, 255–256
Sprawl, 9
  central city neighborhoods and, 52–55
  civil rights and, 59–64, 104
  concentrated poverty and, 55–57 (*see also* Poverty)
  defined, 1
  as dominant growth pattern, 1–2
  environmental justice and, 23–44
  food justice and, 171–186
  future issues for, 371–378
  gentrification and, 7, 61
  Hobson's choice of, 60
  legal issues and, 117–118
  limits to, 114–115
  low-density, 110
  magnitude of incentives for, 348–349
  migration and, 299–301
  more efficient growth and, 349–350
  patterns in, 52–55
  place-based leadership and, 114–120
  policy's contribution to, 108–110
  political desirability of, 110–114
  political fragmentation and, 57–58
  proximity factors and, 59
  racialized space and, 57–59
  residential segregation and, 103, 106–107
  revitalization tools and, 345–363
  social desirability of, 110–114
  social justice advocates and, 59–64
  transportation and, 34–41, 299–315 (*see also* Transportation)
  zoning abuses and, 30–33
Sprawl City (Bullard, Johnson, and Torres), 9

Squires, G., 235
Standing Peachtree, 215
Stanford, D., 37
Star Tribune, 52
State and Territorial Air Pollution
    Program Administrators, 42, 279
State Farm Insurance, 202, 235
Steering, 323–324
Stoll, Michael, 39
Stolz, R., 35–36, 38, 93
Strategic racism, 66
Streeter, K., 39
Subsidies, 2–3, 7, 300
    donor regions and, 36–37
    environmental justice and, 26
    FHA and, 54, 109–110
    location-efficient mortgages and, 356
    transportation and, 351, 354
Suburbs
    coalitions and, 323–342
    future issues for, 371–378
    land use reform and, 331–336
    Latinos and, 80–87
    migration and, 299–301
    more efficient growth and, 349–350
    regional coalitions and, 323–342
    transportation and, 40
    white flight and, 53–55, 58, 120, 356
Sugre, T. J., 64, 66
Sulfur, 280
Sullivan, B., 199
Superfund sites, 28, 32–33
Supermarkets, 13–14, 116
    food justice and, 173–186
    Nashville and, 142–143
    Nutrition and Your Health: Dietary
    Guidelines for Americans and, 180
Surface Transportation Policy Project,
    267, 303
Suro, Roberto, 80–82
Sustainable development, 2–3, 8–9,
    52, 90–91
Swanstrom, T., 4, 24, 75

Taft, G. A., 24
Tagami, K., 240

"Tale of Two Airports" (Hendricks),
    231
Tang, S., 282
Tarbet, V. E., 355
Taxes, 1–2, 58
    base sharing and, 359
    brownfields and, 358
    bus system cuts and, 38
    California and, 88
    coalitions and, 325–331, 340
    discrimination and, 377
    fiscal equity and, 325–331
    gasoline, 36–37, 220
    homogenous neighborhoods and, 114
    housing and, 323–324, 340
    lower, 112–113
    new market credits and, 360
    private activity bonds and, 359
    race to the bottom and, 8
    segregation, 4
Tax increment financing (TIF), 361–
    362
Taylor, J., 62
Tennessee Department of
    Transportation, 136–137
Tennessee State University Geographic
    Information Sciences Laboratory
    (TSU GISL), 127, 137, 141
Tennessee Valley Authority (TVA), 140
Tettey-Fio, E., 4
Texas Citizen Action, 304
Texas Citizen Fund, 304
Thevenot, B., 191
Thomas, E., 193
Thomas, K. B., 202
Thomson, K., 117
Tierney, J., 333
Tilly, C., 4
Times-Picayune, 191–192
Torres, Angel O., 103
    Atlanta's transportation sprawl and,
    215–247
    environmental justice and, 24–25
    equity and, 1, 4, 9, 14, 37–38, 307
    Latinos and, 76
    revitalization tools and, 348, 357

Toxic air contaminants (TACs), 279
Toxic Release Inventory (TRI), 224–225
Transit Workers Union, 288
Transportation, 1, 3, 8–10
 air quality and, 41–43, 351
 alternative fuels and, 282–285
 Anderson v. Rochester–Genesee Regional Transportation Authority and, 117
 BART, 92–93
 buses and, 34, 38–39, 43, 79, 103, 105, 116–118, 192, 273–294
 central city neighborhoods and, 25, 40
 coalitions for, 302–310
 congestion and, 24
 cost of, 39–40
 cycling and, 313, 359
 DART system and, 38
 diesel fuels and, 273–294
 dismantling apartheid of, 37–39
 efficiency and, 24
 employment and, 39–41, 301–302
 environmental justice and, 24, 34–41, 249–268, 309
 federal expansion and, 249–250
 Federal Highway Administration (FHWA), 35, 252–253, 268, 303, 313
 food justice and, 116, 172–173, 178–180
 fund leveraging and, 356–357
 gasoline tax and, 36–37, 220
 Good News Garage and, 302
 greenfields and, 351, 354
 Hartsfield–Jackson Atlanta International Airport (ATL) and, 223–242
 Hurricane Katrina and, 190–192
 institutional strategies for, 312–313
 integrated access approach for, 302–305
 Intermodal Surface Transportation Efficiency Act (ISTEA) and, 35, 251–253, 257–258, 268
 job flight and, 39–41
 Labor/Community Strategy Center v. Los Angeles Metropolitan Transit Authority and, 118
 Metropolitan Planning Organizations (MPOs) and, 249–268
 money trail in, 35–37
 MPOs and, 35–36, 41
 Nashville and, 136–138
 National Highway Traffic Safety Administration and, 375
 New Orleans and, 190–192
 Parks and, 34, 38
 pedestrians and, 307, 313, 359
 Plessy v. Ferguson and, 34
 private sector and, 313–314
 Rapid Transit Authorities (RTAs) and, 192
 Richland County, South Carolina, and, 152, 157–158
 spatial mismatch and, 39–41
 state DOTs and, 36, 41
 subsidies for, 351, 354
 suburban flight and, 54
 traffic congestion and, 52, 54
 traffic deaths and, 42
 urban infill benefits and, 359–360
 U.S. Department of Transportation (USDOT) and, 35–36, 221, 223, 251–252, 261, 286, 292, 347, 354, 357
 U.S. expenditure on, 34–35
 whole community approach and, 310–312
Transportation Equity Act for the Twenty-First Century (TEA-21), 35, 252–253, 257–258, 268, 292
Transportation Riders United, 340
Tri-State Transportation Campaign, 303, 311–312
Troutt, D. D., 173
Turner, M. A., 332–333
Turner Broadcasting Systems, 221
Twombly, R., 32

Underground storage tanks, 355
Unequal Protection (Bullard), 9

Union of Concerned Scientists, 291
United Kingdom, 261–262
United States. *See also specific city*
  American Dream and, 112–113,
    299–300
  Civil War and, 111, 215
  diet and, 180–185
  dominant growth pattern in, 1–2
  FEMA and, 198–201
  homeland security and, 378
  infrastructure decline in, 2
  Latino demographics and, 80–87
  mass consumerism and, 111–112
  racial issues and, 4–8 (*see also* Racial
    issues)
  slavery and, 111
  urban infrastructure issues and, 2
University of Denver, 253
University of Michigan, 140–141
University of Texas, 32
Urban Affairs Review, 89
Urbanization
  central city neighborhoods and, 52–
    55
  coalitions and, 323–342
  community development
    corporations and, 116
  diesel fuel and, 273–294
  environmental issues and, 75–76 (*see
    also* Environmental issues)
  future issues for, 371–378
  land use and, 249, 331–336 (*see also*
    Land use)
  Latinos and, 80–87
  livability and, 107–108
  marketing advantages of, 358–359
  middle-income housing and, 64–67
  migration and, 299–301
  more efficient growth and, 349–350
  new urbanism and, 87–89
  race to the bottom and, 8
  regionalism and, 87–89 (*see also*
    Regionalism)
  revitalization tools for, 345–363
  transportation and, 34–41
  zoning and, 30–33

Urban Land Institute (ULI), 193–194,
  230–232, 238
Urban League, 120
Urban renewal projects, 133
Urban Zoning Overlay (UZO), 132–
  133
USAA, 235
U.S. Army Corps of Engineers, 194
USA Today, 127–128
U.S. Census Bureau, 4, 37, 107, 128,
  162, 165
U.S. Centers for Disease Control and
  Prevention, 193
U.S. Commission on Civil Rights
  (USCCR), 28–29
U.S. Conference of Mayors, 312
U.S. Congress, 35, 173, 338, 349,
  358–359
U.S. Department of Agriculture, 2,
  174, 185
U.S. Department of Commerce, 236
U.S. Department of Energy, 284, 291,
  349
U.S. Department of Environmental
  Health, 174
U.S. Department of Homeland
  Security, 204
U.S. Department of Transportation
  (USDOT)
  Atlanta International Airport and,
    221, 223
  diesel fuel and, 286, 292
  environmental justice and, 35–36,
    251–252, 261
  revitalization tools and, 347, 354, 357
U.S. Environmental Protection Agency,
  3, 334, 346
  diesel fuel and, 275–282
  emissions regulations and, 279–280
  environmental justice and, 26, 29, 32,
    42–43, 308, 311
  hydrocarbons and, 279–280
  Nashville and, 141
  new emission standards and, 279–
    282
  New Orleans and, 194–195

revitalization tools and, 350–351, 357–361
Web site of, 279
U.S. General Accountability Office, 29
U.S. General Accounting Office, 31–32, 253, 254
U.S. Office of Comptroller of Currency, 360
U.S. Supreme Court, 34, 109, 118, 133

Van Vliet, P., 42
Varney, J., 195
Vehicle miles traveled (VMT), 275
Verma, N., 301
Vidal, A. C., 59
Vigdor, J. L., 106
Vogel, R. K., 75
Voith, R., 54, 77, 330
Volatile organic compounds (VOCs), 224, 275–276, 280

Walesh, K., 75
Waller, M., 258
Wal-Mart, 205
Warrick, J., 203, 281
Warth v. Seldin, 109
Washington, J. M., 111
Washington Post, 205
Waste management, 1, 306–307
Nashville and, 139–142
sewage, 2, 158–160
toxic, 27
Water, 1–2, 24
Clean Water State Revolving Fund (CWSRF) and, 346
Hurricane Katrina and, 195–196
Richland County, South Carolina, and, 158–160
Watsonville, California, 92
Weiher, Gregory, 56–58, 65, 68
Weinhold, B., 287
Welfare, 301–302
Wernett, D. R., 41
West Harlem Environmental Action, Inc. (WE ACT), 43, 273, 285–288, 292–293

Wheeler, Heaster, 40, 75
White, M. C., 193, 223
Whitman, Christie, 308
Wievel, W., 348, 358
Wiggins, Cynthia, 39
Wiley, Maya, 13, 149–169
Willis, G., 200
Willis, N., 258
Wilson, William Julius, 54, 79, 103, 300
Wing, Steve, 13–14, 142, 171–188
Win Win Partners, 360
Wolch, J., 2–3
Wolf, James F., 15, 249–271
Woman's College of the University of North Carolina, 105
Woodbury, C., 171
Working Partnerships, USA, 78, 94
World War II era, 114, 172
Wright, Beverly, 14, 189–211

Yago, G., 236
Yinger, J., 332
Young Ministries for Peace and Justice, 311

Zegeer, C. V., 173
Zero-emission vehicles (ZEVs), 291
Zoning, 3, 113, 351
brownfield sites and, 31–32
environmental justice and, 30–33
exclusionary, 30–31, 109–110
inclusionary, 373
Latinos and, 74
New Orleans and, 193
Richland County, South Carolina, and, 155–156
sacrifice zones and, 378
schools and, 32–33
Urban Zoning Overlay (UZO) and, 132–133
Warth v. Seldin and, 109